Great American Motorcycle Tours

Gary McKechnie

with a foreword by Peter Fonda

Second Edition

AVALON
TRAVEL

Great American Motorcycle Tours
Second Edition

Gary McKechnie

Published by
Avalon Travel Publishing
1400 65th Street, Suite 250
Emeryville, CA 94608, USA

Please send all comments, corrections, additions, amendments, and critiques to:
Great American Motorcycle Tours
AVALON TRAVEL PUBLISHING
1400 65TH STREET, SUITE 250
EMERYVILLE, CA 94608, USA
email: atpfeedback@avalonpub.com

Text © 2002 by Gary McKechnie.
Illustrations and maps © 2002 by Avalon Travel Publishing, Inc.
All rights reserved.
Photos and some illustrations are used by permission
and are the property of their original copyright owners.

Printing History
1st edition—2000
2nd edition—October 2002
5 4 3 2 1
AMA edition—February 2004
5 4 3 2

ISBN: 1-56691-741-7

Editor: Jeff Lupo
Copy Editor: Kim Marks
Graphics Coordinator: Susan Snyder
Production Coordinator: Darren Alessi
Cover Designer: Darren Alessi
Cartographer: Mike Morgenfeld, Donald Patterson
Map Editor: Olivia Solís
Proofreader: Jeff Lupo
Indexer: Vera Gross

Front cover photo: © 2002 D2 Productions/Getty Images
Distributed by Publishers Group West
Printed in the United States by Worzalla

Photos not otherwise credited were provided by: © *Nancy Howell, title page, p. 1, 7, 29, 53, 111, 131, 175, 195, 219, 237, 251, 269, 287, 321, 345, 365, 379;* © *McKechnie family archives, p. 5;* © *Helen Addison, Cape Cod Chamber of Commerce, p.79;* © *PA Dutch CVB, p. 95;* © *Georgia Department of Industry, Trade and Tourism, p. 151;* © *Don Laine / Taos County Chamber of Commerce, p. 307*

Contents

With immeasurable love and gratitude, this book is dedicated to my mom, Lois Ann Mercier McKechnie, who gave everything and deserved more, and to my wife, Nancy Howell McKechnie, my loving travel companion on the road and in my life.

Acknowledgments

Although I could have easily written this book without anyone's assistance, my publisher wouldn't extend the deadline until 2038. Therefore, I owe a great deal of gratitude to hundreds of people across the country. I would like to acknowledge the assistance of the following folks, listed in order of their favorite Beatle.

John Lennon: John McKechnie, Bud McKechnie, Ian McKechnie, all McKechnies everywhere, Peter Fonda, Cassandra Conyers, Dianna Delling, Donna Galassi, Peg Goldstein, Jean James, Lin Lee, Susan Albrecht, Patricia Kiderlen, Lynn Dyer, Judith Swain, Suzanne Elder, Phyllis Reller, Karen Baker, Gwen Peterson, Tony Fortier, Ken McNenny, Susan Sullivan, Pepper Massey-Swan, Karen Connelly, Liz Porter, Karen Hamill, Sue Ellen Peck, Tom Hash, Rick Gunn, Mark Kayser, Lisa Umiker, Rich Gates, Ray Towells, Julie Smith, Carrie Wilkinson-Tuma, Mike Dorn, Wendy Haase, Jan Dorfler, Steve Lewis, Shelly Clark, Jenny Stacy, Susan Belanski, Jack Dunlavy, Phillip Magdali, Jr., Paula Tirrito, Steven Skavroneck, Valerie Parker, Joel Frey, Lenore Barkley, Jan Osterman, Howard Gray, Christine DeCuir, Sandy Tucker, Don Sparks, DeRoy Jenson, Ed and Minna Williams, Rennie Ross, Didi Bushnell, Jim Pelletier, Stan Corneil, Chris Mackey, Amy Ballenger, Jeff Ehoodin of BMW of North America, Inc. . . .

Paul McCartney: Jeff Webster, Nina Kelly, Todd Morgan, Dave Blanford, Nancy Borino, Tom Lyons, Krista Elias, Shannon Mackie-Albert, Rachel Keating, Maureen Oltrogge, Mike Finney, Julia Scott, Sue Bland, Natasha Johnston, Laura Simoes, Wyndham Lewis, Dennis Cianci, Marjie Wright, Mary Cochran, Robyn McPeters, Jody Bernard, Sarah Pitcher, Nancy Brockman, Paul Schreiner, Bev Owens, Traci Varner, Dirk Oldenburg, Mark Reese of American Suzuki Motor Corporation, Ty van Hooydonk of Paine and Associates, Scott Heath and Linda Adams of Yamaha Motor Corporation USA . . .

George Harrison: Rick Wilder, Ken Crouse, Donna Bonnefin, Pettit Gilwee, Keith Walklet, Amy Herzog, Susan Carvalho, Kathy Langley, Kirk Komick, Jennifer Franklin, Mike Pitel, Billy Dodd, Heather Deville, Joel Howard, Annie Kuehls, Bob and Paula Glass, Troy Duvall, Jeff Lupo, John and Diane Sheiry, Croft Long and Mel Moore of Kawasaki Motors Corp. . . .

Ringo Starr: Trevor and Regina Aldhurst, Rosemary and Fabrizio Chiarello, Frank and Mary Newton, Mary Beth Hutchinson, Anna Maria Dalton, Karen Hedelt, Emily Case, Pauli Galin, Elmer Thomas, Nancy and Tom Blackford, Karen Suffredini, Mike McGuinn, Susan Williams, Virginia Mure, Ron and Sue Ramage, Leslie Prevish and Joe Hice of Buell Motorcycles . . .

Pete Best: Every engineer, surveyor, road crew, and chain gang that helped build America's beautiful back roads.

A Cross-Country Wish

Ride free, under a guiding sun
Revel in the serenity of boundless space
Savor the infinite beauty of earth's gifts
Let the wind rejuvenate your soul,
Unburden your mind
And illuminate your heart.

—Nancy Lutz

Why I Ride

By Peter Fonda

A motorcycle is the only way to see America. If you ride, you already understand how the feelings of freedom and nature are enhanced. When traveling by car or plane these feelings are missing. Gone.

Which is why I ride.

When I travel by motorcycle, I feel the wind and see the endless skies and stop when I want and where I want, fetching my rod from the saddlebag and fly-fishing for an hour or two. Hours don't matter, really, because on the road I develop a more natural use of time and never feel as if I have to be anywhere.

Which is why I ride.

I have a friend who joins me each year on a long run from Los Angeles to Montana. On this ride, we have only two rules: We will ride only back roads (a lengthy process when exiting L.A.), and we have no fixed destination on Day One—only the desire to return to the open road. Within a few hours we've extricated ourselves from the city and its traffic and are cruising north on 395, threading the needle between the Inyo Mountains and the Sierra Nevada. A motorcycle may be just a vehicle, but it is also the instrument we use to experience life, to explore, to discover new people and places, and to affirm our friendship.

Which is why I ride.

Gary McKechnie has written the first national motorcycle touring guide, and I trust it will lead you to moments like these. It's fun to read and filled with pertinent information for riders, and the 20 tours he describes can rescue you from the interstate highways and deliver you into the heart of America. He's traveled the country and found back roads and general stores, national parks and small town diners, cowboy saloons, and British pubs. He leads you to roads laced with the smell of pine trees and bordered by rushing streams, where you can park your bike, fetch your rod out of your saddlebag, and spend a few hours fly-fishing.

Which is why I ride.

Read this book, and you will too.

Preface

To the Second Edition

As I explored new roads and traveled to regions of the country I had never seen, the pride and sense of privilege I felt was overwhelming. However insignificant it may seem in the scheme of things, I felt my individual responsibility to the country was to report what I saw with honesty and to the best of my ability.

I trust I did my part, and my personal satisfaction coupled with the awards and recognition the first edition of *Great American Motorcycle Tours* received may be a testament to having fulfilled this obligation. This pride continues to grow in light of the profane events of September 11th and the steady stream of letters from readers here and abroad who have written to share their own plans and dreams for an American motorcycle journey.

In regard to letters, I stand corrected by comments citing my reluctance to include more varied lodging. It was my admiration of independent merchants and my quest to "break the links" with chain hotels and restaurants that found me steering clear of franchises and chain businesses. Of course, having asked for reader input to help fine tune future editions like this, I've accepted this advice and greatly expanded selections for "Blue Plate Specials" and "Shut-Eye." For each town or city highlighted, you'll find new diners and a reference list for every chain hotel within a ten-mile radius. Collectively, hundreds of new motorcycle shops, area codes, prices, attractions, and adventures have replaced outdated or worthless information.

Finally, no matter what you ride, drive, or pedal, please do not deny yourself an opportunity to see the United States. While my suggestions here will only scratch the surface, I promise when you embark on your own voyage of discovery, the best of America will become the best experience of your life.

Introduction

No single defining moment marks the Big Bang in the universe of motorcycle touring, but it may have been the day Malcolm Forbes settled into the saddle of his own Harley-Davidson. That's the day the image of bikers transformed from Marlon Brando into Marlin Perkins.

Other factors played a supporting role: Baby boomers' incomes afforded them small luxuries, and soon they added motorcycles to their toy collections. Harley-Davidson, after years of decline, turned into one of the business success stories of the century, embodying the strengths of American enterprise.

Those of us who had ridden for years watched all of this with fascination. We were already on the road, riding Yamahas, Suzukis, BMWs, Kawasakis, and Hondas. A few free spirits straddled Triumphs, Ducatis, and Moto Guzzis. We had long recognized that travel and motorcycling combined two passions that offered similar benefits: adventure, freedom, and the thrill of exploration.

My great-granddad John Philip McKechnie (born 1877) grew up to ride a motorcycle, which I find fascinating. Equally impressive was finding pictures of his son Ian C. McKechnie (my granddad) riding his new Harley across the New Mexico desert in the 1920s. Later, in the 1950s, Ian's son John (my dad) rode an AJS 500 while he was in the army.

Genetic coding was in full swing, and I started riding when I was 14, teaching myself on my brother Craig's 1972 Yamaha 250. I had to teach myself because Craig didn't know that I knew where his motorcycle key was hidden (the top left drawer of his desk). Riding around my neighborhood while he was out with friends, I soon grew tired of this bike and wanted something larger and faster. There was only one way to get it. Displaying diligence and a strong work ethic, Craig was finally able to afford a Honda 360. So I found the key and started riding that.

Years later, I finally bought my own 1976 RD 250, and later still a 1982 Suzuki 650. By then I was old enough to hit the road. I took short trips and, when my other brother, Kevin, bought a BMW R65, I expanded my range, skimming up the Atlantic Coast with him, turning left across Canada, then heading down along the Mississippi. So began an undying fascination with travel by motorcycle.

That others have come to share this fascination is supported by figures compiled by the Motorcycle Industry Council. The sale of new motorcycles has increased every year since 1991. More than 31 million Americans ride motorcycles, scooters, or ATVs. And about a hundred motorcycle touring/rental businesses operate in the United States alone.

What sparked my own voyage of discovery was the realization that one element was missing.

Travel guides had been written about tours of baseball fields and historic Native American sites. You could buy a specialized travel guide if you were disabled or traveled with pets. There were books on how to pack your clothes and where you could take your kids. But there wasn't a single national touring guide for motorcycle travelers.

Sure, there were articles in motorcycle magazines, but they tended to discuss bike mechanics, not the experience of the ride. In the few books that did describe tours, the theme invariably turned to the author's coming of age and the remarkable discovery that America wasn't such a bad place after all.

Personally, I never gave a flip about gear ratios when I was riding through Amish Country, and it didn't take a mid-life crisis to assure me that the United States is the greatest nation in history. That's why this book needed to be written. In my year on the road, I dealt with countless physical, logistical, and financial challenges, and I also had to face the fact that I would be sharing my findings with independent spirits who were reluctant to follow someone else's road map. I pressed on because I knew that there were millions of miles of roads to travel, and some riders might waste months trying to find which were the best and why. I knew that valuable two-week, two-wheeled vacations could be squandered on boring roads leading to ordinary places.

Of course, there are no special roads for motorcycles, just as there are no special roads for RVs. But as a rider you know what you're looking for. You want to ride on back roads where you shed routine and adopt a lifestyle in which every minute is an adventure.

When I had a desk job, I followed the same route to work day after day. Slowly this habit seeped into my travels: If an interesting road suddenly came into view, I'd pass it by to remain true to my self-inflicted schedule. I rarely strayed from the chosen path.

After I finally escaped from my cubicle and hit the road on a motorcycle, things were different. I was free to travel where and when I wanted. Released from the confines of airplanes and climate-controlled automobiles, I developed a sense of discovery and learned that everything worked out all right even when things went wrong. For every flat tire, broken chain, or wrong turn, I was rewarded with an unexpected kindness from a stranger or a detour leading to a better road.

I also found that, after a few days in the saddle, everything waiting back home seemed trivial, routine. I relished the feeling of adventure, of living in the moment. For me, these events came at unexpected times. When you meet a real live prospector in a Western town or talk to a Maine clamdigger about his work, you'll encounter one of those unexpected moments, too.

Selecting the Best Tours in America

Since freedom is the foundation of this book, you're sure to wonder how I selected the runs and roads included. How can I say with certainty that these tours represent the best rides and roads in America? I couldn't then and still can't now. I've included only a few tours in the Midwest and Pacific Northwest, and none in vast Texas. And thousands of back roads and blue highways, because of limited space, have been left out.

Understand that when selecting these tours, I relied on the advice of riders, motorcycle rental companies, and personal bias for routes that would expose you to places offering culture, history, and scenery. I've also tried to be equitable in representing different regions of America, so you'll get a good overview of our nation.

So use this book as a guide, not the gospel. If I neglected to mention the general store where you buy Moon Pies in South Carolina, make a note of it. Add your own routes and make your own discoveries. It was physically and logistically impossible to visit every biker-friendly business along these routes. You'll find that in this edition, however, reader response has helped flesh out these rides and I've included suggestions for new runs to follow.

I think you'll find that these rides offer spiritual pleasures as well as physical ones. The roads will speak to you often, whether you're on your bike or in a town. In Lenox, Massachusetts, you may experience this pleasure while listening to the Boston Symphony Orchestra at Tanglewood, or in Lone Pine, California, when you sit down at a diner and watch the sun set over the mountains.

Variety is the benchmark here. Restaurants and lodging options are as diverse as the roads and states and cultures you'll encounter. My recommendations are based on the tempo and tone of the area. Depending on the town, I'd just as soon point you toward a greasy spoon and an ordinary motel as a casual restaurant and a unique inn.

What I have tried to produce is a guide to essential information that you can access more quickly than by surfing the Internet—and one that won't weigh you down when you're on the road. Lodging options, nightspots, and motorcycle dealers are included in each chapter. As for on-the-road repairs, you'll need to attend to those on your own. Comprehensive warranties and roadside assistance should keep you out of trouble. Plus, there are other books—your owner's manual, for instance—that offer useful and in-depth repair information.

A few things to note as you're reading—and riding:
• Don't let lodging prices fool you. They represent peak season, double occupancy, so deduct approximately 10–15 percent if you're a solo traveler and even more if you can travel in an off or shoulder season.
• Admission prices listed are for adults.
• Don't be shy—ask for a senior discount if you qualify.
• If you plan to visit more than one national park, spring for the $50 National Parks Pass. It's good for admission to any national park for one year.
• It's nice to wear full leathers and clothes that reflect the hard riding you've done, but use common sense and courtesy and dress appropriately when at certain restaurants.

I did my best in writing about the highlights of these runs, but I'm sure I missed something along the way. If you have any suggestions for material to include in future editions of this book, or if you'd like to suggest one of your favorite rides, email me at elvis4all@aol.com, or check www.gamtours.com.

There you have it.

Now open the garage, saddle up, and go meet your country.

The Tours

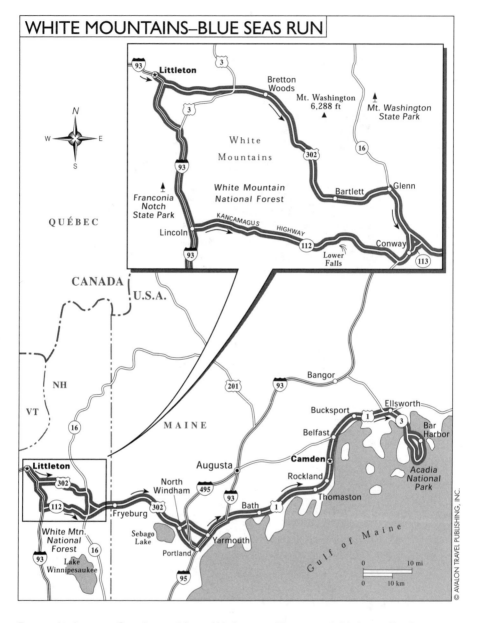

WHITE MOUNTAINS–BLUE SEAS RUN

Route: Littleton to Camden via Mount Washington, Kancamagus Highway, Fryeburg, Yarmouth, Waldoboro, Thomaston

Distance: Approximately 282 miles; consider four days with stops.
   •Day 1—Littleton •Day 2—Travel •Day 3—Camden •Day 4—Bar Harbor

First Leg: Littleton to Camden (210 miles)

Second Leg (optional): Camden to Bar Harbor (72 miles)

Helmet Laws: No helmets are required in New Hampshire or Maine.

White Mountains—Blue Seas Run

Littleton, New Hampshire to Camden, Maine

From the mountains to the oceans white with foam, this summer run is a relatively short one, but with distinct changes in landscape and cultures. Individually, the two legs described here offer thoroughly enjoyable, though not breathtaking, experiences. When combined, they create a perfect balance of mountain rides, coastal runs, and an opportunity to get off your bike and head out to sea. If you plan to ride either in late spring or early fall, you'll have relative peace and quiet. Note that many stores and restaurants—especially in Maine—are closed from mid-October to Memorial Day.

Consider alternate routes and side trips that will add some horsepower to your ride—particularly down some of Maine's peninsulas. I've included some options, and you're ever so welcome to add your own.

Some long stretches of road will give you time to think. I thought about New Hampshire's license plates stamped with the state motto, "Live Free or Die." It's appropriate, considering New Hampshire has no helmet law, no state sales tax, and no state income tax.

It's quite ironic, however, when you consider who's stamping out those tags.

Littleton Primer

At first glance, Littleton, New Hampshire, looks like a blue-collar town that never experienced a recession. A Main Street program has kept up the town's appearance, and the lack of a mall (amen!) brings many of the more than 6,000 citizens downtown throughout the day. One hundred sixty miles from both Boston and Montreal, Littleton is nestled in the Connecticut River Valley, and sits at the doorstep of two great roads leading to the 780,000-acre White Mountain National Forest. This alone is worth the ride.

Historically, Littleton has stayed in the shadows. Named after the region's surveyor, Colonel Moses Little, the town made its first contribution to American history during the Revolutionary era, when its unusually straight tree trunks were used for sailing ship masts. If you happen to be building a sailing ship, strap one of these bad boys onto your handlebars. Prior to the Civil War, Littleton was an essential stop on the Underground Railroad. If you're invited into some of the town's older homes, check out the basements where runaway slaves were shielded until they could continue their trek to Canada. At the turn of the century, two companies—one manufacturing stereoscopic view cards and the other, gloves—did their part to keep the town in the black. Aside from those highlights, things stayed pretty quiet around here until an author named it among his hundred favorite small towns, and retirees and families started taking a second look at the place. Now it's your turn.

On the Road in Littleton

Route 302 (Main Street) barrels through the center of town, which makes it unappealing for a leisurely cruise. So take advantage of the cheap curbside parking—drop a dime in the slot, and you'll own that section of God's black pavement for the next hour. The bargain rates extend from parking meters into the restaurants, inns, and hotels. Littleton isn't an upscale village; it is a working town that happens to attract a handful of tourists. The town's independent merchants don't put on a show for your cash; they are genuine and friendly.

Logistically, Littleton is a perfect starting point for a ride, since it's the largest town on the western end of Route 302 and close to the Kancamagus Highway (112). Visually, this is a town that seems locked in the 1950s. When night falls, you can listen to the Ammonoosuc River flowing, order a burger, fries, and chocolate frappé at a Main Street diner, then walk across the street to catch the evening picture show. And don't forget to say "Hey" to Wally and the Beav.

Pull it Over: Littleton Highlights
Attractions and Adventures

The Littleton Conservation Commission tends three trails that showcase different aspects of the outdoors, from bird-watching to geological history to scenic overlooks. A free trail guide is available at the Chamber of Commerce. A self-guided walking tour takes you past a dozen historically significant buildings.

I can't promise a Smithsonian-sized experience at the **Littleton Area Historical Society,** 1 Cottage St., 603/444-6586, since it's open only on Wednesdays. Built in 1905, the old opera house/fire station was renovated in 2001. If you're motivated, seriously motivated, the local society members will show off artifacts from the local glove company, a Victorian melodeon, and will share the story of the Kilburn Brothers who kicked off the DVD of their day— the stereographic view card.

Shopping

You could travel all over the nation to verify it, but it might be simpler just to believe **Chutter General Store,** 603/444-5787, www.chutter.com, when it claims to be one of three general stores in America that still sells penny candies from a jar. They feature New Hampshire-made products and also boast the world's longest candy counter. At a penny apiece, that's 1,000 pieces of candy for a fin. Double that if you've got a sawbuck.

Blue-Plate Specials

Drop by the **Littleton Diner,** 145 Main St., 603/444-3994, www.littletondiner.com, for New England-style home-cooked food and a tasty reminder that not every restaurant needs million-dollar ad campaigns. Here since 1930, the diner serves breakfast anytime (try the pancakes), a roast turkey dinner, soups, salads, and sundaes, all amidst the satisfying clatter of diner flatware. The place is open daily for breakfast, lunch, and dinner, a testament to their tagline: "There's always something cooking."

Unlike most American towns, Littleton isn't reluctant to promote home cooking. **Topic of the Town,** 30 Main St., 603/444-6721, offers another all-day breakfast, along with daily specials and turkey dinners, jumbo sirloin, Greek salads, chicken, ribs, and lovely frappes—all served in a generic diner setting. Perfect.

Watering Holes

You'll find scant options for nightlife in Littleton, but, as a local observed, "This is New England and that's how people like it." There's a lounge attached to the

Clam Shell Restaurant, 274 Dells Rd., 603/444-6445, a mile outside of town, as well as a tavern adjoining the **Italian Oasis Restaurant** at 106 Main St., 603/444-6995, inside Parker Marketplace. The Oasis also has a microbrewery, and both serve mixed drinks.

Since there's not much shaking after dark, if a good flick is playing at **Jax Junior Cinema,** 33 Main St., 603/444-5907, you'll want to stop in and relive the days when you hung out at the Saturday matinee. Quirky fact: This theater's claim to fame is that it premiered the 1930s Bette Davis movie *The Great Lie.* Locals are still abuzz.

Shut-Eye

Chain hotels are scarce in and around Littleton, but the choices below should suffice. For more options, call Lodging and Campground Information at 888/822-2687.

Motels and Motor Courts

Thayer's Inn, 136 Main St., 603/444-6469 or 800/634-8179, www.thayers inn.com, would seem perfectly at home in Mayberry. It opened in 1843 as a stagecoach stop, and some traditions continue. A few rooms still have shared baths, but all are clean and comfortable, with rates from $60–80. This is a great place to stay if you're on a budget—and even if you're not. President Grant gave a speech from the front balcony, but ask for a room in back—a lot of traffic rolls down Route 302.

No unwanted surprises await at **Eastgate Motor Inn,** Exit 41 at I-93, 603/444-3971, www.eastgatemotorinn.com. This family-owned operation offers nicer-than-average rooms (some with a fridge) and above-average service, and is usually booked by tourists who like a clean room, pool, free breakfast, and cash in their pocket. If you'd rather save your money for the road, consider this inn, with rates from around $50.

Inn-dependence

One cozy option is the **Beal House Inn,** 2 W. Main St., 603/444-2661 or 888/616-BEAL, www.bealhouseinn.com. Owners Catherine and Jose Luis Pawelek run a large, friendly, fireplace-rich inn a few blocks from the village. You'll find five suites and three rooms with private baths, two common rooms, a great library, and an eclectic bistro (Flying Moose) with a dynamite menu and wines. Considering the owners come from South Florida, you can expect Southern hospitality. Rates start at $105.

On the Road: Littleton to Camden

Get ready for a most excellent ride. This run offers three options: You can take Route 302 across the White Mountains, drop south to reach Highway 112—the famed Kancamagus—or make a day trip of both roads and double back the following day to reach Maine. If you can take only one road, take 112.

The ride starts slowly. As you roll out of Littleton on Route 302 east, you'll pass the Kilburn Brothers Stereoscopic View Factory. It's an apartment building now, but if you have any of these cards in your attic, now you'll know where they came from.

I had vowed to ride interstates only to serve the national interest or to pick up time. Interstate 93 is the exception. It rivals any back road you'll find. Follow it south toward the town of Lincoln.

A detour at Exit 38 leads to the **Frost Place,** 603/823-5510, www.frost place.org, once the home of poet Robert Frost who read his poem *The Gift Outright* at JFK's inauguration. Three bucks will get you in the front door. On display are first editions of his books, photos, memorabilia, and a poet-in-residence who hosts readings in the old barn. Credit the harsh New Hampshire winters for a summers-only schedule: Memorial Day through Columbus Day.

Back on I-93, subtle hints such as towering mountains, plummeting roads, and a reduction to two lanes tell you you're entering Franconia Notch and the dazzling eight-mile-long **Franconia Notch State Park,** 603/823-5563, www.nhparks.com. Stuffed between the highest peaks of the Franconia and Kinsman Ranges, this section of earth allows you abundant places to explore. Pull off at the first exit (34C), and you'll have access to swimming, camping, fishing, picnicking, and hiking around Echo Lake. Back on I-93 you'll jump on and off the road as you work your way south, taking the next exit (34B) to see the **New England Ski Museum.** The base for the aerial tram here doubles as an information center for details on camping, hiking, and access to Profile Lake, and passage to the 4,200-foot peak of Cannon Mountain. The next exit (34A) puts you near an 800-foot gorge called The Flume. Try to make time for roughing it. This is a stunning park, and it's worth the layover to breathe fresh air and experience nature. There are no hotels in the park, but **Lafayette Campground,** 603/823-9513, with 97 tent sites, showers, and a store, places you at "Notch Central." From here you can check out the "Old Man of the Mountain" (Nathaniel Hawthorne's Great Stone Face), and The Basin, which, like Keith Richards, is a 25,000-year-old glacial pothole.

Afterward, the going gets tricky, but stay on I-93 and for a flirt with the past, watch for **Clark's Trading Post** (603/745-8913), www.clarkstradingpost.com, in North Woodstock. It may seem corny, but this is a throwback to the days when you took road trips with your parents. Clark's has been at it for more than 70 years with trained bears, steam trains, and old-fashioned gadgets that tourists (circa 1962) love. Admission is $7. At Clark's, turn left onto a well-named connector road called "Connector Road" and at the next T, turn left to access Highway 112, the western tip of the Kancamagus Highway.

Since "The Kank" has no gas stations, stores, or hamburger clowns on its 34-mile stretch to Conway, the town of Lincoln has thoughtfully added a flood of ugly stores and smelly things. Race past these and into some of the most mind-boggling alpine scenery and rideable roads you'll encounter. Goose it to 60 and get into the rhythm of the road, but be prepared to brake when you reach some 20 mph hairpin turns that deliver you to scenic viewing areas, such as the Hancock Overlook.

Pack It Up

A few pairs of jeans, a jacket, boots, rain gear, sunglasses, and gloves are naturals to pack for your ride, but what about a video camera? As a person who likes to chronicle my tours, I carry what others may call luxuries, but I call them tools of the trade.

- **Video camera:** It's vulnerable to water and weather, but you'll get good images of your trip. Super 8 cameras are fairly compact.
- **Binoculars:** A small pair can enhance images, especially when you're riding through a national park or across a desert.
- **Tape recorder:** I do some of my best and most productive thinking as I ride, capturing my thoughts through a small recorder looped around my neck.
- **Journal:** They're easy to start, but hard to sustain. If you can keep up the writing, you'll have a great record of what could be the ride of your life.
- **Traveler's checks:** Not an original idea, just a smart one.
- **ATM/credit card:** Along with traveler's checks, it's easy money.
- A copy of *Great American Motorcycle Tours.*
- And, for reasons completely unrelated to motorcycling, a **life-sized cutout of Tina Louise.**

Soon you'll learn that the road switches more frequently than Little Richard. You may head east, northwest, southeast, then northeast to go east again. With The Kank's multiple turns and seven-degree grades, you'll be hugging the center line and shifting like a maniac.

After you cross Kancamagus Pass at 2,855 feet, you'll swoop down the mountain like a peregrine falcon, snatching great views to your left and following the road that now skirts the Swift River. To backtrack to Littleton and enjoy a nine-mile run winding through forests and scenic overlooks, turn left onto Bear Notch Road and head up to Route 302.

Continuing east on The Kank, you'll pass the **Rocky Gorge Scenic Area,** which leads to a wooden footbridge. Just over a mile later you'll be at the Lower Falls, which is a great spot for a dip in the Swift River.

Picnic spots, campgrounds, and riverfront rest areas mark the eastern edge of the highway, and with little fanfare you'll reach the end of the road at Highway 113. The majority of traffic will be heading north to reach the outlet town of North Conway—but there's urban ugliness in this direction, my friend. Instead, start heading for the Maine coast via Highway 302.

As state lines go, the entrance to Maine is minimalist—just a stark sign reading "Maine." My image of the state had been a frozen tundra where housewives carve blubber from dead seals. However, at first glance you could put this road in Vermont or the Adirondacks. Only after riding for several miles do you realize that the roads are not especially scenic. As you follow Highway 302 past Fryeburg and toward the Sebago area and Portland, there are no towns, no billboards, no nothing.

But you have to think like a "Maineiac." Just when you think you're out of scenery, huge Sebago Lake opens up. You'll see cabins, nearby mountains, and folks out restoring old buildings. Seems like a decent place to stop for a sodee pop.

Sadly, the scenery doesn't last. Welding shops and snowmobile garages replace natural beauty. You can bypass some of Portland's congestion by taking Route 35 north at North Windham to Gray, riding toward Yarmouth and the coast. When you've passed east of the I-495 interchange, Route 35 becomes 115 and turns out to be a nice road with dips and hills and an occasional pasture for variety. I-95 (which is also U.S. 1) picks up outside Yarmouth, so follow it until you can veer off onto U.S. 1 toward Bath, Rockland, and Camden.

One stop worth making is in Waldoboro at **Moody's Diner,** U.S. 1, 207/832-7785, www.moodysdiner.com, a 24-hour weekday eatery. Since 1934, Moody's has been cooking up good road food, including ribeye steaks and sirloin, crabmeat rolls, hamburgers, meat loaf, stew, and breakfast—all served in an authentic diner setting. While it's not much to look at, Moody's is definitely a staple among Maine residents.

Advice From a Road Scholar

A few decades on the road and several thousand miles in the saddle have given me some insights that may improve the quality of your own ride.
• Even if you're in a hurry to reach Point B, try not to leave Point A after mid-afternoon. Chances are you'll be racing the sun, and you'll miss the moments you're riding for. If you leave in the morning, you'll have a full day to make unscheduled stops and discover points of interest.
• If you get off schedule, don't worry. The purpose of touring isn't to reach as many places as possible, it is to experience as many sensations and places as you can. Don't kill yourself with a self-inflicted schedule.
• Reward yourself. Every so often, stop at a place you don't think looks very interesting at first. Take a break and meditate. Watch what's going on around you. A conversation with a general store clerk, a swim in a pond, or the sight of glistening pebbles in a riverbed can be just as pleasing as a good stretch of road.
• Have a contingency plan in case your day gets rained out. Write postcards; see a museum or a movie; read, rest, or go to the library; talk to locals. If a day gets screwed up, roll with it.
• Take wrong turns. Get lost. Make discoveries.

Your next stop should be the **Maine State Prison Showroom** in Thomaston, U.S. 1, 207/354-3131. Guests at the Graybar Hotel have a lot of time and talent on their hands and display it through desks, toys, nautical figurines, bar stools, and lamps. It's cool stuff, and you just might bump into some of your old riding buddies or former congressmen.

You'd think Maine's oceanfront road would offer ocean views, but these are hidden far behind trees and land. Up here, U.S. 1 is a nondescript highway, which makes it all the more pleasing to ride into such a beautiful town as Camden.

Alternate Route: Route 302

Although the Kancamagus is an obvious choice, following Route 302 out of Littleton is a close second. After passing through the center of town, turn left at the Eastgate Motor Inn. It's an inauspicious beginning, but soon the road turns mighty pretty.

- Yes, the boots do make you look like Fonzie, but if you plan on joining any walking tours or beating your feet around a town, you'll appreciate the comfort of a pair of walking shoes.
- If you use a magnetic tank bag, never toss your wallet in it. Never. The powerful magnets that can withstand 90-mile-an-hour winds can also de-magnetize ATM and credit cards in a flash.
- It can be maddening when a truck ahead of you slows you down to its pace. If you pass, often the truck speeds up, and then you've got to worry about a tailgater. Instead, just pull over for a few minutes and take a break. It'll give the truck time to move on and allow you to return to scenic roads unobstructed by Yosemite Sam mud flaps.
- It gets mighty cold—especially out West—when the sun goes down. Even if you don't think you'll need them, bring along long underwear.
- If you can't avoid the small animal in front of you, grit your teeth and go for it. It's not worth laying down your bike to save a squirrel.
- And remember that loose gravel, wet leaves, and oil slicks don't care how long you've been riding. Don't get so swept up in the ride that you neglect safety.

Route 302 leads to Fosters Crossroads, where you'll start a southeast descent toward Bretton Woods and the famous **Mount Washington Inn,** 603/278-1000 or 800/258-0330, www.mtwashington.com, which sits majestically off to your left. If you can't spot the white frame palace and its red roof, follow the sightline of tourists who have it pinned down with cameras and binoculars. With rates starting at $269, the grand hotel is a mighty expensive option, but looking is free. The inn boasts fantastic views of the White Mountains bordered by the Presidential Range, as well as all the amenities that make this a resort: horseback riding, tennis, entertainment, and an 18-hole Donald Ross course. Add to this the 900-foot white-railed veranda and broad porte-cochére, and you know you're riding into the lap of luxury. If the inn is full, they book the Bretton Woods Motor Inn and Townhomes at Bretton Woods as well.

On your left you'll see the ingenious **Mount Washington Cog Railway,** 603/278-5404 or 800/922-8825, www.thecog.com, which takes passengers to the chilly peak of Mount Washington. At 6,288 feet, this is the highest point in the Northeast—called *Agiocochook* by Native Americans and believed to be the home of the Great Spirit. Settlers Abel Crawford and his son Ethan carved out the first footpath to its summit in 1819. That footpath is still in use. If you're fascinated by all things mechanical, you'll be impressed by how this railroad can ascend a 37-degree grade. The three-hour tour isn't cheap—$49 for adults. Then again, it is the highest peak in New England. . . then again, it is $49. Then again, the train *is* called "Old Peppersass. . ."

Further on, you'll ride past Saco Lake and enter dazzling Crawford Notch, as the road slices into the folds of the mountains and begins to loosely follow the Saco River toward Bartlett. For the next six miles you'll encounter the unspoiled rugged beauty of the Presidential Range. **Crawford Notch State Park,** 603/374-2272, offers picnic areas, hiking, waterfalls, and a visitors center. After an exhilarating run through the notch, you'll reach Glen and the junction of Route 16, which leads north to the Mount Washington Auto Road. Although it's several miles north in Gorham, it's worth the detour if you're willing to pay $8 to tackle eight miles of 12-degree grades and wind speeds clocked (back in 1934) at 231 mph.(!) Open only from mid-May to late October, the road provides killer views of the White Mountains, Presidential Range, and beyond. If you haven't been blown off the mountain, double back to Route 302 and head for the coast.

Camden Primer

Tourism bureaus usually go overboard promoting their town or state. Camden is different. It delivers on its promise of beauty. This harbor town is where the mountains (Appalachians) meet the sea (Atlantic), and the confluence makes a dramatic setting.

Although Camden is approximately the same size as Littleton, the village is far more active. Robert Ripley once estimated that if all the Chinese marched four abreast, they could walk around the world and the march would never end. That's about true for traffic here during Camden's peak season. Of course, that's on a nice day with warm weather. Fog and gray rains wash in and out frequently and can turn a great ride into a desolate and depressingly wet mess.

As in most New England towns worth visiting, the central district is best seen on foot. Adjacent to the marina you'll find a large parking lot with motorcycle-reserved spaces. From there you can set off to eat seafood, drop into bookshops, check out local crafts, eat seafood, cruise on a schooner, and eat seafood.

Summertime, obviously, is peak tourist season, with a very affluent group setting up shop. Big, fat money rolls in from banking families, cruise-line owners, and personalities like John Travolta, Kirstie Alley, and Martha Stewart, who arrive to buy large properties and even whole islands.

But after they've left and the tourists are gone, the locals get back to work. The town keeps busy with its service industry, windjammer cruises (lots of seafarers here, cap'n), and the Maryland Bank of North America, which took over the old woolen mill.

So here it is. It's not a wild town, but if you appreciate nature, you won't find a better base for day trips to search out Maine's best roads and natural attractions.

On the Road in Camden

To see the best of Camden, you'll need at least two very full days. Reserve the first sunny day for a ride to Mount Battie. Leaving town on U.S. 1, you'll enjoy nice elevation changes for about two miles before reaching **Camden Hills State Park,** 207/236-3109. Fork over $2, and you can ascend the 1.6-mile road in a steady, steep climb and reach the 790-foot summit of Mount Battie a few minutes later. Although the ride is short, you'll remember the view for a thousand years. From a stone tower lookout, you'll see the ocean meeting the mountains a few miles distant. The effect is spiritual. The sun shines so brightly on the

At Home in Maine

Maine's residents are called "Mainers" or "Maineiacs." If you're not from here, friend, you're "from away."

Like the rest of America, Maine is threatened by the "national village." The Maine accent ("Ayuh, the clomms ah hahmless") is turning into a Midwestern drone as kids pick up vanilla speech patterns from the tube. The other assault comes from rich outsiders who made their stash and now want to buy a piece of charming Maine. After they arrive, instead of appreciating the state for what it is, they try to re-create what they left behind, sometimes posting "No Trespassing" signs on beaches where natives had walked for years. According to one Maineiac, "It pisses us off." The bright side, he adds, is that folks "from away" usually last only four or five years before leaving "'coz they can't take the weather anyway."

water that the ocean looks like an endless white desert. Small islands break off from the mainland; roofs sprout through the tops of fir trees; small coves shelter schooners; and the wakes of clipper ships look like wisps of cotton. On a clear day it seems as if you can see forever as your eyes follow the coast northeast to Bar Harbor's Cadillac Mountain, more than 40 miles away.

Pull it Over: Camden Highlights
Attractions and Adventures

There are two Maine businesses which, while a few hours from Camden, may be worth a side trip if you're inspired to further explore the great outdoors. **Northern Outdoors,** 800/765-7238, www.northernoutdoors.com, arranges adventures for all things Maine. You can go rafting, fishing, climbing, canoeing, and kayaking. **New England Outdoor,** 207/723-5438 or 800/766-7238, www.neoc.com, is another adventure company hosting daily whitewater trips, hunting, fishing, and a canoe and kayak school.

Of course, you can stay in Camden and be tempted to quit the hustle and bustle of your workaday life for the satisfaction of seeing the world by bike and boat. A fleet of schooners takes two-hour cruises around Penobscot Bay past coastal mountains, seals, eagles, porpoises, and hardworking lobstermen. As you

Why Do Them Leaves Look Funny?

If you want to battle motor homes for rights to the road, arrive during fall foliage when "leaf peepers" descend on New England like locusts on Kansas corn. They're here to watch the leaves change from a uniform green to an autumnal palette of oranges, reds, and yellows. Why do leaves change color? They don't, Gomer. Here's the skinny: About two weeks before they "turn," a cell layer forms at the base of each leaf that prevents moisture from entering. The chlorophyll, which makes the leaf green, isn't able to renew itself, so the leaf's true color can be seen. Depending on exposure to the sun, elevation, and the chemical make-up of the tree, different colors appear. Sugar maple leaves are primarily red and orange, white ash turns yellow and purple, and the pin cherry's purple-green leaves turn yellow. Most color changes start at higher elevations and work their way down the mountains and hills.

check out different charters, ask if you'll be able to help raise the sails, take the wheel, or simply kick back with a beer or wine. Costs range from about $20–30. Options include the 65-foot windjammer *Appledore,* Camden Town Landing, Sharp's Wharf, 207/236-8353, and Schooner *Lazy Jack,* Camden Town Landing, 207/230-0602, www.schoonerlazyjack.com, a 1947 Bahamian charter boat restored and brought to Camden in 1987. A 13-passenger capacity and $20 ticket is the draw for this boat, which takes a two-hour cruise around Penobscot Bay. The schooner *Surprise,* Camden Town Landing, 207/236-4687, www.camdenmainesailing.com, is a 57-foot, 1918 classic. Captain Jack serves cookies and fruit and spins yarns. Schooner *Olad,* Camden Town Landing, Sharp's Wharf, 207/236-2323, www.maineschooners.com, offers 55- and 75-foot windjammers that depart every hour with 21–40 passengers. Want to stay at sea overnight or longer? Check out the deluxe **Maine Windjammer Cruises,** Camden Town Landing, 207/236-2938, 888/692-7245, www.mainewindjammercruises.com, for weeklong, four-day, and weekend cruises departing Monday and Friday. They've been around since 1936 and have several ships to choose from. Lewis R. French, Camden Town Landing, 800/469-4635, www.midcoast.com/~windjam, offers four- and six-day cruises for up to 22 nonsmoking crewmembers. Schooner yacht *Wendameen,* Rockland, 207/594-1751, www.schooneryacht.com, runs overnights for $170, including dinner and breakfast. The schooner *Ellida,* 178 E. Pond Rd., Jefferson, 207/549-3908 or 888/807-6921, www.maineclassicschooners.com, sails out of Rockland (next to Camden) and offers four-day cruises, lunch and dinner cruises, and customized excursions.

For fishing trips, contact **Georges River Outfitters,** 1384 Atlantic Hwy., Warren, 207/273-3818, www.sportsmensgifts.com. Native Maineaic Jeff Bellmore is a United States Coast Guard Captain and Master Maine Guide who hosts customized fresh and saltwater excursions and limits boats to two passengers for one-on-one (or -two) advice. Freshwater catches include salmon, bass, trout, and perch; ocean runs are for stripers, bluefish, and mackerel. If you've got $175–350, you've got a captain, boat, and guide.

The Farnsworth Art Museum, 16 Museum Street, Rockland, 207/596-6457, www.farnsworthmuseum.org, several miles east of Camden, displays one of the larger collections of works by the Wyeths of Maine, recognized as the first family of American art. Additional works reflect all eras, from colonial to American Impressionism to the present, with 8,000 items on display. Admission is $9.

Owls Head Transportation Museum, Rte. 73, Owls Head, 207/594-4418, www.ohtm.org, is located a few miles south and west of Camden. The mechanical menagerie here includes a 1937 Mercedes 540K, a World War I Fokker triplane, a Stanley Steamer, a 1963 prototype Mustang, and a mint-condition World War II Harley-Davidson. The displays are dazzling—and fun. Summer events include an antique motorcycle show featuring more than 200 vintage bikes.

Blue-Plate Specials

Cappy's, 1 Main St., 207/236-2254, is the place for bikers, sailors, locals, and anyone who likes good food and good service. You'll find real clam chowder, crab skins, shrimp—and these are just the munchies. Come here at night, and the lively bar talk will surely include conversation about boats, bikes, and microbrews, such as Old Thumper, Goat Island Light, and Blue Fin Stout. Microbrew tastings are held in Cappy's crow's nest from 4–6 P.M.

Besides Mount Battie, the best view in town is of the harbor. Sit on the deck at the **Waterfront Restaurant,** Bayview St., 207/236-3747, and the harbor is yours—along with lobster, steak, and an oyster bar. The full bar is open until the customers go home.

Watering Holes

Sea Dog Brewing Company, 43 Mechanic St., 207/236-6863, www.seadog brewing.com, has won more than 30 awards for its beers, but bottom line, it's good. Have 'em pump a pint of Old Gollywobbler Brown Ale, Sherman's Dry Hopped Pale Ale, or any of the dozen or more choices. The setting overlooks the Knox Mill and if you're not hanging out at Cappy's, this is a good alternative.

Shut-Eye

Motels and Motor Courts
Camden still has some old-fashioned motels. Consider the **Towne Motel,** 68 Elm St., 207/236-3377 or 800/656-4999 www.midcoast.com/townemotel. In the heart of town, they have 18 rooms that go from $89–115 in season. A light continental breakfast is included. North of town is the **Birchwood Motel,** Belfast Rd., 207/236-4204, where their 15 rooms go from $50–77.

Chain Drive*
A, C.

*Chain hotels in, or within ten miles of town. See cross-reference guide featuring phone numbers and web addresses on page 405.

Inn-Dependence

The Belmont Inn, 6 Belmont Ave., 207/236-8053 or 800/238-8053, www.thebelmontinn.com, is two blocks off U.S. 1 and offers 10 times the solitude you might expect. Wraparound porches, a great sitting room, breakfasts on the porch, and 99 windows give this private house a serious breath of fresh, outdoor air. The large rooms have a distinctly homey feel and rates start at $125. If the day's ride has worn you out, the in-house restaurant will be a welcome—and tasty—break.

Blue Harbor House, 67 Elm St., 207/236-3196 or 800/248-3196, www.blue harborhouse.com, doesn't look like a motorcycle traveler's first choice. But Jody Schmoll and Dennis Hayden know everything about Camden and Maine and can point out back roads and local joints to explore. Request a large room or, better yet, a carriage-house suite, since their smallest room is just that. Rates are $95–165

Indulgences

Norumbega, 61 High St., 207/236-4646, www.norumbegainn.com, is perhaps the most photographed home in Maine. The 1886 Victorian castle is a stunning piece of architecture and a great place to spend the night if you've got the wherewithal—or a credit card (summer rates run $125–310). Built by Joseph B. Stearns (the inventor of duplex telegraphy, no less), the oak-paneled common rooms are reminiscent of an English manor house, and the 13 rooms and suites (some with king-size four-poster beds) will have you sleeping in the lap of luxury. You'll enjoy great water views and a filling country breakfast. If this is a once-in-a-lifetime ride, live it up.

On the Road: Camden to Bar Harbor

Stay long enough to get your soul recharged, then it's time to hit the road, Jack. Although you're heading up one of the most striking coastlines in America, you won't see much of it unless you're offshore on a lobster boat. If you sift through the rubble, the mundane views reveal a few jewels, such as the bridge at Verona, but mostly you'll see traffic clogging the main artery to Mount Desert Island, part of Acadia National Park. Stick with U.S. 1 until Ellsworth, where you can take Route 3 south into "Baa Haabaa."

Cheap motels and crosswinds mark the bridge entrance to Mount Desert Island. At Hulls Cove, look for the **Visitors Center,** 207/288-3338, www.nps.gov/acad. It may be an illusion, but tourists in Bar Harbor seem heartier than most—they wear hiking boots and often look like bearded mountain folk. So do the men.

Rangers at the center offer volumes of material, from the *Beaver Log* newspaper to information on ranger-led programs, weather, tides, fishing, and camping. A free film narrated by Jack Perkins (of *A&E Biography* fame) tells the history of the island and how it was settled by "Rusticators" from the social circles of Philadelphia, Boston, and New York. Money from the likes of Pulitzer, Ford, Vanderbilt, and J. P. Morgan financed mansions patronizingly called "cottages."

For motorcycle travelers, the most relevant information pertains to the 27-mile Park Loop Road, which follows the island coast, then knifes its way through the center of the park. You could race it in an hour, but allow three

Rally: Laconia Motorcycle Rally and Race Week

A year after 400 riders spent a few days at Weirs Beach, New Hampshire, the first sanctioned "Gypsy Tour" was held in Laconia in 1917. Popular with America's few thousand riders, the "Gypsy Tour" developed a following through the 1920s and 1930s. In 1938, motorcycle hill-climber Fritzie Baer and his partners (the Red Hat Brigade) started a 30-year effort to keep the rally at full steam. But during the 1960s, the hill climbs and road races were cancelled as the Rally fell out of favor with local police. A week before the 1965 rally, a state law was passed allowing police to arrest riders loitering in groups of three or more. The law was bound to spark trouble and it did. At the "Riot of Laconia," motorcyclists battled police and the National Guard, leading to Motorcycle Week becoming Motorcycle Weekend. In 1975, camping along Highway 106 was outlawed and attendance dropped to a new low of 25,000. But as the Sturgis and Daytona rallies grew in size and popularity, locals took a fresh look at Laconia. In 1991, Motorcycle Week was back, the term "Gypsy Tour" was restored in 1992, and in 1993 the hill climbs returned to Gunstock. Held the second week of June, by 2001, 375,000 motorcyclists arrived for eight days of motorcycle events including races, hill climbs, touring, parades, vintage bikes, swap meets, demo rides, and the blessing of the motorcycles.

603/366-2000
www.laconiamcweek.com

for abundant photo ops. If you have a tape player, spring for the $13 rental of the Acadia tape tour; if not, a $1.25 booklet should suffice. Either will fill you in on the island's history and natural beauty. A few highlights:

John D. Rockefeller designed 45 miles of carriage roads with the stipulation that no motor cars would be allowed. He never mentioned motorcycles. In any event, this was a summer haven, and folks here felt so privileged that in 1919 they decided to donate well over 30,000 acres of mountains, lakes, and sea to the government, making Acadia the first national park east of the Mississippi.

Everything was going swell until the Great Forest Fire of 1947 swept over most of the island and burned more than 17,000 acres to cinders. Also gone were the mansions of "Millionaire's Row." Good heavens, Lovey... Charcoal!

A $10 fee grants you access to the Park Loop Road, and you'll immediately appreciate the efforts of the people who gave us the gift of Acadia. The road leads to great cliff corners, dips, and rises. Scenic ocean views are frequent, and if you time it right the normally silent Thunder Hole will boom with the fury of the sea. If there's fog, the landscape becomes an Impressionist painting. And if you're riding on a clear day, the peak of Cadillac Mountain (1,532 feet) may afford a matching view of Camden's Mount Battie—and exposure to the first rays of sunlight to fall on the United States.

When you finally reach downtown Bar Harbor, you'll discover tourist central is comprised of a village green and mismatched buildings that house bookstores, drugstores, and the ever-present gift shops. Since you've ridden this far, it's worth checking out. Look for curbside parking or the free two-hour municipal parking lot between Route 3 (Mount Desert Avenue) and Cottage Street.

Pull it Over: Bar Harbor Highlights
Attractions and Adventures

Like Camden, Bar Harbor's season runs from about mid-May to late October—weather willing. The best attractions here are the outdoor activities. Deep-sea fishing charters, windjammer cruises, island cruises, lighthouse cruises, and kayak rentals abound. The town pier is the best place to pick up brochures and make your selection.

Want to get out of the saddle and up a mountain? You can learn the ropes at **Atlantic Climbing School,** 26 Cottage St., 207/288-2521, www.acsclimb.com, with beginner to advanced programs that take you to Acadia for instruction on spectacular cliffs. Prices run from $95–160, depending on skill level and number of people in the class. If you've got time, get a piece of the rock. Reservations are required.

Ocean Drive,
Acadia National Park

© NATIONAL PARK SERVICE

If you prefer getting away from the crowds and captains, charter a boat. Ask what's included—fuel can be expensive. **Mansell Boat Rentals,** Main St., Southwest Harbor, 207/244-5625, www.mansellboatrentals.com, rents boats that range from an 11-foot inflatable with a 25-horsepower Mercury engine to a 19-foot Seaway with bucket seats and a 75-horsepower Mariner. Sailboats and Boston Whalers are also on the list. Experience is necessary, and a deposit is required.

Coastal Kayaking Tours, 48 Cottage St., 207/288-9605 or 800/526-8615, www.acadiafun.com, Maine's oldest sea kayak outfitter, has more than 100 sea kayaks, 20 trainers, guides, and tours that can last a few hours to a few days. You'll get a hearty upper-body workout and the opportunity to watch the sea life from sea level.

Several whale-watching charters depart from the marina, and all host similar excursions. Offered from late May to late October, trips last around three hours. Some charters will refund your money if no whales are spotted. Options include **Acadian Whale Adventures,** www.whalesadventures.com, 207/288-9800 or 866/710-9800; or the **Bar Harbor Whale Watch Co.,** 207/288-2386 or 800/508-1499, www.whalesrus.com. Wear your leathers—it can get cold on the boat. Did you hear me? Wear your—I heard you, Mom!

The Wendell Gilley Museum of Bird Carving, Southwest Harbor, 207/244-7555, www.acadia.net/gilley, is slightly out of the way, but if you need a fantastically detailed bird carving for your office. . . . Gilley, a late native son, earned a national following, and here you'll see why. The museum shop sells bird carvings, carving tools, and field guides for nature lovers. Hours vary, so call ahead.

Shopping

If you're a devotee of America's million-plus microbreweries, visit **Atlantic Brewing Company,** 30 Rodick St., 207/288-9513, www.atlanticbrewing.com, and stock up on Bar Harbor Real Ale, a nut brown ale with a round, malty body. Other brews include Blueberry Ale and Ginger Wheat. Free tours are given at 4 P.M. daily.

After a hard ride, it's time for the great indoors and a good cigar. In the summertime, **Joe's Smoke Shop,** 119 Main St., 207/288-9897, has enough cigars to fill a walk-in humidor and an intimate bar, where you can enjoy a glass of wine, brandy, port, scotch, or a martini.

Suffering withdrawal because you're cruising without a dulcimer? If you like Irish and/or Appalachian music, drop in at **Song of the Sea,** 47 West St., 207/288-5653, www.songsea.com. Beautiful hand-crafted Irish harps, bagpipes, chanters, flutes, CDs, and other unusual instruments are worth seeing—and shipping home.

Blue-Plate Specials

How many diners can back up a "Get In Here And Eat!" sign with great food? Since 1969, **Freddie's Route 66,** 21 Cottage St., 207/288-3708, a funky, collectibles-filled diner, has served roadhouse specialties like chicken pot pies and hot turkey dinners as well as fish and pasta. It's open for lunch and dinner, with happy hour from 5 until "66 minutes past" (6:06 P.M.).

The Thirsty Whale Tavern, 40 Cottage St., 207/288-9335, offers fine spirits, sandwiches, and beer in a basic bar—uh, tavern—setting. You'll find chicken, burgers, haddock, clams, and a dozen beers—including some microbrews—on tap. Avoid it if you don't like smoke.

Galyn's Galley Restaurant, 17 Main St., 207/288-9706, was constructed inside an 1890s boarding house, so you can check in and check out fresh lobster, scallops, fish, and their specialty prime rib. Upstairs, the intimate lounge features an antique mahogany bar. If you don't drink alcohol, just order one of the homemade, super-sweet desserts, chased by a shot of insulin.

Shut-Eye

If you have to stay over, Bar Harbor has more than 3,000 hotel rooms. Check www.barharborinfo.com for listings. If the weather's right, camping is another option. Campsites within Acadia National Park need to be reserved well in advance. Call the National Parks Reservations service at 800/365-2267, or go to reservations.nps.gov. (no www.)

Chain Drive*
A, E, L, M, S, DD.

*Chain hotels in, or within ten miles of town. See cross-reference guide featuring phone numbers and web address on page 405.

Side Trip: Port Clyde and Monhegan Island

Between Brunswick and Rockland, several peninsulas hang off the coast like icicles. If you can make one trip, head south on U.S. 1 to Route 131 to Port Clyde, a part of Maine that's relatively tourist-free ("pretty old school," says a local). From here you can catch the mail boat(!) to Monhegan Island (207/372-8848, www.monheganboat.com). The $25 round trip runs seven days a week from May through October (call ahead for departure times).

Monhegan has been home to the Wyeth Family for years, and artists from around the world come here to draw and paint. You can't see this rugged and rustic island on bike since no vehicles are allowed. Set off on foot and hike down seldom-walked trails, visit galleries in the artists' colony, and meet true lobstermen. It's a great place to get your creativity in gear and peace in your heart.

Resources for Riders

White Mountains—Blue Seas Run

Maine Travel Information
Maine Campground Owners Association—207/782-5874,
    www.campmaine.com
Maine Office of Tourism—888/624-6345, www.visitmaine.com
Maine Road Conditions—207/287-3427

New Hampshire Travel Information
New Hampshire Fall Foliage Report—800/258-3608
New Hampshire Fish and Game Department—603/271-3421,
    www.wildlife.state.nh.us
New Hampshire Office of Travel and Tourism—603/271-2343 or
    800/386-4664, www.visitnh.gov
New Hampshire Road Conditions—603/271-6900
New Hampshire State Parks—603/271-3628, www.nhparks.state.nh.us

Local and Regional Information
Acadia National Park Information—207/288-3338, www.nps.gov/acad
Bar Harbor Chamber of Commerce—207/288-5103 or 800/288-5103,
    www.barharborinfo.com
Camden Chamber of Commerce—207/236-4404 or 800/223-5459,
    www.camdenme.org
Littleton Chamber of Commerce—603/444-6561,
    www.littletonareachamber.com
Mount Washington Valley Chamber of Commerce—603/356-5701 or
    800/367-3364, www.mtwashingtonvalley.org
White Mountain National Forest—603/528-8721, www.fs.fed.us/r9/white

New Hampshire Motorcycle Shops
Littleton Harley-Davidson/Buell—Rte. 116, Littleton, 603/444-1300,
    www.littletonharley.com
Manchester Harley-Davidson/Buell—115 John E. Devine Dr., Manchester,
    603/622-2461 or 800/CYCLE93, www.manchesterhd.com

Maine Motorcycle Shops
Big Moose Harley-Davidson/Buell—375 Riverside St., Portland,
    .207/797-6061, www.bigmooseharley.com
North Country Harley-Davidson—N. Belfast Ave., Augusta, 207/622-7994.
    www.northcountry.com
Reid's RV Center (Ducati, BMW) —1300 Atlantic Hwy., Lincolnville,
    207/338-6068, www.reidscycle.com
Smith's Sno & Grass Yamaha—984 Barnestown Rd., Hope, 207/763-3428,
    www.smithssnograssyamaha.com

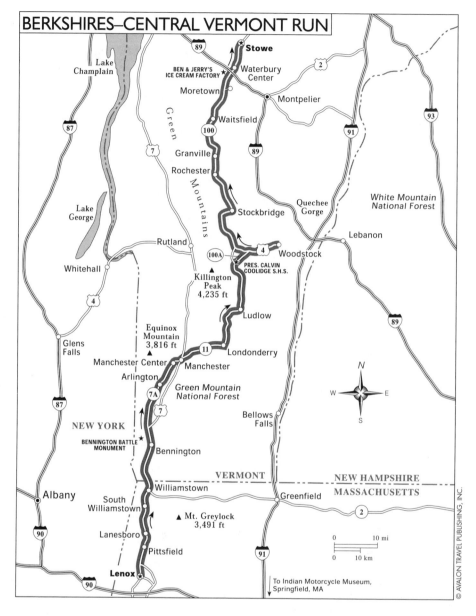

BERKSHIRES–CENTRAL VERMONT RUN

Route: Lenox to Stowe via Williamstown, Arlington, Manchester Village, Plymouth Notch, Woodstock, Rochester, Waitsfield

Distance: Approximately 210 miles; consider five days with stops.
• Day 1—Lenox/Stockbridge • Day 2—Travel • Day 3—Woodstock • Day 4—Travel • Day 5—Stowe

First Leg: Lenox, Massachusetts, to Woodstock, Vermont (122 miles)

Second Leg: Woodstock to Stowe, Vermont (88 miles)

Helmet Laws: Massachusetts and Vermont require helmets.

Berkshires—Central Vermont Run

Lenox, Massachusetts to Stowe, Vermont

If you live west of the Mississippi or south of the Mason-Dixon line, reaching your region's best road can take hours. This is where New England is different. The dense concentration of rivers, hillocks, and mountains compresses a nation's worth of ideal motorcycling roads into a relatively small area. Of course, it's not just the roads that make this trip one of the best in America. This tour offers the criteria for a perfect run: culture, history, and scenery.

Lenox is where you'll find The Mount, novelist Edith Wharton's home, along with summer stock theaters, wildlife preserves, and Tanglewood, the summer venue of the Boston Symphony Orchestra. A short ride away is Stockbridge, Norman Rockwell's final hometown. From the heart of the Berkshires, the road leads to Vermont and Plymouth Notch, the preserved village and birthplace of the reticent, yet surprisingly eloquent, Calvin Coolidge. Neighboring Woodstock is the quintessential New England village. Stowe's peak travel time is ski season, which means that summer and early fall free up the forest and mountain roads for some of the best riding in America.

Lenox Primer

In the latter half of the 1800s, this tranquil farming region was "discovered" by famous and wealthy residents of Boston and New York. First, Nathaniel Hawthorne wrote *The House of Seven Gables* and *Tanglewood Tales* while living near Lenox, and then Samuel Gray Ward, the Boston banker who later helped finance the purchase of Alaska, built a summer home near Hawthorne's cottage. Through Hawthorne's words and Ward's wealthy friends, Lenox became the place to establish summer homes, which were, in fact, gigantic mansions their owners dismissed as "cottages." In Lenox, actors, actresses, authors, bankers, and industrialists like Andrew Carnegie added flash to the Gilded Age.

With the turn of the century, a federal income tax overturned the fortunes of many of these families and the mansions were later sold and converted into the schools, hotels, and resorts you'll see today. Although they lost a few millionaires, Lenox found new life through music. In 1937, locals enlisted the Boston Symphony Orchestra to make Tanglewood—an estate between Lenox and Stockbridge—their summer home. Today, Tanglewood hosts one of the world's leading music festivals and has made this town the summertime cultural capital of the Northeast.

If you travel here in the peak season of July and August, be warned that prices—especially at restaurants—rise dramatically. Then again, the upscale attitude hasn't sidelined locals' favorites like cheap pizza gardens, breakfast diners, and working-class bars.

In the evening when the streets are quiet and the moon is rising over the Berkshire hills, walk through the Lenox streets. The evening mist, historic buildings, and peaceful silence will transport you back 200 years.

On the Road in Lenox

The core of Lenox is small. Small, I tell ya, just two blocks wide and about four blocks long. You could goose it and clear town in under 10 seconds. But that's not what Lenox is about. And since parking is free, rest your bike. The longer you stay, the more you save.

Take your time and see the primary street (Church Street); walk along Main Street (Route 7A); and drop down back alleys to discover less trafficked antique shops, art galleries, and coffee bars. Stop by the circa 1815 Berkshire County Courthouse, which now houses the Lenox Library. You may run across Lenoxians Gene Shalit and Maureen Stapleton. I did. Really.

Since Lenox proper doesn't offer a wealth of roads, take a half day for an extremely casual—and educational—14-mile loop to neighboring Stockbridge. Even during peak tourist season, back roads are lightly traveled and immensely fun.

From the heart of town, the Patterson memorial obelisk marks the intersection of Route 7A and Route 183 South. Head down 183 and into a canopy road that runs past the Stockbridge Bowl, reached by turning left down Hawthorne Street. This glacial lake is reserved for the residents of Stockbridge, but I doubt you'll get carded. Be discreet and you'll find it's a perfect place to swim, blessed with an amazing vista of the surrounding Berkshires.

Back on Route 183, Tanglewood will be on your left, but since concerts don't begin until dusk, keep riding straight for several more tree-lined miles until you cross Route 102 to reach the Norman Rockwell Museum on your left. Farther down 183 on your right is Chesterwood, the equally fascinating home and studio of sculptor Daniel Chester French—best known for his masterpiece, the *Lincoln Memorial*. His studio is still cluttered with several Lincoln studies and other striking pieces.

Return to Route 102 East, and you'll enter the village of Stockbridge, where you can stop for a drink at the Lion's Den at the famous **Red Lion Inn,** 413/298-5545, www.redlioninn.com, serving travelers since 1773. Naturally, there are a few gift shops and restaurants in town—none of special note—so when you're ready to ride back to Lenox, return to Route 7 North (turn left at the fire station) and watch for Berkshire Cottages Blantyre and Cranwell on your right.

Now you're home. Bow to your partner. Then bow to your corner. And promenade.

Pull It Over: Lenox Highlights
Attractions and Adventures

During July and August, the Boston Symphony Orchestra gets the hell out of Bean Town and heads to **Tanglewood,** West St./Rte. 183, 413/637-5165 or 617/637-5165, www.bso.org. Now the site of the world's leading musical festival, Tanglewood has been drawing crowds since 1937 and is a must-see if you're here in season. Guest conductors including Andre Previn and John Williams have taken the lead beneath The Shed, and non-BSO summer nights feature such artists as Bob Dylan and James Taylor. Lawn tickets are reasonably priced, which makes this perhaps the best outdoor concert venue in America—and the best musical picnic you'll ever enjoy. Before you go, pack a blanket and swing by **Loeb's Food Town,** 42 Main St., 413/637-0270, a great little fully-stocked grocery where you can pick up a baked chicken, beer, wine, and everything else.

Edith Wharton is one of America's most celebrated authors (foreshadowing this book's success), winning the 1921 Pulitzer Prize for *The Age of Innocence*. Wharton's estate, **The Mount,** Plunkett St. (Rts. 7 and 7A), 413/637-1899 or 888/637-1902, www.edithwharton.org, was built in 1902, based on the classical precepts of her book *The Decoration of Houses*. Hourly tours ($6) are conducted June and October and if you're a lady rider traveling through in July and August, the "Women of Achievement" lecture series is held on Mondays.

Highbrow bikers may look forward to **Shakespeare & Company,** 70 Kemble St., 413/637-1197, www.shakespeare.org, which is near The Mount and stages 10 plays by Shakespeare and six by Berkshire playwrights in an outdoor amphitheater between late May and October. Wherefore art thou, spark plug cleaner?

Berkshire Wildlife Sanctuaries, 472 W. Mountain Rd., 413/637-0320, $4, is just a few miles from town and is open Tuesday–Sunday, dawn–dusk. Part of the larger 1,500-acre Pleasant Valley Sanctuary, Berkshire offers several miles of trails and abundant wildlife. It's a quiet and natural destination to ride your bike.

Norman Rockwell was the Charles Kuralt of canvas, capturing an America that existed only in our minds. While the somewhat sterile **Norman Rockwell Museum,** Rte. 183, Stockbridge, 413/298-4100, www.nrm.org, doesn't capture his sincerity, it does display the world's largest collection of his original art, with nearly 500 works, including the original Four Freedoms—well worth the ride and a few hours. Rockwell's former studio was moved to this site and appears as he left it when he died. Hint: His autobiography is excellent for road reading. The museum and store are open daily 10–5. Admission is $10.

You may not know the name Daniel Chester French, but I guarantee that you know the work of this American sculptor. A few blocks from the Rockwell Museum is **Chesterwood,** 4 Williamsville Rd., Stockbridge, 413/298-3579, www.chesterwood.org, a 122-acre Italian-style villa where he created masterpieces, such as the *Lincoln Memorial* (1922) and *Concord's Minute Man* (1875). After viewing his home and seeing the 500-plus works in the well-stocked studio, stroll the grounds and you'll likely sense the power of the natural surroundings that inspired these works of Americana. Open daily 10–5; admission is $8.50.

Herman Melville lived in **Arrowhead,** 780 Holmes Rd., Pittsfield, 413/442-1793, www.mobydick.org, from 1850–1862, writing books such as *Moby Dick.* Sadly, the world traveler and gifted writer found it difficult to raise a family on modest royalties so he packed it up for a desk job in New York City, where he worked for the last 20 years of his life as a customs inspector. Arrowhead is loaded with many of Melville's personal artifacts, and if you like his books, then it's worth the detour—although the tour can drag. The home is open 9:30–5, Memorial Day–October 31, with tours on the hour. Admission is $5.

Blue-Plate Specials

The Village Snack Shop, 27 Housatonic St., 413/637-2564, serves great food from 6 A.M.–2 P.M., Monday–Saturday. Its motto: "Where friends meet for a cup of coffee." Not just coffee, but eggs, juice, sandwiches, hot dogs, hamburgers, and milkshakes. A simple diner, the kind that's just right on a ride.

For some of the best Southern cooking in the North, try the **Great Lenox Diner,** 30 Church St., 413/637-3204. No wimpy, washed-out New England food here—at dinnertime look for fresh turkey, chicken, potatoes, stuffing, gravy, and vegetables. Lunch features sandwiches and homemade soups.

At **Carol's Restaurant,** 8 Franklin St., 413/637-8948, you'll find all-day breakfast, good simple food, and waitresses who'll probably call you "Honey." Carol's serves deli sandwiches, fried fish, and basic meals at a fair price.

And don't miss **Dakota,** 1035 South St., 413/499-7900, located a few miles north of Lenox en route to Pittsfield on Route 7, where they serve big food in a big Pacific Northwest setting. Here since the 1960s, the featured items include fresh salmon, prime rib, lobster, and hand-cut steaks. Expect to wait for a table. Expect the meal to last for days.

Watering Holes

Want to look like a local? Pull up a barstool and order a Fat Boy Burger at the **Olde Heritage Tavern,** 12 Housatonic St., 413/637-0884. It offers all the ingredients of a neighborhood bar: Foosball, darts, jukeboxes, local characters, pub grub, liquor, and pitchers of Newcastle Brown Ale and others. Did I say bar? Sir, this is a tavern!

Shut-Eye

Lenox has dozens of inns and a healthy number of independent motels. In season, many inns and hotels require minimum stays on weekends, and prices rise accordingly. Check in advance. Two lodging services can help you: Go to www.lenox.org/lodging/ for the Chamber's listing of local digs, or, if you prefer to stay south of town (Lee, Lenoxdale, Stockbridge, Great Barrington), the Berkshire Lodging Association at 888/298-4760, www.berkshirelodging.com, offers a list of inns, hotels, and motels.

Chain Drive*
A, C, E, S, U, CC, DD.

*Chain hotels in, or within ten miles of town. See cross-reference guide featuring phone numbers and web addresses on page 405.

Inn-Dependence
Before Edith Wharton built The Mount, **The Gables,** 81 Walker St., 413/637-3416 or 800/382-9401, www.gableslenox.com, became her home when she

married wealthy young Teddy Wharton. Frank and Mary Newton restored it and now it offers everything an inn should: an enclosed heated pool, garden tables, large rooms adorned with antiques and collectibles, hard-surface parking, tennis—plus a huge breakfast and a short walk to the village. Rates run $90–210.

Although **Garden Gables Inn** is on the main drag, 135 Main St., 413/637-0193, www.gardengablesinn.com, the setting is secluded and peaceful. Five acres provide a buffer from the tourists, and a swimming pool and comfortable rooms make this a safe and relaxing choice, with rates from $110–225.

On the Road: Lenox to Woodstock

When you leave Lenox, Route 7A merges with Route 7 on the road to Pittsfield. Tense traffic is the price you'll pay to reach the Berkshire County seat, but you'll be duly rewarded at the nondescript **King Kone,** 413/496-9485, at the corner of Fenn and 1st. Just $1.10—that's only 11 dimes, friends—buys a small, medium, or large ice cream cone. Go for the large. It's nearly a foot tall and, damn, she's a pretty sight.

After escaping the pit of Pittsfield, head north on Route 7. Two miles past Lanesborough you can detour right onto North Main Street and ride an additional nine switchback-rich miles to reach the summit of Mount Greylock. At 3,491 feet, it's the state's highest peak, and a 100-foot-tall war memorial offers a view of five states. If you have neither the time nor the inclination to scale the summit, continue on Route 7. When you reach New Ashford, get ready for several miles of great elevations and terrific plunges surrounding the Brodie Mountain ski area. Further up the road at Routes 7 and 43, watch for the **Store at Five Corners,** 413/458-3176, www.thestoreatfivecorners.com, a general-store anomaly. Basic staples (thread, detergent, tape) rest beside gourmet groceries, and the market has become an attraction unto itself. No pork rinds in sight, but if you're looking for fine wines, garlic parsley pasta, and other imported fare, you'll find plenty to peruse.

Just a few hundred yards past Five Corners is the most visually appetizing sight you've seen in a while. Scan the horizon to your right and the valley looks like a Dali painting as it melts into low hills a mile away. In fall, the view will prepare you for upcoming scenes of old men in overalls selling pumpkins by the roadside, cornstalks stacked like teepees, and dogs sleeping on the porches of cozy homes. Sunflowers sag under their own weight, and flower gardens speckle yards. The smell of fresh air mingles with the spicy aroma of trees, sweet corn, and smoking chimneys.

Soon you are in Williamstown, a tranquil village built around Williams College (circa 1793). If you're ahead of schedule, take a break downtown, where the antiques are pricy and the merchandise is available elsewhere. Still, the town is cool, and the **Sterling and Francine Clark Art Institute,** 225 South St., 413/458-9545, www.clarkart.edu, is well worth a visit. Even if your walls are hung with paint-by-number masterpieces, this is where you can relive college art appreciation class, viewing works by artists of the caliber of Sargent, Remington, and Degas. Open daily except Monday until July 1, then seven days a week through summer. Admission varies based on exhibit, but is usually five bucks.

You know life is good when Route 7 continues north, its steep grades dropping you into the thick of purple and yellow and green hills. The hues reveal that you are entering Vermont, the name derived from the French words vert (green) and mont (mountain). Within a few miles you'll notice that something's missing; there are no billboards in Vermont. None. Natural beauty is the state's best advertising.

Replacing the billboards, however, are maple syrup sellers. Maple syrup is sold from front porches. Maple syrup is sold from car trunks, at diners, in gas stations, schools, prisons, basements, attics, duck blinds, churches, tollbooths, and bomb shelters. The proliferation of maple syrup packaged in jars, jugs, bottles, and canisters will stay with you years after Vermont disappears from your memory.

For now, however, you are approaching Bennington and its 306-foot-tall Bennington Battle Monument. Directions to the monument are tricky, but since you can see it from 50 miles away I don't think you need much help finding it.

When you roll into the north end of town, watch the road signs and veer onto parallel route 7A. Now you can relax again as you begin your voyage through

Cool Calvin

Vermont's Calvin Coolidge didn't say much, but when he did, you can rest assured he knew what he was talking about . . .

"Nothing in the world can take the place of persistence. Talent will not; nothing is more common than unsuccessful men with talent. Genius will not; unrewarded genius is almost a proverb. Education will not; the world is full of educated derelicts. Persistence and Determination alone are omnipotent. The slogan 'Press On,' has solved and always will solve the problems of the human race."

Vermont. As you approach the village of Arlington, you sense there are no worries here—just mountains to watch and a quiet back road that's coaxing you along. The riding here is sublime and you may never want to stop, but I suggest that you should since you're fast approaching **Snow's Arlington Dairy Bar,** 3176 VT Route 7A, 802/375-2546. A favorite with bikers, Snow's has been on the ground since 1962, serving hot dogs, chili dogs, fries, and shakes. Pull it over, grab a picnic table, and enjoy the surrounding woods. If you carry an AARP card, time your ride for Tuesday's Senior Day (a generous 10 percent off).

Less than a mile up the road is Arlington's **Norman Rockwell Exhibit,** 802/375-6423, www.normanrockwellexhibit.com, which I believe is much more sincere than the larger version in Stockbridge. Allow an hour for this stop. The exhibit is housed in a converted church, and what makes it different is that the guides here were once models for Rockwell who lived in Arlington from 1939–1952. According to the docents, he'd pay them $5 to pose for his paintings (a fortune for kids) and when he and other artists set up easels on the town green to raise money for Arlington's Community House, Rockwell would draw pictures for $1. Because these pictures reflect an idealized Americana, be prepared for an emotional visit.

Nine miles later you'll reach Manchester Village, but not without passing hills colored with countless shades of green and bordered by the flowing Batten Kill River. Park your bike and explore the river with the full-service **BattenKill Canoe Ltd.,** 800/421-5268, www.battenkill.com. They lead tours—or will turn you loose—on the crystal clear, trout-rich waterway that flows beside lonely country lanes, quiet meadows, and into deep woods. Although Manchester is a small town, there are other detours to make. To experience 5.2 miles of steep grades and sharp curves, take a scenic ride to the summit of 3,816-foot Mount Equinox (802/362-1114, $5), which is the highest peak in the Taconic Range. The toll road leads to a restaurant, walking trails, and picnic sites, but the Carthusian monastery is off limits to travelers. Tell 'em you wanna be a monk and maybe they'll let you in.

Hildene, 802/362-1788, www.hildene.org, the 24-room Georgian Revival home of Robert Todd Lincoln (Abe's kid), is on your right. Home to Lincoln's few descendants, the house features original furnishings and family effects, as well as formal gardens.

A few miles farther north, the merchants of Manchester Center (est. 1761) tricked out their outlet stores so that wealthy shoppers would think they were getting a good deal. Although outlets no longer mean savings, say that to anyone leaving Polo, Bass, Izod, Calvin Klein, Nautica, Big Dog, or Godiva, and expect to be jerked off your bike and beaten with a sack of size 34 Jordache jeans. Aside from this, with its river, side streets, and non-outlet stores and restaurants, Manchester is well worth a break.

When you leave Manchester, turn right at the roundabout and say *au revoir* to 7A and howdy-do, Route 11. You've cleared the orgy of outlets and dodged swarms of shoppers and once again it's just you and the positive strokes that come with traveling by motorcycle. Your bike is scaling the hills northeast of town and as you enter the Green Mountain National Forest, a scenic pull-off provides a glorious aerial view of Manchester. Since you won't be traveling here in winter, the rising and falling road will give you a chance to practice 1,000-cc ski jumps. On any hill, just tap it into neutral, stand on your foot pegs, and stretch forward as you feel the smooth fall, soft dip at the base, and the slow rise. Feels just like the real thing.

At Londonderry, Route 11 stops, zigs to the left, then introduces you to State Road 100. That's the most *righteous* State Road 100. Never before in the history of motorcycling has one road done so much for so many. SR 100 cleaves a path through the center of the Green Mountains and plunges you into the heart of Vermont, where apple trees and general stores and Holstein cows create a new, yet strangely familiar, landscape.

Running toward Ludlow, a riverside ride takes you through wide-open spaces to the junction with 155, where you'll veer right to continue on SR 100. In the weeks leading to fall foliage, apple trees are brilliant red, and scattered colors change from dark green to bright red to greenish yellow. Unfortunately, the Tom Joad–style shacks don't inspire a sense of awe.

Although Ludlow's seen better days, the Okemo Mountain Ski Resort is here and offers nice elevations, just as upcoming Tyson provides a pleasing ride beside Echo Lake, which I'm sure is perfectly suitable for swimming at least two hours a year. This brings up a point: Sunny, pleasant Vermont can become *Night on Bald Mountain* in moments. Stow some warm clothes or carry a butane torch in your saddlebags to stave off frostbite.

This is where SR 100 gets interesting. Very. As you near Killington, you'll realize that the ground was laid out by God and the road designed by an engineer who probably rode an Indian Chief. You'll experience great twists, exhilarating turns, frequent rises, and thrilling drops. The ride gets even more exciting when you turn right to Route 100A.

On the run, you'll see tarpaper shacks with cords of firewood so massive you'd be hard pressed to tell where the kindling ends and the homes begin. Mountains towering along the roadside are straight from *The Land of the Giants*. Don't spare the horsepower as you ride northeast toward Plymouth Notch and the **Calvin Coolidge State Historic Site**, 802/672-3773, www.historicvermont.org, $6.50, a turn-of-the-century village preserved in honor of its famous son.

If you doubt that just about anyone can become president, witness this. A sleepy village tucked in the folds of sleepy hills is where Coolidge was born on the Fourth of July. Even if you don't know a thing about our 30th president, I guarantee you'll spend more time here after you read his observations about government and the United States, and learn that he was the last president to write his own speeches. As you tour the village, you may even buy some cheese from the small factory that Calvin's son John operated until he passed away in May 2000. Afterward, take a few minutes at the cemetery across the street. The Coolidge family fronts the road, with Calvin's headstone marked with the presidential seal.

The 100A adventure continues to the junction of Route 4, where you'll turn right for the final 10-mile trip to Woodstock. This winding, level road follows the flow of the Ottaquechee River. Be careful: The curving river can be hypnotizing, and there's no guardrail. Keep your eyes on the road and soon you'll be in Woodstock—a most interesting town.

Woodstock Primer

If ever a town was sent from Central Casting, it's Woodstock. Everything is here: the church steeple, village green, lazy river, covered bridge, American flags. This is Currier and Ives country.

History made this town what it is. It was chartered in 1761 and settled in 1768. The colonial homes, many of which are still standing, were built well and inexpensively using abundant natural materials. Early Woodstock was like a commune, in which bartering replaced cash purchases. Small businesses, including hatters, silversmiths, printers, cabinet makers, tanners, and jewelers, took up residence in town, while,on the outskirts, lumber and sawmills, cider presses, brick kilns, and iron casting furnaces came into operation.

Self-sufficiency and ingenuity are hallmarks of Woodstock's history. The earliest Morgan horses were stabled here (as were Jersey cows and Merino sheep), but farming and industry dropped into the background in 1934, when the first ski tow in America was installed here. That's when Woodstock became a center for tourism.

And it still is.

On the Road in Woodstock

Woodstock is a perfect stop for motorcycle travelers because the roads are right; the beauty is omnipresent; the streets are clinically clean; and great restaurants and neighborhood bars let you kick back after a day on the road.

There are only minor flaws in this dream state. Some locals grumble that merchants cater more to wealthy tourists. But more prominent is the fact that Route 4, the road you came in on, is also the primary truck route. Every few minutes, distant rumblings and the squeal of jake brakes announce the arrival of a semi. If you can block out the truck traffic, take solace in simple touches such as a picture of Calvin Coolidge in a storefront window.

As in Lenox, the town center is best seen on foot, and you'll find plenty of metered parking (and a convenient information booth) at the village square. If the booth is closed, the Woodstock Town Crier on Elm Street is, in reality, just a blackboard on which locals list such newsworthy events as raffles, chicken dinners, hayrides, and garden club meetings. Even the local movie venue—the town hall—is a throwback to the 1920s.

Outstanding shops include the **Village Butcher,** 18 Elm St., 802/457-2756, with a few hundred types of wines, cheeses, and meats. **FH Gillingham & Sons,** 11 Elm St., 802/457-2100, www.gillinghams.com, an old-time general store selling everything from fresh milk in bottles to hardware, wine, and microbrews, has been a Woodstock landmark since the late 1800s. If you've been inspired by the scenery, drop by **Pleasant Street Books,** 48 Pleasant St., 802/457-4050, which has two floors filled with more than 10,000 old volumes—from Civil War, to travel, to Vermontiana.

For many reasons, small towns such as this are better viewed after dark. Though the shops may be closed, you'll have a chance to distance yourself from tourists, pause by the bridge, and watch the Ottauquechee roll past.

For a short ride, join the caravan of bikers on the six-mile run east to **Quechee Gorge,** www.quecheegorge.com, and the **Simon Pearce Glass Factory.** The gorge is a popular spot for motorcycle travelers—but why? The 1960s tourist shop is weighted down with Quechee Gorge spoons, Indian mocassins made in Taiwan, and cedar altars sporting plastic Jesuses. Despite the lack of quality gifts, there's no dearth of visor-clad tourists ready to buy a geegaw for the breakfast nook in Idaho.

Here's why they come: The appeal is the hike down to the gorge, a 168-foot vertical drop below Vermont's oldest steel span bridge or a safer half-mile descent down a trail to the Ottauquechee River below. Walking down isn't too bad—smokers do it. Hikers do it and bikers do it. But all are far less enthusiastic hiking up.

At the bottom, take a break and just recline on one of thousands of wide river rocks. The dry river bed is a good place to think, as evidenced by all the people writing, sketching, and painting. When you want to ride the road again, further up Route 4 the Quechee Gorge Village features an antiques center,

Ready, Set, Go

Practical advice on packing and pre-ride preparations comes from Ray Towells, a dedicated rider and founder of Orlando's **Iron Horse Rentals.** *Call 407/426-7091 or check www.hogride.com for more information. Ray's British, so read this with an accent.*

Pre-Ride
Have your mechanic check your bike and make sure it's ready for the road. Don't ask for a comprehensive tune-up, just have him check the brake linings, pads, tires, oil, fuses, and spares.

Let someone know how long you'll be away and leave a rough itinerary. If you're planning a three-day trip, and it's been five days since you called, your friend will know something's wrong.

Clothing
If you wear full leathers in Florida in summer, you're an idiot. Dress for the climate. Try to find a leather jacket with a removable lining or sleeves that zip off. Beyond that, you won't need much—a few pairs of jeans, shorts, and T-shirts. When riding in a cold climate, bring thermal underwear. The average biker doesn't want to dress up, but casual shoes, Polo shirts, and khaki pants can pass in a nice restaurant.

country store, hyper-cool diner, and candle shop. When you're done, tie down your plastic Jesus with a bungee and return to Woodstock.

Pull it Over: Woodstock Highlights
Attractions and Adventures

Thankfully, in this pristine countryside most things worth doing are done outdoors. Even though some may seem like grade school field trips, these excursions are intriguing.

Billings Farm, Rte. 12, 802/457-2355, www.billingsfarm.com, is slightly interesting for laypeople, absolutely fascinating if you like cows and chickens. This pastoral parcel of land was created to educate the public on the value of responsible agriculture and land stewardship (the passions of lawyer, railroad entrepreneur, and philanthropist Frederick Billings). The circa 1871

Safety and Practicalities

As for supplies, I always carry a water container, foam earplugs to protect against noise, and a small flashlight. In remote areas, I pack a small first-aid kit with bandages, aspirin, sunscreen, and water purification tablets. A cell phone is great in an emergency. I also carry a roll of reflective tape. If you lose power to your lights, the tape will be a godsend.

When people see a $20,000 touring bike, they get ideas. Carry a Kryptonite lock. Bring an extra set of keys for your bike and hide them. Use heavy-duty tape to stick them under your saddle, for instance, or inside your headlight or spotlight.

If you break down and have to leave your bike, try to hide it off the road and cover it. A dark bike cover will come in handy.

Tool Kit

Bring a standard tool kit that includes, at minimum, vise grips or pliers; Allen wrenches, hex wrenches, and an adjustable wrench; a small screwdriver kit with multiple heads; small, medium, and large hose clamps; a roll of speed tape or electrical tape; wire; and two or three feet of electrical wire and a few connectors. You should also carry a puncture repair kit for your tires.

working farm is a living museum, hosting demonstrations of how they did it in the old days—from rug hooking to butter churning to wooden-tool making. The guides toss out useful data as well: "Count the number of fogs in August, and you can match the number of snows in the winter." Surprisingly fascinating. It's open May–October daily 10–5; admission is $8.

Marsh-Billings-Rockefeller National Historic Park, Rte. 12, 802/457-3368, Vermont's first national park, was donated to the United States a few years ago by Frederick Billings' granddaughter, Mary French Rockefeller, and her husband, Laurance Rockefeller. The park interprets conservation history using the 1870 forest established by Billings as a case study. Take a guided tour of the family mansion and gardens, or of the forest. The park is open June–mid-October, 10–4:30. The cost is $5.

Out toward the Gorge, the **Simon Pearce Gallery,** Rte. 4, Quechee, 802/295-2711, www.simonpearce.com, is open daily 9–9. While the name suggests a colonial-era factory, this gallery didn't open until a few years ago. That doesn't diminish the quality of the work, however. After watching the artists whip a glass out of molten sand, you'll want to raise a glass to their skills. Quality glassware as well as off-kilter factory seconds are sold in the gift shop. If your house has settled at a slant, spring for the seconds.

If you firmly believe that the pleasure's in the journey and not the final destination, saddle up on South America's favorite mammal and embark on one of six excursions into the Green Mountains. **Woodstock Llama Treks,** Rte. 4 (two miles west of Woodstock), 802/457-5117, www.woodstockllamatreks.com, features breakfast, lunch, romantic, and half-day treks, including meals, music, or picnics along meadows and hills. It's not an adventure, but a llovely way to see the llay of the lland. Rates run $15–40 per person during their season from mid-May–October.

Instead of heading to a mega-mall Googolplex, locals gather to enjoy movies in a refined setting at the **Town Hall Theatre,** the village green, 802/457-2620. Where else could you watch *Perils of Pauline* in Dolby?

Blue-Plate Specials

Here since 1955, **Wasp's Snack Bar,** 57 Pleasant St., 802/457-9805, has diner stools at the counter, and eggs, bacon, pancakes, hash browns, and coffee cooking and brewing behind it. A hangout for locals, you'll have to look for it since the signage is minimal. No dinners here, but lunch offers anything the cook can make, homemade specials, and homemade soups. Nothing fancy, but just right.

Homemade "rich super premium" ice cream (served in the basement) is the foundation—as it should be—for **Mountain Creamery,** 33 Central St., 802/457-1715. Upstairs, you can eat country breakfasts until 11:30 and big sandwiches noon–6:30. If you like your road food sweet, load up on pies, cakes, muffins, cookies, and brownies.

Full lunches and dinners are also served at Bentley's (see Watering Holes a half-inch below).

Watering Holes

Here since the '70s, **Bentley's,** 3 Elm St., 802/457-3232, is Woodstock's neighborhood bar. A few couches, a long bar, 1920s style, and creaky wooden floors give this place after-hours appeal. Lunch and dinner are served, but the microbrews (try Bentley's Elm Street Ale), wines, and casual setting make this spot equally enjoyable for an evening conversation and a good drink—although it can often get wicked busy.

Shut-Eye

Motels and Motor Courts
The large and clean **Shire Motel,** 46 Pleasant St., 802/457-2211, www.shire
motel.com, has been here since 1963. Located in the heart of town, it has 33
rooms with all sized beds. Summer peak rates are $78–125.

Chain Drive*
A, C, S

*Chain hotels in, or within ten miles of town. See cross-reference guide featur-
ing phone numbers and web addresses on page 405.

Inn-Dependence
Nancy and Tom Blackford are über-hosts who make their **Woodstocker
B&B,** 61 River St. (Rte. 4), 802/457-3896, www.scenesofvermont
.com/woodstocker, seem like home by laying out home-baked cookies and
breads each afternoon. Board games, a whirlpool tub, and a friendly house
dog add to the effect. You'll also enjoy killer breakfasts with oven-puffed
pancakes, a great location within walking distance of the village, and spacious rooms with queen or two double beds—although sounds can carry.
Rates range from $85–175.

Smack dab on the village green, the largest hotel in town, **Woodstock Inn,**
14 The Green, 802/457-1100 or 800/448-7900, www.woodstockinn.com, also
includes Richardson's Tavern, a restaurant, and premium rooms overlooking a
putting green. With 144 rooms, this inn is a popular spot for tourists, but its location and amenities may coax you to join them. Rates run from $159–303.

On the Road: Woodstock to Stowe

The moment you get home and put your bike in the garage, write a letter to the
Vermont highway commissioner and give thanks for the additional 90 miles of Route
100 beyond Woodstock. At the intersection of Routes 4 and 100, you'll find a Citgo
Food Mart. If you arrived by car, you'd get gas and snacks and leave. But on a bike
you'll want the experience to last. I sat on the porch, read the local bulletin board,
watched people buy maple syrup, and enjoyed the reprieve from my routine. You'll
have these experiences on the road, too—and often. Take advantage of them.

Routes 100 and 4 are the same for several miles, and you'll turn right at Phil's
Country Store to follow them. The road is slow and curving; the idea of a

straightaway is foreign in Vermont (credit this fact to Vermont's 1964 sale of surplus straightaways to Kansas).

As you swing into satisfying turns, you'll question whether this ride is actually the shortest route between Points A and B. It's not—and that's good. Route 100 rolls through gorgeous farmland, fields, and forest. It rides beside rivers and mountains. And it introduces you to the protectors of the free-enterprise system: individuals who live miles from the shadow of a mall and make their living as independent merchants. In the yards of unpainted frame houses and log cabins, signs advertise bread, carved flutes, honey, antiques, artwork, and, of course, maple syrup. This short stretch slowly reveals the diversity of the nation and confirms that this motorcycle tour is a great American adventure.

You'll have little time to contemplate the sensations you feel, because roughly five miles past the split of Routes 4 and 100, you're in the thick of it. South of Pittsfield you'll see yellow warning signs and the twisting black line that herald a series of quick turns that'll shift your bike beneath you like a hopped-up pendulum. Working the throttle, clutch, and brake in a symphony of shifting makes for a magical experience.

The bucolic nature of Vermont is on display. The roads weave randomly through this countryside, where tin roofs rusted on the edges sag lazily and crumbling mortar flakes off red chimneys. You'll see broken barns and unpainted covered bridges spanning rivers strewn with boulders.

The road leads to tight turns and cramped quarters, changes in elevation compensating for monochromatic greenness. Cornfields and farmland don't offer much visual appeal, but if you're not a local, it's strangely satisfying to watch Vermont farmers turn the earth, work the combines, and roll tractors weighted beneath bales of hay.

Depending on its mood and the lay of land, the wide White River will surface on your left or right. With no guardrails to keep you out of the drink, keep one eye on the road and one on the river. The flowing road leads to a small village, the town of Rochester, which is worth putting on the brakes and taking a break. This commercial district is only about two blocks long, but it has everything a motorcyclist needs: a gas station, small market, and the **Rochester Cafe and Country Store,** 802/767-4302, which features an old-fashioned soda fountain and serves breakfast and hot and cold sandwiches.

The ride north from Rochester leads to ordinary towns and villages, which arise every few miles, but the highlights you'll remember are the long stretches of emptiness. On the sloping roads south of Granville, gravity sucks you into a vortex of trees, leaves, and wild grass until you're completely enveloped by the environment. The Granville Gulf Reservation promises "six miles of natural

Beside a frigid waterfall along Highway 100 in Vermont.

beauty to be preserved forever." And it delivers. The force of nature is strong here: As you coast downhill, a stream on your right goes uphill. A great waterfall is on your left and offers a great place to stop for a picture—and a frigid spray of Vermont water.

The region changes from rural to upper class near Waitsfield. Between here and Morefield is the sesquipedalian (it means "lengthy") "1800 to 1850 Mad River Valley Rural Historic District." Along with the nice homes and a sense of wilderness, the smell of pine mingles with the scent of stables.

This journey is now coming to a close. When you reach Route 100B, Stowe is just 18 miles away. That's 18 more miles of mountains, smooth roads, Vermont farmlands, and Waterbury—home of Ben & Jerry's, and the ice cream capital of the world.

Life is good.

Stowe Primer

When it's not wintertime, Stowe is a cross between Lenox and something less than Lenox. It's not a rich town by any means, but it's not poor. It's pooch.

The lower village—the center of town—lies about four miles southeast of the ski area, and the road north (Route 108) merits a visit as much as the village. Compared to Lenox and Woodstock, there's not much ground to cover here, but motorcycle travelers like Routes 100 and 108, which intersect at the center of town.

The town was chartered in 1763 and named after descendants of England's Lord Stowe. Although known as a winter resort today, Stowe was a summer place 100 years ago. Then, like now, the main activities were shopping in the village, swimming in swimming holes, and riding up the mountain road to the peak of Mount Mansfield—at 4,393 feet, Vermont's highest point.

It's worth noting that in my visits here, the friendliness of innkeepers and chamber officials has never varied: They have always been indifferent. On the other hand, shopkeepers are courteous—especially if you're in the mood to buy.

On the Road in Stowe

You've already ridden some of Vermont's best roads on the way up, but if you're like me and can't get enough of mountain riding, turn onto Route 108 and head to Smuggler's Notch. This is a most excellent road for motorcycles and was a favorite route for independent Vermonters who smuggled goods from the United States to Canada during the 1807 Embargo Act. The road proved to be just as popular for transporting escaped slaves in the 1800s and bootleg liquor during Prohibition. This narrow, isolated road threads the needle between Mount Mansfield and Sterling Peak, rock formations created about 400 million years ago. At the summit, you may be able to make out outcroppings like Elephant's Head, Singing Bird, and Smuggler's Face. You may even run across some lost bootleggers.

Pull it Over: Stowe Highlights
Attractions and Adventures

Most of the town's attractions involve natural pursuits. At **Fly Fish Vermont,** 954 S. Main St., 802/253-3964, www.flyfishvt.com, Bob Shannon and staff offer a complete selection of equipment, including locally tied flies and rod and wader rentals. May–October, guides can take you to the best fishing spots in the area. But do you have room in your saddlebags for a 20-pound king salmon? Do you, punk?

At **Catamount Fishing Adventures,** Barrow's Rd., 802/253-8500, www.catamountfishing.com, Willy Dietrich offers four- to eight-hour fly-fishing or spin-fishing excursions in backwoods Vermont. The eight-hour trip includes a free lunch. Trips are based on your level of expertise, so if you normally fish with a shotgun, you're a beginner. Choose from canoe, float tube, small motorboat, or side stream tours in pursuit of trout, bass, and northern pike.

In the middle of adventure, when you're hugging the road, the chance to soar like an eagle is a damn fine thrill. Glider rides at **Morrisville-Stowe State Airport,** Rte. 100, Morrisville, 802/888-7845 or 800/898-7845, range from

$54 for 10 minutes to $179 for an hour, with $20 increments in between. When the rope pops off the glider, the serene and wild ride begins. Look for the Adirondacks to the west, Jay Peak to the north, Mount Washington to the east, and nothing but air below. Friends fly free (split the cost, get it?).

I bet you'll dig the ride up Route 108, and here's an option for getting back down: Ride the Lamoille River. Based at the Mann's View Inn, **Smuggler's Notch Canoe Touring,** 802/644-8321 or 888/937-6266, www.manns view.com, gets you paddling the clear streams past pine and maple forests, dairy farms, and majestic mountains. No thrashing white water, but it's one way to become Grizzly Adams. The $50 runs can last up to four hours and cover up to 12 miles, or you can really do it with an overnight canoe excursion and camp on the river's edge. Shuttle service takes you back to your bike.

If you're saddle sore, put on your walking shoes (or in-line skates) for a trip past mountains, woods, and farms. A 5.5-mile greenway stretches from Main Street along the West Branch River and Mountain Road to the covered bridge at Brook Road. Unless you've got a lift, it's another 5.5 miles back, though. The greenway was named by *Travel & Leisure* as one of the "19 Great Walks of the World."

When you've had enough sightseeing, head to **Ben & Jerry's,** Rte. 100 (one mile north of I-89), 802/244-8687 (244-TOUR), www.ben jerry.com. It's not in Stowe, but it's close enough. With $5 business diplomas from a correspondence course and a collective life savings of $8,000, Ben Cohen and Jerry Greenfield opened an ice cream parlor in an abandoned Burlington gas station in 1978. Not only did they vow to use only fresh Vermont ingredients, they also pledged 7.5 percent of pretax profits to em- ployee-led philanthropy. This is the way a business should be run—and the way ice cream should taste. Take the half-hour first-come-first-served tour for $2 and score some free ice cream straight from the production line. Beats touring a fertilizer factory.

Blue-Plate Specials

The gathering spot for locals, **McCarthy's,** Mountain Rd., 802/253-8626, serves the best breakfast in town. Stick around and you can chow down on homemade breads, soups, and pie at lunch. The food is cheap but healthy.

At dinnertime look for **Cactus Cafe,** 2160 Mountain Rd. (Rte. 108), 802/253-7770, known as much for its 16-ounce handmade margaritas as for its food. Along with Mexican standards (enchiladas, fajitas, quesadillas), pan-fried trout, pork chops, and Southwestern stir fry appear on the menu. If you can't get enough of the great outdoors (who can?), dine in the perennial garden.

If you've got a hankering for wild boar, venison, or pheasant, skip McDonald's and park it at **Mr. Pickwick's,** 433 Mountain Rd., 802/253-7064, www .englandinn.com., open daily for lunch and dinner. There are other restaurants within Ye Olde England Inne, but Mr. Pickwick's serves up more than 150 varieties of ale, including fresh wheat beer and lambic ales from Belgium. If there's a designated rider in your group, try one of each. Gotta cigar? Complement it from the selection of vintage ports, rare cognacs, and single malt scotches.

Watering Holes

The Whip Bar and Grill, Main St., 802/253-7301, www.greenmountain-inn.com, is downstairs at the Green Mountain Inn. Sure, it's a hotel bar but it feels more like a pub with its high-back chairs and English riding club design. They serve meals here, but the brews are better.

Gracie's on Main Street (basement of the Carlson Building), 802/253-8741, is a great little smoke-free basement bar featuring draft beer, bottled beer, and specially brewed beers. Gracie's also has a full menu of burgers, nachos, fish, and steak, but, damn, the bar looks so inviting. A canine theme runs throughout the place, as evidenced by "South of the Border Collie" fare.

The juke-joint atmosphere at the **Backyard Tavern,** 395 Mountain Rd., 802/253-9204, hasn't stopped celebs like Steven Tyler, Daryl Hannah, Matt Dillon, Tom Selleck, Mick Jagger, and Keith Richards from hanging out here. You'll find a basic bar menu with cheeseburgers and chicken fingers, a pool table, a great jukebox, pinball, and $1.50 draft pints daily.

Try the **Sunset Grille & Tap Room,** 140 Cottage Club Rd., 802/253-9281. You'll find a restaurant here, but the Tap Room is where you can get wings, bar pizzas, and burgers while watching sports on a variety of TVs. Summer Saturday night BBQ cookouts are held on the secluded patio, and pickup horseshoe and volleyball games shape up out back. When you're bored with that, check out the huge domestic beer selection.

Shut-Eye

Stowe's visitor information center also assists travelers with lodging. Call 802/253-7321 or 800/247-8693, or check www.gostowe.com. **Stowe Country Rentals** represents more than a dozen rental cabins, farms, and resorts. If you're traveling with a large group and need a base, check 'em out. Contact 800/639-1990 or www.stowecountryrentals.com. There are also 40-plus independent inns, hotels, and motels in town.

Motels and Motor Courts

Located about 2.5 miles north of the village is the clean and basic **Stowe Motel,** 2043 Mountain Road Stowe, 802/253-7629 or 800/829-7629, www.stowe motel.com. Sixty rooms and efficiencies are spread between three properties, with king and queen beds at each. Rooms start at about $70 and include a continental breakfast.

Chain Drive*

L

*Chain hotels in, or within ten miles of town. See cross-reference guide featuring phone numbers and web addresses on page 405.

Inn-Dependence

There's always the **Green Mountain Inn,** Main St., 802/253-7301 or 800/253-7302, www.greenmountaininn.com, with rates from $109–169. Right in the heart of town, this 1833 home-turned-inn has been renovated to feature 76 antiques-filled rooms and suites. The decor is rapidly becoming passé, but this location, with its health club, heated outdoor pool, canopy beds, fireplaces, and Jacuzzis, is just right after the ride. So is the pub. There's a two-night minimum on summer and fall weekends.

After Julie Andrews and Christopher Plummer escaped from the Nazis—no, wait. . . that was the movie—anyway, after the Von Trapp family left Austria, they wound up in its American counterpart, Stowe, and opened the **Trapp Family Lodge,** Rte. 108—up two miles from town, left at the white church, then two more miles—802/253-8511 or 800/826-7000, www.trappfamily.com. In-fighting among family members is a given now, but the lodge has sustained itself in large part on the strength of the family's story. Included on the 2,200 acres are 93 rooms with spectacular mountain views, nightly entertainment, a fitness center, three pools, tennis courts, and hiking trails. The dining room, lounge, and tearoom feature a European theme. Rates start at a Stowe-steep $180.

Related Side Trips

Vermont

Contributed by Ken Aiken

Route 110

Route 110 is a narrow, twisting road that begins at Route 14 in South Royalton, Vermont, and follows a churning river through the Vermont Piedmont. Lasting only 29.6 miles, the old wagon road runs through the historic villages of Tunbridge and Chelsea, and ends near the granite quarries of East Barre.

Route 17

Waitsfield, Vermont

Route 17 heads west from Route 100 in Waitsfield, climbs over the spine of the Green Mountains through the Appalachian Gap, then snakes and undulates across Champlain Valley, crossing Lake Champlain at historic Crown Point to Route 9 in New York. Dynamite.

Route 133

Routes 133 and 140 wind through Vermont's Taconic Mountains, and since neither gets too much traffic, they're perfect for cruising and enjoying the fall foliage. The slice of Route 140 just east of Route 7 is a sport rider's dream.

Resources for Riders

Bershires—Central Vermont Run

Massachusetts Travel Information

Massachusetts Department of Travel & Tourism—800/447-6277,
www.massvacation.com
Massachusetts Road Conditions—617/374-1234
Massachusetts State Park Campgrounds Reservations—877/422-6762,
www.reserveamerica.com

Vermont Travel Information

Vermont Attractions Association—802/229-4581, www.vtattractions.org
Vermont Campground Association—www.campvermont.com
Vermont Chamber of Commerce—802/223-3443, www.vtchamber.com
Vermont Department of Forests, Parks and Recreation—802/241-3655,
www. vtstateparks.com
Vermont Department of Tourism—802/828-3237 or 800/837-6668
Vermont Fall Foliage Hotline—802/828-3239
Vermont Fish and Wildlife—802/241-3700, www.vtfishandwildlife.com
Vermont Road Conditions—802/828-4894 or 800/429-7623

Local and Regional Information

Berkshires Visitors Bureau—413/443-9186 or 800/237-5747,
www.berkshires.org
Lenox Chamber of Commerce—413/637-3646, www.lenox.org
Stowe Chamber of Commerce—802/253-7321 or 800/247-8693,
www.gostowe.com
Woodstock Chamber of Commerce—802/457-3555 or 888/496-6378,
www.woodstockvt.com

Massachusetts Motorcycle Shops

North's Service—675 Lenox Rd., Lenox, 413/499-3266,
www.northsservices.com
Ronnie's Cycle Sales & Service—150 Howland Ave., Adams, 413/743-0715,
and 501 Wahconah St., Pittsfield, 413/443-0638, www.ronnies.com
RPM's Cycle Sales & Service—326 Merrill Rd., Pittsfield, 413/443-5659

Vermont Motorcycle Shops

Hillside Motorsports (Kawasaki and Suzuki)—1341 Rte. 14, White River Jct.,
802/295-0860, www.hillsidemotorsports.com
Jarvis Speed & Sport Center—142 Merritt Rd.,Hartland, 802/674-5572
Ronnie's Cycle—200 Northside Dr., Bennington, 802/447-3235,
www.ronnies.com
Twin States Harley-Davidson—351 Miracle Mile, Lebanon, NH,
603/448-4664, www.twinstatesharley.com

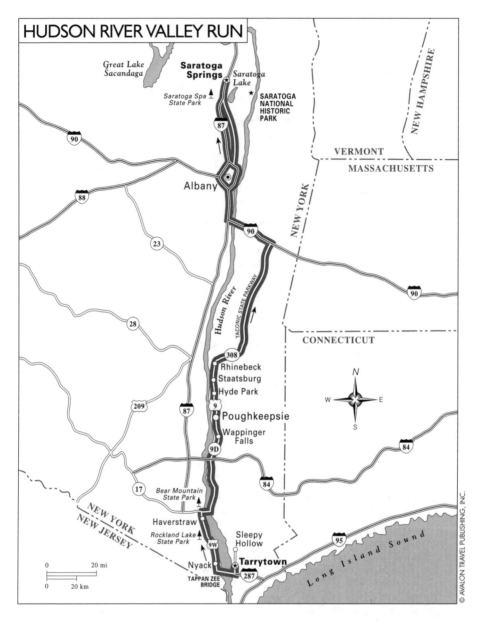

HUDSON RIVER VALLEY RUN

Route: Tarrytown to Saratoga Springs via Nyack, Bear Mountain State Park, Hyde Park, Staatsburg, Rhinebeck, Taconic State Parkway

Distance: Approximately 180 miles; consider four days with stops.
- Day 1—Tarrytown/Travel • Day 2—Hyde Park • Day 3—Travel
- Day 4—Saratoga Springs

First Leg: Tarrytown to Hyde Park (88 miles)

Second Leg: Hyde Park to Saratoga Springs (92 miles)

Helmet Laws: New York requires helmets.

Hudson River Valley Run

Tarrytown/Sleepy Hollow to Saratoga Springs, New York

If you've avoided touring the state of New York because friends convinced you there was nothing but the traffic of New York City, tune them out, tap your bike into gear, twist the throttle, and head up the Hudson River.

Twenty-five miles north of NYC are the neighboring communities of Tarrytown and Sleepy Hollow, a perfect base from which to begin a tour of the Hudson River Valley. Though close to the capital of capitalism, it's worlds away in texture and feel. You might think you took a wrong turn in Bavaria, but this is indeed America—an America that began more than 150 years before the nation existed. The villages and the following 180 miles will introduce you to a world of distinctive literature, art, history, and cuisine. They will also offer great river roads, hills, scenic vistas, pubs, and diners and lead you into the outstanding Adirondacks. Savor the ride in summertime and early fall.

Tarrytown Primer

The sense of history here is omnipresent. In the early 1600s, this area was home to a tribe of the Mohegan family, the Weckquaesgeek (whose tribal name, roughly translated, means "Christ! What a lousy tribal name!"). They lived, fished, hunted, and traded along the Pocantico, relatively undisturbed until 1609, when Henry Hudson, navigating without the aid of a GPS system, sailed up the river searching for the northwest passage to India. Settlers began arriving soon after. The Dutch named the area Slaeperig Haven (Sleepy Harbor) for its sheltered anchorage. Other Dutch settlers arrived, and by 1685 Frederick Philipse I owned nearly half of what is now Westchester County. In the 1730s, members of the Livingston family began building riverfront estates, such as Clermont, Wilderstein, and Montgomery Place, all of which are open for tours.

Fast forward to the American Revolution. British soldier/spy John André was captured here, and the papers he was carrying revealed Benedict Arnold's traitorous plan to capture West Point. A half century later, in 1820, Rip Van Winkle's creator, Washington Irving, drew further attention to the region with the publication of *The Legend of Sleepy Hollow.*

The tranquil area continued to grow. The second half of the 1800s saw freight arriving and departing by river and rail. Factories were built, followed by estates built by the people who built the factories. With the likes of Jay Gould, William Dodge, and John D. and William Rockefeller taking up summer residence, Tarrytown became a destination for the wealthy until the Great Depression, when new income taxes forced many of the "nouveau poore" to give up their estates.

In the mid-1950s, the Tappan Zee Bridge and New York State Thruway were built, opening up the town for commuters. City workers began driving up from NYC and driving up real estate prices. Today, Tarrytown still displays a distinct degree of affluence. So look sharp.

On the Road in Tarrytown

When you arrive in Tarrytown, give yourself a moment to adjust to your surroundings. Couples walk past carrying bags of fresh produce; neighbors stop and pass the time outside antique shops; and merchants thank God they're not

A 30-Second History: BMW

Bayerische Flugzeugwerke (Bavarian Aircraftworks) was founded March 7, 1916 with a blue and black logo suggesting a rotating airplane propeller in the blue Bavarian sky. Their first bike, the R 32, premiered at the Paris Motor Show and stood out with its two-cylinder, horizontally opposed piston engine—a style which continues today.

working in a mall. You may think you've entered Pleasantville, but you're cruising through one of the oldest villages in America.

Tarrytown's main drag isn't really Main Street but Route 9, the road of choice for buses, trucks, teens, tourists, seniors, and soccer moms hauling vanloads of ball-kicking kids. With this buzzing traffic, it's best here just to park your bike and explore on foot. If you follow the scents emanating from bakeries, gourmet shops, ethnic restaurants, and coffee bars, you'll eventually arrive in the heart of downtown, encompassing about six square blocks.

Like many small American towns, Tarrytown has turned to antiques dealers to fill in storefronts in the commercial center. Antiques are in such high demand here that one espresso bar displays a sign informing customers, "This is not an antiques shop. But we do have an old guy who works here."

Since Tarrytown is primarily a residential area, amusing diversions are few, but give yourself at least a few hours to roam the streets. The **Sleepy Hollow Chamber of Commerce,** 914/631-1705, www.sleepyhollowchamber.com, is a smart first stop. Located in a narrow building next to the fire station on Main Street, this is where you can score information from the rack of informational brochures. If something sparks your interest, track it down. If there's little for you here, consider this the perfect starting line for an extraordinarily full ride.

Pull it Over: Tarrytown Highlights
Attractions and Adventures

Sometimes, there's a whole lotta shakin' going on at the **Music Hall,** 13 Main St., 914/631-3390, www.tarrytownmusichall.org. Built in 1885, this hall is one of the oldest in Westchester County and has hosted a century of performances by artists like Chuck Mangione, Tito Puente, Dave Brubeck, Tony Bennett, Judy Collins, Dizzy Gillespie, Lionel Hampton, Lyle Lovett, Wynton Marsalis, Tom Paxton, and Leon Redbone. Folk and classical concerts are performed here as well, and the acoustics are alleged to rival those of Carnegie Hall. If there's a show in town, listen up.

For music of a different sort, head to the banks of the Pocantico River in **Rockefeller State Park Preserve,** 914/631-1470, www.friendsrock.org. Washington Irving described it as "one of the quietest places in the whole wide world. A small brook glides through it, with just murmur enough to lull one to repose." If you stow a rod and reel, brown trout are here for catch-and-release flyfishing, and you can find bass in Swan Lake. Non-resident day licenses ($11) can be purchased at the park office or Sleepy Hollow Village Hall.

Kuralt: BMW R 1100 RT

"Kuralt"* for the New England and Mid-Atlantic rides was a 1998 BMW R 1100 RT. Blessed with BMW's mainstay, the horizontal four-valve flat twin boxer, this bike has a sound and feel as unique as the V-Twin's throaty roar. Cruising in top gear, it runs like a power drill with 20-inch biceps. The sturdy support of the central suspension strut is immediately noticeable, providing super-solid handling.

Though some historians claim Gutenburg's printing press is history's greatest invention, I'd argue that this bike's automatic windshield deserves that honor. You press a handle-grip button and the windscreen rises up to 22 degrees to deflect wind noise, pressure, and chill. The only hassle I encountered was in adjusting the saddle, which requires removing the seat and then shifting the metal bars that raise the elevation. Then again, unless a fondness for chocolate increases the width of your ass, you should have to do this only once.

For water adventures, **Hudson River Recreation,** 247 Palmer Ave., Sleepy Hollow, 888/321-4837, www.kayakhudson.com is your ticket. Between May and October, you can follow the path of Captain Kidd as you paddle with the Great Yellow Fleet of kayaks on the Hudson River. Paddle south past Kidd Rock and the Tarrytown lighthouse and north to the Rockefeller Estate and Sing Sing prison. A training session precedes the three-hour guided tour. No experience necessary; the $45 fee includes an instruction class and gear.

Back on land you can ride your bike onto an estate to see how the other .01 percent lives. When John D. Rockefeller got tired of living in a dumpy fixer-upper, he had Johnny Jr. build **Kykuit** (pronounced KI-cut) which means "high place." The neoclassical country mansion and gardens, which overlook the Hudson, were completed in 1913 and were home to four generations of Rockefellers, including Nelson A., who added 20th-century sculptures to the estate's gardens. Vintage carriages and cars (such as a 1918 Crane Simplex) are on display in the Coach Barn and there's a café on site. Reservations are suggested. Located on Route 9, **Kykuit,** 914/631-9491, is open May–October daily except Tuesday. Admission is $20.

When you're in Tarrytown, remember that next door is Sleepy Hollow. For a road story you'll tell later, retrace the route Ichabod Crane used to flee from the Headless Horseman in *The Legend of Sleepy Hollow.* To duplicate Ichabod's

This bike has several other distinct advantages. A generous 6.6- gallon tank allows it to go for 267 miles (my average) on a tank, far surpassing the nominal 150 miles I've experienced on other bikes. Large diameter discs and motorcycle ABS provide a welcome sense of safety. And, judging from the appraising glances of strangers, I'd say the R 1100 RT is the best-looking bike on the road. Though it doesn't have the "cruiser" look, its Deutschland design is classic in itself. *Das ist ein schön* bike!

For details on new BMW models, check www.bmwusacycles.com.

*It was the travels of CBS correspondent Charles Kuralt that inspired me to explore America. I named each motorcycle I rode in his honor.

flight, take Route 9 from Patriot's Park (along the old Albany Post Road) to the Sleepy Hollow Bridge under the shadow of the Old Dutch Church.

Shopping

Tarrytown is already a nice town to begin with, and a good smoke can make it even nicer (provided you don't get that pesky cancer). At **Main Street Cigars,** 8A Main St., 914/366-4381, open daily, check out the walk-in humidor and then recline on the comfy smoking couch.

Get within 25 feet of fragrant **Novello's Market,** 45 Broadway, 914/366-6800, and your schnozz will go into olfactory overdrive. Have the clerk pack a picnic for the road. Provisions include fresh pears, mangos, sweet red plums, olive oil, hot pepper oil, teas, cookies, gourmet pizzas, olives, salami, imported cheeses, candies and cakes, ice drinks, and coffees. Here's a place to get fat and happy.

Blue-Plate Specials

Go figure. Since 1985, **Santa Fe Restaurant,** 5 Main St., 914/332-4452, www.ezpages.com/santafe, has succeeded by serving Mexican and Southwestern cuisine in the heart of Dutch country. Home-cooked without flavor enhancers, all dishes can be spiced to your satisfaction and tolerance for pain. The comfortable neighborhood feel is complemented by a full range of Mexican beers and more than 30 premium tequilas. Muy bueno! Open daily for lunch and dinner.

Horsefeathers, 94 N. Broadway, 914/631-6606, www.horsefeathers restaurant.com, is what you look for when you ride: pub-style atmosphere with home-style comfort foods like meatloaf, burgers, and mashed potatoes, along with soups, pasta, steaks, and chicken. The big draw is the extensive collection of beers—more than 100 micros—from across the country and around the world. Homey and comfortable, Horsefeathers is open daily for lunch and dinner.

Featuring Italian food with a Mediterranean flair, the riverside **Sunset Cove,** 238 Green St., at Washington Irving Boat Club, 914/366-7889, www.sunset-cove.net, may have the nicest view on the Hudson. Dining here can be just as enjoyable as riding your bike down to the river; pull up a chair on the patio and peer beneath the Tappan Zee Bridge for a view of the New York City skyline 25 miles away. A definite stop for riders.

Shut-Eye

There are few inns in Tarrytown, so if you need to stay the night you'll probably wind up at one of the chains below—the less expensive options are across the Hudson in Nyack.

Chain Drive*
A, C, D, G, K, U, CC

*Chain hotels in, or within ten miles of town. See cross-reference guide featuring phone numbers and web addresses on page 405.

Indulgences

If you're anxious to escape generic motels, storm **The Castle at Tarrytown,** 400 Benedict Ave., 914/631-1980, www.castleattarrytown.com. Built in two stages, in 1897 and 1910, the humble abode was formerly the home of playwright/author/journalist/socialite General Howard Carrol. Evoking an elegant gentleman's club, the inn boasts Gothic windows, tapestries, rich woods, and a baronial setting—you may even pick up a dueling scar during your stay. From the backyard garden, take in the fantastic view, which stretches down the

Hudson and back into history. Rest assured that the name of the signature restaurant, Equus, doesn't suggest entrée ingredients. Resting your head here will set you back $205–595 a night.

On the Road: Tarrytown to Hyde Park

Like John Lennon, New York has a fascination with the number 9. Within a few miles of Tarrytown, you'll discover Route 9, Route 9A, Route 9W, Route 9G, and Route 9D. Right now, head to Route 9W by going west over the Tappan Zee Bridge (a.k.a. 287/87/New York State Thruway) into Rockland County, and let the joy begin.

As you roll over the Tappan Zee Bridge, the mighty Hudson River rumbles 150 feet below. The setting captured on canvas by 19th-century Hudson River School artists will no longer seem embellished as you begin your ride through a landscape that rivals the magnitude of a Greek epic poem. When you peer downriver to the hazy outline of New York City, you'll picture—if not Odysseus and his crew—then Hudson's ship, the *Half Moon,* under full sail.

A few miles past the bridge, 9W branches north off 287 and heads into the hills. The road twists through the village of Nyack and rises slightly in elevation, but Nyack itself offers little. If you need a place to rest and watch the river, pull over a few miles north into Rockland Lake State Park, accessed via two entrances about three miles apart.

A few miles before Route 9W merges with 202, you'll reach the town of Haverstraw, which shoves you in the midst of dense, tedious traffic and a Christmas strand of stoplights. The payoff: You won't encounter an uglier town for several hours. (Memo to Haverstraw city council: I am available for promotional appearances.)

Once you run the Haverstraw gauntlet, you'll return to more curves and a relaxed mental state as you cruise at a casual 40 mph. Soon you'll reach a stretch of road that starts you cooking. Changes in elevations will propel you up and to the left, then drop you down to the right. Revel in the pleasure of the ride. Feel the fresh air on your skin and in your lungs, listen to the hum of the bike, watch the never-ending river drop off nearly 200 feet to your right.

When you see signs telling truckers to use a lower gear, you know you're nearing **Bear Mountain State Park,** 845/786-2701, www.hudsonriver .com/bearmtn, a must-see for a high altitude ride and stunning views of the valley. This may be the first of many times you'll "find the zone" as you begin swinging into corners, diving into short stretches of canopy roads, and cowering beneath boulders looming over the road.

After entering Bear Mountain State Park, make a brief detour down Seven Lakes Drive to the inn for no other reason than to score a great souvenir picture—its rock and wood construction recalls a Yosemite lodge. Picnic tables, a pool, and Hessian Lake are adjacent to the inn, and there are trails where you can stretch your legs. You can even take a walk.

For motorcycle travelers, the real appeal of the park is ascending Bear Mountain. Be forewarned: If you suffer from vertigo, dropsy, or the shakes, don't take this ride since the road twists like your drunk uncle at a wedding reception. While the speed limit is a sensible 25 mph, you could push it to 26 since small boulders have been thoughtfully placed along the road's edge to keep you from going over it.

A half mile up, turn onto Perkins Memorial Drive. This road introduces another memorable motorcycling moment: If you drive it between summer and fall foliage season, it is nearly empty and the forest is moist and cool. The downside: On the ride up, sheer drops fall off to your left, and branches and wet leaves can send you skidding. Still, the road is worth the price of admission (free) since you'll be treated to a kaleidoscope of majestic vistas. The beautiful valleys stretched out like long, verdant branches must have been touched by the finger of God. This is America.

When you reach the peak, your pleasure will derive from the solitude and serenity found here. An abundance of table-sized boulders makes it easy to spread out a picnic, and if you travel off-season or just after a holiday weekend, chances are only a few random travelers will join you.

When it's time to descend, place your bike in neutral and coast; the silence is satisfying. Though it may be slightly dangerous to pull over, do so if there's no traffic behind you—the view of the Hudson River and Bear Mountain Bridge will stay with you forever. Bear Mountain Circle returns you to the park, where you'll follow Route 9W north toward the king-sized American flag draped above the bridge. Like crossing the Tappan Zee, crossing the Bear Mountain Bridge to Route 9D reminds you why you're on a bike. If your timing is right, you may even ride over the speeding Montrealer, the train that skids up the Hudson between NYC and Canada.

Now you're in Putnam County and on Route 9D (a.k.a. the Hudson Greenway Trail), a beautiful mountain road. Passing Phillipstown, the Hudson darts in and out of view nearly as often as the white picket fences, evergreens, and estate homes. The road hugs the Hudson as you drive north, passing small general stores hawking beer and sandwiches, a castle on a hill and, in Garrison, **Boscobel**, 845/265-3638, www.boscobel.org, an ongoing restoration of an estate showcasing design arts of the Federal period. You may be tempted to speed, but force yourself to relax. You can hurry at work but when you're traveling. . . please take your time.

The twists and turns continue into Wappinger Falls, where you'll reach a bridge in the center of town. If you turn left and continue to follow Route 9D, the road is scenic, not as fast, and eventually leads to your first major commercial center: Poughkeepsie. You, being an adventurer, will not settle for this. Keep heading north after hooking up with Route 9 to your first overnight: Hyde Park.

Hyde Park Primer

Just as fans of Mark Twain trek to Hannibal and worshippers of Donny Osmond pilgrimage to Utah, students of history head to Hyde Park. Along with World War II veterans and Depression-era children who grew up on relief packages, baby boomers, scholars, and foreign tourists whose countries were saved by Franklin Delano Roosevelt, arrive to pay their respects to the 32nd president, whose home and grave site are located here.

Most of us have heard of Hyde Park, so it's a bonus that it turns out to be a perfect place to rest your bike, stay the night, enjoy a decent meal, and get an education. In 1705, New York provincial governor Edward Hyde presented this parcel of land to his secretary, Peter Fuconnier. Hyde's munificence earned him a namesake estate and later, a namesake town, which was established in 1821. Mills sprang up on Hudson River tributaries, and, by the turn of the century, Roosevelts, Vanderbilts, and other wealthy families were settling in.

On the Road in Hyde Park

Sorry, there is no true commercial district within Hyde Park—which is one of its assets. The town rests along a straightaway that's highlighted by the attractions listed below, so take it for what it is: a quiet and historically significant stop between Tarrytown and Saratoga.

Pull it Over: Hyde Park Highlights
Attractions and Adventures

Had FDR never achieved national prominence, you may never have heard of Hyde Park. But he did, and today the **FDR National Historic Site**, 4079 Albany Post Rd. (Rte. 9), 845/229-9115 or 800/337-8474, www.nps.gov/hofr, is a shrine for those who want to see how this pastoral countryside helped shape an extraordinary man. With the exception of 13 years in Washington and a few more in Albany, FDR spent his entire life here. This is also his resting place; he and Eleanor are buried in a rose garden adjacent to the house.

The home is filled with original books, china, paintings, and furniture; look for the simple kitchen chair FDR fashioned into a wheelchair. In the **FDR Museum and Presidential Library** (the first presidential museum ever built), the desk demands special attention. It's just as it was left the day he died in April 1945. Motorcyclists may get a kick out of the 1938 Ford Phaeton shown in the basement: It's equipped with manual controls for the disabled president. After hours spent roaming the estate, however, I found the most intriguing and touching displays were the letters and gifts the president received from average Americans expressing gratitude for the relief programs that put them back to work. The site is open daily 9–5. Admission costs $10 ($18 gets you into the FDR site, Val-Kill, and Vanderbilt Mansion; see details on next page).

It's odd, but FDR and his mother froze Eleanor out of their world, despite the fact that the First Lady won the 1934 Washington Wives kickboxing title. The tacit agreement was that Eleanor would reside a few miles away at Val-Kill (Stone Cottage). Established as a furniture factory to provide work to local craftsmen, Val-Kill served as Eleanor's retreat from 1926 until 1945. After FDR died, it became her primary residence and a gathering place for world leaders, including Churchill, JFK, Krushchev, Nehru, and Marshall Tito (who left the Jacksons to lead Yugoslavia). **Val-Kill,** located on Route 9G, 845/229-9422, www. nps.gov/elro, now serves as the Eleanor Roosevelt National Historic Site. It's open daily in summer 9–5, Thursday–Monday off-season. Admission is $5.

Art of the Valley

During the 1800s, popular imagination considered the Hudson to be the American Rhine. Its imposing country estates surely rivaled those of the German river or the chateaux of the French Loire district. Frederick Church and fellow artists captured this prevailing sentiment in an art movement called the Hudson River School. Images of trees and lakes, waterfalls and rivers of the Hudson and Catskill Mountains were adorned with Grecian temples and sweeping panoramas. As you ride through the valley, the essence of those images will reappear time and again—minus the Grecian temples.

Nobody muttered, "There goes the neighborhood" when the Vanderbilts moved to town. **Vanderbilt Mansion,** Rte. 9, 845/229-7770, www.nps .gov/vama, reflects that family's obsession with building homes large enough to drain the kids' inheritance. The Beaux Arts mansion was the home of Louise and publicity-shy Frederick, recognized primarily for being a splendid yachtsman, a gentleman farmer, and an "unassuming philanthropist." Louise died in 1926, Freddy in 1938, and Louise's niece inherited the property a year before she told her neighbor (FDR) that she was donating it to the nation. As you leave the grounds, on your left is an overlook with a tremendous view of the mighty Hudson. The home is open daily 9–5 (Thursday–Monday, November–April). They'll let you through the door for $8.

I've always wanted to be a double-naught spy, so I was anxious to reach the CIA. Damned if I didn't learn this is actually the **Culinary Institute of America,** 845/452-9600, www.ciachef.edu. Cruise down the road on Route 9 and you'll reach the only residential college in the world devoted entirely to culinary education. Founded in 1946 in New Haven, Connecticut, the school moved into this turn-of-the-century former Jesuit seminary in 1972. Today, college-age apprentice chefs, servers, and maitré d's at the 150-acre campus are—surprisingly—studying alongside doctors, lawyers, and stockbrokers who dropped out of their careers to do something fun. Tours ($4) are available Mondays at 10 A.M. and 4 P.M. Of course, you can also see the campus when you drop in to eat (see Blue-Plate Specials).

If you want to catch your own meal, Crum Elbow Creek is well stocked with rainbow, brook, and brown trout, as well as bluegills, sunfish, bullhead, and small, large, and rock bass. For equipment rental and guides, check out the good ol' boys at **Don's Tackle Service** in Red Hook, 845/758-9203.

Blue-Plate Specials

At the **Culinary Institute of America,** Rte. 9, 845/471-6608 (reservations), www.ciachef.edu, four student-staffed restaurants are open to the public. If you travel with a dinner jacket (or appropriate dress) in tow, take a break from the roadside diners and enjoy a classic meal at the American Bounty (regional and seasonal), St. Andrew's Cafe (casual contemporary a la carte), Escoffier (French cuisine), or Caterina de Medici (fine Italian). Prices are slightly lower than they will be when your CIA chef begins working for a five-star restaurant a few weeks hence. The restaurants are closed the first three weeks of July, December 20–January 5, and some holidays.

The retro-1930 Deco decor is right on target at **Eveready Diner,** Rte. 9, 845/229-8100, and the menu just right for motorcycle travelers, featuring soups, burgers, and daily specials (beef stew is great on a cold day). The diner is open 24 hours Friday and Saturday, 5 A.M.–1 A.M. weekdays.

An ordinary restaurant with a varied menu, **Easy Street,** Route 9, 845/229-7969, has been serving up comfort foods since 1974 that appeal to everyone, including hamburgers, steak, seafood, pastas, and on Tuesdays and Saturdays the road food holy trinity: turkey, mashed potatoes, and stuffing.

Watering Holes

In 1933, FDR was quoted as saying, "I think this would be a good time for a beer." Six decades later, some locals at the **Hyde Park Brewing Company,** 4076 Albany Post Rd., 845/229-8277, www.hydeparkbrewing.com, took up the cause in this microbrewery across from Roosevelt's birthplace. One of Hyde Park's rare nightspots to boast a full bar, the pub serves six beers—all brewed rightcheer. Open daily.

Sports fans hang out at **Toucan Grill,** Rte. 9 (Colonial Plaza), 845/229-2118. The standards (wings, fries, burgers, etc.) are washed down with $6 draft pitchers. Open 'til the wee hours, Toucan's features bands on Friday, a jukebox, a pool table, and even a Tiki Hut! Crazy, man, crazy.

Shut-Eye

The choices of lodging in Hyde Park range from motels to. . . motels. Head north to find larger inns or backtrack to Poughkeepsie to find pricy chain hotels.

Motels and Motor Courts
Roosevelt Inn, 4360 Albany Post Rd., 845/229-2443, www.rooseveltinnof hydepark.com, is a good, old-fashioned American motel. Rates here run $80–100 for one of 25 clean rooms, some with king beds, some with fridges. Get off to a good start at the coffee shop, serving breakfast 7–11.

The **Super 8** at 528 Albany Post Rd., 845/229-0088, is clean and cheap ($60–78). Along with their 61 basic economy rooms, they toss in a comp continental breakfast, cable TV, and a clerk on duty 'round the clock.

Chain Drive*
A, G, L, CC, DD

*Chain hotels in, or within ten miles of town. See cross-reference guide featuring phone numbers and web addresses on page 405.

Inn-Dependence

If you have an urge to splurge, stay at the **Belvedere Mansion,** 10 Old Route 9, Staatsburg, 845/889-8000, www.belvederemansion.com, where the hillside setting offers a great view of the Hudson. Rates at this spa-turned-inn run to $275. The first floor of the main house is a restaurant (as well as a handy pub), and the upstairs features six rooms adorned with 18th-century French antiques and trompe l'oeil cloud-painted ceilings. Riders who share my budget may opt to bunk down in the converted stable, which is now a row of reasonably priced rooms (from $75) featuring queen beds, private baths, and patio. The gravel driveway is a nuisance for kickstands, but if you're riding solo, a single concrete slab will hold your bike.

On the Road to Saratoga Springs

Leaving Hyde Park, the two-lane road has some slow curves accented by stands of pines. The village itself—just a few stores and shops—can be bypassed in order to embark on the next leg of your journey. Although there are no identifiable signs, from here to Germantown in neighboring Columbia County you'll be riding through the Mid-Hudson Valley, a 32-square-mile area recognized by the Department of the Interior as a National Historic Landmark District.

Miles north you'll cruise through the village of Rhinebeck, which—midway between Albany and New York—was a logical stop for commercial river and road traffic. At the corner of Route 9 and East Market Street (Rte. 308) is the intersection of the old King's Highway and Sepasco Indian Trail. On your left,

Congress Park in Saratoga Springs

© NANCY HOWELL

the circa 1766 **Beekman Arms,** 845/876-7077, www.beekmanarms.com, boasts that it's the oldest inn in America. Although you'll find a few hundred other "oldest inns" around the country, "The Beek" gets points for hosting George Washington, Benjamin Harrison, and FDR—who wrapped up each gubernatorial and presidential campaign with a front porch speech. In 1775, this was the Bogardus Tavern, a bar that stayed open while the 4th Regiment of the Continental Army drilled on its front lawn before the war. If you're tired enough to stop but not tired enough to stay the night, kick back with an ale in the warm, rich setting of the Colonial Tap Room.

If your schedule allows, take Route 9 north and detour onto Stone Church Road and head to the **Old Rhinebeck Aerodrome,** 914/758-8610, www.old rhinebeck.org, an antique aircraft museum that displays World War I and Lindbergh-era aircraft, such as a 1917 Fokker DR-1 triplane, a 1915 Newport 11, and a 1918 Curtiss-Jenny, as well as old cars and vintage motorcycles. Saturdays and Sundays at 2 P.M. from mid-June–October, they also present a flying circus reminiscent of the Great Waldo Pepper. If you're ready to get off

West Point

I never was in the military, but my mom took me to Marineland once. If you're interested in military history, **West Point,** 845/938-2638, www.usma.edu, is worth the detour. Washington garrisoned his troops here during the Revolutionary War, and in 1802, President Jefferson signed the act of Congress creating the U.S. Military Academy. And that's not all: Lee, Grant, Patton, Eisenhower, and Schwarzkopf all learned to march here.

Since September 11th, the grounds have been closed to outsiders unless you've called in advance for the one-hour, $7 tour. If you have, continue north on 9W to Route 218 and enter West Point at Thayer Gate. The tour starts at the museum (open 10:30 A.M.–4:15 P.M.) and a guide will lead you to see the Cadet Chapel and the world's largest church organ, and then to Trophy Point, a favorite overlook for artists. The visitors center, which features a 30-minute movie, is open 9 A.M.–4:45 P.M. On Saturday mornings in the fall, take time to watch the "Long Gray Line," the parade of cadets marching prior to the football game. You'll need to buy tickets for the game well in advance, since you'll need them to get on the grounds. Either that, or enlist.

the bike, climb into a 1929 open cockpit biplane for a 15-minute barnstorming ride. The aerodrome is open daily mid-May–late October from 10–5. Admission costs $6 Monday–Friday, double that on weekends.

If time is tight, just past the Beekman Arms, turn right onto East Market Street (Rte. 308) and motor past splendid examples of Italianate Revival homes and Victorian architecture. If you've spent the morning in Hyde Park, it may be afternoon as you head east, so as the sun settles over the Hudson you'll feel the warmth on your back and smell the scent of the forest as you cruise down the road. Long shadows fall before your bike and Little Wappinger Creek occasionally skims into view. In the early fall, acres of harvested cornfields accent the landscape and the country ride becomes distinguished by its even, level serenity. Six miles after turning onto Route 308 in a lazy loop towards Rock City, the road becomes Route 199.

The pleasure of cruising through four more miles of farmland will adjust your attitude and prepare you to ride one of the most beautiful roads in America. The Taconic State Parkway cautions it is for "passenger cars only," but the sign is obviously the work of some corrupt anti-motorcycle administration. Rest assured that motorcycles are allowed.

Even as you forsake river views, the road is faster and less congested than Route 9. The result is that you'll enjoy a ride that acknowledges that life may be short, but it can be big.

The road is so pristine—so perfect—that the sweeps and dips and gentle drops affirm your existence. The cool air and sweet smell of the surroundings are only part of the adventure. You'll drop close to a hundred feet in less than a mile; you'll encounter stunning views and roadside wildflowers, black ash, slippery elm, arrowwood. Scenic overlooks punctuate the parkway. Look for the one in Columbia County, where the historic Livingston Manor once stood. It was the focal point of a 160,000-acre estate along the Hudson River.

Just as you pass over Routes 2 and 7, past the signs for Ancram and Taghkanic, the view will not only knock your socks off, your boots will fly, too. On a clear day, at least 50 miles of rolling hills unfold to the horizon and possibly to the next galaxy. The view is yours. Use it.

Mea culpa: If I didn't have to take you on the following roads, I wouldn't. The TSP connects with Interstate 90 and, to make time through Albany, you'll be shoved onto Interstate 87. The switch from pastoral scenes to six lanes of fast, tense traffic will change your karma in an instant. Unfortunately, seeking alternate routes would be even more disrupting, so bite your lip and run the gauntlet of urban ugliness, selecting either I-87 or returning to Route 9 to complete your run to my favorite American city, Saratoga Springs.

Saratoga Springs Primer

Saratoga Springs, named a "Great American Place" by *American Heritage* magazine, is what America is all about. Unlike freak towns that have bulldozed historic districts in favor of strip malls, this city recognizes beauty in its past and has placed more than a thousand buildings on the National Register of Historic Places. If you can understand this, Saratoga Springs is so real it looks fake.

Broadway, the town's main boulevard, is an artifact that gains the most attention. When Gideon Putnam laid out the thoroughfare in the early 1800s, he ensured that a team of four horses could make a U-turn (a qualifier shared in Hendersonville, NC). The 120-foot-wide avenue and broad sidewalk makes this the most enjoyable street in the nation for walking, riding, or dropping into a neighborhood bar for a post-ride refreshment. Further up Route 9, you can also ease away the demands of the ride by dropping into a mineral bath at the 2,200-acre Saratoga Spa State Park.

In the early 1900s, this was the place to "take the waters." Now it's the place to kick back after a day on the road. Salty water from ancient seas is trapped beneath limestone layers and sealed by a solid layer of shale. The Saratoga Fault zigzags beneath the town and releases water made bubbly by carbon dioxide gas. Local Iroquois Indians knew well before the 1700s that minerals entering the water also added to the spring's therapeutic value.

Although Saratoga had earned its historical stripes in the Revolution ("Gentleman Johnny" Burgoyne surrendered his Crown Forces nearby on October 10, 1777—more below), it was during the Civil War that John Morrissey, a street fighter who had been indicted twice for burglary, once for assault, and once more for assault with intent to kill, channeled his destructive energies into a horse racing track. His gamble worked and by the turn of the century, the Saratoga Race Track complemented his Saratoga casinos.

Reform politicians later closed the track—which quickly reopened through a loophole. The track's fortunes rose and fell until well after World War II, when the New York Racing Association formed and changed the focus from gambling to the love of horse racing. With the track drawing summer visitors and the spas providing warm relief year-round, Saratoga keeps on running.

On the Road in Saratoga Springs

One of the payoffs on a good motorcycle tour is discovering towns that would be a perfect vignette in a Mark Twain novel or Charles Kuralt feature.

Saratoga Springs would top this list. It was awarded "Great American Main Street" by the National Trust for Historic Preservation, named a top destination by *Facilities* magazine, and chosen as one of "America's Most Walkable Cities" by *Walking* magazine. In 1997, *American Heritage* (an essential magazine if you want to understand this country) honored it as the first "Great American Place." Even without the ponies racing on America's oldest track, Saratoga is a must-see. Hoof it for the best experience.

Within blocks of Broadway, you'll find side streets dotted with cool shops, Congress Park featuring a sculpture by Daniel Chester French (of Lincoln Memorial fame), and slices of Americana that will make you wonder if you've wandered onto the set of *It's A Wonderful Life*.

But this *is* Bedford Falls. When you pass the stunning Adirondack Trust at Broadway and Lake, you'll expect to peer in at Mr. Potter counting George Bailey's bankroll. As you walk or ride the avenue, the preserved architecture, liveliness of the street, and pleasant look on townspeople's faces as they actually shop along the main street is emotionally powerful and thoroughly satisfying.

Two streets are worth exploring by bike. Head toward Skidmore College on North Broadway to view grand homes reflecting architecture from the Greek Revival, Arts and Crafts, and postmodern periods. The second is Union Avenue, a broad boulevard bordered by palatial homes accented with gazebos, Gothic gables, gingerbread trim, and stained-glass windows.

Check at the Visitors Center in **Drink Hall,** 297 Broadway, for the fact-filled brochure titled "A Stroll Through Saratoga Springs." It suggests five walking tours that will acquaint you with the very best of what this town has to offer.

Pull it Over: Saratoga Highlights
Attractions and Adventures

Don't pass up a visit to the **Saratoga Race Course,** Union Ave., 518/584-6200 (July and August), 718/641-4700 (off season), www.saratogaracetrack.com. Where else can you sit back and bet on thoroughbreds shaking the ground just 10 feet away from you? And all for two bucks admission! The "sport of kings" is held at the oldest racetrack in the country, and the sense of tradition is omnipresent. From the swells in the box seats to the two-bit bettors clenching their tickets trackside, this surreal spectacle guarantees a good time. The racing season lasts slightly more than 30 days in July and August, so if you insist on competing with van-driving tourists during peak season, be sure to reserve one morning for "Breakfast at the Track," and stick around for the famed Travers Stakes in August. The track is closed Tuesday.

After a hard day's ride—hell, even after an easy day's ride—Congress Park on Broadway is therapeutic. The turn-of-the century setting is enhanced by the Canfield Casino, favorite hangout of larger-than-life Diamond Jim Brady. Numerous quiet spots beckon you to stretch out on the lawn and enjoy nature. Settle back and listen to the groundskeepers trim the lawn, and watch geese overhead slicing their way south. Another peaceful place is by the Daniel Chester French statue erected in memory of Spencer Trask, a man, says the inscription, whose "One object in life was to do right and observe his fellow man. He gave himself abundantly to hasten the coming of a new and better day." Not a bad legacy.

Save time after the racetrack, Congress Park, and Broadway's shops and pubs to explore **Saratoga Spa State Park,** S. Broadway, 518/584-2535. The 2,000-plus acres encompass an 18- and a 9-hole golf course (518/584-2008), the Gideon Putnam Hotel (518/584-3000 or 800/732-1560), a performing arts center (518/584-9330), and the circa 1930s Lincoln Bathhouse (518/583-

Rally: Americade

Another late arrival, the first "Cade" came in May, 1983. Originally called "Aspencade" for a New Mexico rally that celebrated the changing colors of the aspen, veteran motorcyclist Bill Dutcher hosted "Aspencade East" at the resort community of Lake George, New York, and attracted more than 2,000 attendees. Distancing itself from typical rallies, this event stressed that it was "not the place for speed shows, attitudes, or loud pipes." In 1986, the name was changed to reflect the multi-brand national-sized rally it had become. The TourExpo trade show is now a big part of the event, as are mini-tours, self-guided tours, seminars, social events, and field events. Now the world's largest touring-focus event, Americade enlisted approximately 200 staff volunteers to prepare things for 50,000 riders in 2001. The placement is perfect. Americade is held at the southern gateway to the Adirondack Park, which is larger than Yellowstone, Glacier, Yosemite, and Olympic National Parks combined. Take a while and count its 2,800 lakes and ponds, 30,000 miles of rivers and streams, and 43 mountains with elevations over 4,000 feet.

718/444-7626
www.tourexpo.com

2880). Just a mile south of town, this is a perfect short run. Riding down Broadway, take a right and enter the Avenue of the Pines, a picturesque road that leads to the Gideon Putnam Hotel. Later, ride the Loop Road past Geyser Creek into the heart of the park.

Next to watching the ponies, the most popular outdoor activity is hanging out at Saratoga Lake, just four miles from the city center. Ride Route 9 South (Union Avenue) to 9P South and head over the bridge. The eight-mile-long lake is great for sailing, rowing, bass fishing, and water skiing. Several small restaurants sport decks where you can enjoy a sandwich and a beer while looking out over the lake. If you're anxious to drop a line, you can rent a boat or hire a charter captain with **Flying M Fishing Service,** Saratoga Lake, 518/583-0632. **Saratoga Boatworks,** 549 Union Ave. (Route 9P), 518/584-2628, www.saratogaboatworks.com, rents a variety of fishing boats and pontoon boats. **Point Breeze Marina,** 1459 Rte. 9P, 518/587-3397, Saratoga's largest marina, rents pontoons, speedboats, fishing boats, and canoes. You can find gear, bait, and tackle at shops near the marinas.

Saratoga National Historical Park, 648 Rte. 32, Stillwater, 518/664-9821, www.nps.gov/sara, commemorates the turning point of the American Revolution. Before the battles of Saratoga on September 19 and October 7, 1777, few colonists felt certain that their ragtag army and militias could forge America into an independent country. But after General John Burgoyne surrendered his 6,000 British soldiers to General Horatio Gates on October 17, it was only a matter of time. The dioramas, exhibits, films, and 10-mile battlefield tour road are emotional reminders of America's quest to be free. Toll for the tour road is $2. The park is open daily 9–5, April–mid-November.

Civil War students will want to ride to the summit of Mount MacGregor to see where Ulysses S. Grant died in 1885, shortly after completing his memoirs. The catch is that had Grant not died here, the **Ulysses S. Grant Cottage,** 518/587-8277, would have been torn down to make room for the adjacent prison. If you can ignore the shouts of the cons, this is a great, steep road. Take Route 9 North (left) onto Corinth Mountain Road, then take a quick right and follow signs to Grant Cottage. Hours are iffy, and summers only. Call in advance. Admission is $2.50.

If you're thrilled by thoroughbreds, then the **National Museum of Racing and Hall of Fame,** Union Ave. (across from Saratoga Race Course), 518/584-0400, www.racingmuseum.org, is a must-see. Open daily, the museum's equine art, special exhibits, and miniature wax figurines of jockeys (at least I *thought* they were miniatures), tell the story of horse racing. You can pay to see the museum, or kick in an extra three bucks for the Oklahoma Track Tour, which is an early morning behind-the-scenes tour of stables, the backstretch, and the area where grooms prepare horses for the race.

It seems cheesy riding a trolley after getting off your bike, but the information shared by the drivers/historians of Trolley Tours will spike your learning curve. And for only a buck! Trolleys run July–Labor Day, Tuesday–Saturday 10–6, departing from the visitors center and various stops along Broadway.

You may wind up at the **Saratoga Performing Arts Center** at Spa State Park, 518/587-3330, www.spac.org, for an outdoor concert by such artists as James Taylor, John Fogerty, the Philadelphia Orchestra, the New York City Ballet, or the Pretenders.

Shopping

Normally I wouldn't recommend a souvenir store, but Saratoga is such an incredible town it's worth a memento or two. Look for them at *Impressions of Saratoga,* 368 Broadway, 518/587-0666, www.impressionssaratoga.com. You'll find great horse and racing prints here for home or office.

Remember Elvis in *Roustabout?* Elvis was riding a Honda 350cc and singing *Wheels on my Heels* when Barbara Stanwyck's jerk husband ran him off the road. Well, The King had a guitar strapped around his back and you can do the same (without that Barbara Stanwyck stuff) after you shop at **Saratoga Guitar,** 8 Caroline St., 518/581-1604, www.saratogaguitar.com. The shop hawks lots of new, used, and vintage git boxes, plus other smaller instruments for making music on the road. Rock-a-hula, baby!

One of the greatest pleasures of an extended tour is escaping someone else's schedule and doing things you can't do when you're on the clock. Reading is one of them. Partially built within a vacated bank vault, **Lyrical Ballad Bookstore,** 7 Phila St., 518/584-8779, is one of the best used and rare bookstores I've seen. Brimming with 100,000 editions, there are more topics here than in a year's worth of Oprah. The bookstore is open Monday–Saturday 10–6, Sunday 11–6.

Two floors of quality merchandise distinguish **Regent Street Antique Center,** 153 Regent St., 518/584-0107, open daily 10–5. And it's not all high-priced junque, either. This is a good place for rooting around for old motorcycle magazines from the '30s—and anything else you want shipped back home.

Gotta jones for a stogie? Fix yourself at **Little Habana,** 6 Phila St., 518/587-4278; **Saratoga Cigar & Pipe,** 170 S. Broadway, 518/584-4716, which has a smoking den; or **Smokin' Sam's Cigar Shop,** 5 Caroline St., 518/587-6450. All are open evenings, Smokin' Sam's until midnight in season.

Ride here during race season and I'll bet you'll bet. To be a better bettor, drop into **Main Street News,** 382 Broadway, 518/581-0133, which features a large collection of horse racing periodicals and racing forms. The shelves are stacked with foreign newspapers, magazines, cigars, paperbacks, souvenirs, and domestic newspapers from around the country.

You don't have to travel to Palm Beach to watch pony boys whacking the ball; they've been doing it around here since 1898. If you're here in June or July, cruise over to **Saratoga Equine Sports Center at Bostwick Field,** 518/584-8108, www.saratogapolo.com, to watch the world's top polo players get a "chukker" going. Granted, it's ritzy, but the action's fast and furious—more so when I rode my bike on the field. Just $5 gets you in, although the action moves to Whitney Field during August and September.

Blue-Plate Specials

Compton's Restaurant, 457 Broadway, 518/584-9632, opens daily for breakfast (served all day) and lunch. This diner isn't old-fashioned, it's really old. You wanted an early start? Breakfast starts at 4 A.M. weekdays and 3 A.M. on weekends. Inhale two eggs, homefries, toast, coffee, plus ham, bacon, sausage, or hash—all for $4.50. Try to throw a leg over the saddle after this one.

Traditional southern food is hard to find even in the South these days, but **Hattie's,** 45 Phila St., 518/584-4790, www.hattiesrestaurant.com, has been serving up Louisiana cuisine like fried chicken, ribs, catfish, pork chops, and homemade desserts since 1938. If you can't tour south of the Mason-Dixon, try a meal here. Enjoy the full bar and outdoor revelry on the patio in the summer. In season, Hattie's is open for breakfast, lunch, and dinner.

In the tradition of paraphernalia-cluttered chain restaurants, **Professor Moriarty's,** 430 Broadway, 518/587-5981, www.professormoriartys.com, sports an eclectic collection of conversation pieces that rivals its menu of steak, ribs, chicken, lamb, seafood, pasta, beers, and ales. A warm bar, sidewalk café, and breakfast during racing season make this place a good bet.

Watering Holes

Opened in 1970, **Saratoga Tin & Lint Company,** 2 Caroline St., 518/587-5897, is Saratoga's quintessential neighborhood bar. A basement setting complete with low ceilings, Tin & Lint features creature comforts like wooden benches and one of the best jukeboxes on the road. If you need more convincing, keep in mind that Soupy Sales—*the* Soupy Sales—downed a brew or two here once. You can buy pints of ale for $3, pitchers for $7, until 4 A.M. daily.

J.R.'s BBQ, 389 Broadway, 518/583-4131, in the middle of town, features pool tables, karaoke, beer, and mixed drinks. A cover is charged on live rock nights. What else? The biggest chicken wings in town, weighing in at 90 pounds apiece.

E. O'Dwyers, 15 Spring St., is a British pub with pool tables, booths, tables, and a stream of import brews on tap—Newcastle, Otter Creek Copper, Bass, Harp, Guinness . . . this is the real MacEwan! Two-for-one draft pints are on special Thursday and Friday 4–7. Open until the wee hours (4 A.M.).

Shut-Eye

Numerous independent motel/spas line Broadway, the majority of them clean and tidy. Motels are great when traveling by bike; just park right out front.

Motels and Motor Courts

Smack dab in the middle of everything is the plain jane **Saratoga Downtowner Motel,** 413 Broadway, 518/584-6160 or 888/480-6160. They have 42 AAA rooms, continental breakfasts, and—get this—an indoor pool beneath a retractable roof that opens in the summer. Close to it all, rates are a nominal $75 until race season, when it leaps to a brain-numbing $185. The **Spring's Motel,** 189 Broadway, 518/584-6336, www.springsmotel.com, has 28 spacious and clean rooms. It's $80 a night ($60 with AAA) but leaps to $185 as well during July and August's races. Ouch.

Chain Drive*

L, AA, CC

*Chain hotels in, or within ten miles of town. See cross-reference guide featuring phone numbers and web addresses on page 405.

Inn-Dependence

A few notable inns and hotels are listed here. (Prices reflect double occupancy during peak season; plan on spending less—often far less—if you arrive before or after racing season.)

Adelphi Hotel, 365 Broadway, 518/587-4688, www.adelphihotel.com, is one of the most stunning hotels in America, not only because of its grandeur, but because of the subtle anachronisms captured in the blend of 1920s Deco style and tropical casualness. The 34 rooms boast high ceilings, private baths, and a far-from-generic decor. The day gets off to a perfect start with breakfast on the verandah and wraps up in a lobby bar that has more character than Sybil. This is the premier spot to relax and relive the 1920s, whether you're passed out on the palm-tree shaded verandah or sampling a cocktail, beer, or daiquiri in the faux-painted bar. All this sumptuousness goes for $110–170 per night, more during racing meets.

Kathleen and Noel Smith are two of the friendliest people running one of the nicest inns in Saratoga. **Saratoga Arms,** 495-497 Broadway, 518/584-1775, www.saratogaarms.com, offers large, comfortable rooms right on Broadway and within walking distance of the action. Rates starts at $150.

For a more natural setting, the **Saratoga B&B,** 434 Church St. (Route 9N), 518/584-0920, sits on five wooded acres a few miles up Route 9N, with rooms for $85–225. Adjacent to the B&B is the **Saratoga Motel,** 440 Church St., which is popular with riders for the motel setting and rates that run $55–135. Both can be seen at www.saratoga-lodging.com.

Indulgences

What takes place at the **Lincoln Baths,** 518/583-2880, may sound like punishment for Cool Hand Luke, but Lordy! does it feel good after a ride. In this old-fashioned spa you can get wrapped up in hot sheets, have someone squeeze the tightness out of your muscles, then plunge into steamy, sweat-inducing water . . . paradise. Prices range from $16 for a mineral bath to $60 for a one-hour massage. Hours vary by season; call in advance. Note: If Lincoln's closed and you gotta have someone rub you the right way, call on the affordable **Crystal Spa,** which is open year-round at 92 South Broadway, 518/584-2556, www.thecrystalspa.com.

Perhaps the most elaborate lodging in Saratoga, **Batchellor Mansion Inn,** 20 Circular St., 518/584-7012 or 800/616-7012, www.batchellormansion inn.com, symbolizes turn-of-the-century luxury—though the rooms sport modern whirlpool tubs. The High Victorian home, built in 1873, was restored by its current owners. Guests enjoy a continental breakfast weekdays and full breakfast on weekends. Compare Batchellor's racing rates—$260–395—to off-season rates of $135–285, and you'll get an idea of Saratoga's seasonal inflation.

Side Trip: Adirondacks

Just because this trip ends at Saratoga Springs, it doesn't mean yours has to. Just north of Saratoga, Americade (www.tourexpo.com), the world's largest tour rally, attracts hordes of riders to the Lake George area in early June.

Even off-season, you can enjoy a nice run up to Lake George via dependable Route 9. The road sweeps through slow curves and a few forgettable towns, campgrounds, and random log cabins that would make Ted Kaczynski drool. The forest is tranquil and peaceful, and smooth back roads lead to the Adirondacks, Vermont, and Great Lake Sacandaga. Some say that I-87 North to Canada is one of the most scenic roads in the United States.

Lake George itself is a tacky tourist town littered with T-shirt shops, mini golf, and high cheese. Motels abound in Lake George and tourist cabins dot Route 9N, but if you want to rough it comfortably, Gene and Linda Merlino at the **Lamplight Inn,** 231 Rte. 9N, Lake Luzerne, 518/696-5294, www.lamp lightinn.com, save rooms for bikers. They even provide hoses and rags for cleaning your bike after a day's ride. All rooms have televisions, some have fireplaces and hot tubs, and the common areas have board games and books. A beer and wine license increases guests' enjoyment. The forested setting among 10 acres is generous enough to help you relax.

Resources For Riders

Hudson River Valley Run

New York Travel Information

New York Camping Reservations—800/456-2267, www.reserveamerica.com
New York State Adirondacks Campgrounds—518/457-2500,
  www.dec.state.ny.us
New York State Parks—www.nysparks.com
New York State Thruway Road Conditions—800/847-8929
New York State Travel and Tourism—800/225-5697, www.iloveny.com

Local and Regional Information

Adirondack Bed & Breakfast Association—www.adirondackbb.com
Dutchess County Tourism—845/463-4000 or 800/445-3131,
  www.dutchesstourism.com
Hudson River Valley Information—800/232-4782, www.hudsonvalley.org
Hyde Park Chamber of Commerce—845/229-8612,
  www.hydeparkchamber.org
Saratoga County Chamber of Commerce—518/584-3255 or 800/526-8970,
  www.saratoga.org
Sleepy Hollow Chamber of Commerce—914/631-1705,
  www.sleepyhollowchamber.com

Motorcycle Shops

Westchester BMW—530 Tarrytown Rd., White Plains, 914/428-4777,
  www.westchesterbmw.com
Rockland County Motorcycle Service—1630 Rte. 202, Pomona,
  845/362-1212
Powerhouse Honda—70 Rte. 59, Nyack, 845/358-0300
Prestige Harley-Davidson—205 Rte. 9W, Congers, 845/268-6651,
  www.prestigeharley-davidson.com
Haverstraw Motorsports—64-66 Rte. 9W, Haverstraw, 845/429-0141
Rockwell Cycles—1005 Rte. 9W, Fort Montgomery, 845/446-3834,
  www.rockwellcycles.com
Kawasaki of Newburgh—28 Windsor Hwy., Newburgh, 845/562-3400
Dutchess Recreational Vehicles—737 Freedom Plains Rd. Poughkeepsie,
  845/454-2810
Ed's Service Motorcycles—600 Violet Ave., Hyde Park, 845/454-6210
Zack's V-Twin Cycles—701 Violet Ave., Hyde Park, 845/485-8517,
  www.zacksvtwin.com
Woodstock Harley-Davidson—949 Rte. 28, Kingston, 845/338-2800,
  www.woodstockharley.com
Albany Honda—390 New Karner Rd., Albany, 518/452-1003
Spitzies Harley-Davidson—1970 Central Ave., Albany, 518/456-7433,
  www.spitzies.com

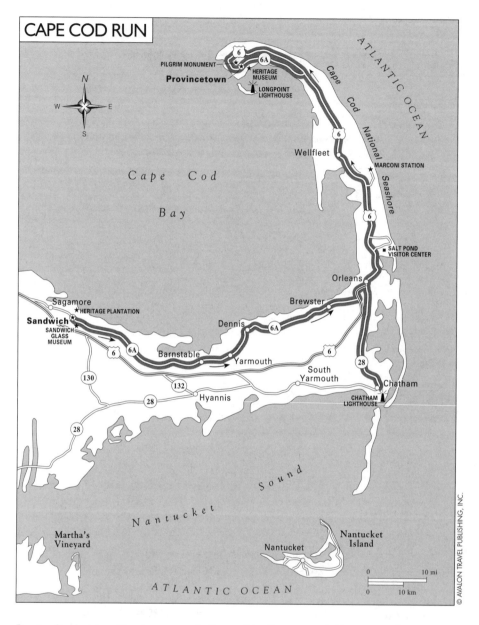

Route: Sandwich to Provincetown via Barnstable, Cummaquid, Dennis, Orleans, Chatham

Distance: Approximately 140 miles (round trip); consider at least three days with stops. •Day 1—Sandwich •Day 2—Travel/Chatham •Day 3—Travel/Provincetown

First Leg: Sandwich to Chatham (40 miles)

Second Leg: Chatham to Provincetown (35 miles)

Side Trip: Provincetown to Nantucket (52 miles)

Helmet Laws: Massachusetts requires helmets.

Cape Cod Run

Sandwich to Provincetown, Massachusetts

About 150 years before John Hancock signed his John Hancock to the Declaration of Independence, freelance whale hunters traversed the waters around Cape Cod. Surrounded by the sea, local boys grew up sailing on home-based market packets, coastal trading ships, and schooners. They graduated to fast Liverpool packets, clippers, and whaling ships. The independence they displayed in advance of their country's formation is readily apparent today on Cape Cod.

The Cape twists like a tree limb thrust 35 miles into the Atlantic Ocean. Removed from mainland America, Cape Codders have developed a distinct cultural identity. Residents value the natural beauty of their cranberry bogs and salt marshes and shorelines. And although whales have descended in economic importance, folks on the Cape still treasure their presence: Witness the fleets of whale-watching charters that set sail from coastal towns.

This trip promises no dangerous curves or sheer drops-offs since the routes are short, straight, calming, and quiet. The draw is the chance to discover circa 1700's towns and turn your bike into a time machine.

Sandwich Primer

Sandwich is a town with an identity crisis: as it enters the 21st century, it lingers in the Colonial Era. Hang around the city center and watch the predominant activities of the townspeople: filling water jugs at an artesian well, slipping into pubs, and catching the action as the grist mill starts grinding away on Shawme Pond.

Founded in 1637, the Cape's oldest town matured into a racy place where people liked to drink and plot to kill the British. The American Revolution might have been the town's highlight had it not been for the arrival of the Boston and Sandwich Glass Company in the 19th century. The glass industry of Sandwich was a natural, not because the town's sands and salt marsh grasses were used for packing but because of the abundance of forests that the factories could slash and burn to stoke the furnaces. When the factory closed in 1888, Sandwich slipped back into the shadows.

On the Road in Sandwich

Cape Cod roads are so sparse, few will explore the region beyond the road you'll ride to reach Provincetown. That said, park your bike in the village and spend a few hours poking around. It won't take much longer than that because museums and nature trails—not bars and roads—are what you'll find here. If you're accustomed to more hyperkinetic activities, you may be disappointed. An afternoon in Sandwich involves a more natural use of time, when you could spend hours doing nothing.

But that's the appeal. When you watch the swans on Shawme Pond, you won't be assaulted by bus fumes. You'll hear the water rushing, the Dexter Grist Mill grinding, and locals filling up on spring water for their coffee. Drop in the mill for a bag of cornmeal. Relax and watch the reflection of the Christopher Wren–inspired church spire on the water. Step into the Sandwich Glass Museum to see that glass can be art. Savor the fresh air as you take a short walk through neighborhoods where even the trash is clean.

While there's a good cross-section of businesses here, two may pique your interest: **Madden and Company,** 16 Jarves St., 508/888-3663, features aisles of scrimshaw, marine paintings, and other marine collectibles. Cool stuff for the office, but the downside is it's only open by appointment. **The Weather Store,** 146 Main St., 508/888-1200, 800/646-1203, www.theweatherstore.com, stocks antique and creatively designed barometers, rain gauges, sundials, and other meteorological goods.

When you're ready to expand your roaming range, hop back on your bike and ride to the Heritage Plantation or down to the bayfront boardwalk, which places you close to the salt marshes and Cape Cod Bay.

Pull it Over: Sandwich Highlights
Attractions and Adventures

Sidewalks start rolling up around 4:30, so aside from the few activities noted below (which actually will occupy most of a day), don't plan on doing much except taking a break from work and experiencing life as a colonist.

On the Cape you're surrounded by water, and there's an undeniable draw to park your bike and go to sea. About 25 miles up the road in East Dennis is the **Albatross,** Sesuit Harbor, 508/385-3244. This deep-sea fishing charter has been family-run since 1965 and leaves twice daily on weekdays for Cape Cod Bay runs for flounder, mackerel, and hake. These charters start when the weather turns warm in June. You can catch sight of a whale with the **Hyannis Whale Watcher,** roughly 15 miles outside Sandwich in Barnstable Harbor, 508/362-6088 or 800/287-0374, www.capecod.net/whales. The plus here is a rain check if you don't spot a whale—and that means right whales, finbacks, minke, and humpbacks, dammit.

I can't believe I liked the **Sandwich Glass Museum,** 129 Main St., 508/888-0251, www.sandwichglassmuseum.org, but I did. At the second largest draw in town, there are intriguing displays of tools that—long before computers and robots—were used to mold, thread, cut, and engrave glass, as well as antique books, maps, shoes, scrimshaw art, cigar holders, and a glass torch from the Lincoln-Hamlin ticket of 1860. Sure you may be surrounded by tourists from Iowa, but you're getting yourself an education there, Jethro. Hand over $3.50 at the door.

The largest draw for any rider is down the road. Pharmaceutical giant Josiah Kirby Lilly Jr. spent 40 years collecting rare books, artwork, drinking steins, stamps, coins, weapons, nautical models, and firearms and all of this is on display at **Heritage Plantation,** Pine and Grove Streets, 508/888-3300, www.heritage plantation.org. Most impressive is his collection inside the replica 1826 Shaker Roundbarn, which houses 35-plus vintage cars including a 1908 Waltham Orient Buckboard, the 1910 Sears Surrey (with the fringe on top), and the $2,000 1915 Stutz Bearcat—the "dream of flappers and college men." Other historical artifacts include a lock of Lincoln's hair (is there a genetic cloner in the house?). Open daily from mid-May–mid-October, admission is $9.

Blue-Plate Specials

Good food and reliable service await you at the **Bee-Hive Tavern,** 406 E. Rte. 6A, 508/833-1184, serving lunch and dinner. Healthy portions of baked stuffed quahog, fried conch fritters, lobster pie, and fish and chips beckon. What's more, meals are affordable. In this colonial tavern setting, you wouldn't be surprised to see a stagecoach roll up. If you're in Sandwich overnight, hoist a Boddington's Pub Ale ($4 a pint) at the low-ceilinged bar.

Five miles west of town on Route 6A, the **Sagamore Inn,** 1131 Sandwich Rd., 508/888-9707, has Colonial-style wooden floors and booths, and mouthwatering Yankee pot roast as well as pasta and seafood dishes.

Shut-Eye

Motels and Motor Courts
In the top 10 of motorcycle lodging options, I'd place the **Spring Hill Motor Lodge,** 351 Rte. 6A, 508/888-1456, 800/647-2514, www.sunsol.com/ springhill/, located three miles east of Sandwich. Reminiscent of an old-fashioned motor court, the juniper-shaded complex features a heated pool, tennis courts, and 24 extremely clean and spacious rooms. Four deluxe cottages boast private porches and fully equipped kitchens. Great for overnight or as a base to explore the Cape, the lodge charges $89–105. The equally clean **Shady Nook Inn and Motel,** 14 Rte. 6A, 508/888-0409 or 800/303-1751, www.shady nookinn.com, has spacious rooms, full baths, cable TV, phones, connecting double rooms, efficiencicies . . . all this from $75–125.

Chain Drive*
A, C, G, DD.

*Chain hotels in, or within ten miles of town. See cross-reference guide featuring phone numbers and web addresses on page 405.

Inn-Dependence
More generic and tourist-oriented is the **Dan'l Webster Inn,** 149 Main St., 508/888-3622 or 800/444-3566, www.danlwebsterinn.com. Rooms ($139–219) are clean, comfortable, and individually decorated. The on-site colonial-themed restaurant has won *Wine Spectator* magazine's Award of Excellence, but its tavern is a replica of the 1770s taproom where local patriots gathered for grog and ale during the Revolution. The setting here is less formal and features soups, sandwiches, and lighter fare.

On the Road: Sandwich to Chatham

As you skirt along the shores and marshes of Cape Cod Bay and leave Sandwich behind, Route 6A is low and lean, slowly swinging into a gentle curve and delivering you into the past. On this leg you'll ride past villages founded in the 1600s, small places such as Barnstable, Cummaquid, and Dennis.

Long before Route 6 arrived to transport people in a hurry, Route 6A had preserved Cape Cod the way it used to be. The roads are as soft and gentle as the scent of the pines. Let the other regions of Cape Cod lure commercialism. Not on this ride. Had you ridden this road 200 years ago, not only would the locals have fled in terror at the sight of your bike, but you would also have been riding the Old King's Highway, the only route mail and passenger coaches took prior to the Revolution. Today it is yours. And it remains imbued with regional flavor. Along 6A you'll still hear native Cape Codders talk about "washashores," the transplants who arrived from "off Cape." Then there are the "boggers," the farmers whose fruitful cranberry bogs have stayed in the family for generations.

As you leave Sandwich heading east on 6A, you'll notice the repetitive uniformity of the unpainted shingled homes. White cedar shingles were plentiful, easily split, and could last up to 60 years. And why paint when your house was going to be sandblasted and sea-sprayed throughout the year? Some people do paint—but only a shade of white that earns the local historic commission's "certificate of appropriateness."

The ride is short, the road level, the landscape dotted with blue spruce, silver maple, firs, Canadian hemlock, and sycamore. The trees are as plentiful as the signage pointing to woodworkers, potters, artists, cabinetmakers, weavers, and other New England craftspeople who work from their homes. There are few changes in elevation, but there are bends in the road that follow the contour of the shore. In Yarmouthport, round the corner and there's a stop you should make. The **Parnassus Book Service,** 220 Rte. 6A, 508/362-6420, www.parnassus books.com, is a place Charles Kuralt would have loved. The building, the books, and the old crusty owner are still the same as they have been for 40 years. You can buy a book inside or, if no one's on duty, grab a book from the outdoor display, check the price, and put your money through a slot in the door.

Next come the minuscule villages of Cummaquid, Yarmouth, and then Dennis. As you roll into Dennis, there's a trace amount of activity in a small shopping plaza but, as in other towns along Route 6A, the doors lock and the sidewalks roll up around five o'clock. That's fine, because a few more miles down the road lies Brewster and the must-see **Brewster Store,** 1935 Rte. 6A, 508/896-3744. In 1852 this opened as Universalist Society church, but a decade later prophets gave way to profits. Since 1866, more or less, this has been a general store outfitted with all the props you'd see at Sam Drucker's. Old-fashioned candy displays are still here, and so is a soda fountain, player piano, peanut roaster, a Station Agent #24 pot-bellied stove, and a jar filled with pickles the size of zeppelins. Out front, locals gather on church pews each morning to eat donuts, drink coffee, trade yarns, and solve the world's problems.

This is the last gasp of individuality as Brewster precedes Orleans, a busy bottleneck that has all the conveniences of home (supermarket, restaurants, motels, etc.). Since it does look like home, that's why you'd want to head south on Route 28 and make your way to the "elbow" of the Cape in Chatham. Fantastic Chatham.

Chatham Primer

Nearly as old as Sandwich, Chatham was settled in 1656 by Pilgrims whose surnames continue to dominate the town's census list of 6,500-plus residents. At first this was a farming community until one egghead looked around, realized he was on the peninsular southeastern tip of the cape, and said, "Aye, Martha, 'tis true. Farming blows."

So for more than 300 years shellfish harvesting and deep-sea fishing have remained a staple for this town. Aside from the sea, Chatham has no major industries to speak of. By being here, you're helping fuel tourism which keeps the town going—at least during the summer months when the weather's right.

On the Road in Chatham

Like Sandwich, Chatham is a town best explored on foot. You'll understand why when you ride in on Route 28, which, in town, is called Main Street. For block after block you'll find bars, nice restaurants, and some of the freshest seafood in America. Sure, you could head 20 miles west to Hyannis and find more people doing more stuff in more chain stores, but you can do that anywhere. Stop your bike and really see what's happening. A local sums it up: "If you're in a hurry, you don't belong in Chatham."

Assuming you'll stay the night, keep your bike at the inn/motel/hotel since parking is at a premium in peak season—it's free. Now you're free to walk the streets and tune into the smells of coffee, bakeries, candle shops, cafés, flowers, and sea. It's a nice mix that rewards you for bypassing Orleans.

As you walk Chatham, look for the highlights. One is **The Spyglass,** 618 Main St., 508/945-9686, where collectors pick up authentic antique ship spyglasses, lanterns, old naval uniforms, admiral's caps, and other rare marine items. Buy some epaulets and change your biker name to "Commodore." For a party back in your room, check out **The Epicure,** 534 Main St., 508/945-0047, which has about eleventy-hundred wines, cigars, gourmet picnic foods, and other essentials.

After soaking in Main Street, cruise over to the ocean, which is a short ride or slightly longer walk away. Head east on Main Street, then south on Morris Island Road to reach the Chatham Lighthouse. Unless you're a native or a member of the Polar Bear Club, you may find the beach here swimmable only a few hours a year. Still, the shore attracts riders who find a good photo op where the tip of Cape Cod meets the Atlantic.

Pull it Over: Chatham Highlights
Attractions and Adventures

If the weather's right, nothing beats a day on the waters of old Cape Cod. Through Cape Yachts, **Nauti Jane's,** Ridgevale Beach Rd., Chatham, 508/432-7079, supplies Hobie Cats, larger sailboats, and power boats. Option B: Leave the sailing to a professional. Capt. Paul Avellar takes the wheel at **Beachcomber Boat Tours,** 508/945-5265, www.sealwatch.com, and Capt. David Murdoch sets sail at **Chatham Water Tours,** 508/432-5895, www.chathamwater tours.net. Unless these men share The Skipper's bad luck and you wind up on an uncharted desert isle, you'll get a waterside look at the natural side of Chatham: a panorama of pristine New England beaches, harbors, and seals. Group riders can pool their cash and customize a cruise.

Blue-Plate Specials

Nothing fancy at **Sandy's Diner,** 639 Main St., 508/945-0631, just three very nice ladies who will whip up a hearty breakfast or lunch for you. Don't expect a four-star meal at this low-key diner, here since 1965. Not a lot of men here, either; they're down at **Larry's PX,** 1591 Main St., West Chatham, 508/945-3964. When Larry left the Culling Board, a lot of the menfolk went with him. If you crave a midnight snack, wait a few hours and be here when he opens at 4 A.M. Larry's serves big breakfasts and overstuffed sandwiches at lunch.

I could recommend a fancy restaurant, but, instead, savor this: fresh seafood for your own Cape Cod clambake. Locals have been shopping at **Nickerson's Fish & Lobster,** Chatham Fish Pier, 508/945-0145, since 1950, and if you wanted seafood any fresher, you'd have to dive for it yourself. Steamers, lobster tails, little necks, mussels, quahog, haddock, cod, flounder, and sweet lobsters are yours for the asking. They load your feast on a beer flat and supply all the accessories you need for a beach cookout or a meal at your efficiency (they can also cook it for the most delicious to-go meal you've ever had). Cash only. Open daily Memorial Day–Labor Day, weekends until mid-October.

Watering Holes

There are fewer than a handful of nighttime hang-outs, primarily restaurants that will keep their bars open until 1 A.M. The largest draw in Chatham village is its only raw bar, the **Chatham Squire,** 487 Main St., 508/945-0942, www.thesquire.com, where they offer "Food for the hungry, drink for the thirsty." That about sums it up. The standard lineup of Killian's, Bass, Guinness, and Pete's Wicked Ale goes for $4.20 a pint. Their restaurant features chowders, sirloin, ribs, chicken, and fish. Lots of fish.

Christian's, 443 Main St., 508/945-3362, is a restaurant created inside an old sea captain's house. What you're looking for is Upstairs at Christian's, a place where you can retreat to a piano bar and hoist an ale at tables tucked in and under the eaves and nooks. Not wild, but a good retreat.

Over in West Chatham, locals are hanging out at **The Sou'wester,** 1563 Main St., 508/945-5761, www.souwester.com. Away from the restaurant, a party atmosphere prevails in the lounge bar, where bands play nearly every night in season. Libations revolve around beer, wine, and mixed drinks. Conversation revolves around fishing, sports, fishing, women, sports, and fishing.

Shut-Eye

Motels and Motor Courts

For a small town, Chatham offers many good lodging choices, although the prices aren't always pleasing. Just over a mile from the village, the **Chatham Motel,** 1487 Main St., 508/945-2630 or 800/770-5545, www.chathammotel.com, stands in a pine grove. The 32 rooms are clean and well equipped, and the grounds feature gardens, BBQ grills, and a pool. Pre-summer rates are $80–95, and jump to $135–165 in season. A five-minute walk from the village is the **Hawthorne Motel,** 196 Shore Road, 508/945-0372, www.thehawthorne.com. Located on the waterfront, they offer 16 motel rooms, 10 kitchenettes, and 2 two-bedroom cottages on four acres overlooking Pleasant Bay. You'll pay $110 before summer, $160 during. Right near the Chatham Lighthouse, the **Surfside Motor Court,** 25 Holway St., 508/945-9757, www.capecodtravel.com/surfsideinn, charges from $90 per night. Within walking distance of the water, you'll get an old-fashioned (but clean) room and easy access to swimming and fishing.

Inn-Dependence

The Moorings, 326 Main St., 508/945-0848, 800/320-0848, www.cape cod.com/moorings, is a bed-and-breakfast that provides privacy via carriage houses and cottages that can sleep up to four. Price tag here is $125–228. One of the most picturesque inns is the **Chatham Wayside Inn,** 512 Main St., 508/945-5550 or 800/391-5734, www.waysideinn.com. The circa 1860 home has lots of room—enough for a pub, restaurant, and 56 guest rooms, many with patios or balconies, fireplaces, and whirlpool tubs, from a low of $95 to an in-season low of $185.

On the Road: Chatham to Provincetown

When you leave Chatham on Route 28 North, the Atlantic Ocean will be on your right. Although you'll be backtracking to reach and bypass Orleans, at least the scenery on the ride is spiced with places such as Pleasant Bay, Pilgrim Lake, hidden coves, and small boats.

After you pass Orleans, you'll reach the end of Route 28 and briefly hook up with familiar Route 6A before locking into Route 6. While the roads are fairly dense with traffic, they're manageable and, a mile past Eastham, will lead you directly to the **Cape Cod National Seashore's Salt Pond Visitor Center,** 508/255-3421. This is the introduction to some 27,000 acres of national park which await you, courtesy of Cape Codder JFK. Like most places along these remote roads, low key diversions like this may not seem appealing to bikers in general, but it's well worth a stop to understand the history of the Cape. At the center, the *Sands of Time* is a short film showing how the Cape was formed by a glacial deposit and how it will one day be reclaimed by the sea (Sunday, May 27, 2012, at 8:04 P.M., to be exact).

A sign helpfully suggests how to plan your visit if your time is limited to an hour, a half day, or even a full day. Options range from touring the museum and watching the movie, to hooking up with a ranger-led program, whale-watching, or hanging out on 30 miles of beach. If you're ready to reach Provincetown, an hour's visit should be enough, slightly longer if the history of the sea intrigues you. The small must-see museum is first-class, with exhibits on the lonely lives of lighthouse keepers, the many uses of whalebone, the area's colonial taverns, and the primitive rescue equipment used to save shipwrecked sailors. On early wooden life preservers, instructions for their use were carved in three languages to give foreign sailors a chance.

Farther up the road in Wellfleet is Marconi Station, site of the first transatlantic wireless telegraph station. In 1903, Teddy Roosevelt sent a message to England's King Edward VII: "Most cordial greetings and best wishes." Edward's memorable reply, "Can you call me back? The game's on," endeared him to generations of American men. Hike up a 20-foot bluff and the site is just a plaque, a platform, and a boardwalk, but you're here, so why not drop in?

Now a warning: If you look at the Cape on a map it seems as if Route 6 would be one of the nation's best oceanfront roads. It's not. It hugs the middle of a thin strip of land and leaves 3,000 miles of Atlantic Ocean hidden behind stands of trees, taffy shops, and T-shirt stores. The reward for your effort is that once you've reached the tip of Cape Cod, you can always point at a map and say, "Yeah, I rode my bike there once."

So, the next 22 miles are uneventful until you get well north, where the sea winds blow in sand from the beach. As you roll into the last curves of the peninsula, just ahead you'll spy the terminus of this trip: Provincetown.

Provincetown Primer

When the Pilgrims landed here in November of 1620, they set in motion the formation of New England. It may not seem that impressive when you consider that the Mayflower only docked here for two months before sailing on to Plymouth, but think about this: That was long enough for the Mayflower Compact to be signed, which was the first charter of democratic government in world history. *World history.*

Absent any Pilgrims, Provincetown later became home to early colonial settlers, who were followed by Portuguese immigrants who showed up to do a little fishing on the Grand, Stellwagen, and Georges Banks. These were hearty people; part-time fishermen who became full-time residents, bold enough to stay here through the harsh, biting winters.

Provincetown now peaks in the summer with day-trippers and others who drive up for lunch and perhaps an overnight. Dense with commercialism but blessed by miles of beaches, the town will speak to you . . . or it will remain very quiet.

I didn't hear much.

On the Road in Provincetown

When you arrive in Provincetown there's a strong possibility you'll be put off by the crowded, narrow streets that make a bike ride nearly as uncomfortable as driving a motor home. The main thoroughfare, three-mile long Commercial Street, is clogged with gift shops, T-shirt stores, bars, and a predominantly gay population. Fine if you're gay, tolerable if you're not, annoying if you just wanted to see a neat fishing village. In Provincetown, outrageous is the norm.

The instantaneous assault on your senses makes it clear that the natural beauty of Cape Cod is far nicer than any man-made creation. With that in mind, you have the option of making this a day trip and returning to quiet Chatham, or staying for the night.

Either way, perhaps the best view of Cape Cod is from the **Pilgrim Monument,** High Pole Hill, 508/487-1310, www.pilgrim-monument.org, dedicated in 1910 to commemorate the first landing of the Pilgrims in Provincetown. At the base of the 252-foot tower is the Provincetown Museum, which is included in the $6 admission. Outside of a few museums, the main attractions in town are walking Commercial Street, dropping in a watering hole for a drink, or getting away from it all on a whale watch.

Pull it Over: Provincetown Highlights
Attractions and Adventures

Whale watches depart from Provincetown Harbor. Provincetown is roughly six miles from the Stellwagen Bank Sanctuary, the main feeding ground for whales and Merv Griffin. Most trips run between April and October and cost around $20. Sign up with **Whale Watch,** 508/349-1900 or 800/826-9300, www.whalewatch.com.

Because P-town's already 50 miles out to sea, several charter boats take advantage of its strategic location by fishing for fluke, flounder, bluefish, mackerel, and striped bass. A fleet of fishing boats stands at the ready to take you out on the high seas. Most provide bait and tackle, but no harpoons.

The highlight of **Provincetown Heritage Museum,** 365 Commercial St., 508/487-7098, is the *Rose Dorothea,* which at 66 feet is the largest fishing schooner model in the world. Why didn't they just make it a boat? Unless there are renovations underway, the museum is open 10–5:30. Admission is $3.

Blue-Plate Specials

An unsophisticated neon exterior announces the **Lobster Pot,** 321 Commercial St., 508/487-0842, which serves lunch and dinner. The local hangout overlooks P-Town Harbor and serves up a medley of Portuguese, Cajun, Japanese, and Mexican seafood-based meals. Go for the clam chowder. Upstairs at "The Pot," the bar gets mighty crowded.

In 1929, the same year the Great Depression kicked in, the **Mayflower Cafe,** 300 Commercial St., 508/487-0121, kicked off. Now run by descendents of the original owners, the sit-down restaurant is a classic with dishes like homemade clam chowder, steamed softshell clams, Portuguese-style fish & chips, crab cakes, oysters, pastas, lobster, pork chops, sandwiches, pizzas, fresh-baked dinner rolls, and plenty of beer. Bring cash, no credit cards.

Watering Holes

There are drinking spots up and down Commercial Street, but when you go in and don't see any women, you've either entered a gay bar or a high-testosterone sports bar. Some bars switch formats, so you're best exploring on your own. A safe bet may be **Bubala's,** 185 Commercial St., 508/487-0773, which has live entertainment nightly; usually jazz, blues, or comedy. Fine for a beer, but they pride themselves on martinis. The **Surf Club,** 315 A Commercial St., 508/487-1367, has been here since the early '70s, and is a local fave. Three TVs play sports, the windows open to the water, and decks are designed for drinking and dancing to the blues bands that play as late as 1 A.M. in the summer.

Shut-Eye

Motels and Motor Courts

In a town where dirty is clean, the **Cape Colony Inn,** 280 Bradford St., 508/487-1755 or 800/841-6716, www.capecolonyinn.com, is clean clean. It's also remote enough (a few miles) to be a good base for P-town, offering seven landscaped acres, picnic areas, a beach volleyball court, heated pool, and 57 loaded rooms at rates from $69–112.

Gonna Have a Clambake

Circle the bikes, grab a shovel, and get started on your own clambake. Dig a large pit and line the bottom with stones, on top of which you'll place wood to burn. A few hours later, after the wood burns and the rocks are red hot, rake away the wood coals and cover them with seaweed. Place your food (clams, mussels, corn, potatoes, onions, sausage, etc.) on top and cover the pit with a tarp. After an hour of steaming, your meal should be ready. Or blow it off, and just go to a restaurant.

Chain Drive*
A, L

*Chain hotels in, or within ten miles of town. See cross-reference guide featuring phone numbers and web addresses on page 405.

Inn-Dependence
The Fairbanks Inn, 90 Bradford St., 508/487-0386 or 800/324-7265, www.fairbanksinn.com, has consistently received high marks from the press and their guests. Amenities include an expanded continental breakfast, sun porch, and 10 wood-burning fireplaces—if you need them in the summer. Rates start at $69 for a double room, the same going for $159 in season. Adding a touch of class, the English country house–style **Beaconlight,** 12 Winthrop St., 508/487-9603 or 800/696-9603, www.capecod.net/beaconlight/, has a few king beds, a video library, voicemail, fridges, fireplaces, a grand piano, outdoor heated spa, and serves a gourmet continental breakfast. Rooms go for $100–200.

Side Trip: Nantucket

Even though you won't need to bring your bike to this island, it's worth the trip—Nantucket is the closest you'll get to a colonial whaling town, complete with 800-odd homes built by whalers between 1740 and 1840. On a day trip, you can walk the area you need to see in about four hours and still have time to kick back at a few pubs or restaurants.

From Hyannis, you can gain a few valuable hours by reaching the island via a 15-minute plane ride aboard **Island Airlines,** 508/228-7575 or 800/248-7779, or **Cape Air,** 508/771-6944 or 800/352-0714, www.flycapeair.com. Both carriers charge $76 for a round trip, and you'll have to take a taxi to reach the center of town. Also from Hyannis, the next best option is catching the **Fast Ferry,** 508/495-3278, www.fastferry.com, which rockets you there in 45 minutes for around $52 round trip. **Hy-Line Cruises,** 508/778-2600 or 888/778-1132, does the same thing for slightly more. Take the slow ferry (2.5 hours/$22) only if you're on a budget or can't swim. The ferry terminals have snacks, coffee, phones, and lockers where you can stow your helmet. Tip: Find a parking spot early or you'll be gouged by the hustlers across the street.

Different ferry services dock at different locations on Nantucket, and there are bicycle rentals nearby (mopeds, too, if you're ready to downsize). But since the streets were made using ballast from the old sailing ships, the cobblestone wobble will rattle your brain right out of your skull.

Find your way to Main Street, the heart of Nantucket. A good first stop is either the **Nantucket Island Chamber of Commerce,** 48 Main St., 508/228-1700, or the **Visitors Services Bureau,** 25 Federal St., 508/228-0925, which have racks of brochures on museums, lodging, and activities. Next, the **Jared Coffin House,** 29 Broad St., 508/228-2400, is an impressive older home, which now serves a great breakfast for a nominal price.

In the heart of town a few stores stand out. **Congdon's Pharmacy,** 47 Main St., 508/228-0020, established in 1871, features an old-fashioned soda fountain. **Murray's Beverage Store,** 23 Main St., 508/228-0071, sells wines, cigars, trail mix, crackers, and bar snacks. **The Brotherhood of Thieves,** 23 Broad St., is a popular spot for locals. It's low-key here: no phone, just walk-in service for burgers, shoestring fries, beer, and mixed drinks.

As you explore, the "Nantucket Historical Association Museum Guide and Walking Tour," available at the museum, will lead you to quiet side streets several blocks from the busy downtown district. This may be where you'll enjoy yourself most. Get lost on the back streets and enjoy the same sense of solitude you can get on your bike.

Resources for Riders
Cape Cod Run

Massachusetts Travel Information
Massachusetts Road Conditions—617/374-1234
Massachusetts State Park Campgrounds Reservations—877/422-6762,
    www.reserveamerica.com
Massachusetts Department of Travel & Tourism—800/447-6277,
    www.massvacation.com

Local and Regional Information
Bed & Breakfast Cape Cod—508/255-3824 or 800/541-6226,
    www.bedandbreakfastcapecod.com
Bed & Breakfast Reservations—800/832-2632, www.bbreserve.com
Canal Region Chamber of Commerce (Sandwich) —508/759-6000,
    www.capecodcanalchamber.org
Cape Cod Area Visitors Bureau—508/862-0700 or 888/332-2732,
    www.capecodchamber.org
Cape Cod National Seashore—508/255-3421, www.nps.gov/caco
Cape Cod Weather—508/771-5522
Chatham Chamber of Commerce—508/945-5199 or 800/715-5567,
    www.chathamcapecod.org
Nantucket Island Chamber of Commerce—508/228-1700,
    www.nantucketchamber.org
Provincetown Chamber of Commerce—508/487-3424,
    www.ptownchamber.com

Motorcycle Shops
Archie's Cycle Service—489 Ashley Blvd., New Bedford, 508/995-9751
Cape Cod Power Sports—92 Barnstable Rd., Hyannis, 508/771-5900,
    www.ccpowersports.com
JMR Honda-Polaris-Suzuki—741 Yarmouth Rd., Hyannis, 508/778-7211

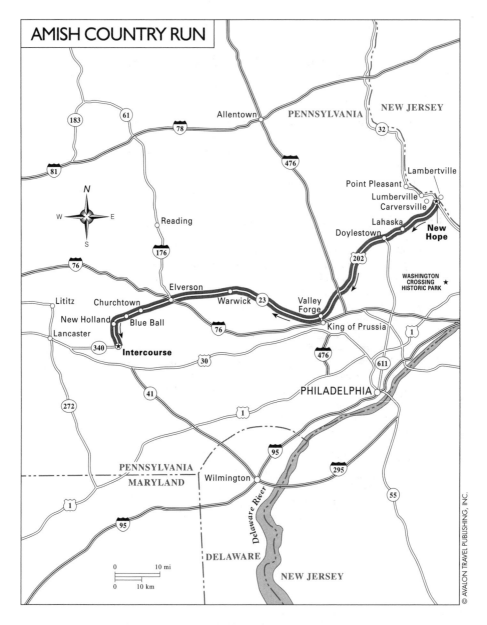

Route: New Hope to Intercourse via Lahaska, Doylestown, Valley Forge
Distance: Approximately 110 miles; consider three days with stops.
   • Day 1—New Hope • Day 2—Travel • Day 3—Intercourse
First Leg: New Hope to Intercourse (110 miles)
Helmet Laws: Pennsylvania requires helmets.

Amish Country Run

New Hope to Intercourse, Pennsylvania

This journey will take you into the past, from the colonial accents an hour north of Philadelphia to 19th-century farms. Along the way you'll ride next to the historic Delaware River and gaze on Pennsylvania's most pristine farmland. Some of the finest back roads and friendliest people reside in this part of America. Time your ride for late summer or early fall and you'll enjoy it even more.

New Hope Primer

Of all the towns in America—at least the ones I've visited—New Hope is clearly the one most at ease with itself. It accepts diversity without question and welcomes all without exception. Locals explain that the feeling is the result of New Hope being on the cross of a "vortex," a positive energy field centered in an underground river flowing 60 feet below the Delaware River. The only other town with such a vortex is Sedona, Arizona—but I hear it's energized by plutonium.

You'll view New Hope through the prism of age. Young riders may see it as a nouveau Haight-Ashbury; couples with kids notice a family-friendly getaway; and older motorcycle travelers will arrive in a charming shopping village.

New Hope is all this, but it is something greater. It is a historic community that predates Philadelphia. It was at Coryell's Ferry where George Washington trained for his fabled crossing, and made the real voyage a few miles south.

A century later the town became the birthplace of the New Hope School of Artists, whose members left Philadelphia to gain inspiration from the summer countryside; later, they fostered the American Impressionist movement. It is an actors' community—as a young man, Robert Redford honed his skills here at the Bucks County Playhouse. It is a walking town that spans the river into Lambertville, New Jersey. And, for your benefit, it is also a town serving as Point B for motorcycle travelers on weekend runs from New York, New Jersey, and Pennsylvania.

On the Road in New Hope

What you'll see beyond the boundaries of New Hope is magical, but you should first know what's in town. New Hope can be high-class, with galleries, cafés, and upscale boutiques, but it can also be down-to-earth, with cigar shops and bars that welcome motorcycle travelers. Collectibles shops line Main Street, providing a field day for antique-shoppers. And, judging from witch shops and tie-dyed kids roaming around, New Hope also could be a breeding ground for the radical.

So take a good look, make some mental notes, then swerve around the tourists, and take off on Route 32 North (a.k.a. River Road), a short and se-ductive ride beside the beautiful Delaware.

The trimmed hedges and manicured lawns of the town soon give way to sharp curves and a tunnel of green. Fresh fields and fat stone walls suggest Britain's Yorkshire Dales as they rise and fall with the earth. The road follows the lead of the walls, pushing you up and dragging you into tight corners and spec-tacularly old scenery.

As you pass cars carrying wooden canoes, you'll find it hard to believe that this landscape is only a few miles from the downtown tourists. Getting into the groove, you soon arrive at Route 263 and **Dilly's Corner,** 215/862-5333 (closed Mondays), where moms, bikers, teens, and tourists alike load up on hamburgers, cheeseburgers, swirls, and sundaes.

Heading north toward Lumberville, you enter primeval woods as green and moist as a rain forest. The corduroy texture of the road travels from the tires up into your body. The Delaware River rides on your right as you pass a flotilla of people drifting downriver in slick black inner tubes and deer grazing on the lawns of magnificent mansions.

Landscaped lawns and untouched grasses grow side by side, and there's ex-treme satisfaction in the knowledge that no one's screwed this up yet. Past the 1740 House and Cuttalossa Inn, just beyond the authentic, old-fashioned

Lumberville Store, 3741 River Road, 215/297-5388, it's time for a detour. On your left, Old Carversville Road rises like the Matterhorn, and a steep drop materializes on the right. As the road changes to gravel and you slow to compensate, cabins suddenly appear in the hollow, unobtrusive because they are built of the earth and not on it.

Just past a wooden bridge, you arrive in Carversville. Downtown's about the size of your backyard, and the center of activity is the **Carversville General Store,** 215/297-5353. Well stocked with groceries and drinks, it's also the town post office and theater. On Friday evenings, moving picture shows are projected on the side of the building. If you haven't caught on, this is a great place to stop for a Yoo-Hoo and a Chunky bar.

Return to Lumberville, turning left on Route 32 North. Beneath the bridge, fishermen in waders cast their lines. When you pass the village of Devil's Half Acre, the stunning view and weaving road introduce some LeMans driving. Drive it at dusk as the fog settles over the Delaware Valley and you sweep through the mist into small bumps and quick ascents. No commercialism here, just the road and you.

You'll soon reach Point Pleasant, home of **Bucks County River Country,** 215/297-5000 or 215/297-TUBE, www.rivercountry.net, the point of origin for the armada of inner tube passengers you passed downriver. Places like this make a tour great. Rent a tube or raft and go cruising down the Delaware, drifting at a lazy 1.5 mph in cool water. There are no rapids here; so you can do nothing but relax and enjoy the soothing, peaceful experience.

From here, you can continue your northward trek toward Upper Black Eddy and Lake Nockamixon. Take virtually any road in any direction for a longer ride, or turn back and head home to New Hope. That's the beauty of New Hope. No matter where you ride, you'll be satisfied.

Pull it Over: New Hope Highlights
Attractions and Adventures

Far enough from Broadway to try out plays and close enough to take them to NYC if they're any good, **Bucks County Playhouse** has been a launching pad for great playwrights like George S. Kaufman and Moss Hart, while hopeful actors Robert Redford, Grace Kelly, Dick Van Dyke, Tyne Daly, and Liza Minnelli caught the stage right here. The playhouse is located at 70 South Main St., 215/862-2041 or 215/862-2046, www.buckscountyplayhouse.com. Tickets average $20–22.

Mountain River Outfitters, 287 S. Main St., Lambertville, 609/397-3366, www.mountainriver.com, rents kayaks and canoes for $55 per day. You can take kayak programs or head off on your own down the Raritan Canal or Delaware River, reliving the glory of Washington's Christmas Eve crossing.

Riders who like all things mechanical should pay a visit to the **New Hope & Ivyland Railroad,** 32 W. Bridge St., 215/862-2332, www.newhope railroad.com. Admission is $9. They have four full-gauge steam locomotives that pull passenger cars through the hills and valleys of Bucks County. If you have vivid dreams about steam trains, give serious thought to the "locomotive cab ride." This is one of very few steam railroads that allows passengers to ride up front with the engineer and see how the original iron horses were driven. Trips depart several times daily in season.

Some would say a barge trip with the **New Hope Canal Boat Company,** 145 S. Main St., 215/862-0758, www.canalboats.com, is as boring as all get out, but it is different—and cheap ($7.95). A mule team pulls your barge down the Delaware Canal and shows you a different side of New Hope. If you're traveling in a group, call ahead to reserve a private barge for a canal party. You may be looking at a mule's ass for a couple of hours, but it doesn't matter if you've loaded up the barge with a cooler full of beer.

It was one of the turning points of the Revolution and the inspiration for an American icon. A few miles south of New Hope on Christmas Eve 1776, George Washington massed the Continental Army and surprised British troops by crossing the Delaware and capturing 900 British soldiers and German mercenaries in Trenton. Adding a feather in the cap of this victory, later that night Washington marched on to Princeton where he caught the British garrison by surprise and captured enough food and supplies to sustain his troops through the brutal winter of 1777. At the **Washington Crossing Historic Park,** 1112 River Rd. (Rte. 32), Washington Crossing, 215/493-4076, you can take a tour, visit historic homes, and see a movie about the event.

Shopping

Shopping is New Hope's lifeblood. The town has many antique shops, none geared toward motorcycle travelers per se, but interesting nonetheless. A place called **Gypsy Heaven,** 115 S. Main St., 215/862-5251, www.gypsyheaven.com, sells candles and incense and even witches' spells. Maybe they've got one to fix a plugged carburetor.

Located in the former OTC Cracker Factory, **Riverhorse Brewing,** 80 Lambert Lane, Lambertville, 609/397-7776, www.riverhorse.com, was founded in 1994 and brews five kinds of beer at any one time. Add one more and they'd have a six-pack. Open from noon–5 P.M., you can walk through the brewery, buy gifts in the store, and get samples in the sampling room.

Aging baby boomers trying to retrieve the junk they threw away when they hit puberty can buy it back at **Love Saves the Day,** 1 S. Main St., 215/862-1399, which is crammed with Beatles memorabilia, lunch boxes, '60s TV merchandise, and rare Star Wars items. And you blew your money on Internet stock . . .

Reading improves any trip, and **Farley's Bookshop,** 44 S. Main St., 215/862-2452, is the place to load up on literature. The store is filled with rooms that are stacked with shelves that are loaded with an uncommonly huge amount of new books and magazines.

Blue-Plate Specials

Walk inside **Sneddon's Luncheonette,** 47 Bridge St., 609/397-3053, Lambertville, and the sounds of dishes slapping and silverware clanging welcome you faster than the friendly waitresses. Cheap paneling, newspapers displayed handsomely on the floor, and heart-shaped wire-back chairs take you back to the 1960s. The home-cooked meals and soups will take you back home, provided your home was a diner.

There are numerous fine dining restaurants around New Hope, but **Wildflowers Garden Restaurant,** 8 W. Mechanic St., 215/862-2241, offers a twist: good food that doesn't cost a fortune. Although the outdoor patio is crowded, the riverside setting is the perfect place to relax and experience New Hope. Entrées feature such diverse fare as Yankee pot roast and extremely tasty Thai food. Good food, great setting, excellent price: about $5 for lunch, $8 for dinner.

Watering Holes

Crowded and cool, **Fran's Pub,** 116 S. Main St., 215/862-5539, entertains with a pool table, juke box, wide-screen TV, and cooler filled with beers. Look around and you'll notice tattoos are as abundant as brands of brew. Enjoy happy hour (4:30–6:30) on the nice outdoor patio. This place is great for people-watching.

Every night at **John and Peter's,** 96 S. Main St., 215/862-5981, is like a talent show audition, with live acts daily. Folks crowd into this low-key joint with low ceilings to be treated to shows by such performers as Leon Redbone, George Thorogood, and Martin Mull—as well as hundreds of forgettable acts. Still, it's got a neat patio and a cool atmosphere—just the place to kick back in the evening.

Parisian silent film star and chanteuse Odette Myrtil Logan created **Odette's,** S. River Rd., 215/862-2432, www.odettes.com, a neighborly restaurant and lounge. If cheap dives aren't your speed, you may prefer this more civilized alternative. Dinner by the riverside is great, but the real fun happens when locals gather at the piano bar each evening and display their talents (which many of them also display on Broadway). It's an old-fashioned singalong. Guess what? Newswoman Jessica Savitch died here when her car plunged into the creek. Anchors aweigh.

Shut-Eye

Motels and Motor Courts
About a mile from the village, **The New Hope Motel in the Woods,** 6661 Rte. 179, 215/862-2800, is a nice, nostalgic and clean place resting before five acres of lush woods. There are 28 rooms of various sizes and bed configurations, a heated pool, AAA rating, a snack lounge, and summer rates from $59–99 on weekdays, $89–129 on weekends.

Chain Drive*
A, AA

*Chain hotels in, or within ten miles of town. See cross-reference guide featuring phone numbers and web addresses on page 405.

Inn-Dependence
Competition among the many inns in New Hope has raised the level of service and comfort—and the prices. A smaller property in a nice setting, **Porches,** 20 Fishers Alley, 215/862-3277, www.porchesnewhope.com, is an 1880s cottage-style home in the heart of town with weekday rates from $95. The pace is informal, and most of the 1920s-decor rooms overlook the Delaware Canal Towpath. After a full country breakfast of fruit, bacon, sausage, grits, pancakes, and fresh bread, you can waddle off to town a few blocks away. The setting for the **1740 House,** River Rd., Lumberville, 215/297-5661, www.1740house.com, is perfect. A little ways out of town, it's located on a beautiful road overlooking the river and features a pool to relax by when you've finished your ride. Each of the 23 rooms ($90–145) is decorated in Early American and has a river view. Back in town, the **Wedgwood Inn** also represents the **Aaron Burr House Inn,** 80 W. Bridge St., 215/862-2343, www.1870wedgwoodinn.com. With 20 rooms to choose from, the rates run from $130–199. Both are traditional with individually

decorated rooms, some with tubs, fireplaces, king beds, and bay windows. The screened flagstone patio is a relaxing setting. To complement the complimentary breakfast, afternoons end with chocolates and a nip of owner Carl's secret-recipe almond liqueur.

On the Road: New Hope to Intercourse

If I were in an episode of *The Twilight Zone*—the kind where somebody's stuck someplace forever—I would hope Rod Serling would send me riding endlessly across the Pennsylvania countryside. This desire starts in the rides above and continues upon leaving New Hope on Route 202 towards Lahaska. On the way out of town, check out **Peddler's Village,** 215/794-4000, www.peddlers village.com. It looks like a tourist trap, but surprisingly, the 70 stores and eight restaurants that spread across a shopping village are not too bad.

Stay on Route 202 and you'll ride into Doylestown, small enough for a manageable and brief stop. Downtown is particularly clean and nice, with a movie theater, bookstore, and various independent merchants. Doylestown native James Michener gave his name to the **James A. Michener Art Museum,** 138 S. Pine St., 215/340-9800, a refurbished 1880s prison. Bucks County residents Pearl S. Buck, Oscar Hammerstein II, Moss Hart, George S. Kaufman, Dorothy Parker, and S. J. Perelman are all honored here. If you like art, literature, and the thee-ah-tuh, you might be tempted to pull over.

Follow Route 202 out of Doylestown toward King of Prussia (the town, not the monarch), and at Bridgeport get on 23 West to ride to the front door of Valley Forge. Though never the sight of a battle, this is where America's pursuit of liberty hung in the balance. By surviving the harsh winter of 1777–78 and the loss of 2,000 men to the elements, Washington's troops proved they were tough enough to see the Revolution through to its conclusion. That's why you should stop at the **Valley Forge National Historical Park,** 610/783-1077, www.nps.gov/vafo. For $2, you can walk through Washington's spartan headquarters and the log cabins that once housed his troops and see statues and monuments to the men who endured the winter without proper food or clothing. You probably won't see this in winter, but you still may feel chills when you think about what happened in this place.

Following Valley Forge, the road gets much nicer as 23 forms a slow arc through soft hills past Warwick, Elverson, Churchtown, and Blue Ball.

Before you reach New Holland, turn left just past the Hollander Motel onto Brimmer Avenue/New Holland Road, and soon the sweet smell of produce gives way to farm smells worse than a frat house bathroom after an all-night kegger. Put the visor down and the nose plugs in. Silos and buggies tell you that you're entering Amish farmland. Keep heading south until you reach Route 340, then turn right.

In a few minutes, you'll be enjoying Intercourse.

Intercourse Primer

It was one of most amazing sights of my journey. As I rode into Intercourse and raised my visor, the blunt chill of the evening air hit my face. I scanned the road and a motion drew my attention to the ridge of a hill. An Amish farmer stood tall on the back of a mule-driven wagon, hay stacked high behind him. Silhouetted against the setting sun, he was a vision from 1820. I was in Intercourse, and in the past.

This place was originally called Cross Key, but the name was changed because of (select one): A) the intersecting roads, B) the entrance to a horse racing track, or C) the "intercourse," or social interaction, and support that's symbolic of the village. The residents can't agree, either. Although Lancaster gets the tourists, Intercourse is the hub of the Amish people. Surrounded by farmlands, Intercourse is a museum without walls—although the walls are closing in. A few miles in any direction are modern buildings and businesses that must surely tempt young farmers, though a Sharper Image is still light years away.

While New Hope's Bucks County thrives on culture and diversity, the strengths of Lancaster County are dining and simplicity. There's not much shakin' at night, but during the day there are great country roads to ride and the most satisfying roadside restaurants you'll ever find.

On the Road in Intercourse

When you hit the road in Intercourse, don't expect to be welcomed into the culture. Unlike Harrison Ford, you won't be asked to strap on a tool belt and help raise a barn. But if you're respectful and keep your camera out of sight, you won't be viewed as one of the rude "English."

The ride is not too far, just an enjoyable one-day excursion that will immerse you in the countryside and introduce you to the culture. In fact, this may be the most "country" country road you can ride. Each road will tempt you, and if you want to go off on a tear, have at it. Get lost. Explore. Wherever you go, the roads are soft and gentle, and the scenery evocative of the 1800s.

One rectangular route leaves Intercourse on 340 East, passing Spring Garden and White Horse and turning left onto Route 10 before Compass. So far the ride reveals nothing out of the ordinary, but when you turn left (north), you'll notice there are no phone or electrical lines running to the homes. Their absence makes the landscape as pure and authentic as any place you'll find.

Take Route 10 North to Route 23 and turn left to head west. You're on the periphery of the Amish farms, returning past small towns like New Holland and Bareville. At Leola, turn left (south) on Route 772 and the road puts you in the thick of the farms. The ride is quiet and calm, interrupted occasionally by a horse-drawn carriage or hay wagon rolling down the lane. You won't tire of the sight, but be very careful riding at night since these black carriages can be hard to see.

Sharp 90-degree curves dividing the farms keep you alert, as will the crop of Amish children who gather near the road to stare at you and your bike when you ride past. Naturally, they assume you are a deity. Route 772 takes a sharp right at Hess Road, where you turn and continue on 772 to a scenic drive called Scenic Drive (really). Now do yourself a favor and get lost. With Highway 30 to the south and Highway 23 to the north, you may pass the Amish equivalent of a commercial district: buggies lined up at repair shops, tobacco drying in barns, and carpenters crafting simple furniture with even simpler tools.

It's ironic, but if you ride far beyond these boundaries you'll enter the domain of chain restaurants and the insensitive real estate developer whose signs urge you to "Think Redy-Bilt Homes!" Considering some men around here could probably build a home with one plumb bob tied behind their backs, it seems like a kick in the gut.

Side Trip: Lititz

One of the peak experiences of touring by motorcycle is discovering new towns that haven't been destroyed by homogenization. From the northwest corner of the previous ride, it's only a short drive to Lititz (north of Lancaster), a town where almost nothing has happened and which sports that familiar Rockwell look. Ride 772 north into this small town and you'll arrive in a busy little shopping district. This is Main Street, containing all of the essential vitamins and minerals to qualify as a neat town. There's the historic **General Sutter Inn,** 14 E. Main St., 717/626-2115, www.generalsutterinn.com, which features the 1764 Restaurant and 16 spacious rooms. It's tempting to stay the night, with rates from $87–120. Around the corner, **Glassmyer's Restaurant,** 23 N. Broad St., 717/626-2345, serves diner meals topped off by creations from an old-fashioned soda fountain.

But the highlight of Lititz is the aphrodisiacal aroma wafting from the **Wilbur Chocolate Factory,** 48 N. Broad St., 717/626-3249, www.wilbur buds.com. Chances are you've never received (or requested) a box of Wilbur Chocolates, but that shouldn't stop you from sniffing your way around museum displays that detail the history of cocoa, the life cycle of a candy bar, and Wilbur's "Wheel of Fortune" candy horoscope ("For the changing moods of Gemini, the best bet is a bag of milk or dark chocolate buds . . . "). Overhead, the ceiling rumbles beneath the weight of Wilbur gears and belts cranking out another delightful, delicious batch of satisfying chocolates.

Provided you don't fall into a diabetic coma, spend an hour bumming around downtown and then take your time riding back on the country roads of your choice.

Pull it Over: Intercourse Highlights
Attractions and Adventures

There's not much else going on in Intercourse, so you may as well not do something at the **Kitchen Kettle Village,** Rte. 340, 717/768-8261 or 800/732-3538, www.kitchenkettle.com. Actually, there's a chance you may find a new pair of handcrafted leather boots, score some fresh-off-the-lathe furniture, or listen to some folk musicians. The village is open daily 10–5, May–October.

It's an expensive diversion ($169), but the **United States Hot Air Balloon Team,** 490 Hopewell Rd., St. Peters, 610/469-0782 or 800/763-5987, www.ushotairballoon.com, takes daily flights over the Amish farmland. You can reach them en route from New Hope at the St. Peters farm launch site, or head to Lancaster to their second lift off location. You can help prepare the balloon for flight and then settle in for a long drift over the rolling countryside, followed by snacks and a champagne toast. You'll have to leave your bike on the ground.

Dutch Wonderland Tour, Rte. 30 E., 717/291-1888, offers $12.95 tours to go—taped ones, that is. If your bike has a cassette player, the 90-minute taped tour combines music, narration, and directions for a ride through Amish Country. The tape is also available at the National Wax Museum or Old Mill Stream Camping Manor, both on Route 30.

Blue-Plate Specials

Although Amish country is shy on tattoo parlors and tanning salons, there's no shortage of great restaurants, the kind you crave when you're on the road or have just raised a barn. In some cases, you'll share a large table with other travelers. So before you sit down, scrub the bugs off your teeth.

Slightly smaller than Beijing, the **Plain & Fancy Farm,** Rte. 340, 717/768-4400, www.plainandfancyfarm.com, serves food nearly as large. The tour buses packed in the parking lot testify to the restaurant's popularity. Lunch and dinner are served at huge picnic tables inside the barn-like building, where you'll eat as much roast beef, sausage, chicken, mashed potatoes, bow-tie noodles, vegetables, and ice cream as your big ol' belly can hold. And how many places do you know that serve shoo-fly pie?

The Smucker family does well producing filling country foods. That's what you'll find at **Bird-In-Hand Family Restaurant,** 2760 Old Philadelphia Pike (Rte. 340), Bird-In-Hand, 717/768-8266, www.bird-in-hand.com. The menu features ham, pork and sauerkraut, lima beans, roast turkey, new potatoes, and the like. Most items are made from scratch (such as the homemade soups), with some ingredients and dishes delivered by Amish farmers.

In a little truck stop in 1929, Anna Miller cooked up chicken and waffles for travelers. Today, **Miller's Smorgasbord,** Rte. 30 (one mile east of Rte. 896), 717/687-6621, serves breakfast, lunch, and dinner daily. Mix and match omelettes, pancakes, french toast, homemade breads, soups, baked apples, roast turkey, baked ham, fried chicken, fish, shrimp, sautéed mushrooms, mashed

Why Are the Amish Doing This?

Despite their identification as the Pennsylvania Dutch, Amish ancestors hailed from Germany, not Holland. They left Deutschland (get it?) to seek religious freedom. Today's Lancaster County "Old Order Amish" stress humility, family, community, and separation from the world. All Old Order members drive buggies, not cars. Their homes do not have electricity, and their children are educated as far as the eighth grade in one-room schoolhouses.

As for personal appearance, Amish women never cut their hair, and they wear a black prayer covering if they're single and a white one if they're married. Men wear dark suits, straight-cut coats with lapels, suspenders, solid colored shirts, and black or straw broad-brimmed hats. It's not a costume, but an expression of their faith. It's also worth noting that they don't avoid change entirely. They just take longer to consider a new product before deciding to accept or reject it. So don't discount an Amish motorcycle gang.

covered bridge in Lancaster County

© PA DUTCH CVB

potatoes, baked cabbage, chicken pot pie, cakes, and pies that'll kick off your very own Ted Kennedy diet plan.

Stoltzfus Farm Restaurant, Rte. 772 E., 717/768-8156, serves big food such as homemade sausage, chicken, hamloaf, chow-chow, applesauce, apple butter, sweet potatoes, and corn, plus desserts like cherry crumb, apple crumb, and fresh shoo-fly pie. That makes two on your list of places that serve shoo-fly pie. Open daily except Sunday for lunch and dinner; closed December–March.

Shut-Eye

Thanks to its relative closeness to Lancaster, there are countless lodging choices. But ask anyone and they'll tell you it's better in Intercourse.

Chain Drive*

A, C, E, G, I, J, L, S, U, Y, CC, DD

*Chain hotels in, or within ten miles of town. See cross-reference guide featuring phone numbers and web addresses on page 405.

Inn-Dependence

I would rank the **Intercourse Village B&B Suites,** Main St., 717/768-2626 or 800/664-0949, www.amishcountryinns.com, as one of America's best inns. Elmer Thomas restored the 1909 Victorian home, and his staff practices courtesy as art. The rooms befit a five-star hotel; the breakfasts are superb; and the top-floor suite is great for couples. Rates start at $119 and reach as high as $279 for the largest suite. Out back, Elmer created themed cottages, which feature large rooms, microwaves, desks, fireplaces, generous baths, whirlpool tubs, fridges, wet bars, and Amish furnishings built specially for the rooms. Suffice it to say that this is first rate for riders. Absolutely. Elmer's son runs the other recommended option in the heart of town: the **Best Western Intercourse Village Motor Inn,** Rtes. 340 and 772, 717/768-3636 or 800/717-6202. A standard hotel, with rates from $109–139, it nonetheless stays true to Elmer's vision of cleanliness and friendliness. An on-site restaurant serves home-cooked breakfast, lunch, and dinner. There are laundry facilities here, too.

Related Side Trips
Maryland

Contributed by Sylvia Henderson

Route 301
On the outskirts of D.C., Maryland SR 301 crosses the Governor Nice Memorial Bridge. From here, follow Route 3 to 202 (which merges with 360) south into Reedville, the tip of the Northern Neck area. Along the way, small towns and historic sites crop up, offering an easy pace to relax and see points of interest like the birthplaces of Washington and Lee. You'll also have access to the Smith Island ferry (wildlife preserve) and Crisfield, an artsy Victorian town.

Route 404
From Maryland SR 50, cross the Chesapeake Bay Bridge and head to Route 404, passing Wye Mills. Great back roads (Routes 18, 9/404, 1) roll through Delaware to the coast. There's a great shoreline ride south into Ocean City and onto Chincoteague and Assateague, sites of wild ponies, quiet beaches, and lots of mosquitoes and flies (bring repellent!).

Mattawoman Natural Environment
Escape D.C. traffic via Route 210, and ride south toward Indian Head, Maryland. From here, head east on Route 227 to Route 224, where 28 great miles of two-lane roads cut through the Mattawoman Natural Environment.

Route 4
Solomon's Island, Maryland
From D.C., take Route 4 South past Calvert Cliffs (a nuclear power plant and state park). If you're not radiated, keep riding south to Solomon's Island, where you'll find a tiki bar, boardwalk, artsy walking town, good road food, and lots of motorcycle cruising through town. After the island, head west on Routes 4 and 5 past 1700s–mid-1800s homes, plantations, and churches.

Route 235
Point Lookout, Maryland
Cruising out to Point Lookout is a surf and turf ride. You'll wind up at a state park, where Ft. Lincoln houses a historic Civil War prison and museum. Then, roll right aboard a ferry to Smith Island, a wildlife preserve, and ride on to historic Crisfield. A nice slice of Maryland for motorcyclists.

Resources for Riders
Amish Country Run

Pennsylvania Travel Information
Pennsylvania Bed & Breakfast Committee—717/232-8880, www.patravel.org
Pennsylvania Fishing Licenses—717/705-7930, www.fish.state.pa.us
Pennsylvania Road Conditions—717/939-9871 or 800/331-3414
Pennsylvania State Parks—717/783-7941 or 888/727-2757,
　www.dcnr.state.pa.us
Pennsylvania Visitor Information—800/847-4872, www.visitpa.com

Local and Regional Information
Bucks County Visitors Bureau—215/345-4552 or 800/836-2825,
　www.bccvb.org
Harrisburg (Intercourse) Weather—814/234-8010
Lambertville Chamber of Commerce—609/397-0055, www.lambertville.com
Lancaster County (Intercourse) Information—717/299-8901 or 800/723-8824,
　www.padutchcountry.com
New Hope Chamber of Commerce—215/598-3301, www.newhopepa.com
Philadelphia (New Hope) Weather—215/936-1212

Motorcycle Shops
Stan's Cycle Shop—4701 Old Easton Rd., Doylestown, 215/348-4136
All Season Motor Sports—2225 N. Fifth St., Reading, 610/921-3149
Classic Harley-Davidson—983 James Dr., Leesport, 610/916-7777,
　www.classicharley.com
Ray's Motor Service—5560 Perkiomen, Reading, 610/582-2700,
　www.raysyamaha.com
Sport Cycle Suzuki—309 Hafer Drive, Leesport, 610/916-5000
B&B Yamaha—791 Flory Mill Rd., Lancaster, 717/569-5764,
　www.bbyamahaktm.com
Cycle Parts—780 Flory Mill Rd., Lancaster, 717/569-8268

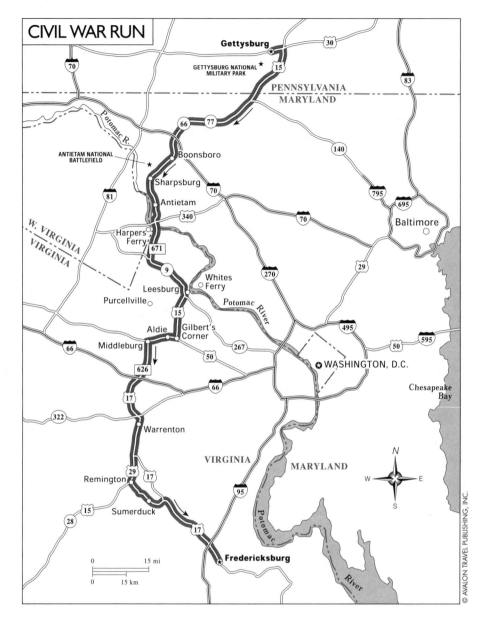

Route: Gettysburg to Fredericksburg via Catoctin State Park, Antietam, Harpers Ferry, Leesburg

Distance: Approximately 170 miles; consider five days with stops.
- Days 1 & 2—Gettysburg • Day 3—Travel • Day 4—Leesburg/Travel
- Day 5—Fredericksburg

First Leg: Gettysburg to Leesburg (92 miles)

Second Leg: Leesburg to Fredericksburg (80 miles)

Helmet Laws: Pennsylvania and Virginia require helmets.

Civil War Run

Gettysburg, Pennsylvania to Fredericksburg, Virginia

As you ease into your second Pennsylvania ride, you get the feeling that the state is a microcosm of American history. From the Declaration of Independence to the Exposition of 1876, from Amish farmland to the fields of Gettysburg, almost everything we're about is contained here.

This is a poignant trip through the killing fields of Pennsylvania, across a mood-changing Maryland state park, past Civil War highlights, and into two historic Virginia walking towns. As you ride in spring or fall for clear roads and clear weather, the route may not reveal all there is to know about the Civil War, but you'll gain an appreciation for the countryside and your country.

Gettysburg Primer

Confederate soldiers searching for new shoes sparked the flash point of the Battle of Gettysburg. By accident, enemy troops spotted one another near the village, word was passed, and three days later the Civil War had reached its turning point.

Robert E. Lee had 75,000 men; George G. Meade had 97,000. At the height of the battle, more than 172,000 men and 634 cannons were spread out over 25 square miles. When the final shot was fired, 51,000 casualties bloodied the fields.

Although the war continued for two more years, the Battle of Gettysburg broke the spirit and strength of the Confederacy. It also gave President Lincoln the opportunity to praise the soldiers and state the essential truths about our experiment with democracy.

To be sure, this has become a tourist town filled with tacky gift shops and tedious attractions. Although it borders on a honky-tonk, when you consider the extenuating circumstances—the volume of heroes, the bravery displayed by men of both sides—well, you just have to see it and accept it.

On the Road in Gettysburg

Gettysburg's legend in American history is so large, it's surprising to find that the actual places of note are confined within a relatively small area. Despite steady growth, Gettysburg at its core is still a village, reminiscent of the 1860s. But it's worth remembering, as you walk through town, that the area in 1863 was more heavily wooded. The forests are long gone; now you must use your imagination to fill in the landscape.

The town square is bisected by Route 15, the main north-south road through town, and by east-west Route 30. This is the perfect place from which to base your tour. Within a few hundred yards you'll experience the richness of history. The battlefields themselves are a mile or so south, too far to walk.

Bordering the roundabout are two sites worth a stop. On the southeast side of the square, the red, white, and blue bunting denotes the **Lincoln Room Museum,** 12 Lincoln Sq., 717/334-8188. This was the home of David Wills, the young lawyer who had extended an invitation to Lincoln to make "a few appropriate remarks." Lincoln stayed in the second-floor room and worked on his speech the night before the dedication of the cemetery. For $3.50, you can visit the room and see related exhibits and mementoes.

Across the street, the **Gettysburg Hotel,** 1 Lincoln Sq., 717/337-2000, www.gettysburg-hotel.com, has welcomed its share of presidents as well, primarily Eisenhower and his staff, who stayed here when the summer White House came to town.

After walking the square, ride south down Route 15 toward the battlefield. Obviously, you'll want to ride the battlefield, but do this only after taking a guided tour. It's important to know where you are to understand what you are seeing. It helps to know about such places as Little Round Top and the site of Pickett's Charge. From here, Union sharpshooters slaughtered 6,000 men trapped below in the Valley of Death, their blood flowing into a small creek renamed Bloody Run.

Following your guided tour, head to the **National Park Visitor Center,** where park rangers will fill in the blanks. They'll tell you about the 3,500 soldiers buried in the cemetery, 1,600 of them known only to God. You'll hear about bodies being eaten by hogs and about looters whose punishment was having to bury dead horses. But what you'll want to hear most is the story of the Address.

You may have read Lincoln's speech, but only after you've seen Gettysburg will you understand its importance. It was Lincoln's "I Have a Dream" speech. He spoke of the nation's past, the present, and the future he saw, and he re-established the concept of democracy. Within two minutes, "the United States are" became "the United States is." Lincoln had unified America.

When you're turned loose, ride later in the day, when the tourist crowds thin. From Little Round Top to the site of Pickett's Charge, this is a spiritual ride. You can take your time and see the roads and retrace the trails forged by soldiers of both sides; and you cannot help but be moved by the experience.

Pull it Over: Gettysburg Highlights
Attractions and Adventures

Gettysburg National Military Park Visitor Center, 97 Taneytown Rd., 717/334-1124, www.nps.gov/gett, is ground zero for your Gettysburg experience, and admission is free. To see what needs to be seen, it is essential to travel with a tour guide. Not surprisingly, the best and most enlightening information comes straight from the park rangers, whose love of history is palpable in their guided tours. Free tours leave from the center, which also contains an interesting museum with muskets, bayonets, artillery fuse plugs, swords, field glasses, flags, the drum of a drummer boy, and pictures of very old veterans from Gettysburg's 75th anniversary, in 1938. From May–September, more and varied tours are added.

If you really want to know the details of the Battle of Gettysburg and not just the overview most tourists get, you'll have to invest in a licensed guide from **Gettysburg National Military Park Guided Tours.** They leave from the center as well, but you have to be serious about this because you'll need to rent a car to transport the guide who will take you on a personalized two-hour tour based on your interests. For Civil War buffs only, it's $40 for up to six people, $60 for 7–15 people.

Gettysburg Tours, 778 Baltimore St., 717/334-6296, www.gettysburgad-dress.com, offers an inexpensive way to get a layout of the area and some background information before you explore on your own. Popular with nearly every visitor, the $17.95 tour is also the cheesiest—tourists pack onto an open-air double-decker bus you would normally make fun of and throw things at. The schedule is punctual and the information factual, though none of it is presented creatively. Keep in mind that stops at historic sites, such as Pickett's Charge and Bloody Run, are brief. The departure point can vary based on the time of year, so call ahead.

Tight Muscles: Work It Out Now

Even though I'm a mighty, mighty man, after a few hundred miles in the saddle, my muscles can get tight and screw up the next day's ride. Richard Cotton, chief exercise physiologist for the American Council on Exercise, www.acefitness.org, explains that muscles get stiff when confined to sedentary positions. Day after day of riding without stretching reduces the length of your muscles, which limits your range of motion and, if you move suddenly, can cause injury. Cotton recommends starting and ending the day with easy stretching exercises. The entire series should take no longer than five minutes and can significantly improve the quality of your ride.

Pre- and Post-ride

Chest: On some bike configurations, your shoulders are rolled forward and your chest muscles tighten up. To stretch your chest, place your palms flat inside a door or against a tree and twist your upper body.

Neck: After fighting the wind and the weight of your helmet, stretch your neck muscles by placing two fingers on your chin and pushing it toward your chest while raising up the back of your head. Next, look over your left, then right, shoulder for 10 seconds on each side.

Upper back: Before and after the ride, do a few trunk twists—keeping your legs slightly spread and hips square to the front while turning your shoulders from side to side.

Lower back: Few bike seats are designed to protect your lower back, so when you dismount, put your fist against your lower back, stretch backward, and raise your chest toward the sky. Don't let your legs bow, since the arching comes from the hips.

Triceps: Stretch your triceps by putting your palm between your shoulders with your elbow pointing up. Pull your elbow behind your head for 10–30 seconds. Do this for both arms.

One of the coolest ways to see the Gettysburg battlefield—besides on a motorcycle—is in a 1930s Yellowstone Park bus. **Historic Tours,** 55 Steinwehr Ave., 717/334-8000, offers two-hour tours for $17. The restored open-top classics are visually appealing, and the tour isn't bad.

If your bike is equipped with a cassette player, you may want to skip the bus tour and trade $13.73 for a two-hour narrative tour of the battle's history from

Quadriceps: To loosen up the top of your thighs, stand next to your bike and grip the handlebar with one hand. Take the opposite leg and pull it backward from the ankle, bringing your heel up to your butt. Do this for 10 seconds with both legs.

Hamstring: To stretch the back of your legs, stand and cross one leg in front of the other. Bend forward from your hips until you feel a comfortable stretch. Reverse positions and repeat to stretch your other leg.

Calves: Find a solid object (wall, tree, etc.), then lean over and push against it while pressing into the ground to alternately stretch each leg behind you.

Back and Butt: While lying on your back, put both hands below one knee and pull that knee toward the opposite shoulder. Do this for several seconds, alternating legs. Follow up by putting both arms behind your knees and drawing both legs toward your chest.

While Riding

Lower Back: Most riders tend to ride with their shoulders down and back arched forward. To counteract the stress of this position, occasionally arch backward and roll your pelvis forward to create a curve in your lower back. Riding with an S curve as opposed to a C curve prevents lower back stiffness.

Legs: Stretch each leg over the foot pegs or swing them back and forth against the pressure of the wind.

Overall

Vibrations can cause numbness in your hands, feet, and butt. At each gas stop take a few minutes to get the blood flowing and the muscles moving. Shake your hands and feet, stretch your fingers, do arm circles forward and backward, and take a short walk.

Auto Tape Tours, 717/334-6245, www.tapetours.com. You can find the tape at the **National Civil War Wax Museum,** located at 297 Steinwehr Avenue. The narrative takes you through the battle's three days, telling you when to turn and where to look.

Hard to believe World War II's most illustrious general could be overshadowed, but when Dwight Eisenhower bought a home in Gettysburg in 1950, he was destined to take a back seat to the battle. He used his farm here (the only home he ever owned) as a weekend retreat and temporary White House. Today it is the **Eisenhower National Historic Site,** 97 Taneytown Rd., 717/338-9114, www.nps.gov/eise. If you grew up liking Ike, you'll like the tour ($5.75). The displays are rich in personal items, such as his World War II jacket and helmet. Why such a noble soldier picked a creep like Nixon as his running mate is beyond me.

Blue-Plate Specials

The Lincoln Diner, 32 Carlyle Place, 717/334-3900, is just right for motorcycle travelers. An actual old diner, it serves staples, such as fried clams, fried oysters, and breaded veal, in the obligatory cholesterol-rich breakfasts. Watch your diet when you get home, but while you're here, become an Elvis impersonator and pig out on a hot fudge banana royal.

Don't miss **Dunlap's,** 90 Buford Ave., 717/334-4816, www.dunlaps restaurant.com. It's been here forever, thanks to a menu that features ham, turkey, and beef cooked and sliced right here; fried chicken, real mashed potatoes, sandwiches, stuffed flounder, steaks, and big breakfasts. They top it off with cheap prices.

General Pickett's, 571 Steinwehr Ave., 717/334-7580, is not a chain, but a genuine honest-to-goodness buffet. Made-from-scratch soups, fresh-baked breads, a salad bar, and down-home entrées are all wrapped up with homemade pies and cakes.

The Honeybee Diner, 3015 Baltimore St., 717/359-9857, is five miles south of town, but they boast the biggest menu in Gettysburg. Homemade soups, desserts, and 15 daily specials span American, Greek, and Italian cuisine. Serves breakfast, lunch, and dinner.

Watering Holes

The Pub & Restaurant, 20-22 Lincoln Square, 717/334-7100, gives you options: Buy a brew at the hammered-copper-top bar or head to the restaurant next door for a traditional entrée (chicken, steak, pasta, etc.). Of course, you can also elect to then return to the full bar for ales, domestic brews, and other spirits. This place is popular with college students who like the $2 pitchers.

As the name implies, the **Spring House Tavern,** 89 Steinwehr Ave., 717/334-2100, www.dobbinhouse.com, is more like a Colonial pub. In the basement of the Dobbin House, tavern waitresses wear Colonial costumes and candles light the room. Although it doubles as a family restaurant, the full bar, a handful of tap beers, and its unique setting makes this worth seeing.

At **Herr Tavern & Publick House,** 900 Chambersburg Rd., 717/334-4332, www.herrtavern.com, is The Livery. During the battle of Gettysburg, the home served as the first Confederate Hospital but time and capitalism have turned it into a faithfully restored pre-Civil War tavern. Saloon keepers serve beer straight from the ice into your sweaty hands. While the lounge is small and comfortable, a large deck can get you outdoors to enjoy the cool summer nights. In addition to bar food, entertainment ranges from darts, Foosball, and video games, to a first for me: a black light poolroom.
\

Shut-Eye

Chain Drive*
A, C, E, G, J, L, S, V, BB, CC, DD

*Chain hotels in, or within ten miles of town. See cross-reference guide featuring phone numbers and web addresses on page 405.

Numerous franchise hotels are located near the battlefield, each offering similar rooms but varying amenities—some feature a pool or Jacuzzi. In the heart of town, the above-mentioned **Gettysburg Hotel,** 1 Lincoln Sq., 717/337-2000 or 800/528-1234, www.gettysburg-hotel.com, is a full-service Best Western, with rates from $99–142. The 1797 landmark has covered parking, a restaurant, and a few suites with fireplaces and whirlpool tubs.

Inn-Dependence
Ride down the street to the **Farnsworth House Inn,** 401 Baltimore St., 717/334-8838, www.farnsworthhousedining.com, if you don't mind a gravel drive and the fact that a Confederate sharpshooter made this his post. The Victorian home has a sunroom and complimentary country garden breakfasts. It also offers a restaurant with dishes like country ham, peanut soup, meat casserole, and pumpkin fritters. Rumor has it some of the rooms are haunted. Rates run $100–165, with or without ghosts. Note: The 100 bullet holes in the house may make it slightly drafty in winter.

For descriptions of and reservations for the majority of area inns, check with **Inns of Gettysburg,** 717/624-1300 or 800/586-2216, www.gettysburgbedandbreakfast.com.

Side Trip: York Harley-Davidson Tour

Next to the Harley headquarters in Milwaukee, York is the site of most interest to riders. The York plant (roughly 30 miles east of Gettysburg) is **Harley-Davidson's**

Final Assembly Plant, the largest H-D facility, where more than 3,200 employees crank out 700 bikes a day.

During the one-hour factory tour, a guide takes you to the shop floor to view the parts manufacturing process and the final motorcycle assembly lines. Slip enough parts in your pocket and you can build your own bike. You can test-sit the newest models and spend as much time as you like in the renovated museum, which focuses on the history, people, process, and product within the York factory. Call 717/848-1177 or 877/746-7937 for tour times and availability. For groups of 10 or more, make reservations at 717/852-6590. The York Visitor Center (located at the plant) can be reached at 717/852-6006. On the tour, you'll need to wear close-toed shoes and leave your camera behind—so don't get any ideas about starting your own motorcycle corporation. The plant is located off Route 30 at 1425 Eden Road, one mile east of I-83.

On the Road: Gettysburg to Leesburg

Business Route 15 South, the level two-lane road leaving Gettysburg, passes statuary and monuments that suggest that the entire town is a cemetery. Just past the town limits, **Rider's Edge,** 2490 Emmitsburg Rd., 717/334-2518, is a Yamaha shop and a convenient stop for last-minute gear. About six miles later you'll reach 15 South, which turns into a larger highway, albeit narrower than an interstate. Although this is no back road, it provides surprisingly beautiful vistas of farmland, which continue eight miles over the Maryland state line, where Route 77 West veers off to the right for a detour to Antietam and positions you for one of the great rides of your life.

Your disappointment over leaving Route 15 dissipates the moment you enter Maryland's Catoctin Mountain State Park. Of all the roads in America, this is one that needs to be ridden like an animal. A two-lane exclamation point, this thrill-a-minute road rolls past valleys, twisties, lakes, sharp curves, deer, and rivers. Past Pryor's Orchards (purveyor of jelly, honey, nuts, and apples), you spot a great river and a setting as intriguing as Sherwood Forest. Glance up at the mountain peaks revealing themselves well above the forest. The road ahead is a grab bag of mild curves and sharp edges, like an abridged version of New Hampshire's Kank.

Too soon, you're out of the woods. Instead of continuing into the traffic of Hagerstown, turn left on State Route 66 and drop south toward the town of Sharpsburg and the Antietam battlefield. The road is marked by apple orchards, hand-painted signs announcing straw for $2.50 a bale, and, a few miles down, a general store in Mount Aetna where you can pull over for a soda pop and to wipe that smile off your face. By the time you reach the I-70 junction, you'll be content to blow past it, knowing there are far better roads up ahead promising farmland vistas and bucolic countryside, bumps and small hills, and sweeping turns that throw you into great straightaways. Here the asphalt is as fluid as a river.

Near Boonsboro, there's a tricky jog south on Alternate 40 and look for Highway 34 West. Although the route switches direction often, you're passing villages and avoiding cities. When you reach Sharpsburg at the intersection of Highway 65, turn right and ride about two miles to the **Antietam National Battlefield,** 301/432-5124, www.nps.gov/anti. Admission is $3. Sadly, even more than the events of September 11, 2001, this site marks the bloodiest day in American history. When Lee made his first invasion to take the war into the North, he brought 40,000 troops. General George B. McClellan led more than 80,000 Union soldiers. When they met on September 17, 1862—a year before the Battle of Gettysburg—more than 23,000 men were left killed, wounded, or missing.

From here, head south on Highway 65 and tighten up for a mountain ride that mimics the flow of the Shenandoah River. You're heading toward the state of West Virginia and **Harpers Ferry National Historical Park,** 304/535-6371, www.nps.gov/hafe, $3. A must-see stop, this is where, in October 1859, radical abolitionist John Brown rounded up 18 slaves and attacked the U.S. Army arsenal, hoping to jump-start a slave rebellion. Didn't happen. However, the Civil War did happen and because of its placement where the Shenandoah and Potomac Rivers meet, the town changed hands eight times during the Civil War. There is not a single museum here. Instead, there are 25 museums in a park that spans three states, West Virginia, Virginia, and Maryland. You'll see a restored town, hiking trails, guided tours, interpretive tours, fishing, and living history programs. While it's open all year, most programs are held in the spring and summer.

From Harpers Ferry, cruise slowly east on US Route 340 so you can eye the ruggedly handsome Shenandoah River. At Highway 671 (a.k.a. Harpers Ferry Road), turn right at the well-stocked Amoco station. Virginia must have gotten a good price on scenery because there's far more of it here than there is in Addis Ababa. Later you may see evidence of the state's wildflower program, which blankets highway medians with flowers, such as black-eyed Susans, daffodils, goldenrods, and ox-eye daisies.

Highway 671 is a fast two-lane road with pretty valleys and canopy roads that are in direct contrast to the sharp twists, weaves, ascents, and descents you'll be making. The road lasts about eight miles until you reach Route 9. Turn left at the Little Country Store toward Leesburg, taking a well-deserved break to see great stone walls stretched across fields, farmhouses dotting the tops of low hills, and cornfields everywhere. If it's dusk and the conditions are right, you'll have the pleasure of watching a great gray fog rolling in over the hills.

Shortly, Route 9 merges with Route 7. It's been a great ride, and now it's time to rest up in Leesburg.

Leesburg Primer

Even someone who knows nothing about the Civil War has probably heard the oft-repeated phrase describing it: "brother against brother." That reality was embodied in the area surrounding Leesburg.

After John Brown's raid on Harpers Ferry in 1859, folks in Loudoun County feared a slave insurrection. Though never the site of a major battle or even a significant skirmish, Leesburg voted 400-22 in May of 1861 to secede from the Union. Just a few miles away, the Germans and Quakers of Waterford voted 220-31 to remain with, and fight for, the preservation of the United States. Thus, the area spawned Virginia's only organized Union force: the Loudoun Rangers, led by Quaker Sam Meade, who scouted, patrolled, and skirmished with Confederate forces in the area.

The conflicts are no longer apparent. Today's lifestyle reflects a more genteel history. And though this may not be the most historical town you'll stay in, it's worth an overnight on your way south.

On the Road in Leesburg

Leesburg is just right for a bike ride. The downtown (at the intersection of Market Street (SR 7) and King Street (U.S. 15) is of manageable size, there's plenty of parking for bikes, and the diners, nightclubs, and riders from assorted clubs are visible reminders that you're in the right place.

You can spend your time conversing with the motorcycle travelers who've rolled into town, but if you want a quick, painless history lesson for just a buck, the **Loudoun Museum,** 16 Loudoun St., 703/777-7427, www.loudounmuseum.org, is a smart first stop. A short video explains the history of the county and the Battle of Ball's Bluff, a small but important skirmish that represents the sum total of Leesburg's active participation in the Civil War. It's a nice small museum, which includes slices of colonial history. Local farmer John Binn wrote a "Treatise on Practical Farming," introducing modern farming techniques that drew praise from the king of gentlemen farmers, Thomas Jefferson. Some of those techniques are still in use.

The remainder of downtown is like a smaller Charleston; the houses have been preserved well, although their scale is not as impressive. Cluttered antiques shops abound. If this run has increased your fascination with the Civil War, grab a book for the road at **Clio's History Bookshop,** 103 Loudoun St., 703/777-1815, which carries hundreds of books on the Civil War, or as some locals call it, "the War of Northern Aggression."

After you take Route 15 a mile north to Battlefield Road and see Ball's Bluff Battlefield (described below), attend to a plan more important than investing in your 401K. Stow some grub in a saddlebag, ride up 15 to CR 655, turn east, and follow it to the water. Scratch around for a buck-fifty and board **White's Ferry,** 24801 White's Ferry Rd., 301/349-5200. You'll take a short and immensely enjoyable ferry ride over the wide and tranquil Potomac. When you get to Maryland a few minutes later, park it and enjoy a picnic—an inexpensive pleasure worth a million bucks.

Pull it Over: Leesburg Highlights
Attractions and Adventures

Who can resist a company with a name like **Butts Tubes**? At Butts, Butts Lane (Harpers Ferry Rd.), Purcellville, 540/668-9007 or 800/836-9911, www.butts tubes.com, inner-tube prices vary according to the size of your butt. You'll pay $1 per size for a tube (sizes 8–20) or more for a canoe. Leave your bike here. They'll bus you up the Shenandoah, tell you where to get off in Maryland, let you drift for two hours and over three rapids, then meet you in Virginia for the bus ride home.

Ball's Bluff Battlefield, 703/779-9372, marks a significant day in Civil War history. In 1861, when Union troops were convinced it wouldn't be long before they'd whip the Rebels into submission, 1,700 Union soldiers crossed the Potomac and came face to face with an equally determined 1,700 Confederate troops defending Leesburg. When the smoke cleared, 155 Rebels had been killed—a pittance compared to the 900-plus casualties suffered by the Union. Some Union troops retreating across the Potomac were killed, and their bodies floated downstream, bringing the war back to Washington, D.C. The stinging defeat had some benefit. A committee was formed to investigate Union defeats and corruption and to tighten up the war effort. There's a park and cemetery here, as well as interpretive trails where you can follow the battle.

The area surrounding Leesburg features dozens of back roads that wind past working farms and working vineyards. Obtain a map of the Loudoun Wine Trail and the county's vineyards from the Department of Economic Development, 703/777-0426, www.rural.loudoun.state.va.us. Leesburg Vintner, 29 S. King St., 703/777-3322, www.leesburgvintner.com, has been recognized as Virginia's retail winery of the year. You'll find barrels of wine (cleverly packaged in bottles), as well as cheese and other gourmet picnic foods.

Blue-Plate Specials

Leesburg Restaurant, 9 S. King St., 703/777-3292, serves breakfast, lunch, and dinner daily. In the morning, equal numbers of riders and locals appear to frequent this place, a down-home restaurant since 1865. I think this is where Grant threw his victory party.

On the outskirts of the historic district is **Johnson's Charcoal Beef House,** 401 E. Market St., 703/777-1116. Since 1963 Johnson's has been a staple of Virginia dining: servers will "honey" and "sugar" you non-stop; you'll dine on from-scratch meals and country breakfasts; and you may spot Washington Redskins players loading up on raw meat.

The perfectly named **Mighty Midget Kitchen,** 202 Harrison St. SE #A, 703/777-6406, is a Leesburg institution. Pull in and order BBQ sandwiches, hamburgers, hot dogs, fries, and soda pops and then dine al fresco at outdoor café tables. Here since 1947, the Mighty Midget isn't much bigger than it was when it was born. It's tiny. Yes sir, real tiny.

Watering Holes

With new money refinishing Leesburg in an upscale veneer, you wouldn't expect to find a biker bar in the heart of town. Yet the **Downtown Saloon,** 5 N. King St., 703/777-9768, has been around since 1965, but recently changed its name from Payne's Biker Bar. No additives, no artificial sweeteners, just a love of motorcycling and the three P's: peanuts, pin-ups, and pool. Come here to enjoy bar food and a comfortable setting where you can kick back and map out your next leg.

The Kings Court Tavern, 2C Loudoun St., 703/777-7747, is less biker than Brit. A pub theme runs throughout, with private booths, a long bar, TVs, and liquor. Downstairs at Ball's Bluff, the underground pub features a well-stocked bar, darts, occasional live music, and traditional English food, such as wings, sandwiches, and salads.

Shut-Eye

Chain Drive*
A, E, L

*Chain hotels in, or within ten miles of town. See cross-reference guide featuring phone numbers and web addresses on page 405.

Inn-Dependence

The **Loudoun County B&B Guild,** 800/752-6118, www.vabb.com, represents 19 inns throughout the county. One of them is the **Norris House Inn,** 108 Loudoun St., 703/777-1806 or 800/644-1806, www.norrishouse.com. With rates of $100–150, this inn features a parlor, library, sunroom, and rambling verandah overlooking the gardens. Antiques accent guest rooms and some have fireplaces. You can tap the innkeepers for inside advice on great roads.

On the Road: Leesburg to Fredericksburg

Unlike the Wild West desert straightaways, where you can strap your handlebars in place and take a nap, roads in Virginia demand your attention.

Leave Leesburg on U.S. 15, the same road that leads out of Gettysburg. It's not impressive to start, just an ordinary road with an ordinary job. Twelve miles later at Gilbert's Corner, turn right and ride toward Aldie and then Middleburg. There are beautiful horse farms here—if you owned an Arabian instead of a bike, you'd probably live here. The passion for all things equestrian is omnipresent. People shopping in the uptown, upscale district are clearly devoted to horses—you can see it in their faces.

When you leave Middleburg behind, nothing is sudden. The road changes like a book, revealing a little at a time until the story is right in front of you. Upon reaching The Plains (which ain't too fancy), look for a service station and then some smooth country riding—nice shallow dips, split-rail fences, sweeping curves, weeping willows, and broken homes.

Take CR 245, a nice road that crosses beneath I-66, turns into U.S. 17, and then veers off to your left on U.S. 15/29 to bypass Warrenton. You'll ride into small towns like Remington and ride out seconds later. Look for SR 651 toward Sumerduck. The remote road mixes things up with some tight twists, graceful curves, inclines, and one-lane bridges. From here the roads are country, and you get the strong feeling you're entering the South. Within a few miles you've switched the channel from Masterpiece Theatre to Hee-Haw. It's hard to believe this change in cultures is all happening less than an hour's drive from the nation's capital.

When 651 rejoins 17, turn right and follow it to Fredericksburg, one of the nicest towns you'll have the pleasure to meet.

Fredericksburg Primer

Why was Fredericksburg so vital to Civil War soldiers? Look at a map, put your finger on this city, and you'll be pointing midway between the southern capital of Richmond and the northern capital of Washington, D.C.

The high banks of the Rappahannock were a natural defensive barrier, and the north/south rail corridor kept both armies supplied. The end result was that four separate battles were fought in and around the city, leaving more than 100,000 casualties and a barren landscape in their wake.

Fortunately, the town has never again been reduced to that level of horror. Today, a good vibe runs throughout: People are friendly, and the pace is slow. That makes this one of the most rewarding stops you can make. People here understand and appreciate history, along with humor, so certain tours are far more enjoyable than any I've seen. Add to this the walkable restaurant- and antiques-filled downtown district and you've arrived at the perfect base to reach other Civil War sites, such as Spotsylvania to the east or the Stonewall Jackson Shrine to the south.

On the Road in Fredericksburg

Of all the historical towns I visited, I'd say Fredericksburg does the best job of making history interesting and entertaining without turning it into a caricature. This town has history down to an art.

Park your bike (parking's free, Pierre) and put on some walking shoes and do the town. If you walk at a good clip, you can see it in a day—but I'd wager you'll stick around for a little longer. For about eight blocks, both sides of Caroline Street, two blocks west of the Rappahannock River, provide numerous diversions, from cheap antiques to a cool diner to historic homes.

Swing by the **Fredericksburg Visitor Center,** 706 Caroline St., 540/373-1776, to buy tickets for everything historical in town, such as the Hugh Mercer Apothecary Shop, the Rising Sun Tavern, Mary Washington House, and Fredericksburg/Spotsylvania National Military Park. These tours are a must while you're in town, and buying a "Pick 4 Ticket" will save you 30 percent. They also have maps for walking tours that highlight different eras of the town's history.

Pick up the necessary maps and tickets, then head north on Caroline, allowing time to drop in shops along the way. At the corner of Caroline and Amelia, step into the Hugh Mercer Apothecary Shop, 1020 Caroline St. Manning the shop while the good doctor is out, wenches demonstrate the "modern medicines" used to treat patients. Thankfully, they never break character, even while discussing the medicinal value of leeches, herbs, amputations, mustard plasters, and a "good puking." If you're a doctor, you'll have plenty to talk to your peers about. If you're a lawyer, you'll find plenty of times to mutter "malpractice."

About three blocks north at the Rising Sun Tavern, 1304 Caroline St., the format is the same and just as entertaining. Anywhere else this would be a brief walk through an old building. Not here. The Rising Sun Tavern was built in 1760 by Charles Washington, the younger brother of George Washington, and, quite likely, the Billy Carter of Colonial America. Anyway, you can learn a lot from a wench—for example, tavern decks had only 51 cards. You had to pay one shilling, six pence for the 52nd card. Otherwise, you were not "dealing with a full deck."

After you've seen the remaining historical sites, hop on your bike and ride to the **Fredericksburg Battlefield,** 1013 Lafayette Blvd., 540/373-6122, www.nps .gov/frsp. The museum is much smaller than the one at Gettysburg, but the introductory video does a good job of explaining the battles that happened here. Outside the back door, you'll take a self-guided tour that starts at the Sunken Road, one of the saddest places in America. Confederate soldiers used the high stone wall to shield themselves from Union troops and cut them down like lambs at the slaughter.

A little farther down, a monument may restore some of your faith in humanity. It's dedicated to 19-year-old Confederate soldier, Richard Kirkland, who couldn't bear to hear the dying cries of the enemy. He scaled the wall and aided the suffering men, granted passage by Union soldiers who held their fire.

That's the final polish on another historical gem. Wrap up your tour with a nice dinner and a quiet evening at your inn.

Pull it Over: Fredericksburg Highlights
Attractions and Adventures

The **Fredericksburg Area Museum,** 907 Princess Anne St., 540/371-3037, www.famcc.org, $5, is housed in the old 1860 Town Hall/Market House, which survived Civil War battles and now contains an interesting collection from Fredericksburg history. The highlights, of course, are the Civil War weapons.

The **Fredericksburg/Spotsylvania National Military Park** maintains nearly 6,000 acres of land. A seven-day pass costs just $4 and provides admission to all local battlefields and the Stonewall Jackson shrine. The **Fredericksburg Visitor Center,** 1013 Lafayette Blvd., 540/373-6122, www.nps.gov/frsp, and **Chancellorsville Battlefield Visitor Center,** Rte. 3 W., 540/786-2880, help interpret the four battlefields: Fredericksburg, Chancellorsville, The Wilderness, and Spotsylvania Courthouse.

After seeing the amputation table lancets, snakeroot, and crab claws at **Hugh Mercer Apothecary Shop,** 1020 Caroline St., 540/373-3362, I asked if Dr. Mercer was ever tempted to practice modern medicine. Without breaking character, the docent answered, "But Dr. Mercer *is* a modern doctor." With the right wench, this is one of the best tours in America. The shop is open daily. Admission is $4. The **Rising Sun Tavern,** 1304 Caroline St., 540/371-1494, is nearly as fun as the Apothecary Shop. The only thing missing is beer on tap. Four bucks gets you in.

Kenmore Plantation & Gardens, 1201 Washington Ave., 540/373-3381, www.kenmore.org, was built by Colonel Fielding Lewis for his wife, Betty, George Washington's only sister. Guides claim that the plaster work makes this one of the most beautiful houses in America, a claim they back up with mention of an official award. This is a bit of an overstatement, however, considering that the honor was given in the 1930s. As the house undergoes restoration until 2006, admission has been cut in half to $3. The tour drags, so it's a crapshoot.

Trade in your iron horse for a real one with **Fredericksburg Carriage Tours,** at the corner of George and Sophia Streets, 540/752-5560. The two-mile, 45-minute narrated tour costs $10 and passes 25 local points of interest.

Left your dulcimer at home? One of the neatest shops in Fredericksburg is **Picker's Supply,** 902 Caroline St., 540/371-4669 or 800/830-4669, www.pickers supply.com. Even if you don't play, you will be tempted to pick up a banjo, mandolin, or fiddle for the road. If you do play, check out the vintage guitars.

Blue-Plate Specials

I knew there was a reason I was drawn to **Goolrick's,** 901 Caroline St., 540/373-9878: It's the oldest continuously operating soda fountain in America. They serve the best milkshakes in the world—just ask the Aussie who said the same (I think he mixed his with a Foster's). Open daily for breakfast, lunch, and dinner, Goolrick's features an abridged menu of sandwiches, soups, homemade macaroni and potato salad, and fresh-squeezed lemonade.

More than 40 years of operation stand as testament to the simple meals and superior service at **Anne's Grill,** 1609 Princess Anne St., 540/373-9621. Big home cooking, breakfast all day, burgers, steaks, seafood at lunch and dinner, sassy waitresses, and lots of locals. Closed Wednesdays and from 2–4 P.M. each day.

Anne's counterpart is down the street at the **2400 Diner,** 2400 Princess Anne St., 540/373-9049. For more than half a century they, too, have been serving good dishes done right. There's a little bit of everything here, from subs and chicken to steaks and fish—ah, the pleasure of road food. Daily from 7 A.M.–9 P.M.

Watering Holes

You know that junk about never discussing politics and religion? Well, when you come to **J. Bryan's Tap Room,** 200 Hanover St., 540/373-0738, throw that chestnut out the window. This place leans to the right, as evidenced by the framed photos of Liddy, Dole, Gingrich, and Reagan. Beyond that, it's a cool place with 12 beers on tap, including Woodchuck Cider, and Bass Ale. Happy hour lasts from 4–9 p.m., and the Wurlitzer juke box is authentic. Oh, yeah—George Washington once owned this place.

Shut-Eye

Motels and Motor Courts
The **Fredericksburg Colonial Inn,** 1707 Princess Anne St., 540/371-5666, www.fci1.com, is one of the best bargains in town. Expect old-fashioned motel goodness with Civil War antiques and a fridge in each room—some rooms with a separate living room—and the atmosphere that comes with being in business since the 1930s. Rates are equally generous, $59–89.

Credit the nearby interstate for providing Fredericksburg with a long list of chains. . . .

Chain Drive*
A, C, E, G, I, J, L, Q, S, U, BB, CC, DD

*Chain hotels in, or within ten miles of town. See cross-reference guide featuring phone numbers and web addresses on page 405.

Inn-Dependence
Fredericksburg has several inns, but if you prefer the modern conveniences of a TV, large bed, and private bath, you may do better at a chain hotel. Call the Visitor Center for listings. Otherwise, the **Richard Johnston Inn,** 711 Caroline St., 540/899-7606 or 877/557-0770, features seven rooms and two suites, some of them uncommonly large, many filled with antiques and reproductions, and all have private baths. Built in the late 1700s, the inn has great placement in the heart of downtown. For $90–175, you get all this and a continental breakfast on weekdays and a full breakfast on weekends.

Related Side Trips
Virginia; West Virginia

contributed by John Weinstein

Virginia
Route 42
Western Virginia's mountainous corkscrew turns and twisties are plentiful near Harrisonburg, where they shoot south down Route 42 to Goshen. Ride Route 39 West across the Appalachians and Allegheny Mountains to Warm Springs and then cruise north on U.S. 220 to Monterey. The reward: breathtaking views of surrounding mountains and pastures and the sound of cowbells ringing from the fields.

Skyline Drive
Atop the Shenandoah Mountains, parallel to the Appalachian Trail, Skyline Drive stretches almost 100 miles from Front Royal in northern Virginia to Waynesboro, where it links up with the Blue Ridge Parkway. At least five major Civil War battlefields are within an hour of the Drive, and Thomas Jefferson's home, Monticello, is in nearby Charlottesville.

West Virginia
Route 33
Seneca Rocks, West Virginia
In Pendleton County, at the intersection of Routes 33 and 25/55, riders hang out at the local eatery before riding around Seneca Rocks, a monolith that rises nearly 1,000 feet straight up from the rolling hills of eastern West Virginia. Climbers consider ascending Seneca Rocks a rite of passage. Riders consider them crazy.

Route 16
War, West Virginia
War! What is it good for? It's good for a great ride. Near Bluefield, at the southernmost point of the Mountain State, Route 16 runs from the Virginia border through War, then Coalwood (home of "Rocket Boy" Homer Hickam), and on to Welch. Aside from Deal's Gap, I'd argue that you won't find a more challenging riding east of the Rockies.

Resources for Riders
Civil War Run

Pennsylvania Travel Information
Pennsylvania Fishing Licenses—717/705-7930, www.fish.state.pa.us
Pennsylvania Road Conditions—717/939-9871 or 800/331-3414
Pennsylvania State Parks—717/783-7941 or 888/727-2757,
   www.dcnr.state.pa.us
Pennsylvania Visitor Information—800/847-4872, www.visitpa.com

Virginia Travel Information
Virginia Camping—800/933-7275, www.dcr.state.va.us
Virginia Civil War Trails—888/248-4592 (CIVILWAR)
Virginia Country Inns Bed and Breakfasts—800/262-1293
Virginia Highway Helpline—800/367-7623
Virginia Scenic Roads Map—804/786-0002
Virginia State Travel Information—800/253-2767, www.virginia.org
Virginia Tourism—800/934-9184, www.virginia.org
Virginia Tourism Bed & Breakfasts—800/934-9184
Virginia Travel Guide—800/847-4882

Local and Regional Information
Fredericksburg Visitor Center—540/373-1776 or 800/678-4748,
   www.fredericksburgva.com
Gettysburg Convention and Visitors Bureau—717/334-6274 or
   800/337-5015, www.gettysburg.com
Loudoun County Visitor's Center—703/771-2170 or 800/752-6118,
   www.visitloudoun.org

Pennsylvania Motorcycle Shops
Action Motorsports—1881 Whiteford Rd., York, 717/757-2688,
   www.actionmotorsportsyork.com
Laugermans Harley-Davidson—100 Arsenal Rd., York, 717/854-3214,
   www.laugerman.com

Virginia Motorcycle Shops
Fredericksburg Motorsports—390 Kings Hwy., Fredericksburg,
   540/899-9100
Loudoun Motorsports—17 Catoctin Circle SE, Leesburg, 703/777-1652,
   www.loudounmotorsports.com
Morton's BMW—9816 Court House Rd., Spotsylvania, 540/891-9844,
   www.mortonsbmw.com

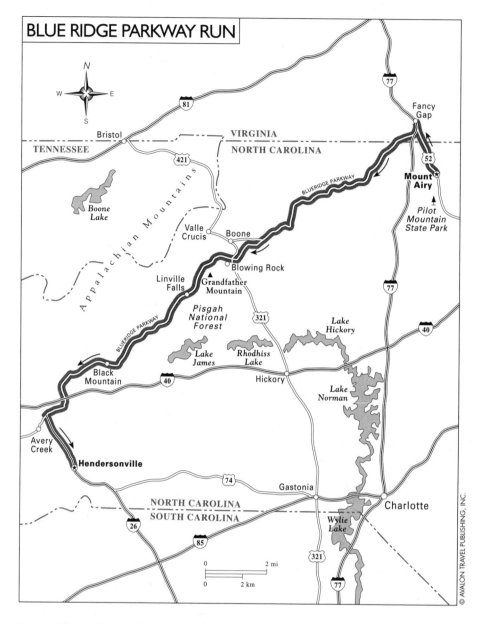

Route: Mount Airy to Hendersonville via Blowing Rock, Valle Crucis, Little Switzerland

Distance: Approximately 200 miles; consider five days with stops.

• Day 1—Mount Airy • Day 2—Travel • Day 3—Blowing Rock • Day 4—Travel • Day 5—Hendersonville

First Leg: Mount Airy to Blowing Rock (100 miles)

Second Leg: Blowing Rock to Hendersonville (90 miles)

Helmet Laws: North Carolina requires helmets.

Blue Ridge Parkway Run

Mount Airy to Hendersonville, North Carolina

Without resorting to hyperbole, the Blue Ridge Parkway is the most beautiful road ever built. This 469-mile-long toll-free dream starts in Front Royal, Virginia, winds its way through the Appalachians, and slithers to a close in Cherokee, North Carolina.

Before I made this run, I had a favorite president. Afterward, FDR was my man—he's the one who got this road-building project going in September 1935 in order to put men back to work. The masterstroke was the decision not to allow commercial vehicles on the road. You don't need to worry about semis or delivery vans here. Just soak in the very best America has to offer as you cruise during the peak riding seasons of spring or fall.

I should point out that it's not just the road that makes this ride. Southern people are inherently friendly; southern women invariably attractive; and the southern vibe so good that on this run, even Harley riders wave.

Mount Airy Primer

There's little you need to know about Mount Airy except this one thing: Andy Griffith was born here. Oh yeah, Chang and Eng Bunker, the original Siamese twins, lived here, but they pale in comparison to Andy Taylor and Barney Fife.

I start here because it's my book; I'm a member of the Andy Griffith Show Rerun Watchers' Club; and the Blue Ridge Parkway (BRP) and other great roads surround the town. I also have learned that genetically, Mount Airy residents can be nothing but friendly and their southern sayings unforgettable.

But Andy is why people are here. Griffith grew up on Haymore Street, and the small-town boy made good. If you're familiar with *The Andy Griffith Show,* you'll recognize the influences that made it to television. There's Floyd's barber shop, a diner, and all the elements of a sleepy North Carolina town.

In recent years, Griffith has repeatedly tried to define the line between the reality of his childhood and the fictional world he inhabited professionally, but that hasn't stopped townspeople from trying to turn their town into Mayberry. The Surry County Arts Council publishes the *Mayberry Confidential,* which includes breaking news on Aunt Bee's bake sale and the Little Miss Mayberry pageant. And then there's the Mayberry Motor Lodge and Mayberry Mall and Mayberry Auto Sales.

You'll find an intriguing blend of fantasy and reality, and you should just enjoy it. Grab a bite at the diner, get a trim at Floyd's, and head to the filling station so Gomer can check out your bike.

On the Road in Mount Airy

For such a small town, there's a surprising amount to experience here. Not thrilling, not magnificent, just . . . American. It won't take long—if you arrived early, you may not even need to stay the evening. A visit downtown and a ride to Pilot Mountain may fill up a day, but at nightfall you'll have a full stomach and a lifetime of memories. Beware of Sunday arrivals, when many downtown businesses are closed.

Ride your bike to Main Street and start with a North Carolina breakfast at **Leon's Burger Express,** 407 N. Main St., 336/789-0849, an old-fashioned diner stuck in the 1950s. Coca-Cola wallpaper, red vinyl seats with silver tacking on back, a pie display—it's all here, plus coffee and friendly waitresses.

Walk back to the **Visitors Center,** 615 Main St., 336/789-4636 or 800/576-0231, www.visitmayberry.com, to see a short video on Andy's contributions to Mount Airy and the collection of one of his boyhood friends, who gathered scripts, records, yearbooks, and wrappers of "Andy Griffith Whole Hog Sausage." The shrine to Andy Griffith is watched over by Bertie McCoy, Mount Airy's de facto Aunt Bee.

Floyd's City Barber Shop, 336/786-2346, should be open by this time, so backtrack past Leon's and drop in to meet Russell Hiatt. Like a Penny Lane barber, he takes a picture of everyone who stops in. With nearly 20,000 photographs on his wall, Hiatt claims he has the world's most important wall since Berlin.

Around mid-morning, saddle up and get on Highway 52 South to start your 15-mile ride to Pilot Mountain. The highway has great curves before you reach the exit at **Pilot Mountain State Park,** 336/325-2355. Admission to the park, open daily 8–8, is free.

The steep ascent to the peak is interrupted occasionally by bicyclists screaming down the mountain road like hornets. It'll take a few minutes to reach the peak, 1,400 feet above the countryside of the upper Piedmont Plateau. Lean back and gaze up the road to the top, watching the mountain unfold before you. As you near the final turn, the view is tremendous. From the peak, you can see Highway 52 darting through the forests towards Mount Airy and glimpse Winston-Salem through the haze on the opposite horizon.

When you return to Mount Airy, it's time to eat again. This time stop at **Snappy Lunch,** 125 N. Main St., 336/786-4931. Oprah's eaten here. So did Hal Smith (Otis) and Aneta Corsaut (Helen Crump). Breakfast is fine, but lunch is mandatory. The pork chop sandwich is fat, greasy, and stacked with coleslaw and other ingredients researchers are still trying to figure out. Damn, it's good. Owner Charles Dowell, one of the nicest restaurateurs in the South, has been cooking here since the 1950s. He's been known to cover your tab if he likes you.

You've just about done it. You could go see the world's largest granite quarry or wait for evening to eat some more. Or, would you believe it? At the old-fashioned **Cinema Theatre,** 142 Main St., 336/786-2222, movies cost a few bucks. Live it up. Maybe you can just relax and realize that you don't have to do a damn thing to enjoy yourself.

Welcome to Mayberry.

Pull it Over: Mount Airy Highlights
Blue-Plate Specials

Pandowdy's Restaurant, 243 N. Main St., 336/786-1993, is the rare downtown restaurant open in the evening, but more than that keeps this place packed every night. Credit the southern hospitality of the waitresses and dishes that outperform even four-star restaurants; the filet mignon is one of the most tender and satisfying I've ever eaten—and it's just 13 bucks! Pandowdy's does lunch and dinner Tuesday–Saturday.

Even though you're on a bike, you can't miss the **Classic Cruise In,** 675 W. Pine St., 336/789-9939, one of the few curb-service restaurants I've seen in my trips around this country. Local girls in cheerleader skirts serve giant hamburgers, but the specialty is hot dogs served with chili sauce, mustard, onions, and slaw. Wash it all down with a "Colossal" shake in your choice of vanilla, chocolate, strawberry, butterscotch, pineapple, cherry, piña colada, Oreo, or peanut butter.

Shut-Eye

Chain Drive*
A, O

*Chain hotels in, or within ten miles of town. See cross-reference guide featuring phone numbers and web addresses on page 405.

Inn-Dependence

If you named your kid Opie, chances are you're destined to stay at the **Andy Griffith Home Place,** 711 Haymore St., 336/789-5999, the small home where Andy grew up. It accommodates up to four people, which is great if you're riding with a group. Rates run $150 a night year-round. Ironically, Andy's place is now run by the **Hampton Inn,** 2029 Rockford St., 336/789-5999, which is nice and clean. Rates from the mid-$60s buy you local calls, access to a swimming pool, and a good night's sleep in a king or queen bed. The Hampton is close enough to the attractions for convenience but far enough away to be quiet.

On the Road: Mount Airy to Blowing Rock

Before leaving Mount Airy on Highway 52 North, grab some sandwiches, fried chicken, soft drinks, and other portable food. Even though restaurants are plentiful off the Parkway, you'll have more fun dining al fresco.

The five-mile ride to Fancy Gap, Virginia, takes you to the Blue Ridge Parkway and to one of life's most enjoyable moments. First, you'll pass signs of the rural South: a drive-in, flea markets, and wrestling flyers tacked to telephone poles. Note another subtle change here. The air starts to smell fresh, perfumed by the grass and flowers of the surrounding mountains and valleys.

The hodgepodge patchwork of businesses and houses and trees and valleys is drawn into clearer focus as you approach the parkway. The mountains rush to greet you, and your bike will rock back and forth every two seconds as you tuck into corners at 45 mph. In the opposite lane, motorcycle travelers are coming around the corners as if they're flying off an assembly line.

Just after the Mountain Top Restaurant, enter the Blue Ridge Parkway, turn left, and the road is yours from mile marker 200 south to mile marker 392. If you travel off-season, it is mind-blowing to realize that, out of 285 million Americans, you're only one of a handful with the intelligence to be on this road. The satisfaction is omnipresent as you pass over the interstate and pity the poor slobs who have no idea what they're missing.

It doesn't take long to realize the BRP represents "the Golden Age of Road Building." To your left you'll spy Pilot Mountain, an acropolis 20 miles distant. If you can't get enough of the views at this early stage, scenic overlooks appear every few miles. But it won't take an overlook to persuade you to stop. Every few miles, cars and bikes have pulled over, and barefoot drivers and riders have settled into the soft grass to enjoy picnics, naps, and nature.

You've felt wind and sun on your face before, but for many reasons it is more satisfying here. Flip up your visor and flood your lungs with fresh air. This road is free of commercial traffic, businesses, and billboards; you have only to pay attention to the dogwoods and evergreens, the meadows, glades, and stone bridges.

As you ride here, you'll recognize that this may be the only road in the country where the speed limit is right. It's 45 mph, the perfect speed to experience everything. At High Piny Spur, elevation 2,805 feet, the vista is grand, a field of varying textures and colors.

The road continues, smooth and flowing. Although there are nice straights for relaxation, it is never boring, never threatening. The Blue Ridge Parkway is absent of restrictions. There are no speed traps, no signs telling you the road is air patrolled. It trusts you to do the right thing. And if you ever want to take a break, exits, such as Alder Gap (3,047 feet) and Sheets Gap (3,342 feet), allow you to get on and off the parkway with ease.

More than 50 miles have passed now, and the BRP has given you greenery and great curves. Just before mile marker 259, the Northwest Trading Post sells crafts and marks the arrival of more tremendous views: The Lump, Benge Gap, and Calloway Gap. You're only a few miles from Blowing Rock, but just after Benge Gap is Bill Watson's Country Store, a convenient stop for gas and food if you failed to pack a lunch.

From here, you have only to enjoy the last few miles until you pass mile marker 291 and start looking for the exit at Highway 221/321 into Blowing Rock.

Blowing Rock Primer

Funny how some towns get started. During the Civil War, Southern soldiers started packing up their families and sending them into the safety of these hills.

After Appomattox, some soldiers joined their families here, and Blowing Rock grew bit by bit until the population hovered around 100.

The number was sufficient for incorporation, but fortunately not nearly enough to spoil the solitude and scenery of the Blue Ridge. Seasonal residents fleeing the South's summer heat headed for the mountains. In turn, a resort town formed, complete with boardinghouses, inns, shops, and restaurants.

Today the commercial district is limited to a handful of stores, and you can park your bike and walk the town in a few hours—but you'd be missing the best of Blowing Rock. You haven't really seen the town until you've entered its forests, climbed its hills, and ridden on its sublime mountain roads. Don't rush it.

On the Road in Blowing Rock

Downtown Blowing Rock isn't that large, but it's a perfect base from which to explore the larger-than-life mountains that surround it. From the center of Blowing Rock, ride south on Highway 221 a few miles to Shulls Mills Road, which leads right onto the Blue Ridge Parkway. Another quick right takes you to the Moses Cone Manor House. There's not much to see here, but the textile magnate's Flat Top Manor comes groovin' up slowly with mountain crafts, such as dulcimers, quilts, and "snake" sticks, as well as a full library of books on the Blue Ridge. Take a moment and relax on the verandah, which overlooks 3,600 acres of riding and hiking trails (also passable on horseback) and a small mountain lake.

Head north on the parkway and just past mile marker 292; exit at Highway 221/321; and ride north toward Boone. Ride about six more miles to the city, which you'll detect when you see the touristy Tweetsie Railroad. Shortly after, hang a left at Highway 105 and stick with it as the winding road leads deeper into the North Carolina countryside. Your destination is a small town called Valle Crucis, so when you reach the corner of Broadstone Road, about two miles later, turn right and head for the hills.

At first the slapdash homes and shaky riverfront cabins will lead to the unshakeable belief that you're leaving civilization behind. Unfortunately, this theory is shattered when you see entrances to "exclusive mountain developments." Ignore them.

Instead, watch the tight turns that whip you into Valle Crucis. At first you'll pass an annex, but keep riding until you see the Esso station sign and old red gas pump announcing that you've arrived at the circa 1883 **Mast General Store**, 828/963-6511, www.mastgeneralstore.com.

Next comes one of those unforgettable motorcycle moments. Housed within the general store is the post office (boxes rent for $1 a year), along with creaking wooden floors, a 1913 pot-bellied stove, and mountain men who sit around and chew Mail Pouch tobacco and talk about what mountain people talk about. The store has been here since bills were paid in produce, roots and herbs, and chickens. But the Mast General Store peddles wares for outsiders as well.

Need a hoe handle? It's here. A Union suit? Check upstairs. They also sell birdhouses, cinnamon brooms, musical spoons, marbles—cat's eye and rainbow shooters—cider mix, leather jackets, and JFK rocking chairs ($175) made by the Ashboro, North Carolina furniture maker that made the president's. Grab a five-cent cup of coffee; sit a spell on the back porch; and watch the fat bumblebees hover above the flowers.

When you leave the past behind, ride back to Highway 105 and head south to Linville, where you hook up to Highway 221 North. It's 19 miles back to Blowing Rock, but there's another stop to make. Approaching on your left is **Grandfather Mountain,** 828/733-2013 or 800/468-7325, www.grandfather.com, at 5,964 feet, the highest peak in the Blue Ridge Mountains. The area is also a wildlife habitat for black bear, white-tailed deer, mountain lions, and bald eagles. More important to you is the road to the top ($12 gets you there), an 18 percent grade(!), far more challenging and twisting than mortals should be able to handle. If put under oath, I would testify that this could be the single most challenging rise because the turns are so tight and inclines so steep that you think you've reached the top several times, but the road keeps rising. Even on the last leg up, the corners continue for miles until you reach the top and the Mile-High Swinging Bridge, a 228-foot-long wooden bridge that epitomizes truth in advertising.

As gusts of wind rock the bridge (record speed is 196.5 knots) and whistle through the protective fencing, those brave enough gain access to an extraordinary view of the Blue Ridge Mountains, views that last light years. Don't let me describe it. See it for yourself.

You'll love the ride back down as much as the ride up, and the ride back to Blowing Rock via Highway 221 is a mental massage—although the optional Blue Ridge Parkway North is more than incredible. Streams and snaking roads form a graceful combination to follow past rural stores like the **Grandfather Mountain Country Store,** 6371 U.S. 221 S., 828/295-6100, where you can stock up on jams, jellies, apple butter, peach cider, and night crawlers.

Pop a few in your mouth and head back to Blowing Rock.

Pull it Over: Blowing Rock Highlights
Attractions and Adventures

At the **Blowing Rock,** U.S. 321, 828/295-7111, www.blowingrock.com, North Carolina's oldest attraction, you can buy genuine rubber tomahawks, cowboy hats, and a book of dirty mountain sayings ("He really crapped in the oatmeal" is a good'un.) Admission is $4. I was skeptical at first, but this really is a windy place, since gusts of powerful mountain air rush in from the valley floor. If you forgot your blow dryer, stop here.

Whitewater rafting expeditions are the specialty of **High Mountain Expeditions,** Main Street and Hwy. 221, Blowing Rock, 828/295-4200 or 800/262-9036, www.highmountainexpeditions.com. Bring a swimsuit or shorts, a T-shirt, and tennis shoes, and you'll be loaded in a van for the ride to Irwin Falls, Tennessee for a half- or full-day adventure. You will get wet.

A dirt and gravel road leads to **Blowing Rock Stables,** off Hwy. 221 (one mile from Main Street), 828/295-7847, where you can rent a horse and ride the trails through Moses Cone Park. A 90-minute gallop is forty bucks; two hours of giddy-upping is fifty.

Blue-Plate Specials

Hankering for a plate of liver mush? You'll find it at **Knight's Restaurant,** N. Main St., 828/295-3869, plus potatoes, grits, baked apples, breads, and cereals—and that's just breakfast. In business since 1949, this is a busy joint, where the staff hustles but you never feel rushed. The best place to get your morning started or ratchet down at night.

Speckled Trout Cafe, Main St., 828/295-9819, features standard appetizers and entrées with an emphasis on fresh trout and seafood. Off-season, tables are easy to come by; peak season, you may starve to death before you get a seat. The fresh rainbow trout is raised in the mountains, then prepared pan fried, broiled, or baked. Open for breakfast, lunch, and dinner.

On a cold, lukewarm, or hot day, swing by the **Blowing Rock Cafe,** 349 Sunset Dr., 828/295-9474. Owner Larry Imeson rides and proudly flies a HOG flag in front of his restaurant. Boasting of a dozen homemade soups and strawberry walnut bran muffins, he adds salads and sandwiches to the mix served inside or on the patio. A diverse clientele ranges from riders to suits to sun worshippers to celebs like Paul Newman, who probably dropped in to hawk a few bottles of salad dressing.

Shut-Eye

Motels and Motor Courts
One of the best places I can recommend is the **Mountainaire Inn and Log Cabins,** 827 N. Main St., 828/295-7991, www.mountainaire-inn.com, provided you stay in a log cabin. Cabins (from $125–200) sleep up to six people and are dressed out for comfort. Some have hot tubs and fireplaces; some have cathederal ceilings; all have a large front porch where you can sit in a rocker and watch your bike. The motel rooms are much smaller. Go for a cabin.

Chain Drive*
A, C, E, J, L, S, V, Z

*Chain hotels in, or within ten miles of town. See cross-reference guide featuring phone numbers and web addresses on page 405.

Inn-Dependence
Crippen's Country Inn, 239 Sunset Dr., 828/295-3487 or 877/295-3487, www.crippens.com, offers a parlor, spacious rooms, and a great location only a few feet from the village. Rates run $99–159. The weekends-only five-star restaurant gets lots of attention.

On the Road: Blowing Rock to Hendersonville

It'll take less than a millisecond to ease back into the feel of the Blue Ridge Parkway. It starts right away with sweeping, slow descents and corners.

A few miles south on the left, Price Lake is one of the first secrets to reveal itself. It's the perfect place to stage a photo of you on your mount; peer over the right side for a view of a small waterfall. Further south, the Julian Price Memorial Park (at mile marker 297) has boat rentals, fishing, and camping.

From here there's so much to see, but so little you have to do. Even if you're accustomed to the overlooks, at mile marker 302 the view is beyond belief. The best views of the parkway are concentrated right here. Yet this isn't the only incredible sight you'll see on the ride.

Only a mile later, look up the road at the Linn Cove Viaduct, a span that rivals the Bixby Creek Bridge of the Pacific Coast Highway. A small parking area and information center lie just over the viaduct, but my gut instinct was to keep riding across the bridge until I passed out from excitement.

Life doesn't get much better for Moses the dog at Christa's Country Store in Pineola Gap, North Carolina, on the Blue Ridge Parkway. He even has pre-serves named after him.

© NANCY HOWELL

So far you haven't even reached the exit for Grandfather Mountain, and you've had a full day's worth of inspiring views. Now the road takes some slow dives and leads to immaculate ascensions. For the next 48 miles you'll be riding through a portion of the Pisgah National Forest.

When you reach mile marker 312 you'll see a stone tunnel ahead, but take the exit at the Pineola Gap to stop at **Christa's Country Corner,** Hwy. 181, 828/733-3353. Although Christa named the store after herself, she accepts that more customers remember Moses, the fat Labrador who sleeps by the counter. The place brims with all the items you'd expect a general store to stock: home-made preserves (featuring Moses's picture), Dr. Enuff soda (I'd never heard of it either), cans of snuff, udder balm, and Moon Pies (which taste great slathered in udder balm).

Getting back on the parkway is like meeting an old friend. You're back to hugging curves and riding at angles even Pythagoras couldn't calculate. You'll reach some roller-coaster drops and commence about 30 miles of the best riding in America.

Granite columns rise on your left, valleys and mountains on your right. You'll want to twist your neck like Linda Blair to see it all, but stop if you want a longer look. Slow down to take advantage of winding roads that validate every reason you concocted to convince your spouse you really needed a bike.

You're riding past apple orchards now, then the North Carolina Minerals Museum at mile marker 321, and then Spruce Pine, a small town six miles off the parkway. Stop if you like, or keep riding and you'll reach towns like Little Switzerland, featuring a café/bookstore and a town the size of a high-school gym.

I kept riding because the hills kept appearing and I wanted to pump the throttle and rocket over them. This is an amazing feat of roadwork. Equally heartening is the relatively scant development in the valleys below.

Starting near mile marker 342, the curves become more frequent, the tunnels more numerous, your exclamations of "Oh, my God!" more urgent. Stop at the Licklog Ridge, then for nearly 40 miles slice through a valley as the road rating changes from PG to R. The world is just beyond your fairing and you're getting close to the end of the run. Make a final (optional) stop at the free **Folk Art Center,** mile marker 382, 828/298-7928, www.southernhighlandguild.org, where the artisans could whip Martha Stewart with one loom tied behind their backs.

At the exit for I-26, say farewell for now to the Blue Ridge Parkway and take the cleanest and most direct route to Hendersonville—the hub of all things good.

Hendersonville Primer

Hendersonville ("The City with a Motto") is an average American town that takes a back seat to Asheville, but I'm not sure why. It has everything a city should have. Chain businesses are relegated to the outskirts of town; the downtown still functions; and it lies in the middle of everything worth seeing.

Hendersonville began as an escape for Floridians who faced yellow fever at the turn of the century; it remains a favorite of Floridians who bring their kids to camp or to escape the heat. Not a bad idea since brisk mountain breezes keep humidity low and summertime temperatures in the comfortable 70s. What's more, the nearby Blue Ridge Mountains block severe weather patterns at Asheville, so folks under Hendersonville's thermal blanket savor a mild climate year-round. The unique weather and geological patterns also affect the foliage, creating a deluge of dogwood, azalea, and apple blossoms in spring and fall.

There's not much more to add, except that you should gas up your bike and commence your own voyage of discovery.

On the Road in Hendersonville

Like Broadway Avenue in Saratoga Springs, Hendersonville's Main Street is a wide avenue designed so a team of four horses could make a U-turn. The street is still touched by small-town nostalgia. Along it you'll find diagonal parking, a movie theater, and a Western Auto store that still sells Radio Flyer wagons and Red Ryder BB guns.

You can get caught up in shopping (antiques emporiums, art galleries, a music store, wine cellar, herb shop, Irish pub, beer brewing store), but you'll have just as much fun on the road.

Consider your location: 3 miles to the Flat Rock Playhouse and Carl Sandburg home, 15 miles to the Blue Ridge Parkway, 17 miles to Chimney Rock, 18 miles to Pisgah National Forest, 19 miles to the Biltmore Estate, and less than 20 miles to Saluda, Tryon, Bat Cave, and Brevard. You're at the center of a wheel with spokes leading to some great places.

A great loop picks up most of these places on a full day's ride. Leave Hendersonville on Highway 64 West toward Brevard, but when 64 turns left, stay straight on Rte. 276 into a portion of **Pisgah National Forest,** 1001 Pisgah Hwy., 828/877-3350, www.cs.unca.edu/nfsnc. Straight and narrow at first, the surroundings then become a canvas of wonderful woodlands, accented with waterfalls and roadside streams.

From the visitors center, on your right, pick up information on horseback riding, hiking trails, camping facilities, and fishing streams. Four miles down the road, look for the photo opportunity at Looking Glass Falls. Pull over for a picture or climb down the rocks and be pummeled into submission by the powerful falls. Another two miles and you'll reach Sliding Rock, where you should stop your bike, put on your trunks, and experience the forest's most exhilarating natural attraction, offering the same sensation as skimming down a 60-foot icicle.

The road is just as exciting, like a luge competition, and 276 continues its asphalt rush for eight fun miles until you once again reach the Blue Ridge Parkway(!) for a mighty great ride north. Enjoy traveling with your old friend until you reach Rte. 74A, where you turn right until you reach Bat Cave at Highway 64. You won't see Adam West or Burt Ward, since Bat Cave is just a stretch of gift shops and restaurants with dining decks overlooking mountain streams, but it's got a great name. And it leads to **Chimney Rock Park,** 828/625-9281 or 800/277-9611, www.chimneyrockpark.com, site of the 1,200-foot-tall, 500 million-year-old rock tower that features hiking trails, catwalks from rock to rock, and a commanding view of the Hickory Nut Gorge. When the skies are clear or the forests are ablaze with color, it's worth the $12 to experience this vision. The town here borders on tacky, but it is home to **Heavenly Hoggs,** 381 Hwy. 64, 828/625-2408 an unexpected find that features antique bikes, parts, and apparel. It's closed on Sunday.

Stay on Highway 64 and ride around the beautiful lakefront curves of Lake Lure; then watch for Highway 9 South. This quiet, country road puts you in the middle of forests, where you should look for Rte. 108 South into Tryon, a community centered on equestrian events. Leave Tryon by Route 176 North (a great country road) and get ready to experience a mighty odd town.

Saluda is the site of the steepest railroad grade in America, but it's better known for Coon Dog Day, a Fourth of July festival that brings families out of the hills to show off their hunting dogs, crown a new Coon Dog Queen, and listen to toe-tappin' mountain music. **J. C. Thompson's Grocery Market and Grill** and the **M. A. Pace** general store are worth a visit, as is **Green River BBQ,** 828/749-9892, serving lunch and dinner.

Stay on Route 176 and the ride returns to its familiar temperament, twisting and turning, diving and soaring as it arrives in the village of Flat Rock. This highly cultured area is home of the **Flat Rock Playhouse,** 2661 Greenville Hwy., 828/693-0403, www.flatrockplayhouse.org, which is also North Carolina's state playhouse. Absent any coon dogs, Flat Rock gets by with the Carl Sandburg home.

"The People's Poet" lived here at **Connemara,** 828/693-4178, www.nps .gov/carl, which has been left just the way he left it. His guitar rests by his recliner, and the house is cluttered with original books, notes, awards, and walking canes, as if he'd just stepped out to feed the goats on his family farm. If you appreciate his poems and Lincoln biographies and the chance to walk through some pleasing North Carolina countryside, it's well worth the $3 admission.

It's been a full day. If you met the challenge of skimming down frigid Sliding Rock, dig the icicles out of your underwear and take Route 25 the last few miles back to Hendersonville.

The Essence of the South

In a newspaper article dated January 18, 1987, Charles Kuralt mentioned his visit to the Mast General Store:

"Where should I send you to know the soul of the South? I think I'll send you to the Mast General Store . . .

"You cannot get to know either the store or the people in it if you are in a hurry to reach the bright lights. In its essence, the South is rural, slow and charming, cluttered and eclectic, rich in old tales, old artifacts, and human friendship. The South cannot be hurried through. Vacationers who take the interstate from New York to Miami miss the South completely. . . ."

Pull it Over: Hendersonville Highlights
Attractions and Adventures

It's hard to improve upon nature, but they've done it at **Pisgah National Forest,** 1001 Pisgah Hwy., 828/877-3350 (ranger station) or 877/444-6777 (reservations), with campgrounds, nature trials, horseback riding, swimming, fishing, and picnic sites. At the ranger station, don't miss the "Cradle of Forestry in America" display describing George Vanderbilt's work with Dr. Carl Alwin Schenck to prevent clear-cutting and encourage area settlers to practice the new science of forestry.

It may be slightly far from your base (30 minutes north of Asheville), but **French Broad Rafting Company,** 828/649-3574 or 800/842-3189, www.frenchbroadrafting.com, offers some great whitewater runs along the French Broad River. You can rent a canoe and do it yourself, take a calm water raft trip for $25, or indulge in a full-day excursion that travels eight miles, rides over Class I–IV rapids, and includes lunch for a low, low $60.

The **Biltmore Estate,** Hwy. 25, Asheville, 800/543-2961, www.biltmore.com, is beyond description. It took six years, 11 million bricks, and a thousand men to build George Vanderbilt's estate. The humble abode encompasses 250 rooms, 65 fireplaces, 43 bathrooms, 34 bedrooms, and three kitchens, covering more than four acres of floor space. Pay $34 to get in, then rent a taped tour and marvel at the mansion's magnitude, unique craftsmanship, painted ceilings, unusual furnishings, and family history. Afterward, you can score some free wine from a

A 30-Second History: Honda

In post-war Japan, Soichiro Honda was one of the first to design a cheap and convenient way to get around. Having bought 500 two-stroke motors (war surplus), he slapped them onto pedal bikes. When those bikes sold out, Honda designed and built his own 50cc engine and placed it on a smoking new bike. Seriously. It was nicknamed the "Chimney" for its prolific exhaust. After starting the Honda Motor Company in 1948, he developed a 90cc version of the A-Type bike (called the "B-Type"), and later introduced the "D-Type" in 1949. Since this was his company's first real motorcycle, the fulfillment of his quest sparked Honda to nickname it "The Dream."

Kuralt: 1984 Honda GL 1200A

"Kuralt"* for the Blue Ridge Parkway was my Uncle Bud's 1984 Honda Aspencade. It was dirty as hell but smooth as glass, so I enjoyed it immensely. It was a revelation to find that the rewards of riding are the same on a bike held together with wood putty and duct tape as they are on a sleek new model. On this bike, the shifting was smooth and the hyper-ergonomic design meant I felt no strain. I also got rough satisfaction from knowing I was riding a bike and not a two-wheeled motor home. If you have an older bike that's mechanically sound, consider touring with it. I did, and I didn't mind at all.

For details on new Honda models, check www.hondamotorcycle.com.

*It was the travels of CBS correspondent Charles Kuralt that inspired me to explore America. I named each motorcycle I rode in his honor.

tapped barrel in the winery. You may assume this'll be just a home tour, but trust me, it's far beyond anything you can imagine.

Shopping

You've got to love a place where the inventory didn't roll off an assembly line. Here since 1924, the **Curb Market,** 221 N. Church St., 828/692-8012, is the place to stock up on great North Carolina goods like blueberry jam, pickled squash, relishes, jellies, chow chow, moonshine syrup and cakes in a jar, and walking sticks. Every item is locally grown, homemade, or handcrafted by Henderson County residents. Call ahead for shopping days.

There are few items at **JRD's Classics and Collectibles,** 222 N. Main St., 828/698-0075, that you could bring home on your bike, but you've got to see it regardless. The store is loaded with vintage game room collectibles and accessories: juke boxes, barber poles, pinball machines, and gas pumps, all cleaned and restored by the hyper-focused young owner.

Blue-Plate Specials

Days Gone By, 310 N. Main St., 828/693-9056, a century-old soda fountain and drug store, has preserved its embossed tin ceiling along with a collection of straw dispensers, milkshake mixers, pie carousels, and hand-dipped ice cream. Remember grabbing a hamburger and shake after school? Kids still do it today. Open for breakfast and lunch.

Renee Ellender was raised down in Louisiana and incorporates her mother's recipes from Bayou Terrebonne to whip up a mess of gumbo, jambalaya, red beans and rice, po' boys, and other south Louisiana dishes at **Cypress Cellar,** 321C N. Main St., 828/698-1005. A full bar helps wash some of that there cayenne pepper down, Antoine. Stop here for lunch or dinner.

If you want to get gussied up ("proper casual") and have a hankering for cuisine instead of food, head to **Expressions,** 114 N. Main St., 828/693-8516. Dinner entrées include filet mignon, herb-crusted rack of lamb, chicken breast stuffed with apples, raisins, and pecans, and sautéed Atlantic salmon. The wine menu boasts some 230 labels; enjoy one in the upstairs lounge.

Watering Holes

Hendersonville's not a partying town, but **Hannah Flannagan's Pub,** 300 N. Main St., 828/696-1665, tries to help, featuring 100 beers, Irish specialties, and live entertainment. This is a friendly place within stumbling distance of your room. I don't like riding after dark, but **Shindig on the Green,** 828/258-6107, is worth the evening ride down to Asheville. Saturday nights between July 4 and Labor Day, bluegrass musicians gather here to play down-home, red-hot-and-blue music.

Shut-Eye

I-26 rolls past a few miles outside of town, so Hendersonville has its share of chain hotels and several large inns.

Motels and Motor Courts
Cottages are always a great find, and I have three clean-as-a-whistle recommendations. Just five minutes from Main Street, **Weeping Creek Cottages,** 65 Snapdragon Lane (off Rte. 25 S.), 828/693-0496 or 800/988-4858, www .weepingcreek.com, has 17 cottages varying in size from small one-bedroom to very spacious three-bedrooms. In an Eden-like setting, all have kitchenettes, and the larger cottages have full kitchens. A riders' favorite, a carport covers all bikes. A heated pool, five wooded acres, and a morning breakfast basket are yours from a low $80 off season to $140 in season. **Bent Oaks,** 1522 Greenville Hwy., 828/693-3458, has 12 cottages, with rates ranging from $55 for a one-bedroom to $150 in peak season for a two-bedroom. The **Mountain Aire Suites,** 1351

Asheville Hwy., 828/692-9173, includes a cottage and two suites, a pool, hot tub, and kitchenettes. Located a half-mile from Main Street, rates range from $55–85.

Chain Drive*
A, C, E, G, J, L, S, U

*Chain hotels in, or within ten miles of town. See cross-reference guide featuring phone numbers and web addresses on page 405.

Inn-Dependence
The **Waverly Inn,** 783 N. Main St., 828/693-9193 or 800/537-8195, www.waverlyinn.com, is just a few blocks from downtown. The owners will kindly put your bike under cover, feed you a breakfast the size of Montana, and lure you to the five o'clock social hour to enjoy free drinks and mingle with fellow guests on the verandah. Room rates vary greatly depending on the season ($109 to a high $195), but all are country comfortable. Innkeepers John and Diane Sheiry are as nice as can be—and John can tell you about great back roads even moonshiners don't know about. Friendlier people you'll never meet—unless these two have twins. Right next door, the 17-room **Claddagh Inn,** 755 N. Main St., 828/697-7778 or 800/225-4700, www.claddagh inn.com, is similar in size and style to the Waverly, with a full breakfast, afternoon wine and sherry, and rooms ($80–140) that border between country and formal. Away from town, **The Lodge on Lake Lure,** 828/625-2789, 800/733-2785, www.lodgeonlakelure.com, recalls a day in the Adirondacks. This former state troopers' retreat has been transformed into an idyllic escape overlooking Lake Lure and Bald Mountain, with rates of $149–250. Vaulted ceilings, hand-hewn beams, evening lake cruises, and a hearty mountain gourmet breakfast await you. Good as gold.

Related Side Trips
North Carolina

Contributed by Darryl M. Lodato

Highways 129, 28
Deal's Gap, North Carolina

Known as The Dragon, Deal's Gap runs 318 tightly coiled turns within 11 miles of
steep mountain passes. Less intense, but dazzling, is the scenery from Deal's
Gap along Highway 28 South.

Resources for Riders
Blue Ridge Parkway Run

North Carolina Travel Information
North Carolina Bed & Breakfasts—800/849-5392, www.ncbbi.org
North Carolina Historic Sites—919/733-7862
North Carolina Parks and Recreation—919/733-7275 or 919/733-4181,
    www.ncsparks.net
North Carolina National Forests—828/257-4200, www.cs.unca.edu/nfsnc
North Carolina Travel and Tourism—919/733-8372 or 800/847-4862,
    www.visitnc.com

Local and Regional Information
Blowing Rock Chamber of Commerce—828/295-7851 or 800/295-7851,
    www.blowingrock.com
Blue Ridge Parkway Information—828/298-0398, www.nps.gov/blri
Hendersonville Information Center—800/828-4244,
    www.historichendersonville.org
Mount Airy Chamber of Commerce—336/786-6116 or 800/948-0949,
    www.visitmayberry.com
Mount Airy Visitor Center—336/789-4636 or 800/576-0231

Motorcycle Shops
Worth Honda-Kawasaki—600 W. Pine St., Mt. Airy, 336/786-5111
Honda Action Cycle—8483 Hwy. 421 N., Vilas, 828/297-7400
Stamey's Cycle Center—836 Kimberly Ln., Boone, 828/264-5847
Harper Cycle and Marine—1108 Spartanburg Hwy., Hendersonville,
    828/692-1124, www.harpercycle.com
Schroader's Honda—220 Mitchell Dr., Hendersonville, 828/693-4101,
    www.schroaders.com
Dal-Kawa Cycle Center—312 Kanuga St., Hendersonville, 828/692-7519,
    www.dalkawa.com
Gene Lummus Harley-Davidson—2130 U.S. 70, Swannanoa, 828/298-1683,
    www.genelummush-d.com

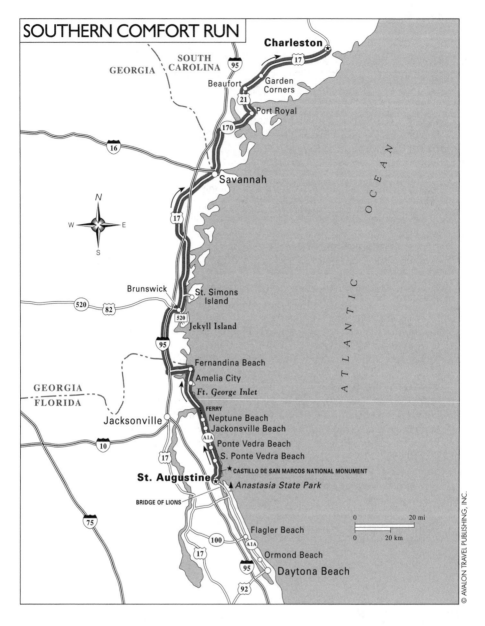

SOUTHERN COMFORT RUN

© AVALON TRAVEL PUBLISHING, INC.

Route: St. Augustine to Charleston via Amelia Island, Jekyll Island, St. Simons Island, Beaufort

Distance: Approximately 250 miles; consider seven days with stops.
- Days 1 & 2—St. Augustine/Daytona Beach • Day 3—Travel
- Days 4 & 5—Savannah • Day 6—Travel/Charleston • Day 7—Charleston

First Leg: St. Augustine to Savannah (150 miles)

Second Leg: Savannah to Charleston (100 miles)

Helmet Laws: In Florida, helmets are not required if you are over 21 and carry a minimum of $10,000 in medical insurance. Georgia requires helmets. South Carolina does not if you are over 21.

Southern Comfort Run

St. Augustine, Florida to Charleston, South Carolina

This run worships the Holy Trinity of the Lower Atlantic's historic walking towns. Ride along the seaside from a historic Spanish colony to Georgia barrier islands to magnolia-scented, mint julep–sipping, well-preserved antebellum towns. Make this run in spring or fall and enjoy perfect riding weather.

St. Augustine Primer

After seeing several dozen "oldest cities," I'd say St. Augustine has earned bragging rights to the title. On April 3, 1513, explorer and body shop owner Ponce de Leon landed here in search of the Fountain of Youth and claimed the region for Spain. Even though he found what he thought was the fountain, eight years later, old Ponce died. It was another half century before Menéndez de Avilés arrived and officially colonized the territory for Spain, in 1565. Local Timucuan Indians attended the ceremony, probably thinking, "These Spaniards seem like such nice people . . . ."

The town was attacked and sacked several times over the next 150 years, until the Spanish got wise and started building the Castillo de San Marcos in 1672. The squat, sturdy fort remains, overlooking Matanzas Bay and the entry into the Atlantic. A flurry of treaties and trades passed the town around from Spain to England, then back to Spain, and finally to the United States in the 19th century. The local Timucuan Indians weren't consulted about any of this.

Traces from these eras remain, but most of what you see took shape during the 1880s. As part of his plan to build railroads and resorts along Florida's east coast, Henry M. Flagler created the magnificent Ponce de Leon Hotel, located a short 24-hour rail journey from New York.

What de Leon and Flagler fostered is still present today: the homes, the Castillo de San Marcos, city gates, grand hotels, and cemeteries. This is one of the rare towns that knew better than to raze 500 years of history in favor of a new parking garage. The result: St. Augustine has character and style.

The town boasts great brewpubs, Key West–style bars, horse-drawn carriages, 42 miles of beaches, a first-class marina, fishing charters, hidden alleys and courtyards, excellent riding weather . . . And the rest is history.

On the Road in St. Augustine

Few other places in Florida rival St. Augustine as a walking town. But it's also a riding town. Take half a day or longer for a coastal run to Daytona Beach. Even if it's not Bike Week (roughly the last week of February through the first week of March) or Biketoberfest (first week of October), there's still enough shakin' to keep you entertained.

Remember these directions: Cross the beautiful Bridge of Lions and head south. That's it. Stay on Highway A1A when it veers to the left and, with the Atlantic Ocean on your side, it's a straight shot down the coast and one of the easiest rides you'll ever make.

At an altitude of six feet above sea level, two-lane A1A takes you along Anastasia Island and 50-odd miles of sandy white beachfront. The county fishing pier, beach ramps, motels, and oyster bars appear in rapid succession.

This is a far gentler ride than the Pacific Coast Highway. Instead of being a few hundred feet above the ocean, you're right beside it, with the Matanzas River creeping along on your right. After passing Highway 206, look to your right for the **Fort Matanzas National Monument,** 904/471-0116. A short boat ride takes you to the fort (free), which was built in 1740 for the Spaniards' southern defense of St. Augustine.

The road remains the same, always pleasing and with little growth to screw up the view. You'll ride through Marineland (pop. 37), a community as well as a former Old Florida tourist attraction. From here, 15 miles of calm riding takes you to Flagler Beach, where the **Pier Restaurant,** 215 S. Hwy. A1A, 386/439-3891, at the junction of Highway 100, is the best place on the coast to rest your bike and enjoy an ocean view with breakfast, lunch, or dinner.

There's little else to note but a world of great riding to savor as you ride south. Savor it now because, 20-odd miles later, after you pass Ormond Beach, you'll enter wide lanes of tourist traffic at Daytona Beach. Stick with it; just past the Ocean Center (a large convention facility) is Main Street. Although the mood is suspiciously quiet when bikers aren't in town, take time to poke around here and the Boardwalk—they're both kinda dirty, but you'd kick yourself if you didn't stop.

Of the several bars on Main Street, there's one you have to see. Remember how thrilling it was to drink your first beer? Well, friend, you can relive yesteryear with a visit to the **Boot Hill Saloon,** 310 Main St., 386/258-9506. If you've fantasized about the bar's decor, you won't be disappointed. There are two pool tables and a ceiling cloaked with bras left behind by female patrons, as well as Polaroid pictures taken of same. Open daily 'til 3 A.M. As you ride the street, keep an eye open for other Main Street landmarks, including Froggy's, Dirty Harry's, Full Moon Saloon, Bank and Blues, and The Wreck.

The Atlantic Ocean and Boardwalk lie a few blocks east. Changing facilities give you the opportunity to swim, tan, or chill. The Boardwalk is pretty grungy, but its bars and pier keep people coming.

Next, head a few blocks south of Main Street to Highway 92 (a.k.a. International Speedway Boulevard). Turn right and follow it for several miles, and when you spot the massive race track, **Daytona USA,** 386/947-6530, www.daytonausa.com, pull over. Open daily 9–7, they charge $20. Despite its slant toward cars and not bikes, it's still pretty damn cool.

The track features interactive displays—following a demonstration by a pit crew, you're challenged to test your skills at cleaning windshields and changing tires. One of the racing movies shown on the 55-foot screen puts you in the driver's seat. A new attraction, Acceleration Alley, costs $5 and is a motion simulator ride that puts you behind the wheel for six minutes as you drive the track at virtual speeds of up to 200 mph. If that's not enough to satisfy your mighty motorcycling soul, invest in the Richard Petty Riding Experience ($105). Although you don't get to drive, you do ride shotgun in a souped-up heap of metal that hits 170 mph on the Super Stretch. I did it and learned several new ways to shout "motherf———!" No side windows, just netting, a helmet, three laps, and comp admission to Daytona USA (you're saving $20, Gomer).

After you wipe that smile off your face, work your way back toward Highway A1A, stopping along Beach Street or Ridgewood Avenue, home to several motorcycle dealers and customizers. When you ride back into St. Augustine and cross the Bridge of Lions once again, you'll get the best view of the city. From the crest of the bridge you can see yachts moored in the harbor, the bayfront promenade, the plaza, and the fort to your right.

Now all you have to do is park your bike, find a quiet restaurant, or sit by the bayside and do what Ponce couldn't: Recapture your youth.

Pull it Over: St. Augustine Highlights
Attractions and Adventures

Flagler College, 74 King St., 904/829-6481, once a luxury resort known as the Ponce de Leon Hotel, is now a four-year school for some lucky punks. They lead tours here and if you like architecture, you'll find fantastic photo ops around campus.

Located on the north end of the island, **Anastasia State Recreation Area,** 1340-A S. A1A Hwy., 904/461-2000, offers picnic areas, a nature trail that crosses above fragile sand dunes, canoes, windsurfing rentals and instruction, four miles of beachfront, and 139 tent and trailer campsites (reservations, 904/461-2033). The park is open daily 8–sundown. Admission is $3.25.

The guys at **Camachee Cove Sportfishing,** 107 Yacht Club Dr., 904/825-1971, can arrange charters on 20-plus boats from 20–48 feet. Charters typically head 9–25 miles offshore to troll or fish with live bait for marlin, sailfish, dolphin, wahoo, kingfish, tuna, and amberjack. This outfit also arranges night, river, and shark-fishing excursions, as well as tournament charters.

Conch House Sportfishing, 57 Comares Ave., 904/829-6989 or 888/463-4742, offers private charters for half- and full-day runs; tackle and bait are provided. Seriously consider this place. The Conch House doubles as a pretty active watering hole—especially on weekends when everyone (including their dogs) head here for outdoor entertainment, drinking, and water sports.

History echoes in the walls of **Castillo de San Marcos,** Bayfront, 904/829-6506, www.nps.gov/casa. Wander around the fort and take a ranger-led tour if possible. There are bastions to climb, cannons to sight, and now-darkened rooms that once housed prisoners and soldiers. After several rounds of pillaging in the 150 years following its founding, the Spanish decided to protect themselves and began construction of the Castillo de San Marcos in 1672. The fort had a dual purpose: to guard the first permanent European settlement in the continental United States and to protect the sea route for Spanish treasure ships returning home. Although never taken by military force, the fortress was ceded to the British—and then again back to the Spanish—before becoming a possession of the United States in 1821. A must-see, the fort is open daily from 8:45–4:45. Admission is $4.

Just up San Marco Boulevard is what Ponce de Leon came looking for in 1513. Past the giant cross marking the explorer's first landfall is Ponce de Leon's odoriferous sulphur water **Fountain of Youth,** 11 Magnolia Ave., 904/829-3168 or 800/356-8222, www.fountainofyouthflorida.com. Across this cool and shaded archaeological site is what's believed to be Ponce's coquina stone cross, as well as the burial grounds of Timucuan Indians. When you're here, it's fascinating to consider what America looked like the very day that de Leon arrived. There were no roads, no cities, no Pilgrims . . . just Native Americans and a continent that stretched unexplored to the Pacific. Today this site is touristy, but you have to see it. Open daily 9–5. Admission is $5.75.

While no single store stands out along **St. George Street,** this pedestrian boulevard in the heart of the historic district is where most everyone goes. An eclectic collection of shops dot the mall, along with a few bars and restaurants. It's also the gathering site for several historic tours.

Blue-Plate Specials

The independent **Gypsy Cab Company,** 828 Anastasia Blvd., 904/824-8244, www.gypsycab.com, does everything right, serving lunch and dinner weekends and just dinner on weekdays. Parking's tight and there may be a wait, but it's worth it. The menu of fish, steak, veal, and chicken dishes changes almost daily and is always good. After trying the Cajun shrimp, call and thank me.

At **Scarlett O'Hara's,** 70 Hypolita St., 904/824-6535, the menu is basic—a little of everything—but even a hamburger or red beans and rice seems extra good when eaten on the front porch here. The service is good, prices are fair, and the patio bar is a nice, shady hideout. Scarlett's serves lunch and dinner.

Watering Holes

Tradewinds Lounge, 124 Charlotte St., 904/829-9336, www.tradewindslounge.com, defies the trend of trendy bars; this is the real deal. Here since 1964, this watering hole for locals also attracts a cross-section of tourists, students, dropouts, and beach bums. Weekdays, happy hour runs from 5–8 with live music playing from then until closing. Tradewinds has it all: a full bar, margaritas, rum punch, and, of course, beer.

O. C. White's, 118 Avenida Menéndez, 904/824-0808, is a restaurant, too, but the patio areas out front are just across from the marina, so it's a great place to have a beer and enjoy the outdoors. Not wild, but perfect for talking and looking.

Yet another restaurant, **A1A Aleworks,** 1 King St., 904/829-2977, is a great place to grab an inexpensive lunch—or dinner, for that matter—and the place is usually crowded with a lot of young locals. As the name implies, it's also a great place to grab a cold one (seven micros as well as domestics) or a drink from the full bar. Upstairs, the balcony seems borrowed from Bourbon Street. Have a drink and watch the yachts sailing in on the bay.

Shut-Eye

St. Augustine has dozens of inns, chain hotels, and moderately priced independent motels—but sometimes it's not enough. Make reservations well in advance, and note that weekday rates are lower than those listed below.

Motels and Motor Courts

The **Monterey Inn,** 16 Avenida Menendez, 904/824-4482, www.themontereyinn.com, has a great bayside location and clean rooms that overlook yachts at anchor, sailboats skimming past the harbor, horse-drawn carriages, and the fabled Bridge of Lions. Fifty-nine units have double, queen or king beds, cable TV, phone, plenty of parking, a swimming pool, and AAA discounts on rooms that go from $49 to the mid-$100s.

The **Bayfront Inn,** 138 Avenida Menendez, 904/824-1681, www.bayfrontinn.com, is a clean, standard hotel with a nice view and good location (two blocks from the Bridge of Lions). Rates range from $59–110 per night. The hotel features a regular array of amenities, including a swimming pool, whirlpool, cable TV, and telephone.

Leaving the city behind, a five minute ride north on Highway A1A takes you to the beach and a selection of smaller and older motels. The 29-room **Ocean Sands Motor Inn,** 3465 Coastal Hwy. (N. A1A), 904/824-1112 or 800/609-0888, www.oceansandsinn.com, has a good location and good rates (from $49). Rooms are complete with private patios, cable TV, coffeemakers, refrigerators, and microwaves. Bring your own food and you may never leave.

Chain Drive*

A, B, C, E, G, J, L, S, U, V, Z, BB, CC, DD

*Chain hotels in, or within ten miles of town. See cross-reference guide featuring phone numbers and web addresses on page 405.

Inn-Dependence

The **Secret Garden Inn,** 56 1/2 Charlotte St., 904/829-3678, www.secretgardeninn.com, borders on the romantic (good for couples). The eclectic, eccentric courtyard hideaway has three suites complete with tiled baths, balconies, queen beds, kitchens, and, each morning, an assortment of pastries, bread, fruits, and juices delivered to your door. Rates run $105–145. The **Casa De La Paz,** 22 Avenida Menéndez, 904/829-2915 or 800/929-2915, www.casadelapaz.com, is a bayside Mediterranean Revival home complete with a private courtyard. This inn is more upscale than most—classical music and complimentary beverages are provided throughout the day—and one of the more popular accommodations due to its service, location, ambience, and on-site parking. The innkeepers also arrange "soft" adventures (kayaking, sailboating, fishing). You'll pay $120–240 here. Next door, the **Casablanca Inn,** 24 Avenida Menéndez, 904/829-0928 or 800/826-2626, www.casablancainn.com, features 20 guest rooms (15 with hot tubs) and, therefore, more camaraderie among guests who take advantage of the bayfront verandah, piano, free beer, soft drinks, and sherry, bicycles, hot tubs, and large breakfast. Rates range from $89–225.

Indulgences

Opened in 1888, the **Casa Monica Hotel,** 95 Cordova Street, 904/827-1888 or 800/648-1888, www.casamonica.com, was vacant by 1932 and was relegated to be the St. Johns County Courthouse from 1968 to 1997. Hotelier Richard Kessler restored this landmark in the heart of downtown and once again the Moorish-Revival accents of the original are clearly visible throughout, from its 137 rooms and suites (including three-story suites in the towers) to its themed dining room, swimming pool, cafés, and shops. Expect elegance, class, and fun. Rates from $129–$169 to almost double that in peak season.

On the Road: St. Augustine to Savannah

As you head north out of St. Augustine on San Marco Avenue, you'll pass the St. Augustine School for the Deaf and Blind, where the young Ray Charles studied. Take a right at May Street and, after scaling a steep bridge (look to your right for another fantastic view of the old city), you'll arrive in Vilano Beach, which features a few motels and restaurants. Far more enticing is the return of the Atlantic Ocean.

The road is a combination of country lane and beach road, two lanes of low-key riding right beside the water. This will be your destiny . . . at least for the next 30 miles. Every so often you'll spy a pullout and steps down to the beach. You'll be hard-pressed to stay on your bike when the waves are right.

By the time you reach South Ponte Vedra Beach, the waves will be hidden by towering walls of vegetation, but if you look closely, you'll see narrow gaps in the brush. If trivial barriers like these don't deter you, prop your bike up on the sandy shoulder and sneak through to find a secluded beach that's close to its natural state.

Within miles, this run comes to a close. Between Daytona and here, you've ridden some of Florida's best uninterrupted shoreline. When you reach Ponte Vedra, Jacksonville Beach, and Neptune Beach, your view is blocked by dense commercial growth. Still, taking Highway A1A is better than riding through Jacksonville, a city that has all the charm of a stomach virus.

After a sharp left after Neptune Beach, A1A weaves up toward the Mayport Naval Station and past a creepy fishing village to reach the **St. Johns River Ferry,** 904/241-9969. As if you needed another reason to justify why you ride, sometimes motorcycles are waved to the front of the line. The crossing doesn't take long, although the ferry leaves only every 30 minutes. The fare for motorcycles is $2.50.

You'll be dropped off at Fort George Island, and within 15 miles you'll be on a nice pine-rich road that enters the southern end of Amelia Island. Fernandina Beach is the only town on the island. The whole place is popular with honeymooners, families, and retirees—why, I'm not sure. There are tidy bed-and-breakfasts, large inns, magnificent resorts, and a downtown district with bookstores, restaurants, and unusual stores, but I'd have preferred this place when it was a "festering fleshpot," so called by the government back when it had a reputation as a hotbed for pirates, brothels, and bawdy ladies.

Highway A1A is called South Fletcher Avenue; from here turn left at Atlantic Avenue. Stay straight and after the road becomes Centre Street, you're in the heart of town. It should be around noon, so I'd suggest lunch at the **Florida House Inn,** 22 S. Third St., 904/261-3300, www.floridahouseinn.com, the oldest operating inn in the state. The meals here epitomize perfect southern dining. A mere $7.98 buys you never-ending platters of filling food served at long tables. Follow your meal with a cold one at the **Palace Saloon,** 117 Centre St., 904/261-6320, perhaps Florida's most impressive watering hole—half grog shop, half historical museum. The oldest continuously operating bar in Florida, its barkeeps have been priming the pumps and delivering frosted mugs of beer to sailors, locals, shrimpers, and travelers since 1903.

Having bypassed Jacksonville, you have to head west on A1A to reach I-95 North, where you can make up some time. At Exit 6, take Highway 17 toward the towns of Brunswick, Jekyll Island, and St. Simons Island, which are all concentrated at the end of the road. **Jekyll Island,** 912/635-3636, www.jekyll island.com, is accessible via Highway 520, which runs straight into the heart of the resort town. Although you've ridden fewer than 40 miles, you've entered the real South, where the pace is molasses-slow. In the 1880s, millionaires like Goodyear, Gould, Pulitzer, Rockefeller, and Morgan paid $125,000 for the island to use as a hunting preserve and family retreat. Today the getaway is a state park and worth a brief detour.

Return to Highway 17 and work your way through Brunswick and past St. Simons Island (unless you want another detour). Stick with 17 for a slow, rural ride away from the coast and into Savannah, the finest city in the South.

Savannah Primer

If you judged by recent events alone, the most important moments in Savannah's history would be the release of the film *Forrest Gump* and *Midnight in the Garden of Good and Evil,* John Berendt's extraordinary book about a local murder case. More important than these two events, however, were the actions of James Edward Oglethorpe and General William T. Sherman.

I'll start with Oglethorpe. In February 1733, he led 114 settlers to a high bluff on the Savannah River to create a new colony settled by poor people, soldiers, and foreign Protestants. Although the colony failed when Parliament cut off all funds in 1751, Oglethorpe's planned city of lush squares bordered by beautiful homes survived and today puts Savannah in a class by itself.

Then there was Sherman. In late 1864, after Sherman had torched Atlanta, he and his men marched to the sea—and Savannah. Savannahians compared their 9,000 soldiers against Sherman's 70,000 and, displaying a remarkable degree of common sense, decided to surrender. Sherman gave the city of Savannah to President Lincoln as a Christmas present. This act surely endeared him to the locals—about as much as when his soldiers tossed aside tombstones in the Colonial Park Cemetery so they'd have room to pitch their tents.

On the Road in Savannah

If you've never been to the real South, Savannah is a great place to start. In spring (when everyone else is here), the dogwoods and azaleas are in bloom, and the Spanish moss clutches at gnarled oak branches. Inside the ordinary brownstones surrounding the squares, elegance and a sense of tradition reveal themselves in the velvet drapes, cut crystal chandeliers, and oil portraits of long-gone ancestors. Savannah *is* the South.

Forsyth Park, Savannah

© GEORGIA DEPARTMENT OF INDUSTRY, TRADE AND TOURISM

Just as Daytona worked you up, Savannah will settle you down. Start by circling the fabled squares between Bay Street and Forsyth Park. You are riding within the nation's largest historic district—more than two miles square. It didn't always look like this. Between 1945 and 1950, some idiots demolished more than 950 homes to make room for parking lots. Then some women got wise and bought a single $22,000 house to jump-start the city's preservation movement. You'll pick up this piece of intelligence at the **Savannah Visitors Information Center,** 301 Martin Luther King Jr. Blvd., 912/944-0455, www.savannahvisit.com.

The visitors center, a restored train station, is the best place to start learning about what you just saw on your ride. There's a historical movie and museum here ($4 for both), and the center is the departure point for nearly a million tours. The bus tour outperforms the actual tours inside historic houses since many docents just point at objects and mutter, "This is a mirror from 1794. This is a table from 1812. This DVD player is from 1799 . . ." Back on board, the driver's narrative should fill in the blanks for you young whippersnappers.

Make mental notes and with leads provided by the tour guide, you'll discover a lot of places to visit on your own during the day. For some reason, I prefer seeing this town after dark. The streets are less crowded, and the squares more attractive. Get a map and walk over to Monterey Square to see the Mercer House. Forsyth Park, with its glistening fountain and ancient oaks, is a perfect romantic setting if you want to fling some woo. G'wan! Fling that woo!

The greatest concentration of nightlife is found at the City Market (check out Vinnie Van Go-Go's for New York–style pizza and Malone's, a big bar/joint). Wednesdays–Sundays at City Market you'll find DJs, live bands, and dancing in the square—but no square dancing.

Down by the riverside, you'll want to park your bike atop Bay Street, since the road to River Street drops 42 feet. It's not too precipitous a plunge, but the millions of bumpy, rounded paving boulders—once used as ballast on slave ships—make parking and riding tough. As you walk this nine-block stretch of shops, restaurants, bars, and tourist traps, it's hard to conceive that this was once a row of cotton warehouses. You may notice a cavernous void amidst the rows of shops. At this site, human misery reached its peak as newly arrived slaves were sold here to the highest bidder.

Here's a way to see another side of Savannah. If the squares slow you down during the day, you may just want to get on your bike and ride about 18 miles east of Savannah on Highway 80 to **Tybee Island,** 800/868-2322, www.tybee visit.com. It's a nice ride out, past very low and wide salt marshes. With little to interrupt your view, you can easily spot the green-and-white **Williams Seafood Restaurant,** 912/897-2219, just before the Bull River Bridge. Here since 1936, it's usually packed with knowledgeable diners scoring fried and broiled seafood, deviled crab, and hush puppies. When you reach Tybee, you'll find a slow-paced, beachside community that focuses not on art and architecture but on fishing, sailing, and swimming.

Hang out here, or ride back to Savannah where you can check into a hotel, find an inn, or follow Sherman's lead and kick over a few tombstones and pitch a tent in the cemetery.

Pull it Over: Savannah Highlights
Attractions and Adventures

Full descriptions of most tours—ghosts, historical, *Midnight* book tours, etc.—are available at the Savannah Visitors Information Center. My luck has been consistently good with **Gray Line Tours,** 912/234-8687 or 800/426-2318, www.graylineofsavannah.com. Like other outfits, they offer a narrated tour through Savannah's historical homes and haunts, and theirs are usually chock full of historical goodness. Tickets range from $18–24.

Blue-Plate Specials

If you come to Savannah and don't eat at **Mrs. Wilkes' Dining Room,** 107 W. Jones St., 912/232-5997, I'll personally track you down and beat you senseless. This is the best food in Savannah and may be the best food in the South. For about ten bucks, they serve everything you need to get fat and happy: huge platters of fried chicken, beef stew, okra, sweet potatoes, cornbread, tea, and banana pudding, all carted to a communal table where you dine with a dozen other visitors. The result is good conversation and great food. Be ready to wait; the line can stretch out the door and down the block. Open for breakfast and lunch.

Since 1903 locals have been heading to **Clary's Cafe,** 404 Abercorn St., 912/233-0402, for down-home cooking and occasional ethnic dishes, such as Teriyaki scallops. Ever since "The Book" came out, tourists have been poking around here, too—this is where Luther, the nut everyone thought was going to poison the town water supply, ate. The drugstore gone, this is just a restaurant now, but it still offers a taste of old Savannah. Try the city's best black bean soup.

The Lady & Sons, 311 W. Congress St., 912/233-2600, follows in the footsteps of Mrs. Wilkes', serving lunch and dinner in a similar style but without the communal seating. Expect good hearty Southern dishes with an emphasis on fried chicken and biscuits. Also expect a line.

Watering Holes

You wouldn't expect it, but Savannah has a large Irish population, so pubs are popular. **Six Pence Pub,** 245 Bull St., 912/233-3156, features standard pub grub, but an atmosphere that'd be just as good even if they served nothing but beer. Live entertainment ranges from Irish folk to rock to blues.

On any given night at **Kevin Barry's Pub,** 117 W. River St., 912/233-9626, you may find U.S. Marines sharing the bar with businessmen smoking big cigars. Beer is sold by the pint, with an emphasis on the Half and Half (Guinness/Harp). Irish music plays nightly starting at 8:30. There's a $2 cover.

Churchill's Pub, 9 Drayton St., 912/232-8501, may be the most authentic in Savannah. To complement a full range of draught ales, try the Bubble & Squeak, Toad in the Hole (a large Yorkshire pudding stuffed with bangers), or roast beef and Yorkshire pudding. A great place to kick back and enjoy darts, drinks, and a fireplace.

A restaurant sits upstairs at the 18th-century mansion known as the **Olde Pink House,** 23 Abercorn St., 912/232-4286, but a buried treasure lies below: Planter's Tavern, a low-key basement piano bar with twin fireplaces and Gale Thurmond playing old Johnny Mercer tunes. Her voice, the setting, the comfortable couches . . . it's the most pleasingly civilized nightspot in Savannah.

Shut-Eye

Savannah features dozens of chain hotels and a greater number of inns. Book well in advance because rooms go fast.

Chain Drive*
A, C, G, J, K, L, P, Q, S, Z, BB, CC

*Chain hotels in, or within ten miles of town. See cross-reference guide featuring phone numbers and web addresses on page 405.

Inn-Dependence
The generic name of the **Bed & Breakfast Inn,** 117 W. Gordon St., 912/238-0518, www.savannahbnb.com, suggests a no-frills approach to inn keeping. Surprisingly, the rooms are spacious, the full breakfast hearty, and the location only a block from Forsyth Park. Rates run $89–115. Formerly a three-story riverfront warehouse, the **Olde Harbour Inn,** 508 E. Factors Walk, 912/234-4100 or 800/553-6533, www.oldeharbourinn.com, was remodeled to house luxury river-view suites. Rates ranging from $169–229 include complimentary continental breakfast and wine and cheese in the evening. Each room overlooks the Savannah River and the freighters passing by. The **Gaston Gallery,** 211 E. Gaston St., 912/238-3294 or 800/671-0716, www.gastongallery.com, is an elegant 19th-century townhouse in the historic district. Some rooms have a balcony, but the entire home enjoys a wide verandah that invites you to pull up a chair and watch the lazy pace of Savannah. Rooms here go for $90–210.

On the Road: Savannah to Charleston

It's a short ride from Savannah to South Carolina. Just find Highway 17 North and ride across the Hugh Talmadge Memorial Bridge and boom—you're there. You're in the Lowcountry now, where the road is as flat as a sheet of paper. 17 shoots past marshland for several miles before retreating into the woods with a right turn onto Alternate SC 170.

You'll see signs of the Deep South: hand-lettered posters for bush hoggers, pine forests, and the El Cheapo general store and gas station. But the enjoyment is hard to sustain because just as you start into a nice run, subdivisions and trailers begin popping up. After passing a trace amount of commercialism, you'll settle back into the South Carolina countryside as you follow 170 to the left toward the town of Beaufort.

Down the Line

Whether you're headed for Bike Week in Daytona or to New England for Laconia or Americade, Amtrak's Auto Train can provide you with a 900-mile shortcut. Several years ago, the Auto Train started carrying bikes on its run between Lorton, Virginia (outside Washington, D.C.) and Sanford, Florida (outside Orlando). The Auto Train departs daily at 4:30 P.M. (from either location) and arrives at 9 A.M. the following morning. Provided your vehicle has at least four inches of ground clearance, a 15 x 8 palette can hold up to four bikes. Just ride up a four-foot ramp and into a tire-wide groove and your bike is firmly confined by canvas straps. No trike bikes or sidecars allowed. Rates for sleepers, Coach, and First Class vary by season and direction. Not only will you save a few days, the meals on board are served in style (on china and tablecloths); the lounge is open late; and the huge seats can substitute for a bed. For current rates and reservations call Auto Train at 800/USA-RAIL (872-7245), or check www.amtrak.com

The savannahs open up, and a few curves appear, along with the requisite Baptist church and adjoining cemetery. Although you're less than a half-hour from Savannah, it's intriguing to think of the people who have lived and died here, believing that the outside world couldn't penetrate their lifestyle. Sadly, the illusion is shattered when you pass the Sun City Hilton Head Retirement Village, followed by I-95. Pass them both with extreme prejudice.

Despite the development, you're soon back to the marshland and crossing the long, low Broad River Bridge. This spot is scenic in an Everglades sort of way. Just after the bridge, turn right on SR 802 toward Port Royal. There's plenty of nothing to see at first, but then you'll begin to follow the waterfront toward downtown **Beaufort,** 800/638-3525, www.beaufortsc.org, which just happens to be South Carolina's second oldest township. While old antebellum homes and the waterfront provide great photo ops, obvious points of interest are hard to find.

Oddly, the setting gets more southern the farther north you go. You want SR 280 to U.S. 21 North—you'll find the roads by looking for the greatest concentration of mobile homes and video stores in North America. At the end of U.S. 21, at Gardens Corner, turn right onto two-lane U.S. 17 and let your mind wander. You'll ride this road into the past, complete with gas stations from the '30s; wisteria vines; peaches, tomatoes, and plums sold out of trucks on the roadside; and men in overalls straight from a Margaret Bourke-White photograph.

Aside from this, there's not a tremendous amount to see here, but all that changes once you roll into Rhett Butler's hometown . . .

Charleston.

Charleston Primer

Grab a history book and study Charleston. This is a city that is English, Spanish, African, Caribbean, Union, Confederate, old, and young.

Like residents of St. Augustine and Savannah, Charlestonians recognize the irreplaceable value of history, and their town changes little, at least in the historic district. Despite being a magnet for disaster—bombings, fires, pirates, earthquakes, hurricanes, tornadoes, war—Charleston seems to be content with itself, even when members of the public works department unearth unexploded Civil War shells beneath uprooted pavement.

If you know the South, you've heard about Charleston's fabled "bluebloods," the native Charlestonians who still talk about the Civil War ("the Woh-ah") as if the damned Yankees still controlled Fort Sumter. Yet, it is their determination to preserve this epoch that makes this town one of America's top travel destinations.

Although the bluebloods would draw my red blood for saying so, they have General Sherman to thank for this. After he gave Savannah a reprieve, he also bypassed Charleston. Some say this was because Sherman had a soft spot for the city since serving at Fort Moultrie in the 1840s.

Come to think of it, speculating as to why Charleston remains the way it is, is irrelevant. It's here. Enjoy it.

On the Road in Charleston

It goes against a biker's independent spirit to rely on a tour guide for the skinny on a town, but that may be your best bet for understanding Charleston's layered history. The city was shaped by events during the American Revolution, the Civil War, the Jazz Age (remember the Charleston?), and, as recently as 1989, by Hurricane Hugo, which nearly ripped the place to shreds.

If you decide to make like the masses and hop on a tour, you'll be fine. They're pretty alright. Most depart from the excellently detailed **Charleston Visitors Center,** 375 Meeting St., 843/724-7174. I had good luck with **Gray Line Tours,** 843/722-4444 or 800/423-0444. For a generic, Ma and Pa Kettle–style

*Jekyll Island
Historic District*

bus tour, the 75-minute ride was surprisingly informative and an easy way to get an overview of the city. The $15 tour passes the standard points of interest for all Charleston tours—such as historic churches, Fort Moultrie, Old Citadel, Battery waterfront, Rainbow Row—but the guides are well read and make it more exciting than your preconceived notions would lead you to believe.

Consider following up this low-pressure tour with another, more detailed one. I can't say enough good things about **The Story of Charleston,** 843/723-1670, www.tourcharleston.com, which demonstrates the difference between studying with a student and learning from a professor. The walking tour ($14) goes well beyond dates and architecture to illuminate Charleston's religious, sociological, and cultural history, filling in enough blanks to make you dangerous. This company also hosts two other $14 walking tours: the Pirates of Charleston and the Ghosts of Charleston.

Other necessary tours beckon (Fort Sumter, USS Yorktown; see pages 167–168), but the evening is just as important here. As you've seen, historic Charleston is a great walking town, and every point can be reached on foot within minutes.

The center of activity takes place along Market Street, which would need little alteration to be a Civil War scene. Black women weaving intricate baskets sit near the edges of the marketplace; horse-drawn carriages clop past; and street preachers shout for lost souls.

From here, walk a few blocks south; at Vendue Range turn left and walk past the fountain to the pier, where large porch swings invite you to take a load off. From the end of the pier, you can see Fort Sumter, which looks like a black birthday cake with a flagpole candle. Beyond it lies the Atlantic Ocean.

Having learned the city's layout, walk a few more blocks south to the Battery, which is far more pleasant at dusk. The cannons, mortars, statues, and oak trees all spell "photo op," and the site provides a relaxing place to view the harbor.

Returning toward the nightlife of Market and Meeting Streets, get lost as you did in Savannah and St. Augustine. Each "single home" has something different to reveal, from the old carriage stepping stones to the second-floor, chandelier-lit "salons" that are cooler and more suitably adorned than any floor below or above. Watch for the barbed iron that was installed on houses when fears of a slave insurrection spread across the city.

After the sun sets, wander the streets until you find a place to settle back, and then give silent thanks to General Sherman for taking the left fork to Columbia.

Pull it Over: Charleston Highlights
Attractions and Adventures

Tradition holds true at **The Citadel,** 171 Moultrie Ave., 843/953-5000, although a few things have changed since 1842 (women!). The best part about a visit here is watching the Dress Parade by the South Carolina Corps of Cadets, which usually takes place Friday afternoons at 3:45. You don't need a ticket; you don't even need to be a man. Just show up early.

The schooner *Pride,* 843/559-9686, www.schoonerpride.com, puts you on the water with style and grace. You can help raise and trim the sails, or even take a trick at the wheel. Two-hour cruises cost $18 and typically sail at 2, 4:30, and 7 p.m. Reservations are highly recommended.

You know where the Civil War was fought, but this is where it started—and led to 600,000 casualties over four years. South Carolina had seceded, yet Union forces occupied Fort Sumter at the entrance of Charleston Harbor. The Confederates wanted them out; the Yankees refused; and on April 12, 1861, they fired from Fort Johnson, sparking a two-day bombardment that resulted in the surrender of Fort Sumter. Of course, the Union wanted their fort back and spent two years pulverizing it with 46,000 shells. The National Park Service maintains the fort, and park rangers are here to answer your questions. **Fort Sumter Tours,** 843/722-2628, www.spiritlinecruises.com depart from City Marina or Patriot's Point. The tour, which costs $11, lasts just over two hours.

It's hard to see everything at the **Charleston Museum,** 360 Meeting St., 843/722-2996, www.charlestonmuseum.com, so pick what piques your interest and focus on that. Items on exhibit include muskets, antique fire-fighting equipment, swords, railroads, and a replica of the *Hunley*—the Confederate submarine that sunk the *Housatonic* before it was sunk itself in Charleston Harbor. The real *Hunley* was found in 1995, raised in 2001, and contained some interesting artifacts from the doomed men on board. The **Hunley Hotline,** 843/723-9797, provides up-to-date information on displays of items found on board. The museum is open Monday–Saturday 9–5, Sunday 1–5.

Four ships and 25 aircraft are on display at **Patriot's Point Naval and Maritime Museum,** 40 Patriot's Point Rd. (via Hwy. 17), 843/884-2727, www.state.sc.us/patpt. The focal point is the aircraft carrier *USS Yorktown,* which replaced the original after it was sunk at the Battle of Midway. Commissioned on April 15, 1943, this *Yorktown* supported American ground troops in the Philippines at Iwo Jima and Okinawa, and in December 1968, was there to recover the crew of Apollo 8. An admission fee of $12.50 buys you access to the flight deck, hangar deck, ready rooms, ship's hospital, and bridge. If you want to take 'er for a spin, I poked around and found the keys under a flowerpot. On deck you'll see carrier aircraft ranging from WWII bombers, fighters, and torpedo planes, to modern jets.

The **Charleston Harbor Tour,** 843/722-1112, offers a cheap ($12) way to get on the bay, and the captain really knows his stuff. The tour (catch it from the foot of Market Street) covers a lot of history you can learn only from the harbor's vantage point. Only problem is, the boat can be very dirty.

Shopping

If you're inspired by the history, architecture, and gentility of this old southern city, you'll find abundant mementoes of them at the **Historic Charleston Foundation Museum Shop,** 108 Meeting St., 843/724-8484. Open daily, the shop carries books, gifts, maps, and other historical items—worth a stop since the staff will ship your purchases back home.

Y'know, it's hard to find Harley merchandise anywhere . . . Fortunately, the **Harley Shop,** 211 Meeting St., 843/722-9472, www.lowcountryharley.com, is filled with motor clothes, gifts, and collectibles.

Tinder Box Internationale, 177 Meeting St., 843/853-3720, www.tinder box.com, is a cigar shop that boasts the largest selection of domestic and imported cigars in South Carolina, as well as humidors, cutters, estate pipes, tobaccos, and the Club Habana. This upstairs martini bar features exotic drinks, coffees, and . . . cigars! Open Monday–Saturday till 1 A.M., Sunday till midnight.

Blue-Plate Specials

Serving lunch and dinner, **Hyman's,** 215 Meeting St., 843/723-6000, has been here since 1890. Judging from the lines winding down the sidewalk, it'll be here until 2090. The menu offers oysters, crabs, mussels, steaks, and okra gumbo, as well as 15–25 fish to choose from cooked anyway you like—broiled, fried, Cajun, scampi, steamed, lightly Cajun sautéed, or Caribbean jerk.

Open for lunch and dinner, **Sticky Fingers,** 235 Meeting St., 843/853-7427, has been named Charleston's best BBQ joint by several newspapers, magazines, and my stomach. Their ribs are Memphis wet, Memphis dry, Carolina sweet, and Tennessee whiskey. This is standard BBQ fare, but southern all the way. If you need a few hours to get the BBQ sauce off your fingers, settle down at the Sticky Bar and try to loosen it up with the moisture on a cold glass of beer. If you're truly inspired by the BBQ, you may want to leave with a souvenir shirt: "Come lick our bones."

Watering Holes

Numerous great clubs dot the historic district, so consider this the short list. **Tommy Condon's,** 160 Church St., 843/577-3818, attracts families during the day, but at night it's the adults who can't get enough British beer and live Irish sing-along folk music. You can hear their howling down the street. At **The Griffon,** 18 Vendue Range, 843/723-1700, you'll find signed money plastered on the walls, people from all over world, small tables for good conversation, and a low-beamed ceiling for effect.

Shut-Eye

You can't avoid the fact Charleston's a popular town; it reaches critical mass in the historic district. There are numerous inns here and several chain hotels.

Chain Drive*
A, C, F, J, K, L, P, Q, S, BB, CC, DD

*Chain hotels in, or within ten miles of town. See cross-reference guide featuring phone numbers and web addresses on page 405.

Inn-Dependence

If you can swing it, stay at **Two Meeting Street Inn,** 2 Meeting St., 843/723-7322, www.twomeetingstreet.com, a nationally recognized inn that symbolizes Charlestonian elegance. Rates run $165–310 and include the continental breakfast and afternoon tea. Stunning inside and out, the mansion features nine spacious bedrooms and a luxurious ambience. G'wan, treat yourself to an afternoon in a rocking chair on the piazza.

Related Side Trips

Georgia

Contributed by Darryl M. Lodato

Highways 19, 180, 60

Suchez, Georgia

Hidden in the Chattahoochee Forest of Northern Georgia, Suchez attracts motorcyclists for some of the nation's best mountain twisties. Head northeast on 180 for 10 miles of narrow hairpins canopied by old-growth trees. If perfectly cambered sweepers are more your style, Highway 60 will let you test the laws of physics while enjoying spectacular scenery.

Resources for Riders
Southern Comfort Run

Florida Travel Information
Florida Association of RV Parks and Campgrounds—850/562-7151,
www.floridacamping.com
Florida Association of Small and Historic Lodgings—281/499-1374 or
800/524-1880, www.florida-inns.com
Florida Division of Tourism—888/735-2872, www.flausa.com
Florida State Parks—850/488-9872, www.floridastateparks.org
Florida State Parks Camping Reservations—800/326-3521 or
866/422-6735, www.reserveamerica.com
Florida Turnpike Conditions—800/749-7453

Georgia Travel Information
Georgia Bed & Breakfast Council—404/873-4482, www.stay-in-ga.com
Georgia Department of Tourism—800/847-4842, www.georgia.org
Georgia Road Information—404/635-6800
Georgia State Parks and Historic Sites—404/656-2770 or 404/656-3530,
www.gastateparks.org

South Carolina Travel Information
South Carolina Bed & Breakfast Association—888/599-1234,
www.southcarolinabedandbreakfast.com
South Carolina Campground Owners Association—803/772-5354 or
800/344-4518, www.sccamping.com
South Carolina Department of Tourism—803/734-0122 or 800/872-3505,
www.discoversouthcarolina.com
South Carolina Road Conditions—803/896-9621

Local and Regional Information
Charleston Convention and Visitors Bureau—843/853-8000 or
800/774-0006, www.charlestoncvb.com
Charleston Weather Bureau—843/744-3207
Jacksonville Weather Service—904/741-4311
St. Augustine Visitor Information Center—904/825-1000,
www.oldcity.com
St. Johns Visitor and Convention Bureau (St. Augustine)—800/653-2489,
www.visitoldcity.com
Savannah Convention and Visitors Bureau—877/728-2662, www.savcvb.com
Savannah Visitor Information Center—912/944-0455, www.savannahvisit.com

Florida Motorcycle Shops
Bill Lennon's Cycle World—2630 U.S. 1 S., St. Augustine, 904/797-8955
BMW Motorcycles of Daytona—118 E. Fairview Ave., Daytona Beach,
386/257-2269, www.bmwcyclesdaytona.com

Cycle Accessories of Daytona—712 N. Beach St., Daytona Beach,
   386/255-4255, www.polarisofdaytona.com
Daytona Blackgold Cycles—541 Ballough Rd., Daytona Beach, 386/258-8020
Daytona Fun Machines—450 Ridgewood Ave., Daytona Beach,
   386/238-0888, www.daytonafunmachines.com
Daytona Harley-Davidson/Buell—290 N. Beach St., Daytona Beach,
   386/253-2453, www.daytonahd.com
First City Honda—210 SR 16, St. Augustine, 904/829-6416
Jim Walker Honda-Suzuki-Yamaha—2385 S. Ridgewood Ave.
   Daytona Beach, 386/761-2411
Tri-City Cycles—308 S. 2nd St., Flagler Beach, 386/439-3967
Harley-Davidson Augustine—3956 N. Ponce de Leon Blvd., St. Augustine,
   904/829-8782, www.hollingsworthhd.com (note: moving this summer)
Honda-Triumph of Jacksonville—8209 Atlantic Blvd., Jacksonville,
   904/721-2453, www.hojax.com
Jacksonville Powersports—10290 Atlantic Blvd., Jacksonville, 904/641-5320,
   www.jacksonvillepowersports.com
US 1 Powersports—2590 U.S. 1 S., St. Augustine, 904/797-3479

Georgia Motorcycle Shops
Beasley Kawasaki Polaris Motorcycles—4317 Ogeechee Rd., Savannah,
   912/234-6446, www.beasleymotor.com
Honda-Yamaha of Savannah—11512 Abercorn St., Savannah, 912/927-7070
John's V-Twin Cycles—77 W. Fairmont Ave., Savannah, 912/925-4666
Savannah Harley-Davidson—6 W. Gateway Blvd., Savannah, 912/925-0005,
   www.rideharley.com
Hinesville Kawasaki—3707 E. Oglethorpe Hwy., Hinesville, 912/876-9898

South Carolina Motorcycle Shops
Southern Scooters—36 Laurel Bay Rd., Beaufort, 843/846-2188
Yamaha of Beaufort—60 Savannah Hwy., Beaufort, 843/525-1711
Low Country Harley-Davidson Buell—4405 Dorchester Rd., Charleston,
   843/554-1847, www.lowcountryharley.com
Luke's Kawasaki-Polaris—7001 Rivers Ave., Charleston, 843/572-4541
Luke's Honda-Kawasaki—1370 N. Main St., Summerville, 843/871-5371
Specialty Motorsports—1286 Fording Island Rd., Bluffton, 843/837-3949,
   www.specialtymotorsports.com

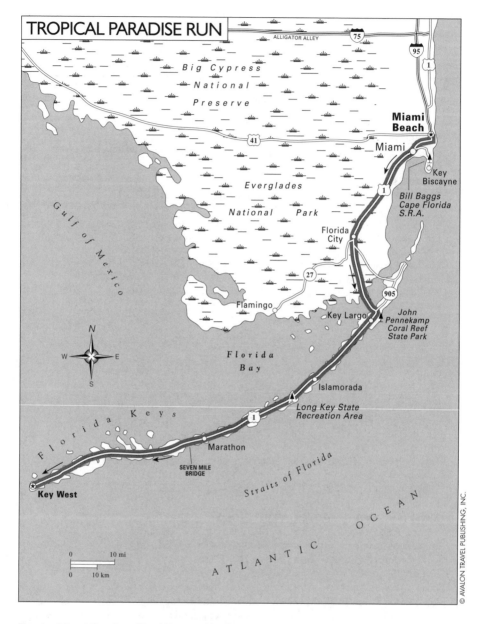

TROPICAL PARADISE RUN

Route: Miami Beach to Key West via Key Largo, Islamorada, Hawk's Cay
Distance: Approximately 300 miles; consider seven days with stops.
  •Days 1 & 2—Miami •Day 3—Travel/Key Largo •Day 4—Travel
  •Days 5 & 6—Key West •Day 7—Return Trip
Helmet Laws: Florida does not require helmets if you are over 21 and carry a
  minimum of $10,000 in medical insurance.

Tropical Paradise Run

Miami Beach to Key West, Florida

It's as far south as you can ride in America, but don't expect to see rednecks, kudzu, and clay roads. Miami Beach is a cosmopolitan city, and the Keys—especially Key West—have managed to hang on to their independent personality despite the efforts of corporations to tame them with generic mega-hotels.

This is a low, level, and not always scenic ride, but if you enjoy sun, snorkeling, scuba diving, and outdoor dining with no dress code, you can't do much better than a wintertime run between Florida's twin cities.

Miami Beach Primer

An insider tip: When you plan your run to Miami, make sure you plan to ride to Miami Beach. Miami is the mainland city, *Miami Beach* is the "Miami" you know, a string of islands separating Biscayne Bay from the Atlantic Ocean. At the southern tip of these islands is South Beach, the revitalized Art Deco district that attracts European jet setters, fashion models, suave Latin playboys, and a nightclub crowd that'll stay up way past your bedtime.

A hundred years ago all this was just a mangrove swamp until some developers got the bright idea to dredge up sand from the ocean floor, pave the swamp, and turn it into a tropical getaway. The idea worked for about three decades until September 1926, when the "No-Name Hurricane" hit and burst

What's Art Deco?

If not for Deco, Miami would be just another of Florida's oceanfront cities noted for a crappy collection of condos. Fortunately, back in the 1930s, hoteliers, desperate to lure northerners to alleviate their great depression, enlisted architects to jazz up staid, boxy buildings. They did so by borrowing accents first unveiled at a Parisian design exhibition a decade earlier. Stealing the shapes they saw utilized on trains, ocean liners, and automobiles, architects accented new hotels with pylons, spheres, cylinders, and cubes. As a bow to the omnipresent ocean, nautical features, such as portholes and images of seaweed, starfish, and rolling waves, were incorporated into the designs. Wraparound windows and glass block became common features. And why the bright colors? Not a Deco idea—give credit to *Miami Vice*, which needed a splashier backdrop for Don Johnson.

the land boom that had been sustained throughout the '20s. Afterward, Miami's fortunes rose and fell and took their most precipitous dive in the 1980s, when Fidel emptied his jails and sent the inmates on a cruise to Florida's sunny shores.

The Mariel Boatlift was the silver bullet that killed Miami tourism. High crime rates and a rapidly aging population sunk the city's image until Crockett and Tubbs arrived. *Miami Vice* depicted Miami Beach as a cosmopolitan, neon-bright tropical city and the shift was on. Art Deco hotels that had fallen out of favor were snapped up by entrepreneurs and turned into chic getaways for European fashion photographers who found a sexy, year-round backdrop.

In South Beach the average age dropped from mid-60s to early 40s in 20 years. Today, cafés crank out Cuban tinto day and night, thong-wearing women glide past on in-line skates, and the beach is revitalized annually with powder soft sands. It's not a great place to actually ride your bike, but it's the best place to kick off a tour down the Florida Keys.

On the Road in Miami Beach

Riding around Miami isn't a great idea—the roads are heavily trafficked and even when you get somewhere you're not seeing much. Your best bet is to ride into South Beach and concentrate your efforts there. Most sites are found between Fifth Street to the south, 17th Street to the north, Ocean Drive on the east, and Washington Avenue, three blocks to the west. Parking tickets are as prevalent as pierced body parts, so consider locking up at a parking garage.

Ocean Drive is the heart of the Art Deco District, a collection of more than 800 buildings that comprise the first 20th-century district to be named to the National Register of Historic Places. If you start here, you can blow off the rest of the day by spreading out a blanket at Lummus Park, the palm-lined stretch of Atlantic Ocean that runs from 5th to 15th Street.

This is Florida's Waikiki. On the wide, white beach, you can hook up with a pickup volleyball game, check out the in-line skaters, and go topless if you're discreet. Women can do this, too. About a hundred yards west, the cafés and hotels of Ocean Drive make it easy to take a break and chill out in the shade.

When you're ready to tour, and not just walk around, staring at historic buildings on Lincoln Road, Espanola Way, North Beach, and the Art Deco District, rent a 90-minute audiotape ($10) at the **Art Deco District Welcome Center,** 1001 Ocean Dr., 305/531-3484, for a walking tour of SoBe. The center is open daily 11–6.

A block north of the Welcome Center, the house at **1144 Ocean Drive** may look familiar if you watched the news the day Gianni Versace was killed here. The Spanish Mediterranean Amsterdam Palace became an eerie tourist attraction and will eventually be a fashionable boutique hotel.

From here, walk two blocks west to Washington Avenue, turn right on 14th Street, then left on Espanola Way. This was the entertainment district for an

*the Vizcaya estate
in Miami*

Rally: Bike Week

The spectacle called Bike Week began in Daytona on January 24, 1937, with the running of the first race across three miles of road and beach. Ed Kretz won the race, but the long distance winner was Bike Week itself.

Although the races were scrubbed in 1942 to save resources for the war effort, fans still arrived to hold an impromptu party called Bike Week. By 1947, when the beach-road races resumed, the party was going at full throttle (no doubt attended by ex-GIs astride surplus military motorcycles). Attendance rose as years passed, but the locals were becoming more leery of bikers. By the late 1980s, fed up city officials and businesses stepped in and reorganized the chaotic drunken bacchanal into a manageable drunken bacchanal. Now Bike Week is a cultural phenomenon that attracts nearly 500,000 riders from around the world. Usually held in the last week of February through the first week of March, festivities revolve around bikes, races, concerts, t-shirts, games, t-shirts, drinking, swap meets, t-shirts, drinking, and contests with some more t-shirts thrown in for good measure. Seeing a blank space on the fall calendar, in 1992 October's Biketoberfest premiered. Although smaller and less threatening than its bigger and older brother Bike Week, Biketoberfest attracts from 80,000–100,000 bikers for a last pre-winter party.

800/854-1234
www.officialbikeweek.com

old hotel and also where a Miami teenager named Desi Arnaz started beating out a conga rhythm. Today, the Mediterranean Revival buildings contain a row of eclectic shops and a Sunday afternoon flea market.

At the next block, Meridian Avenue, turn right and head three blocks to the **Lincoln Road Mall.** Next to Ocean Drive, this is the center of the most activity in Miami Beach, complete with sidewalk cafés, street performers, bookstores, and cigar bars. If you choose the mall over Ocean Drive, the **Van Dyke Cafe,** 846 Lincoln Rd., 305/534-3600, features great food, a busy sidewalk café for people watching, and jazz music up on the second floor seven nights a week.

After that, just saunter back to Ocean Drive and keep an eye out for them thongs.

Pull it Over: Miami and Miami Beach Highlights
Attractions and Adventures

It's a short ride inland from Miami Beach, but the **Venetian Pool,** 2701 De Soto Blvd., Coral Gables, 305/460-5356, is easily one of Miami's most beautiful havens. Created from a rock quarry in 1923, the stunning community pool conjures visions of an Italian waterfront village. Swim here if you hate saltwater. Lockers, concessions, showers, and vintage photos round out the perfection of this shaded, quiet retreat. Open daily; hours vary. Winter admission is $5.50.

In Miami, before there was fashion there was fishin'. Head out to the edge of the Gulf Stream and fish for sailfish, kingfish, dolphin, snapper, and wahoo. Charters are expensive, averaging about $350–400 for a half day. You may do better on a larger fishing boat, where you'll pay about $25. Don't bother with a fishing license since the captain's blanket license should cover all passengers. You'll find several boats at the marinas listed below.

Crandon Marina, 5420 Crandon Blvd., Key Biscayne, 305/361-1281, offers deep-sea fishing and scuba-diving excursions. **Haulover Marine Center,** 15000 Collins Ave., Sunny Isles (North Miami Beach), 305/945-3934, is low on glamour, but high on service with a bait-and-tackle shop, marine gas station, boat launch, and several deep-sea fishing charters.

Here's a way you can fish out of Miami Beach and save yourself a few hundred bucks. For cheaper excursions, check out the **Reward Fleet,** 300 Alton Rd., Miami Beach Marina, 305/372-9470, www.fishingmiami.com, which operates two boats at moderate prices: $30 per person including bait, rod, reel, and tackle.

The beach is the best bet for free activities. The water is usually a gorgeous aquamarine, and the sands are soft and white. Lummus Park along Ocean Drive is fantastic, and beaches run north from here for about 20 miles. If these are too crowded, consider heading south to the remote and sparsely populated sites listed below.

At the far southern end of Key Biscayne, **Bill Baggs Cape Florida State Recreation Area,** 1200 S. Crandon Blvd., 305/361-5811, is worth the ride. Open daily 8 A.M.–sunset, the area features boardwalks, a café, picnic shelters, a fishing pier, and the Cape Florida Lighthouse, all for $2 admission.

North of Bill Baggs and also open daily 8–sunset, **Crandon Park,** 4000 Crandon Blvd., 305/361-5421, has a marina, golf course, tennis center, ball fields, and a 3.5-mile beach with soft sand and a great view of the Atlantic. Parking is both inexpensive and plentiful. Admission is $4.

Just past the tollbooth for the Rickenbacker Causeway, **Sailboards Miami,** Key Biscayne, 305/361-7245, boasts that they can teach anyone to windsurf within two hours. They haven't met my fat cousin Ricky. A one-hour lesson costs $20, two hours $49. Open daily 10–5:30.

Summer diving off Miami is as good as it gets. Explore great natural reefs and "wreckreational" artificial reefs created by sinking water towers, tankers, tanks, a jet, and other recycled structures. There are too many dive shops to list; call the **WaterSports Marketing Council** at 305/672-1270 for information.

Chicago industrialist James Deering built **Vizcaya Museum and Gardens,** 3251 S. Miami Ave., 305/250-9133, www.vizcayamuseum.com, a neoclassical 70-room winter mansion, for a cool $20 million; it'll cost you only $10 to tour it. Vizcaya has entertained the likes of Ronald Reagan, Pope John Paul II, Queen Elizabeth II, Bill Clinton, and Boris Yeltsin. It's a huge house that everyone sees—but the tour verges on boring. Nice if you like big houses, it's open daily 9:30–4:30.

Little Havana's **Calle Ocho** (Eighth Street) is crowded and kind of dirty, but on a motorcycle can seem like an international expedition. If you puff, the draw here is the cigar shops where rows of Cubans at wooden benches rip through giant tobacco leaves, cut them with rounded blades, wrap them tightly, and press them in vises. One of the more authentic is **El Credito,** 1106 SW. 8th St., 305/858-4162 or 800/726-9481, which sells gigantes, supremos, panatelas, and Churchills to dedicated smokers like Robert De Niro, Gregory Hines, and George Hamilton.

Blue-Plate Specials

In South Beach the **11th Street Diner,** 11th St. and Washington Ave., 305/534-6373, serves breakfast, lunch, and dinner in a low-key, working-class setting. Specialties include such classics as meatloaf, burgers, shakes, and blue-plate specials. The 24-hour joint attracts night owls and budget-minded locals who don't need the attitude found at other eateries. The 1948 Deco dining car suggests a Miami institution, but it's only been here since 1992.

The fourth-generation landmark **Joe's Stone Crab Restaurant,** 227 Biscayne St., 305/673-0365, serves tons of stone crab claws daily, as well as an equal amount of drawn butter, lemon wedges, and mustard sauce. Perhaps the greatest ad headline I've seen: "Before SoBe, Joe Be." Joe's is open for lunch Tuesday–Saturday, dinners daily, but is closed September–mid-October.

At the 24-hour beachside **News Cafe,** 800 Ocean Dr., 305/538-6397, you dine on breakfasts, sandwiches, and light appetizers while watching the parade of people pass by. A favorite with locals, tourists are slowly taking over their seats. Still, it's a great setting and features great service.

Watering Holes

You may hear a lot about Miami nightlife, but the "hot clubs" drone with the repetitive thump-thump-thump of techno-pop music. Here are some spots that are better for bikers.

In the middle of South Beach, you wouldn't expect to find **Mac's Club Deuce,** 222 14th St., 305/673-9537, a dark, dirty, working-class bar where men drink and—believe it or not, super models drop in to shoot a game of pool. It sits around the corner from Ocean Drive and within stumbling distance of your hotel.

Opened in 1912, **Tobacco Road,** 626 S. Miami Ave., 305/374-1198, holds Miami's oldest liquor license: number 0001! Head west across the bridge from the beach and you'll find this bar in Miami's downtown (which can look creepy at night). The upstairs Prohibition-era speakeasy today is the stage for local and national blues bands.

South of downtown is hyper-cool Coconut Grove. At the epicenter is CocoWalk, where you'll find several chain bars and lounges, such as **Hooter's** and **Howl at the Moon Saloon,** along with an outdoor bar called **Fat Tuesday,** 3015 Grand Ave., 305/441-2992, which serves beer and 190-proof margaritas that have the strength of 10 men.

Shut-Eye

Chain Drive*
A, B, C, D, F, H, I, J, K, L, N, O, P, R, S, T, U, X, BB, CC, DD

*Chain hotels in, or within ten miles of town. See cross-reference guide featuring phone numbers and web addresses on page 405.

Inn-Dependence
Miami was reborn on the strength of its hotels, so finding nice digs shouldn't be too hard. Stay on Ocean Drive if you want action. If you want a quiet, out-of-the-way place, check out **Indian Creek Hotel,** 2727 Indian Creek Dr., 305/531-2727, www.indiancreekhotel.com. With rates from $140–240 and more charm than a teenager's bracelet, the hotel features a Pueblo Deco setting, courteous staff, and a secluded oasis of a pool out back.

Indulgences

If your second passion is sailing, hit the high seas with **Florida Yacht Charters,** 1290 5th St., Miami Beach Marina, 305/532-8600 or 800/537-0050, www.floridayacht.com. After completing a checkout cruise and paperwork, slap down a deposit and take off for the Keys or Bahamas on a catamaran, sailboat, or motor yacht. Charts, lessons, and captains are available if needed.

On the Road: Miami Beach to Key West

Miami is a progressive city (albeit on the politically corrupt side), but it still hasn't progressed to the point of building a scenic highway down to the Keys.

You have two route choices: The Florida Turnpike bypasses a lot of traffic but costs a few bucks to reach Florida City, the step-off point for the Keys. Then there's Highway 1, the one and only road you need to reach Key West (or Maine). You make the call. Although I suggest a straight 120-mile shot to Key West, there are several places to stop for lodging and daytime activities. On the other hand, towns in between are not that interesting and the clutter of commercialism is taking its toll.

Leaving Miami, the traffic is horrible at first but becomes tolerable after running a gauntlet of urban ugliness. When you reach Florida City, the **Farmer's Market Restaurant,** 300 N. Krome Ave., 305/242-0008, provides the perfect kick-off to the Keys. The servers have degrees in southern hospitality and the home-cooked food is farm fresh; the place serves breakfast, lunch, and dinner. If you thirst for something other than 100 percent pure Florida golden orange juice, you can find a 100 percent pure Wisconsin beer a few miles south at **Skeeter's Last Chance Saloon,** 35800 S. Dixie Hwy. (U.S. 1) 305/248-4935. Here since 1945, it's a most popular destination for riders.

Mile markers that start in Key West at mile marker 0 lead to here, mile marker 127. You'll ride through a 19-mile buffer zone between mainland America and Key Largo at mile marker 108. You may want to wear full leathers, son, but trust your old man. In the winter, the temperature is just right for riding naked, but otherwise it's too damn hot. I wore shorts, a T-shirt, and sneakers and was still covered with flop sweat.

The speed limit is 55, and the road is as level as a flattop from Floyd's Barber Shop. Along this road, motorcycles pass you so often, your frequent waving will help combat global warming. What's missing here are passing lanes. You can tell by the skid marks that some people can't wait. Be patient and pace yourself since, as you well know, motorists can be notoriously stupid.

*Nancy sips on fresh
coconut milk in Key West.*

Two miles past a drawbridge at mile marker 106—one of 42 bridges you'll cross to reach Key West—is the **Key Largo Chamber of Commerce and Florida Keys Visitor Center,** 305/451-1414 or 800/822-1088. Open daily 9–6, the center features information on attractions, lodging, and diving excursions—the lifeblood of Key Largo. Most dive centers host snorkeling trips (about $26) and scuba excursions (around $40, equipment extra).

A few miles south on your left is the **John Pennekamp Coral Reef State Park,** mile marker 102.5, 305/451-1202, www.pennekamppark.com, the most active site between Miami and Key West. The only underwater park in America starts a foot offshore and stretches three miles into the Florida Straits. Most Key Largo dive stations come to this underwater preserve to show divers 55 varieties of coral, 500 species of fish, and shipwrecks dating back to the 1600s. The park is open daily 8–5. Admission is $4.

From the main building, you can book boat tours, snorkeling expeditions, and scuba dives, as well as rent a canoe, kayak, and even swim fins, snorkels, and masks—some with prescription lenses. Or you can skip all this and retreat to one of several shallow swimming areas and use their picnic pavilions or rest rooms. If you have the time, experience, and a bathing suit—dive. The water's perfect and this is where you'll find the oft-pictured underwater Christ of the Abyss statue. Allow at least half a day if you dive, less if you don't.

If you're sidetracked by the sea and want to postpone your trip to the end of the line, I'd highly recommend crashing at the **Largo Lodge,** mile marker 101.7, 305/451-0424 or 800/468-4378, www.largolodge.com, Harriet Stokes's low-key collection of cottages that are locked in the 1940s. Harriet has been here since the mid-1960s, the lodge longer; she's a doll, and the rooms are a bargain at $105 per night. You and your buddies can rent secluded, house-sized units with rattan furniture, kitchenette, large living room, bedroom, and screened porch, all beside an indulgently relaxing bayside setting.

Key Largo offers few other sights. The original *African Queen,* next to the Holiday Inn on your left at mile marker 100, is worth a brief, free glance.

At mile marker 86.7, look on your left for a bodacious lobster statue that lures people into a shopping center but, for your purposes, is better utilized for a funky Florida snapshot. At the collection of Keys called Islamorada, there's less diving and more fishing. You can pick up information on sports-fishing charters at the **Islamorada Visitors Center,** mile marker 82.5, 305/664-9767, www.islamoradachamber.com, which is open daily 8–5.

Almost as large as the lobster you saw earlier is the big-ass mermaid on your right at mile marker 82. The restaurant/bar **Lorelei,** 305/664-4656, open daily 7 A.M.–11 P.M., is a gathering spot for Miami riders, and for good reason. Every night there's a sunset celebration and every weekend the backyard band sets the stage for a Frankie and Annette beach movie. There's a restaurant next door, but on a hot day you'll be just as content having a cold one and dancing the frug.

The Keys start to become more scenic as the road affords longer glimpses of waters that shift from emerald green to azure blue. The commercial growth narrows with the islands, and at times you're only a few feet from the water-line. If Wyoming is Big Sky country, this is Big Sea country, a watery Death Valley.

a sidewalk in Key West

© NANCY HOWELL

If it's getting dark and you want to see more of the Keys, at mile marker 61, **Hawk's Cay,** 305/743-0145 or 800/432-2242, www.hawkscay.com, is a large resort that's far more upscale than Largo Lodge, but can be rewarding with its Dutch East Africa setting, fully equipped condo units, hot tubs, marina restaurant, poolside lounge, power boat rentals, wave runners, and parasailing. Not for everyone, the rates here start in the low $200s.

A few miles down on your right, at mile marker 59, the **Dolphin Research Center,** 305/289-1121, www.dolphins.org, has welcomed enough stars to outfit the Hollywood Squares. President Carter, Jimmy Buffett, and Arnold Schwarzenegger have all swum with the dolphins here—a $135 experience that requires reservations made well in advance. Otherwise, $15 affords admission to look at sea lions and dolphins who stare at you in curiosity. If you book a swim, allow about two hours for your training class and count on roughly 15 minutes in the water, being pushed, pulled, and spun around by friendly dolphins. The center is open daily 9–4.

From here, the road rolls through Marathon, a crowded island to be endured, and unleashes you to the pleasures of the Seven-Mile Bridge. This impressive span presents you with a prime opportunity to soak up vistas stretching far out into the Florida Straits. Remnants of Flagler's original railroad bridge are visible to your right. Enjoy this while you can—once you reach land, the scenery begins to suffer.

At mile marker 4, you'll cross a final bridge and you'll have done it—you've ridden as far south as you can ride in America. At the light, Highway 1 turns to the right, passing strip malls, hotels, a Yamaha dealership, and a Harley-Davidson shop before merging with Truman Boulevard, which delivers you to Duval Street—the heart of Key West.

Key West Primer

There are few islands that can match the legends associated with Key West. Before the 1900s, it was associated with pirates, who were followed in the 1930s by Ernest Hemingway, who was followed in the 1940s by Harry Truman, who was followed in the 1970s by balladeer Jimmy Buffett.

Each of these men contributed something to Key West and, in turn, helped erode what had been here before. The publicity surrounding their infatuation with this remote and character-filled retreat opened the floodgates to tourists. As a result, in many ways the island has become a parody of itself. Trying to get off this three-by-five-mile island without hearing Jimmy Buffett is like trying to tap dance through a minefield without losing a limb.

His songs drone on longer than Muzak in elevators, and tourists young and old arrive here seeking Margaritaville, a fictional utopia that exists only in a beer-shrouded fog.

Likewise, thoughts of paradise have lured the nouveau riche, who have driven the price of real estate beyond reason—to wit, 800-square-foot cottages sell for $200,000.

But all hope is not lost. There are still plenty of characters here who will remain long after the cruise ships set sail and drunken "Parrotheads" return to their cubicles. They'll still be lounging around the Green Parrot or Capt. Tony's or Mallory Square—vagabounds, drifters, and dropouts; writers, artists, and independent thinkers freeing their spirits and feeding their creativity off of the streets of Key West.

On the Road in Key West

Well, you've made it this far, so now what do you do? There's no best way to see Key West, but here's one way I think is USDA okey-dokey. As corny as it sounds, the $20 **Conch Train Tour,** Mallory Square, 305/294-5161, www.historictours.com, might be designed for your folks, but for 90 minutes it gives you a very good historic and geographic overview of the island. Less kitschy is the **Old Town Trolley,** 6631 Maloney Ave., 305/296-6688, www.trolleytours.com, which takes a $20, 70-minute tour, and can navigate some places the train can't. The advantage here is that you can board and reboard at a dozen stops along the way.

After the tour, head down Duval Street to board a snorkeling, diving, or fishing charter. These half- or full-day excursions usually provide all the equipment you'll need. The charters don't go out too far—they don't need to; great diving sites surround the island.

At sunset, there's only one place to be. Mallory Square is where everyone congregates, placing the island in danger of flipping right over. Supposedly the draw is the sunset, but the real show is the street performers, vendors, and local characters hustling for hat money. Fire jugglers, gymnasts, magicians, performing dogs, trained cats, men with pierced nipples carrying iguanas, pot-bellied women in bikinis with pot-bellied pigs in their baskets . . . they're all here looking for their shot at stardom or a few bucks of your tour money.

Follow up the cheap thrills with dinner at a sidewalk café, and then a late evening doing the "Duval Crawl." There are great bars here, sidewalk stands where you can get a temporary tattoo or a good cigar, secluded courtyards hiding restaurants and martini bars and, if you look closely . . . Margaritaville.

Pull it Over: Key West Highlights
Attractions and Adventures

This "Odditorium" is a kick. At **Ripley's Believe It Or Not,** 527 Duval St., 305/293-9694, check out shrunken heads, a display of natives eating a crocodile, and a Birth of Venus made out of 66 slices of browned toast. You'll especially enjoy the cartoon explaining that one Dan Jaimun of Bangkok locked himself in his room for 22 years because his parents refused to buy him a motorcycle. Idiot—21 years was enough for me.

Key West thrives on aquatic adventures, ranging from glass-bottom boat trips to kayak excursions, snorkeling trips, and scuba dives. The competition means that each group offers roughly the same experience at the same cost, so you'll do better to pick up a handful of flyers at the welcome center and make your own selection.

One outfit I can recommend over the competition is **Fury Catamaran,** 305/294-8899, www.furycat.com. The huge, steady boat departs from the Hilton Marina to sail out a mile or two for the sunset, serving free champagne, beer, wine, and soda along the way. Prices vary from $30–40 since Fury also features a slick snorkeling/sunset cruise combination.

Schooner Western Union & Schooner America, Schooner Wharf, 305/292-1766, www.schoonerwesternunion.com, charges $30–45 for cruises aboard the 130-foot *Western Union,* the last tall ship built in Key West. Varnished mahogany decks and canvas sails are part of the appeal; the fact that you can help hoist the sails is part two. Thankfully, there's little Buffett-ing aboard the boat—the entertainer sings old sea chanties. Beer, wine, and soft drinks are served.

No single tour explains all things Key West, so in addition to the Conch Train, consider filling in the blanks with **Island City Strolls,** 305/294-8380. Sharon Wells, the state historian in Key West, is an author and tour guide who knows more about the island than Buffett, Hemingway, and Truman combined. Various tours ($18) are available, ranging from architectural tours to writers' residences to the cemetery.

David Sloan is sincere about his job with **Ghost Tours of Key West,** 305/294-9255, www.hauntedtours.com, and the fact he and his henchman dress like undertakers and drive hearses persuades me to plug this tour. I don't believe in spooks, but, gee, Wally, I kinda felt sorta creepy when he described the guy who married a corpse (and later consummated his marriage).

Ernest Hemingway moved to the house at 907 Whitehead Street in 1931 and, when he wasn't at Sloppy Joe's, wrote *For Whom the Bell Tolls, To Have and Have Not,* and *A Farewell to Arms* in his second-story writing room.

Hemingway Home, 305/294-1575, www.hemingwayhome.com, is a must-see in Key West, so I'm listing it—even though on my tour the guide crammed us in a room, ignored our questions, and started talking before we reached the next room. Unless you're a fan, skip it and save yourself $9.

After years of searching, the late Mel Fisher discovered the circa 1622 wrecks of the *Nuestra Senora de Atocha* and *Santa Margarita,* ships that happened to be carrying a lot of gold and emeralds. Fisher fought the state of Florida for rights to the treasure, and won. Since he didn't need to cash in all the booty to make himself a multimillionaire, he put some on display at the **Mel Fisher Maritime Museum,** 200 Greene St., 305/294-2633, www.melfisher.org. Pay $7.50 at the door for the chance to ogle a six-pound gold bar and a 77-carat uncut emerald. Open daily 9:30–5.

Key West was President Harry Truman's winter pressure release from Washington. His home on the former naval base, today known as the **Harry S. Truman Little White House,** 111 Front St., 305/294-9911, is open for guided tours through nearly every room. If you're as slick as I am, you can sneak a seat at his desk or at the table where he played poker with his buddies. Ante up ten bucks to get in. Open daily 9–4:30.

Shopping

It's leather forever at **Biker Image,** 121 Duval St., 305/292-1328, open daily 9 A.M.–midnight, and carrying sexy clothes for the women-folk, manly leathers for mighty men, plus shirts, hats, caps, shoes, and thongs a-plenty. **Beach Club,** 210 Duval St., 305/292-7975, also peddles an assortment of

A 30-Second History: Harley-Davidson

The world's most popular motorcycle corporation began in Milwaukee when William Harley, 21, and Arthur Davidson, 20, designed an engine to "take the work out of bicycling." In 1903, they built three motorcycles. In 1909, they unveiled the seven-hp V-twin engine, which could rocket riders up to 60 mph. Over the years, innovations, such as the teardrop gas tank, and engines with names like knucklehead, shovelhead, and panhead cemented the allegiance of riders who believe that H-D is the only real motorcycle company.

Kuralt: Harley-Davidson Electra-Glide Classic

"Kuralt"* for the Florida Keys was a 1999 Harley-Davidson Electra-Glide Classic from Orlando's Iron Horse Rentals, www.hogride.com. A massive bike, it has everything you'd find in a city bus. Within finger's touch are a tape deck, AM/FM radio with treble/bass adjustment, weather band, clock, horn, and turn signals. It also has a voltage meter, air and oil pressure gauges, running lights, and an easy-to-read fuel gauge. Master this and you're a shoo-in for the world thumb-wrestling championship.

The hard bags (saddle and trunk) are large, the footrests wide, the styling fine, and the seat so comfortable you'll be tempted to string a hammock. There's so much power to spare that if you're an experienced rider you may be a bit disappointed that the bike does most of the riding for you. After a hundred miles, it's still skimming easily down the road, removing you from the elements and the challenges of riding. It's not the bike's fault—this is a well-tuned piece of machinery—but if you're ready for a long ride during which you want to feel the environment, look for a bike that's less well dressed.

For details on new Harley-Davidson models, check www.harley-davidson.com.

*It was the travels of CBS correspondent Charles Kuralt that inspired me to explore America. I named each motorcycle I rode in his honor.

stuff for riders, including backpacks, saddlebags, boots, and jackets. Open daily 9 A.M.–11:30 P.M.

Blue-Plate Specials

Jimmy Buffet's **Margaritaville,** 500 Duval St., 305/292-1435, www.margaritavillekw.com, isn't "authentic" Key West, but if you like Buffett you'll want to check out the offerings: fish sandwiches, yellowfin tuna, Key West pink shrimp, ribs, beer . . . and margaritas!

Actress Kelly McGillis opened **Kelly's Caribbean Bar & Grill,** 301 Whitehead St., 305/293-8484, which serves both lunch and dinner. Lunch centers around sandwiches and salads with a Caribbean twist, and dinner ranges from pasta to large steaks to four types of fresh fish. The main draw is outdoor dining in a courtyard or on the upper deck—a great spot to test Kelly's microbrews, Golden Clipper and Havana Red.

Off the beaten path, locals and tourists hang in the **Half Shell Raw Bar,** 231 Margaret St., 305/294-7496, a cavernous dockside barn, and pig out on raw oysters, chicken, burgers, ribs, crab, lobster, conch, dolphin, grouper, mako, wahoo, and other fish broiled, grilled, blackened, and fried. Beats them damn Fish McNuggets.

Watering Holes

Sloppy Joe's, 201 Duval St., 305/294-5717 or 800/437-0333, capitalizes on its connection to Hemingway—he drank and gambled here. This loud and noisy bar is filled with barflies and college kids and middle-aged tourists who get along well because everyone's drunk. Plan to drink here if you don't have to wake up until noon the next day, although you can find quiet upstairs in the semiprivate speakeasy. You'll find lots of pix and Ernie memorabilia, live entertainment, and a specialty drink called the Sloppy Rita. You can carouse here daily until 4 A.M.

Captain Tony, namesake of **Capt. Tony's Saloon,** 428 Greene St., 305/294-1838, www.capttonyssaloon.com, remains a hard-drinking, woman-chasing, Key West icon known for being Hemingway's fishing guide and for giving Buffett a break by letting him perform in this morgue-turned-bar. Bring a business card or a bra to leave with the rest. Tony stayed true to keeping this a bar, not a tourist attraction, and his rumrunners and pirate's punch prove it. Trivia time: The bar opened the morning after Prohibition ended: November 15, 1933. Open daily 'til 4 A.M.

For a place with a biker name, **Hog's Breath Saloon,** Front and Duval Sts., 305/296-4222 or 800/826-6969, www.hogsbreath.com, is surprisingly tame. Still, you know you're gonna go, so here's what you'll get: entertainment from start to finish, a patio bar, bar food, and a drink called the "Hogarita." Everybody has an angle. Doors close at 2 A.M.

A few blocks from the commercial center, the **Green Parrot Bar,** Southard and Whitehead Sts., 305/294-6133, www.greenparrot.com, is what Key West bars probably looked like before outsiders showed up, featuring pinball, pool, locals, and drinking that starts early and lasts late. Open shutters bring in the outdoors, and paraphernalia, including Bahamian art and motorcycle collectibles, make this a sanctuary well away from the cruise-line passengers.

Down and dirtier than dirt, **The Bull,** Caroline and Duval, has little charm but a great location and an open-air bar that's great day or night. Upstairs, The

Whistle places you above the madding crowd that flocks along Duval Street during festivals and most any other night. The rooftop Garden of Eden is opened to naturists who want a tan sans tan lines.

Shut-Eye

Lodging options run from chain hotels to small motels to inns. Don't arrive and try to make a reservation—do it in advance if you can. Two complimentary services to help are the **Key West Welcome Center,** 3840 N. Roosevelt Blvd., 800/284-4482, and the **Key West Information Center,** 1601 N. Roosevelt Blvd., 305/292-5000 or 888/222-5145. They also make reservations for diving, snorkeling, sailing, and other activities.

Motels and Motor Courts
Before large resorts shoved their way in, there were quiet motels around Key West. Several still exist, although their in-season rates are quite inflated. Beware. You'll find numerous other (perhaps better) options via the Visitors Center, but here are a few choices: the **Blue Marlin Motel,** 1320 Simonton St., 305/294-2585 or 800/523-1698, www.bluemarlinmotel.com. Rates aren't very motel-y, with a low of $89 and a leap to $169 in season. A block off Duval Street and the Atlantic Ocean, its 54 rooms are motel simple, with a/c, cable, fridge, and some with kitchenettes. A lush tropical courtyard contains a large heated pool. The **El Rancho Motel,** 830 Truman Ave., 305/294-8700 or 800/294-8783, www.elranchokeywest.com, is slightly further from the action, but is still a part of "Old Town." Rates at this motel run from $129–179. The **Key Lodge Motel,** 1004 Duval St., 305/296-9915 or 800/845-8384, is also well placed, and has 22 ground-level rooms, a pool, a free continental breakfast, and off-street parking. Low season rates start at $99 and go as high as—gulp—$199 in the winter and spring.

Chain Drive*
A, C, D, I, J, K, L, N, S, T, AA, DD

*Chain hotels in, or within ten miles of town. See cross-reference guide featuring phone numbers and web addresses on page 405.

Inn-Dependence
Then there's the **Island City House,** 411 William St., 305/294-5702 or 800/634-8230, www.islandcityhouse.com, a nice, laid-back inn consisting of three large buildings hidden within a tropical garden. A pool and free continental breakfast

complement the large and comfortable rooms. Look for the alligator at the bottom of the pool. Rates run $115–210.

The **Center Court Historic Inn & Cottages,** 915 Center St., 305/296-9292 or 800/797-8787, is between Duval and Simonton Streets, just off U.S. 1. The two block street makes this an oasis, with just 17 Caribbean-style rooms arranged in the Cistern House, Honeymoon Hideaway, The Cottage, and the Family House. A heated pool, spa, exercise pavilion, tropical garden, and sun decks raise prices from $98–148 for an inn room to $128–178 for a deck-side efficiency. Group riders may want to check out the cottages.

Indulgences

About 20 miles north of Key West is an island retreat that'll dissolve a lifetime of stress in less than five minutes. **Little Palm Island,** Little Torch Key, 305/872-2524 or 800/343-8567, www.littlepalmisland.com, is accessed by a retro Chris Craft that delivers you to a Fantasy Island setting of spacious thatched-roof Tiki huts, secluded pool, tropical gardens, and a white sandy beach. A sunset dinner on the beach is pure, undiluted paradise. Although activities are available, if you can afford to do absolutely nothing, there's no better place not to do it than here. What's the catch? The privilege will cost you from $650–800 a night.

Resources for Riders
Tropical Paradise Run

Florida Travel Information
Florida Association of RV Parks and Campgrounds—850/562-7151,
   www.floridacamping.com
Florida Association of Small and Historic Lodgings—281/499-1374 or
   800/524-1880, www.florida-inns.com
Florida Division of Tourism—888/735-2872, www.flausa.com
Florida State Parks—850/488-9872, www.floridastateparks.org
Florida State Parks Camping Reservations—800/326-3521 or
   866/422-6735, www.reserveamerica.com
Florida Turnpike Conditions—800/749-7453

Local and Regional Information
Key Largo Chamber of Commerce—305/451-1414 or 800/822-1088,
   www.keylargo.org
Florida Keys and Key West—800/352-5397, www.fla-keys.com
Greater Miami Convention & Visitors Bureau—305/539-3063 or
   800/283-2707, www.miamiandbeaches.com
Key West Visitors Bureau—305/294-2587 or 800/527-8539,
   www.keywestchamber.org
Key West Welcome Center—800/284-4482
Miami Beach Visitor Information—305/672-1270,
   www.miamibeachchamber.com
Miami Weather Service—305/229-4522

Motorcycle Shops
Peterson's Harley-Davidson of Miami—19400 N.W. 2nd Ave., Miami,
   305/651-4811, www.miamiharley.com
Harley-Davidson of Miami South—17631 S. Dixie Hwy., Miami,
   305/235-4023, www.harleymiami.com
Motoport USA—1200 N.W. 57th Ave., Miami, 305/264-4433,
   www.motoportusa.com
Riva Yamaha—3671 N. Dixie Hwy., Miami, 305/651-7753,
   www.rivayamaha.com
Southwest Cycle—8966 S.W. 40th St., Miami, 305/226-9542
M.D. Custom Cycles—102670 Overseas Hwy., Key Largo, 305/451-3606
Florida Key Cycle—2222 N. Roosevelt Blvd., Key West, 305/296-8600
Horne's Harley-Davidson—1113 Truman Ave., Key West, 305/294-3032

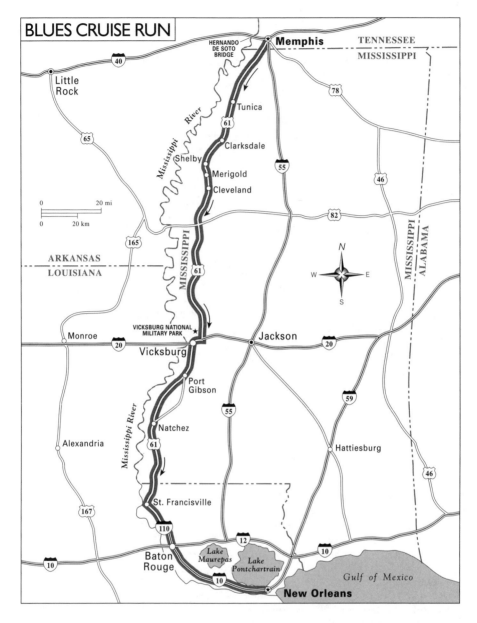

Route: Memphis to New Orleans via Tunica, Clarksdale, Vicksburg, Natchez Trace Parkway, St. Francisville

Distance: Approximately 480 miles; consider seven days with stops.
  • Days 1 & 2—Memphis • Day 3—Travel • Day 4—Vicksburg • Day 5—Travel
  • Days 6 & 7—New Orleans

First Leg: Memphis to Vicksburg (226 miles)

Second Leg: Vicksburg to New Orleans (253 miles)

Helmet Laws: Tennessee and Mississippi require helmets. Optional in Louisiana if over 18 with proof of $10,000 of medical insurance.

Blues Cruise

Memphis, Tennessee to New Orleans, Louisiana

This ride is unusual in its theme, following a single purpose—to immerse you in the birthplace of American music. In Memphis, you have as much chance avoiding the music of Elvis as you do missing Jimmy Buffett tunes in Key West. When you ride Highway 61 into the vast emptiness known as the Mississippi Delta, you'll understand how this landscape nurtured the blues. And New Orleans? Well, that's a whole different story . . .

You can concentrate on music, not frostbite, by riding any time between March and November.

Memphis Primer

I could talk here about Hernando de Soto and paddle wheelers and King Cotton, and all of it would be relevant to Memphis. But the city's history, like that of Vicksburg and New Orleans, is detailed in hundreds of books; being definitive is impossible, so I'll limit my comments to this: You need only know that Memphis gave birth to the blues, then later to its wild sibling, rock 'n' roll. The city set the bar so high—achieving so much so quickly—that the town now seems tired. I doubt it could score a hat trick by creating another musical genre, but I hope Memphis proves me wrong.

Tired or not, Memphis is one of the most intriguing cities in America. In addition to the larger-than-life influences of Elvis and W. C. Handy,

Memphis offers simpler pleasures like fabulous BBQ joints and places like A. Schwab, where you can still buy celluloid collars and voodoo supplies. *American Heritage* magazine named Memphis a "Great American Place" in 1998. The city may be living on past glories, but who has a problem with that?

On the Road in Memphis

Because I love music, I could spend weeks here hitting great record stores and talking to older Memphians. If you have limited time, I'd suggest that you build a day around Elvis and an evening around the blues.

Memphis's streets are confusing, but if you ignore all but a few roads, you'll see nearly everything worth seeing. From the riverfront, look for Union Avenue, which shoots inland. Take this road and when you reach Marshall Avenue, look to your left and you'll see a small red brick building. Stop here because this is where rock 'n' roll was born.

Sun Studio, 706 Union Ave., 901/521-0664 or 800/441 6249, www.sun studio.com, was Sam Phillips's labor of love. When he wasn't recording weddings and political speeches, he was looking for unique black voices from the farms and fields surrounding Memphis. In the back of his mind he was thinking about finding "a white man with a black man's voice."

On July 18, 1953, 18-year-old Elvis Presley dropped by Sam's "Memphis Recording Service" and paid $3.98 to record "My Happiness." A year later, on July 5, 1954, Phillips asked Elvis to jam with guitarist Scotty Moore and bassist

Elvis and His Music

Before his fall, Elvis was passionate about his life and his music. Consider this reference to rock n' roll from a 1956 interview . . .

"The colored folks been singing and playing it just like I'm doing now, man, for more years than I know. They played it like that in the shanties and in their juke joints and nobody paid it no mind until I goosed it up. I got it from them. Down in Tupelo, Mississippi, I used to hear Arthur Crudup bang his box the way I do now and I said that if I ever got to the place where I could feel all old Arthur felt, I'd be a music man like nobody ever saw . . ."

Bill Black. That evening the trio changed history by blending hillbilly and blues to create rock 'n' roll. Not bad for a night's work.

The tour ($8.50) is fascinating not just because of Elvis, but because of "Rocket 88," "Great Balls of Fire," "Blue Suede Shoes," and other breakthrough songs recorded here in a burst of talent by artists such as Carl Perkins, Johnny Cash, Roy Orbison, and Jerry Lee Lewis. Thank God it's still a recording studio. You can even record your own songs here (CD $50, cassette $20). Before you leave, check out the upstairs museum, gift shop, and the picture of Elvis on his 1956 KH Flathead Sportster.

From Sun, head up Union and turn right on Highway 51, a.k.a. Bellevue Boulevard. A few miles up on your left is a bike shop that deserves special mention. **Super Cycle,** 620 Bellevue Blvd. S., 901/725-5991, sells sexy customized Harleys, parts, accessories, and collectibles. Elvis loved cruising the night streets of Memphis on his customized motorcycles—bikes souped up right here. Lew and Ronnie Elliott still service Elvis's bikes at Graceland and love talking motorcycles. The shop is open Tuesday–Friday 8:30–6, Saturday 8–5.

Now that you've primed yourself with Elvis lore, it's time for the payoff. Ride several miles south on 51 and look to your right for the parking lot for **Graceland,** 3763 Elvis Presley Blvd., 901/332-3322 or 800/238-2000, www.elvis-presley.com. The only bad part about being here is that Elvis's image is everywhere, which makes the rest of us look like a race of Elephant Men.

For less than $25, the "Platinum Tour" takes you through the mansion, the Elvis museum, the auto and motorcycle museum, a movie, and his airplanes and tour bus. The tour is very streamlined: You buy a ticket, stand in line, get a headset and a taped tour, get on a bus, cross the street, and tour the house and museum. Aside from feeling like a herded cow, it's all pretty cool. In 1957, the Presleys moved to this 14-acre $100,000 estate, where Elvis commenced two decades of all-night parties, recording sessions, and big food that ended when he got everything he wanted but not a thing that he needed.

Take time in the house, in the museum, and especially at Meditation Gardens, where Elvis is buried beside his father and mother. When you return to Graceland Plaza, check out the auto museum, where you'll see his Honda 300 (from Al's Cycle Shop on Summer Avenue), a cool Honda chopper, and his membership cards to the American Motorcyclist Association and Memphis Motorcycle Club.

There's far more of Elvis's Memphis to see—his first home at Lauderdale Courts (185 Winchester, #328) and Humes High (659 Manassas)—but you also need to see Beale Street. The transition is eased by the hyper-cool Elvis statue on Beale near Main Street. This is Elvis as the Hillbilly Cat, replacing the circa 1970s Elvis whose crotch was polished to a shiny gold by the fondling hands of female fans.

Time Beale Street for the afternoon and again for later that night. This was, and still is, the entertainment center of Memphis. When the town was segregated, the whites didn't know what they were missing. Blacks had turned this into a commercial district with tailors (birthplace of the Zoot Suit), bars, banks, insurance companies, newspapers, beauty parlors, and medical and dental offices. At night, the music would start.

In 1905, W. C. Handy was playing at PeeWee's Saloon when he was commissioned by E. H. Crump, a mayoral candidate, to write a campaign song. Handy recalled the stark music of the Delta singers and used his formal training to complement it with rich instrumentation and voila!—the blues were born with "Mr. Crump" (soon to be known as "Memphis Blues"). Handy later wrote "St. Louis Blues" and "Beale Street Blues."

To honor W. C. Handy, the city has moved his shack to the corner of Beale and 4th Street. The **W. C. Handy House and Museum,** 901/522-1556, $2 admission, is open Tuesday–Saturday 10–5. When you see the simplicity of his home, you'll know that genius comes from within.

During the day there are few places to hit on Beale Street, and **A. Schwab,** 163 Beale Street, 901/523-9782 is a most incredibly essential stop. It was established here in 1876, and I doubt the inventory has changed much since: celluloid collars, bloomers, lye soap, skeleton keys, and my favorite—voodoo potions, candles, and soaps. A gentleman named "Sonny Boy" has cornered the market on a full range of customized voodoo soaps designed for specific purposes. Buy a few bars and scrub up with "Pay Me Now," "Drive Away Evil," "Come to Me," or, the best-seller for litigants, "Win My Lawsuit Court Case."

At night, Beale Street becomes a completely different place. Street musicians play anywhere and everywhere, and blues, rock, and jazz blow the doors off of juke joints and nightclubs.

Go ahead. Get all shook up.

Pull it Over: Memphis Highlights
Attractions and Adventures

A for-profit welcome center, the **Map Room,** 2 S. Main St., 901/543-8686, www.memphismaproom.com, invites you to just sit and relax in its overstuffed chairs. It also offers simple food, magazines, and dozens of books on Memphis's history. Open 24 hours, it attracts local riders who drop in and hang out. While you're here, pick up a copy of *Kreature Comforts,* billed as "the Lowlife Guide to

Elvis and His Bikes

Lew Elliott, owner of Supercycle, a Memphis bike shop, never took a picture with Elvis; he thought it wasn't right for a businessman to ask for a picture with a customer. Elliott recalls:

"Elvis was real easy to get along with. He always was a gentleman the whole damn time, and he made the other guys the same way. They'd come in, and not one of them would sit on a motorcycle unless they asked—including him. Never ever. He would always ask, 'Can I sit on this one?'

"When he'd come in, the ladies at the building across the street would see his trike and know he was here. Elvis was sitting on the windowsill when one of 'em came over and asked my brother Ronnie, 'Is that Elvis?' He said, 'I don't know what his name is. He's just delivering Pepsis.' Then Elvis says, 'Yeah, how many cases do you want, anyway?' Ronnie said, 'I don't know, you'll have to check it.' That's when Elvis started laughing and said, 'Yeah, c'mon over. I'm Elvis.'"

Memphis," which provides details on local haunts and history. It's worth much more than the $2.50 price.

The **Center for Southern Folklore,** 119 South Main St., 901/525-3655, www.southernfolklore.com, combines a nonprofit museum of Southern folk art with a beer and coffee bar and a stage for local bluesmen like Mose "Boogie Woogie" Vinson. Grab a book, settle back, and dig it the most. Open daily 10 A.M.–4 A.M.

The chance to drop by different religious services is one of the perks of touring. At the **Full Gospel Tabernacle,** 787 Hale Rd., 901/396-9192, worship while you dance and sing along with the Reverend Al Green. *The* Al Green. Pay a visit Sunday at 11 A.M. Ride four lights south of Graceland, turn right on Hale Road and it's a half-mile down.

The **National Civil Rights Museum,** 450 Mulberry St., 901/521-9699, www.civilrightsmuseum.org, is located in the old Lorraine Hotel, where Martin Luther King Jr. died. Visiting this place is like making a pilgrimage to the Dakota, where John Lennon was killed. This museum is cluttered with displays, so you'll only be able to skim it. Sit on the bus and feel what it was like to be told to "move to the back," and take time to see Dr. King's room the way it was left on April 4, 1968. The museum is open Monday–Saturday 9–5, Sunday 1–5, closed Tuesday. Admission is $8.50.

Shopping

While a teenager, Elvis couldn't afford many records, so he spent hours and hours at **Poplar Tunes,** 308 Poplar Ave., 901/525-6348, listening to platters by white crooners, hillbilly singers, and black R&B artists—later putting this mix on his own disks. In 1954, "Pop Tunes" was the first store in the world to carry an Elvis record. He returned the favor by dropping in often to sign autographs. Great shirts here, too.

Dr. Malcolm Anthony, proprietor of **Memphis Music,** 149 Beale St., 901/526-5047, www.memphismusicstore.com, is a "bluesologist" with a mighty collection of music books and blues and gospel CDs by artists like Fats Waller, Mighty Clouds of Joy, and Little Charlie and the Nightcats. The good doctor also carries movie posters, such as the one for *Beale Street Mama*—which boasted an "all-colored cast!" Great stuff peddled by a nice guy.

Blue-Plate Specials

Memphis is known for BBQ, and **Cozy Corner,** 745 N. Parkway, 901/527-9158, is a local fave, serving lunch and dinner Tuesday–Saturday. Raymond Robinson Jr. runs this chicken and ribs joint, which attracts blacks, whites, blue- and white-collar workers, and celebrities like BB King, Robert Duvall, and Hank Williams Jr. Get a slab of two, four, or six ribs with coleslaw, bread, and beans or BBQ spaghetti. Have mercy!

Thanks to Chef Bonnie Mack, the **Blues City Cafe,** 138 Beale St., 901/526-3637, is a legend. Diners drop by just for Mack's mean mess of ribs, steaks, shrimp, catfish, tamales, liquors, beer, and burgers. Serving lunch and dinner, this greasy spoon sports cheap formica tables and office chairs; there's a bar and stage next door. Good food, plus great ad copy: "The Best Meal On Beale" and "Put Some South In Your Mouth."

Sure, it's for tourists, but the food's down-home and good at **Elvis Presley's Memphis,** 126 Beale St., 901/527-6900 or 901/527-9036 (entertainment line), www.epmemphis.com. Lunches and dinners feature roasted Dixie chicken, pecan-crusted catfish, baby back ribs and . . . a fried peanut butter and banana sandwich! It's gooey as all hell, will block your arteries, and too many can kill you. Check out the nighttime rockabilly entertainment.

Watering Holes

Along Beale Street, take your pick from a great concentration of nightclubs within walking distance of downtown. Also consider **BB King's Blues Club,**

143 Beale St., 901/524-5464, www.bbkingclubs.com, a restaurant that borders on a juke joint. Lots of BB's ("Blues Boy's") gold records are on display, along with guitars from Keith Richards, Memphis Slim, and Stevie Ray Vaughn. The stage hosts blues acts, of course. Oh yeah. There's a full bar and lots of beer.

A cavernous Irish joint, **Silky O'Sullivan's,** 183 Beale St., 901/522-9596, jumps at night, with imports on tap (Guinness, Fosters, Bass, Newcastle, Harp), a full liquor bar, and a 30-year-old house secret called "the Diver"—a gallon pitcher that contains a little of everything. After you finish the $18 concoction, call a taxi, stumble back to your room, or go to the hospital.

Shut-Eye

On most trips, I try to avoid downtown areas, but in Memphis most attractions are downtown, down by the riverside. Finding a chain here isn't a problem.

Chain Drive*
A, C, D, E, G, H, J, K, L, P, Q, S, O, T, U, W, X, BB, CC, DD

*Chain hotels in, or within ten miles of town. See cross-reference guide featuring phone numbers and web addresses on page 405.

Indulgences

If you can swing it, stay at the legendary **Peabody,** 149 Union Ave., 901/529-4000, www.peabodymemphis.com, where rates run $245–350. Fancified like the rest of Memphis probably used to be, the hotel features plenty of class in its deluxe rooms and suites. The ducks march at 11 and 5. Right across from The Peabody, the generic **Holiday Inn Select,** 160 Union Ave., 901/525-5491 or 888/300-5491, has covered parking and rates from $149–159. In midtown, a few miles from downtown, the **French Quarter Suites,** 2144 Madison Ave., 901/728-4000 or 800/843-0353, are a good option and right next to Overton Square, another site for Memphis nightlife. Some rooms have king beds and all have double-sized whirlpool tubs. Rates range from $99–119.

On the Road: Memphis to Vicksburg

Before leaving Memphis, take a few minutes and set off on a tour to the western United States. The Mississippi River flows past Memphis, so after you've crossed the Hernando DeSoto Bridge into Arkansas, in less than 10 minutes you've ridden to the other side of the continent. Take Front Street to Adams, turn left, and keep going. It's an impressive sight considering the mighty Mississippi is 2,350 miles long, receives water from 300 rivers, drains 1,250,000 square miles of the nation and every day near its mouth dumps enough sand, gravel, and mud to fill a freight train 150 miles long. Just like my bathtub.

When you return to Memphis, take 2nd Street south, pass the National Civil Rights Museum, and watch for Highway 61. Following about 15 miles of congestion, the road clears up and you enter one of the most unusual regions of the country, the Mississippi Delta.

Almost instantly the buildings disappear and the farmland commences. The landscape is completely flat, the only structures of prominence the repetitive billboards for Tunica's casinos followed by billboards for pawnshops.

With so little to look at, the sight of the casinos on the horizon may tempt you, but it'd be more fun to spend the money you'd lose here on a trip to Las Vegas. Tunica is like a comet; it flares up and disappears quickly.

Five miles south of Tunica, Highway 61 goes two lane but the scenery doesn't change. This is about the time you'll understand why Muddy Waters and John Lee Hooker started singing the blues—there was nothing else here to do.

About 60 miles south of Memphis, watch for the sign to Clarksdale where 61 splits from 49. Veer to the right and follow the signs to the Delta Blues Museum. On your ride through this old town, you'll turn right at the intersection (DeSoto) where Robert Johnson supposedly sold his soul to become a great guitar player. That's just one of the stories relayed within the surprisingly impressive, must-see **Delta Blues Museum,** 1 Blues Alley, 662/627-6820, www.deltablues museum.org. Open Monday–Saturday 10–5, the free museum is also a research facility and a library of the blues. It's stocked with CDs, books, magazines, vintage photos, more books, one of BB King's guitars, exhibits on juke joints and harmonicas, and a map showing the birthplace of famous blues musicians. If you don't understand the blues, check out the display on who owes a debt to this local creation: John Lennon, Keith Richards, Bob Dylan, Eric Clapton . . . It also impressed Led Zeppelin's Robert Plant and Jimmy Page, who dropped by the museum and had their picture taken for the local paper.

On Highway 61, you're back to the flatlands of the Delta. There's nothing to see, but it's strangely calming out here. The wind is powerful because there's nothing to stop it but you, and the only distraction is your radio—if you have one—which you can tune to WNIX (1330 AM) and listen to the static sound of old '50s and '60s doo-wop, rock, and R&B records—the perfect soundtrack to this stretch of the ride.

Shelby is the next town of any size, full of future blues musicians. After Shelby is Merigold, where the center of commerce is a crawfish cooler, and then there's the metropolis of Cleveland, which is a good place to buy a tractor. In the town of Shaw you may see some cows, which vary the scenery slightly, but then it returns to the Delta again.

Although I make this ride sound slow and empty—and geographically it is— it took a few weeks to reflect and realize that it was one of my favorite rides. Why? Because this isn't the same shaded back road or wide open desert. This is different and it is real.

As you ride the final 80 miles to Vicksburg, stopping at any of the plentiful food and fuel stores, you'll have time to think about the despair and the hope that permeate this area. Despite the lack of culture as most of us define it, the people here have developed their own. Their culture, more than opera or ballet or Broadway, spoke to young people around the world who, in turn, channeled the music into a social and political force that changed the way we live. And it all started right here. In towns like Panther Burn and Nitta Yuma and Hushpekena.

Suddenly the Delta doesn't seem so empty anymore.

Vicksburg Primer

How valuable was Vicksburg to the Union? President Lincoln observed that "Vicksburg is the key. The war can never be brought to a close unless that key is in our pocket." Ulysses Grant took Lincoln at his word and the Siege of Vicksburg began.

That's what this sleepy town on the banks of the Mississippi is still known for. Originally, Grant tried to ford the Mississippi River and conquer the city, but bluffs 200 feet high stopped him cold. Grant wanted Vicksburg so he moved downriver and crossed to Port Gibson, worked his way to Jackson, and came up behind Vicksburg to shell and starve the city into surrender.

When the siege began on May 18, 1863, citizens went underground, hastily digging caves to escape the bombing. Literally known as the "cave people," they were reduced to eating rats, but surfaced when the siege finally ended on July 4 and Grant nearly received the "unconditional surrender" he had requested. Five days later Grant captured Port Hudson and the commerce of the Mississippi River belonged to the Union.

Today Vicksburg looks as if it's seen better days, but the people here practice Southern hospitality without thinking of it as a cliché.

On the Road in Vicksburg

Vicksburg is the perfect-sized riding and walking town. Park in the historic downtown district and you can hoof it nearly anywhere. When you want to ride, saddle up and head out for a great run through the military park. One nice thing about Vicksburg is that you can see most of it in a day and not feel you're missing too much.

To get an idea of what happened here in 1863, see *Vanishing Glory*, 3201 Clay St., which starts daily every hour on the hour; tickets cost $5. The slide show gives you an overview of the battle and prepares you for the **Vicksburg National Military Park,** 3201 Clay St., 601/636-0583, www.nps.gov/vick, open daily 8–5. To get there, head east on Clay Street (Highway 80) about 10 blocks and look for the plaques, markers, and cannons announcing it on your left.

In the visitors center, you can view an 18-minute film and exhibits on the "cave people," along with the usual collection of Civil War books (with an obvious emphasis on the heroic battles here). If your bike has a cassette player, invest in a taped tour that will fill in the blanks as you ride.

The roughly circular road passes 1,300 monuments, of which the Illinois Monument is most impressive. To avoid glorifying the war, the memorial's builders created a model of Rome's Pantheon and inside listed the names of the Union soldiers who died here.

In light of what happened on these grounds, it seems sacrilegious to tell you this is a great motorcycle road, with nice twists and dynamite blacktop single lanes, but it is. Now back to the war. At the *Cairo,* you'll see the remnants of the Union ironclad sunk in 1862 and raised 100 years later. Next door, within the 40-acre cemetery are the burial sites of 17,000 Union soldiers who were reburied here with honor after the war. The Confederate dead rest in a city cemetery.

If you're a Civil War buff, continue the ride and return to the entrance; otherwise, from the cemetery, you can skip out a side exit and return to town. It should be lunchtime now, and there's only one place to eat.

Walnut Hills, 1214 Adams St., 601/638-4910, www.walnuthillsms.com, serving lunch and dinner, is like Mrs. Wilkes's in Savannah. Settle down at a round table where a lazy Susan the size of a satellite dish holds the finest in road food: fried chicken, rice and gravy, fried corn, purple hull peas, green beans, mustard greens, okra, coleslaw . . . It's good eating, but you'll have to remember to adjust your bike's springs afterward.

Downtown lies just a few blocks away, but ride over to the **Old Courthouse,** 1008 Cherry St., 601/636-0741, www.oldcourthouse.org. For $3 you'll see exhibits that cover the Civil War and more, since locals contributed a lot from personal collections. The most disturbing artifact is from an administrator's sale on December 29, 1842: "Selling church pew, town lot, and at the same time and place, selling 160 Negroes consisting of men, women and children. Also horses and mules." Incredible.

Humanity got its turn in the Vicksburg newspaper that taunted the seemingly impotent General Grant. On July 2, the paper claimed he'd never take over the city. Two days later, Grant and his Union troops were in town and released the suspended paper, having added their own editorial advising the Rebels to respect their Yankee guests.

After you reach Washington Street, take about an hour to drop in at places like the Corner Drug Store (see below), then stick around. The beautiful Mississippi River is calming, and places to socialize at night are few. Besides, why should you be in a hurry to leave? This is an adventure.

Pull it Over: Vicksburg Highlights
Attractions and Adventures

Joseph Gerache, proprietor of the **Corner Drug Store,** 1123 Washington St., 601/636-2756, is a born salesman and, according to his business card, also an apothecary, bon vivant, collector par excellence, entrepreneur, and raconteur avec savoir faire. He's also a collector. His drugstore is crammed with moonshine whiskey jugs, Civil War shells, projectiles and cannonballs, rifles, shotguns, quack medical curiosities, and potions like Dr. Sanford's Liver Invigorator and Indian Chief Kidney and Liver Tonic.

Blue-Plate Specials

Inside a converted biscuit company, the aptly named **Biscuit Company,** 1100 Washington St., 601/631-0099, mixes Southern standards with creative dishes. Waitresses with accents as thick as molasses will tell you all about fried dill pickles, corn and crawfish chowder, shrimp and oyster po'boys. When you're done with dinner, belly up to one of several bars, shoot a game of pool, and listen to local blues bands. No set closing hours. The bar's open "until the last man falls."

Watering Holes

Like other towns along the Mississippi, Vicksburg has built casinos. If you like crowds and drinks and intrusive video game noises, waste your time at

Harrah's, 800/843-2343; **Ameristar,** 601/638-1000 or 800/700-7770; **Isle of Capri,** 800/946-4753; or **Rainbow,** 800/503-3777. Otherwise, settle down with some friendly locals back at Walnut Hills or the Biscuit Company.

Shut-Eye

Motels and Motor Courts
The **Battlefield Inn,** 4137 I-20 N. Frontage Road, 601/638-5811 or 800/359-9363, www.battlefieldinn.org, is a sure bet. Locally-owned, it offers a clean room, two free cocktails per person per night, and a full Southern breakfast for just $58–73. *That's* Southern hospitality.

Chain Drive*
A, C, E, G, I, Q, U, Z, CC

*Chain hotels in, or within ten miles of town. See cross-reference guide featuring phone numbers and web addresses on page 405.

Inn-Dependence
In Vicksburg, even prices at the fancy places are fairly reasonable. **The Corners,** 601 Klein St., 601/636-7421 or 800/444-7421, www.thecorners.com, lets you sleep in the main house or the former slave quarters for $90–130. Either is great, but the massive rooms on the top floor afford a great view of the Mississippi River.

Across the street, **Cedar Grove Mansion,** 2200 Oak St., 601/636-1000 or 800/862-1300, www.cedargroveinn.com, is *Gone-With-the-Wind* fancy, with sumptuous furnishings and a sprawling estate to calm you down. The dining room is usually packed with Vicksburg society, and the piano bar is a nice spot to sip a mint julep. If you stay the night, suh, the tariff ranges between $100–190.

On the Road: Vicksburg to New Orleans

Riding out of Vicksburg on Washington, watch for the Mississippi River Overlook, a quick stop where you can take a picture of you and your bike that'll stay on your desk for years. Follow Highway 61/I-20 to Exit 1B, which puts you back on 61 South toward Natchez. You'll notice a marked difference in this leg of the trip. Instead of fertile plains, the road is bordered by

These signs are posted at spots where riders get killed.

trees and gas stations, warehouses, and manufacturing plants. After about five miles the growth stops and the scenery changes to small houses, oak trees, and kudzu.

It's an uneventful ride to Port Gibson, the small town that Grant said "was too beautiful to burn." Once you hit the canopy of trees and see some of the antebellum homes of this true Southern town, you'll understand why Grant put the lighter away.

Two miles south of Port Gibson, watch for the entrance to the **Natchez Trace Parkway,** www.nps.gov/natr, on your right. The parkway began as a path used by animals and Native Americans and then, in the late 1700s, the way home for traders who had taken the Mississippi downstream but didn't have the muscle or machinery to get back. One of Franklin Roosevelt's public works projects, it doesn't match the Blue Ridge Parkway for beauty, but it's still nice to ride through the woods.

Expect lots of bikes on the road, mostly on weekends when local riders hit this for a good run. If you grew up in the South, you'll recognize the smell of these woods—as familiar to us as the scent of maple syrup to a Vermonter.

Every so often a pleasant field appears, and at Coles Creek, mile marker 17.5, there's a shaded picnic area and restrooms. Watch for the entrance to Emerald Mound, mile marker 10.3, the second-largest temple mound in America and worth a stop for the nice view from the top.

About two miles south of the mound, the parkway slides you back onto Highway 61 toward Natchez. This stretch is not nearly as scenic as what you left—it's just a collection of flea markets and radiator shops.

Follow the signs into the historic district and you'll be riding toward the Mississippi River. The overlook is as impressive as any I've seen; climb on top of a gazebo and you can look for miles upstream and down.

Natchez is a city where time seems to have stopped a few minutes before Lee surrendered at Appomattox. You get a sense of this at the **Visitors Reception Center,** 640 S. Canal, 601/446-6345 or 800/647-6724, www.natchez.ms.us, which provides an introductory movie ($2) and sponsors tours that drive past antebellum homes.

You'll find a slice of Americana in Natchez at a restaurant called **Mammy's Cupboard,** 555 Hwy. 61 S., 601/445-8957. Opened in 1940, the place fulfills every man's dream by ushering diners beneath the bustle of a 28-foot tall woman's skirt. The huge roadside art is funky, but hours are short: Open for lunch Tuesday–Saturday 11–2.

When you leave Natchez, Highway 61 returns to its slow and lonely character, getting narrower, shadier, and more verdant. There are few things to note here, although the razor wire atop the Wilkinson County Correctional Center looks beautiful in the last rays of daylight.

With little else to see, settle in and enjoy the ride. At the junction of 61 and 24 in Woodville, there are three gas stations and a grocery store, but not much to the town.

A few miles south puts you in Louisiana; the road becomes nicer, offering wide pullouts and more forest. Within minutes you'll reach St. Francisville— where I'd recommend that you just follow the signs to the historic district. One of those towns where everything seems to be just right, it's a perfect place to ride your bike and get lost in neighborhoods. The streets are wide; the homes are pretty; and outdoor cafés coax you to stop. Take advantage of the opportunity because after this, when you get back on Highway 61, the road begins to fizzle out as you approach Baton Rouge.

I try desperately to keep you off the interstates, and I seek spiritual and psychological counseling when I fail. I needed therapy for this next recommendation: Because Baton Rouge is a mess of urban hillbilly density, it's far easier to detour onto I-110 to I-10 for the final leg into New Orleans.

It's not really a bad ride, although traffic begins to build about 10 miles outside the city. Stick with it and in a few minutes, *laissez les bons temps rouler!*

New Orleans Primer

Early New Orleans must have been a pretty amazing place. Why else would colonists—English, French, and German citizens, political exiles, and criminals—

stick around despite storms, yellow fever, insects, snakes, alligators, and flooding? Even if I lived in Monte Carlo, I'd pack it up after the first chigger bite.

The reason most stayed is because they had been duped into coming here and didn't have a way back. The French later improved conditions with lavish displays of wealth (coupled with corruption and graft), and the city's notorious reputation for decadence and immorality increased.

Things got even more confusing in 1763. A war treaty forced France to surrender everything east of the Mississippi River to the English, but King Louis XV had already given New Orleans to Spain on the sly. The Spanish arrived; the early French settlers (Creoles) rebelled and were defeated; the Spanish thrived. The Creoles stuck to their language and social customs and later convinced Napoleon to regain their city. He did, but then he sold it to Thomas Jefferson through the Louisiana Purchase in 1803.

There you have it. New Orleans is populated with the ghosts of French settlers, Spanish explorers, British soldiers, African slaves, and Caribbean immigrants, as well as modern-day hustlers, gamblers, artists, musicians, dancers, and riverboat captains who wring maximum pleasure out of each day.

On the Road in New Orleans

While Memphis rocks, New Orleans jazzes things up. You'll hear jazz played in the streets and in the clubs and in courtyards and at funerals. It is everywhere, all the time—like Muzak, but good.

Unfortunately, New Orleans is not a riding town. Park your bike (and lock it), then take tours of the French Quarter and the Garden District to get an overview of the city before you descend into it alone later or the following day. I've had good luck with Gray Line Tours in several cities, and this is another one.

The town is far too large for me to cover in depth here. If you want to delve deep into it, stay a week and invest in volumes of travel guides. For now, I can only suggest an approach to the French Quarter.

Start early. Very. Hitting the streets by 7 A.M. gives you control of the city before the buses arrive. You'll actually find a seat at the **Cafe DuMonde,** 813 Decatur St., 504/587-0833, www.cafedumonde.com, which is open 24 hours a day. It's been here since 1862 and as more than a century of customers can attest, it's the place to relax over a café au lait and hot beignet. Wipe the sugar off your lips and head a few blocks east to the **French Market,** 504/522-2621, www.frenchmarket.com. More than 200 years old, this is where you shop for essentials: turtle shells, gator on a stick, dried snakes, voodoo potions. . . Unfortunately, a lot of crappy new stuff has crept into the market as well.

Double back to Jackson Square (across from the Cafe DuMonde). The **French Quarter Hospitality Center,** 529 St. Ann St., 504/566-5031, on the south side of the square, is the place to load up on literature and maps. Take a break in Jackson Square and watch artists, street performers, and musicians set up on the sidewalks as the morning progresses. Or take off into the French Quarter and let yourself go. Go anywhere and see everything you can in this 90-square-block historic district, keeping in mind that Chartres, Dauphne, and Royal Streets are longer (hence more diverse) than other avenues in the area.

The French Quarter represents the third try at establishing the city—fires in 1788 and 1794 razed the original buildings. Although it attracts tourists, it isn't solely a tourist attraction. More than 7,000 people live and work here, and the Vieux Carré Commission keeps tabs on preserving the architecture. You'll pass antique galleries, private apartments, guest houses, gift shops, cheap dives, legendary nightclubs and restaurants, con men, pickpockets, and prostitutes. Watch your wallet, chief. And your zipper.

When you return here after dark, Bourbon Street, like Memphis's Beale Street, is a different world. Fats Domino, Irma Thomas, Wynton Marsalis, and Harry Connick Jr. all call New Orleans home, and there's always a chance of hearing them at a local club if you know where to look. Tipitina's, perhaps best known for appearances by the Neville Brothers, serves up live R&B, jazz, Cajun, reggae, and rock seven days a week. The most famous jazz venue of all, however, **Preservation Hall,** 726 St. Peter St., 504/522-2841, www.preservationhall.com, strikes up late-night jam sessions in a crowded, poorly lit room where you can dig an ever-changing ensemble of genuine jazz masters. Open nightly 8–midnight, Preservation charges a $5 cover.

Beyond this, experience, more than words, describes the area best. If you're ready to get looped, you're in luck. With no closing laws, bars can stay open night and day—a distinction that may explain why New Orleans has the third-highest alcohol consumption rate in America.

Pull it Over: New Orleans Highlights
Attractions and Adventures

In a macabre mood? A high water table necessitated Lestat-of-the-art above-ground tombs, which are often elaborate, highly photogenic, and historically informative. Half museum, half mausoleum, the city's 42 bone orchards include several historic cities of the dead: Greenwood, Oddfellows Rest, St. Louis Number One and Number Two, and Cypress Grove. You can invest in a guided tour (recommended) or pick up a brochure with cemetery locations at the

Jackson Square Louisiana Visitors Center or at the **New Orleans Visitors Center** at 529 St. Ann Street, 504/568-5661. The www.visitneworleans.com.

Burial may be an art form in New Orleans, but so is living it up. Blaine Kern, known in New Orleans as "Mr. Mardi Gras," has filled a cluster of warehouses with colorful giant heads, floats, and figures to create a photographer's playground. Across the river in Algiers at **Blaine Kern's Mardi Gras World,** 233 Newton St., 504/361-7821 or 800/362-8213, www.mardigrasworld.com, learn the origins of Mardi Gras, how a Krewe commissions a float, and the safest way to pick up a doubloon (step on it first to avoid broken fingers). Park your bike here and you've got some big-headed backdrops. Admission is $13.50. To get here, you can scam a free 30-minute Mississippi River excursion by hopping aboard the Canal Street Ferry, located next to the New Orleans Aquarium near Jackson Square.

Gray Line Tours, 504/569-1401 or 800/535-7786, www.graylinenew orleans.com, offers tours of nearly every area: French Quarter, Garden District, cemeteries, swamps and bayous, and river cruises. Note that walking tours (starting at $18) will be cheaper than van tours.

In addition to Gray Line's, outside the city several swamp tours are available. The trick here is finding a certified Cajun who can make your trip the difference between an adventure and a travelogue at the senior center. Out in Westwego, about 20 minutes southwest of the city, Captain Jerome V. Dupré of **Chacahoula Swamp Tours,** 504/436-2640, is the real deal—a Cajun whose ancestors arrived in the Louisiana wetlands in 1785. Dressed in faded overalls and a shapeless coonskin hat, Dupré loves the swamps and you'll like him. Tours run $22.

The *Higgins Boat,* the landing craft developed by New Orleanian Andrew Higgins to get soldiers ashore on D-Day, sparked historian Stephen Ambrose's desire to create the **National D-Day Museum,** 923 Magazine St., 504/527-6012. www.ddaymuseum.org. A wealth of WWII memorabilia, oral histories from the men who were there and at Iwo Jima and other battles, and an Academy Award–winning film, *D-Day Remembered,* make this a historically vital stop. Admission is $7.

Shopping

Shop 'til you drop on **Magazine Street,** 504/897-6915 or 800/828-2311, a six-mile stretch of antiques shops, java huts, galleries, bakeries, bistros, book shops, health food stores, music shops, newsstands, pawnshops, and secondhand stores. Considered the "Antique Attic of New Orleans," as one shopkeeper puts it, "If you can't find it on Magazine Street, you can't find it anywhere."

Blue-Plate Specials

In Creole cooking, most meals include oysters, redfish, flounder, crawfish ("mudbugs"), catfish, snapper, crab, shrimp, spices, or jambalaya—a stew-like mix of tomatoes, rice, ham, shrimp, chicken, celery, onions, and seasonings. Po' boys are crispy sandwiches stuffed with fried oysters, roast beef, softshell crabs, or other ingredients. Gumbo is a thick soup prepared with chicken, shrimp, okra, or anything else. New Orleans boasts hundreds of great restaurants, so consider those listed below a very limited endorsement.

A cheap place to snag chicken andouille gumbo and hot french bread, the **Gumbo Shop,** 630 St. Peters St., 504/525-1486, serves traditional Creole cuisine for lunch and dinner.

Ralph Brennan's Red Fish Grill, 115 Bourbon St., 504/598-1200, is a casual seafood restaurant in the heart of the French Quarter. After sampling the BBQ shrimp po'boy and sweet potato catfish, check out the oyster bar. Then have another po' boy.

Croissant d'Or, 617 Ursulines, 504/524-4663, is a little hole in the wall, but popular with locals who drop in for a quick sandwich or pastry, or to hang out on the patio. A good place to stop if you're on the run—or want to keep lunch under five bucks.

Camellia Grill, 626 S. Carrollton Ave., 504/866-9573, a local diner famous for its breakfasts and pecan waffles, opened its doors in 1946. At lunch, burgers are big and messy, and at dinner the specials always change. For insomniacs, it's one of the Big Easy's popular night dining destinations.

Watering Holes

New Orleans has more clubs than a deck of cards. Here are a few—but not the only ones—to hit. **Johnny White's Bar,** 733 St. Peter St., 504/523-0839, is a bar for riders, as evidenced by the line of bikes in the street. It's been open since 1967—never closing and still cranking 24 hours a day. Hang out at the back bar, which was salvaged from an old whorehouse.

At **Pat O'Brien's,** 718 St. Peter St., 504/525-4823 or 800/597-4823, www.patobriens.com, here since 1933, you'll be hanging out with frat boys and conventioneers, but when you're nice and looped, you'll all join in a sing-along on the dueling piano patio bar. Then again, you can just chill out with a Hurricane by the flaming fountain. No cover, no time.

What can a nationally known act do for a club? When it was the Neville Brothers or Professor Longhair, it could make the place a hot spot. They did it here, and in addition to its original location, **Tipitina's,** 501 Napoleon Ave., 504/895-8477, www.tipitinas.com, has two other clubs in New Orleans, with live music every night, ranging from blues to rock, jazz to Cajun/Zydeco. Cover charge varies.

Shut-Eye

Major hotel chains are represented throughout New Orleans, although staying in a Garden District bed-and-breakfast can be a more memorable experience. A reservation service can save you time and money. For inns, try **Bed and Breakfast Access,** 888/766-6707, www.bnbaccess.com, which represents about 20 locals inns, or **Bed & Breakfast, Inc.** at 800/729-4640, www.historiclodging.com, which can point you to about 30 local bed-and-breakfasts. For hotels, try **French Quarter Hotel Reservations,** 877/728-2274, www.bigeasy.com, which has prices and info for more than 75 downtown hotels. There's also a nationwide service at 800/964-6835 that can work a deal for you. Each of these services can find you rooms cheaper than you'd find by yourself.

Chain Drive*
A, B, C, D, E, F, G, H, I, J, K, L, N, O, P, Q, S, T, U, V, X, AA, BB, CC, DD

*Chain hotels in, or within ten miles of town. See cross-reference guide featuring phone numbers and web addresses on page 405.

Inn-Dependence
A nice, quiet retreat, the **Beau Sejour,** 1930 Napoleon Ave., 504/897-3746 or 888/897-9398, www.beausejourbandb.com, has a tropical setting matched by Southern hospitality. Kim and Gil Gagnon's home is in a great neighborhood near the St. Charles streetcar. Rooms are actually suites, with rates from $120–180.

Indulgences

It's a ride out of town into a part of Louisiana that conjures *Deliverance,* but if you want to witness a different culture, stay the night in a plantation out by the bayous. Keep in mind that most are located far out in the country, so stock up on food and gas and definitely stay off these unmarked roads after dark. **Tezcuco,** 3138 Hwy. 44, Darrow, 225/562-3929, www.tezcuco.com, which ironically means "Resting Place," is a rather small plantation, built in 1855.

Options include sleeping in what were once slave quarters or living it up in the main house, where you can rent the entire upper floor. Rates run $65–165. Nearby **Nottoway Plantation,** 160 W. River Rd., White Castle, 225/545-2730, www.nottoway.com, billed as the largest in the South, was a 7,000-acre sugar plantation for years after its completion in 1859. For $125–250, you can stay in a spacious main house suite or the rustic outbuildings. The most elaborate plantation is **Oak Alley,** 3645 LA 18, Vacherie, 225/265-2151 or 800/463-7140 www.oakalleyplantation.com, where the entrance is lined with 28 ancient oaks. Although the main house is unavailable to guests, the fully equipped cottages ($105–135) are delightful, and the toasty breakfast beignets are the best.

Related Side Trips

Arkansas; Louisiana; Mississippi; Tennessee

Contributed by Darryl M. Lodato

Arkansas

Highways 7, 62, 23

Eureka Springs, Arkansas

One of the 10 best rides in the nation, Highway 7 cuts a sinuous swath through the rugged mountains and remote backcountry that characterize the Ozarks. Turning west on 62, you'll reach historic Eureka Springs. Founded in the 1800s as a resort, it retains its European character with restored hotel-spas and turn-of-the-century architecture along steep, narrow streets. A southward departure on 23 returns you to a roller-coaster ride through the ancient Ozarks.

Louisiana

Highways 31, 182

Breaux Bridge, St. Martinville, Louisiana

Come on don to de baYO, cher, and pass a good time! In bayou country, start just east of Lafayette in Breaux Bridge on Highway 31. Fill your tank with Crawfish Etouffee at Mulate's, then work it off by doing a Cajun two-step to Beau Soilleau's fiddle. Follow Highway 182 South along Bayou Teche's curvaceous banks, moss-covered live oaks, and magnificent plantation homes.

Mississippi

Highway 35, Natchez Trace Parkway

Sturgis, Mississippi

With no commercial traffic on Natchez Trace Parkway, you can enjoy a leisurely ride through Mississippi. Veer east on Highway 12 near Kosciusko and head into Sturgis, a quaint town and unlikely home to Benchmark Works, a vintage BMW motorcycle museum that you do not want to miss.

Tennessee

Highways 165, 143, Cherohala Skyway

Telico Plains, Tennessee

Take Highway 165 out of town as it follows along the Telico River then ascends to meet Highway 143, becoming the truly awesome Cherohala Skyway. At an elevation averaging more than 4,000 feet, this flawless, serpentine roadway crosses and sweeps around rocky summits for more than 45 miles. It offers breathtaking vistas of the Nantahala and Cherokee National Forests.

Foothills Parkway, Highway 129

Tennessee (just north of Deal's Gap)

A relatively obscure scenic roadway, the Foothills Parkway follows part of the western border of the Great Smoky Mountain Park. This road is a great place for higher speed sport-touring, presenting a series of sweeping turns that twist, dip, and ascend through the mountains. In the fall, the mountainsides are ablaze with color.

Resources for Riders

Blues Cruise

Tennessee Travel Information
Tennessee Department of Tourism—615/741-8299 or 800/462-8366,
www.state.tn.us/tourdev
Tennessee Road Conditions—800/858-6349
Tennessee State Parks—888/867-2757, www.tnstateparks.com
Tennessee Weather Conditions (Memphis)—901/544-0399
Tennessee B&B Innkeepers—800/820-8144, www.tennessee-inns.com

Mississippi Travel Information
Mississippi Department of Tourism—800/927-6378,
www.visitmississippi.org
Mississippi Road Conditions—601/987-1212
Mississippi State Parks—800/467-2757, www.mdwfp.com
Mississippi B&B Association—601/638-8893, www.missbab.com

Louisiana Travel Information
Louisiana Office of Tourism—225/342-8119, www.louisianatravel.com
Louisiana Road Conditions—985/379-1541
Louisiana State Parks—225/342-8111 or 888/677-1400, www.la.state.parks.com
Professional Innkeepers Association of New Orleans—www.bbnola.com

Local and Regional Information
Memphis Visitors Bureau—901/543-5300 or 800/873-6282,
www.memphistravel.com
New Orleans Visitors Information—504/246-5666 or 800/672-6124,
www.neworleanscvb.com
Vicksburg Visitors Bureau—601/636-9421 or 800/221-3536,
www.vicksburgcvb.org

Tennessee Motorcycle Shops
Al's Cycle Shop—3155 Summer Ave., Memphis, 901/324-3767,
www.alscycle.com
Bellevue Suzuki-Kawasaki—2319 Elvis Presley Blvd., Memphis, 901/774-1870
Bob's Honda-Yamaha—3270 Elvis Presley Blvd., Memphis, 901/346-1126,
www.motorsportsinc.net
Bumpus Harley-Davidson—2160 Whitten Road, Memphis, 901/372-1121,
www.bumpusharleydavidson.com
Super Cycle—624 S. Bellevue Blvd., Memphis, 901/725-5991

Mississippi Motorcycle Shops
Cycle Service Plus—2607 E. Hwy. 80, Pearl, 601/939-5077
Harley-Davidson of Jackson—3509 I-55 S., Jackson, 601/372-5770

Jackson Honda-Yamaha—113 Briarwood Dr., Jackson, 601/362-6492
Sevier's Outdoors (Honda-Yamaha) —580 Hwy. 27, Vicksburg,
    601/636-2722
Vicksburg Kawasaki-Suzuki—1670 Hwy. 61 N., Vicksburg, 601/630-9490

Louisiana Motorcycle Shops
Boyce Honda—3011 N. I-10 Service Rd., Metairie, 504/837-6100
Cycle Center—3011 Loyola Dr., Kenner, 504/461-0011
Harley-Davidson of New Orleans—1208 Lafayette St., Gretna,
    504/362-4004, www.hdno.com

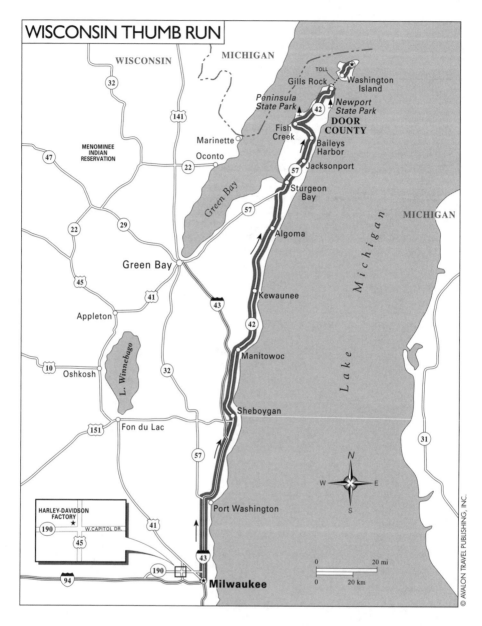

Route: Milwaukee to Door County via Port Washington, Sheboygan, Manitowoc, Two Rivers

Distance: Approximately 175 miles; consider four days with stops.
  • Day 1—Milwaukee • Day 2—Milwaukee/Travel • Days 3 & 4—Door County

First Leg: Milwaukee to Fish Creek (175 miles)

Helmet Laws: Wisconsin does not require helmets.

Wisconsin Thumb Run

Milwaukee to Door County, Wisconsin

Milwaukee makes a rough start to this run, but if you ride a Harley and don't come here, you'll have hell to pay at your next poker run, since this is where Harley-Davidson was born and reborn. As you follow the curve of Lake Michigan, you'll escape the din of the city and find yourself in a European slice of America. Bear in mind that Wisconsin weather (especially on the northern peninsula) can change quickly—even in summer. Pack for two seasons.

Milwaukee Primer

Bratwurst. Beer. Baseball. Blue-collar workers. Most Americans have a pretty good idea what makes Milwaukee tick. We learned about it by watching beer commercials, face-painting cheeseheads, and Fonzie on TV.

But the 611,000-plus citizens here don't see themselves as beer-guzzling Norwegian-, German-, and Polish-Americans. They see their city as a smaller, friendlier version of Chicago, and their museums, galleries, and ethnic festivals as proof that they are, in fact, patrons of the arts and a people proud of their cultural diversity.

This all may be true, but chances are you won't appreciate any of it. You'll be here just long enough to see a brewery, catch a ball game, eat some bratwurst, and go watch the blue-collar workers stick a hydraulic lifter on a new Harley engine.

Dat's a purdy good day dere den, eh?

On the Road in Milwaukee

It's hard to find a great ride inside a metropolitan area, but in exotic cities like Miami and Las Vegas, you just have to go for it. Milwaukee certainly isn't exotic, but an act of Congress mandates it as a stop for Harley riders.

Despite the interstates and some less than attractive neighborhoods, it's fairly easy to get around on your bike and see a few sights. If you truly detest city riding, blow out of town before nightfall to more peaceful environs.

Either way, the day should begin in the suburb of Wauwatosa with a free tour of **Harley-Davidson's Capitol Drive Powertrain Operations,** 11700 W. Capitol Dr., 414/535-3666 or 800/621-2034. Sportster and Buell engines take shape here (the new V-Rod comes out of Kansas City). Tour days and times vary greatly by season; call in advance. Take I-94 west out of town and turn north onto I-45. There are no directional signs to the plant, so watch for Capitol Drive, where you exit, then double back beneath the overpass. The factory entrance is on your right.

Although they claim there's a museum here, in reality there are just a few bikes, signage, and archival pictures. Under discussion are a $30-million museum complex, café, and rally park to be situated downtown. Until that appears, satisfy yourself with the 14-inch Hamilton lathe, "the oldest existing asset in powertrain operations." To its credit, the "museum" does spark intrigue through diagrams showing the hundreds of parts (hydraulic lifters and guides, cylinder push rods, cams, oil pump, rocker pump, connector rod, etc.) designed to create motion out of fuel and air, "a chrome and black miracle."

See displays of flatheads, panheads, knuckleheads, and shovelheads, as well as H-D photos and memorabilia solicited for the archives. And you know how H-D merchandise is as scarce as Starbucks coffee? Well, the folks here thoughtfully sell pens, T-shirts, mugs, bandanas, and caps.

Even though the final product takes shape in York, Pennsylvania (see pages 117–118) and the Twin Cam 88 engines are made eight miles north on Pilgrim Road, the XL engines for H-D and Buell are born here. The hour-long tours, which fill up quickly, begin with a 10-minute video explaining the origins, history, and future plans of the company. After the video, you'll don safety glasses and headphones for a tour of the factory floor, individual work stations, and the Genuine Parts Manufacturing plant, which produces more than 1,300 parts for older Harleys (including a kick starter for a 1916 model).

Both the gifted mechanic and the mechanically illiterate will be impressed by the detail and ingenuity displayed here. My toolkit consists of a hammer and a spoon, so it floors me that early machinists, without the benefit of a computer, could create anything that moved, but they did.

When you leave H-D (with a few component pieces shoved down your trousers), you may be inspired to see what else Milwaukee's known for: breweries. About 80 of them were here in the 1880s, but most have faded away. For a visit to a macrobrewery, ride over to the **Miller Brewing Company,** 4251 W. State St., 414/931-2337, www.millerbrewing.com. The free 50-minute tour (hours vary; call ahead) includes a walk through the packaging line and shipping centers, brew house, museum, and historic caves. Memories should come flooding back of your college party days, if you and your buddies ever ponied up enough cash for a half million cases of beer, that is. Yes, a *half million cases* are stacked in the shipping center. There are also giant brew kettles, high-speed bottling lines, and best of all, free frosty samples served at the Miller Inn.

Milwaukee hasn't forgotten its brewing roots, and microbrewery tours are equally popular. Opened in 1985, **Sprecher Brewery,** 701 W. Glendale Ave., 414/964-2739, www.sprecherbrewery.com, has one of the more popular tours. Located five miles north of downtown, they brew traditional beers and gourmet sodas and wrap up their tours with samples of any 14 beers (Black Bavarian, Pub Brown Ale, Irish Stout, Russian Imperial Stout . . .) served amidst oompah music in an indoor Oktoberfest-style beer garden tent. Tour times vary, so call in advance for reservations. The $2 admission goes to charity.

Opened in 1987 with a total output of 60 barrels, the **Lakefront Brewery,** 1872 N. Commerce St., 414/372-8800, www.lakefrontbrewery.com, now cranks out handcrafted beer in traditional and innovative styles. Depending on the season they brew up pilsners, stein beer, cherry beer, pumpkin beer, ales, coffee stout, and root beer. Tours are Fridays at 3 P.M., and Saturday at 1, 2, and 3 P.M. Admission is $3.

Provided you're not looped by now, wrap up the day the way the locals do: digging into a bratwurst, sitting in the stands at a game, hanging out in the historic Third Ward or on Water Street . . . or dancing a polka at an ethnic fest.

Pull it Over: Milwaukee Highlights
Attractions and Adventures

Milwaukee is a fascinatingly diverse city. If you visit nearly any time between June and September, you're sure to hit one of the several massive ethnic festivals, 414/273-3378 or 800/273-3378, www.summerfest.com, that take place at the lakefront Henry W. Maier Park. Each fest revels in the music, games, and foods of a foreign land: Asia, Mexico, Germany, Ireland, Africa, Poland, Italy . . . The biggest blowout of all is Summerfest, the largest musical festival in the world, with national acts appearing on a dozen stages.

In this town, the most popular outdoor activity is watching one of several professional teams. If you ride in on game day, you may want to join the fans of the **Milwaukee Brewers** (baseball), 414/902-4000 or 800/933-7890, www.milwaukee brewers.com. Tickets range from $5–35. The **Milwaukee Bucks** basketball team are at 414/227-0500, www.bucks.com, and you can go puck yourself at a **Milwaukee Admirals** hockey game, 414/227-0550, www.milwaukeeadmirals.com.

Hungry after the game? Swing by **Usinger's Famous Sausage,** 1030 N. Old World 3rd St., 414/276-9100, to buy a string of meat shoved in a thin, edible sheath. Mmmmm, boy! Cranking out the meat since 1880, Usinger's boasts more than 75 varieties sold in its turn-of-the-century store.

Blue-Plate Specials

Harley isn't the only Milwaukee institution. According to Glenn Fieber, stepson of the original Solly, "people from all over, everywhere" check into **Solly's Coffee Shop,** 4629 N. Port Washington Rd., 414/332-8808, before checking into their hotels. Since 1936, locals and savvy travelers have been settling in at Solly's twin horseshoe counters, where Milwaukee waitresses serve up hearty breakfasts, buttery sirloin burgers, and hand-scooped malts served in the steel can.

The oldest lunch counter in Milwaukee is at **Real Chili,** 1625 W. Wells St., 414/342-6955. This independent purveyor of chili has been here since 1931, serving celebrities, pro ball players, politicians, and on-the-road travelers. Subs, tacos, chili dogs, and chili served over spaghetti and beans come in mild, medium, and hot. If you need a beer to take the sting out, head to their second location at 419 East Wells Street.

In the heart of downtown on the revitalized Riverwalk, **Rock Bottom,** 740 N. Plankinton Ave., 414/276-3030, is a hoppin' spot, especially on the waterside patio where most people dine during good weather. Open for lunch and dinner, it's a good place to hang out, and their five microbrews, brick oven pizzas, prime top sirloin, pork chops, and short ribs put it over the top—although the setting edges out the food.

Watering Holes

Milwaukee's too large a city to ride around looking for a place to party, so you might want to settle down near the greatest concentration of nightspots.

Along Water Street, between State and Knapp, you'll find a number of worthy choices. This is the short list; the **Water Street Tavern Association,** www.onwaterstreet.com, represents fourteen pubs, bars, taverns, and wing joints.

Water Street Brewery, 1101 N. Water St., 414/272-1195, www.waterstreet brewery.com, is a pub-style micro that serves eight varieties of its own brews plus an assortment of other micros. In addition to beer, they serve an extensive menu of fish steaks, ribs, pizza, nachos, and other bar food. A big screen TV comes out for big sports events.

McGillycuddy's, 1135 N. Water St., 414/278-8888, www.onwaterstreet.com, is the largest pub on the block. They combine the best elements of an Irish pub with an American sports bar, serving Guinness on tap, other Brit ales, and Irish stew. Order a mug and settle down on the huge patio.

Flannery's Bar, 425 E. Wells St., 414/278-8586, www.flannerysmilwaukee .com, has live jazz and blues and makes it all sound better by serving $2.50 pints of Guinness, Harp, Bass, and Foster's until midnight.

Looking like a gentlemen's club, the **Oak Barrel,** 1211 N. Water St., 414/224-0535, features single malt scotches, double barrel bourbons, imported beers, and microbrews.

Shut-Eye

Motels and Motor Courts
Although it's not a motel, the **Hotel Wisconsin,** 720 N. Old World 3rd St., 414/271-4900, is priced like one. Located in the heart of the downtown district, rates range from $69 during pre-summer to $79 in May to a still reasonable $89 in high summer season. Opened in 1913, the Victorian hotel has rich woods, plaster medallions, in-room fridges, and large rooms.

Also downtown is the **Astor Hotel,** 924 E. Juneau Ave., 414/271-4220 or 800/558-0200, www.theastorhotel.com. The Astor is one of two buildings in Milwaukee still remaining that were designed to serve as apartment house/transient hotel room combinations. Rates range from $89 prior to the season to $99 for the same room at the height of summer.

Chain Drive*
A, B, C, D, E, G, H, J, L, Q, T, U, W, X, CC

*Chain hotels in, or within ten miles of town. See cross-reference guide featuring phone numbers and web addresses on page 405.

Indulgences

In historic old cities like Milwaukee, Gilded Age hotels are plentiful. If your life has been leading to a Harley tour and you really want to live it up, the **Pfister Hotel,** 424 E. Wisconsin, 414/271-8222 or 800/558-8222, www.the pfisterhotel.com, has been a local legend since it opened in 1893. The lobby is elegant and the rooms follow suit—celebs and sports stars stay here when they're in town. Peak summer rates start at $264.

On the Road: Milwaukee to Door County

Considering from whence you came, you'll be amazed that a single tank of gas can deliver you to such a bucolic setting. Leaving on I-43 North, it takes about 10 miles to shake the Milwaukee dirt off your boots. There's not much between Milwaukee and Exit 306, which you should take east to reach Route 32 for a four-mile run to Port Washington.

There's no reason to stay very long, but the harbor is picture-perfect and Franklin Street features blocks of interesting stores on the shores of Lake Michigan. It'll take about an hour, slightly longer if you drop in at **Harry's Restaurant,** 128 N. Franklin St., 262/284-2861, which serves breakfast, lunch, and dinner. Here since the '50s, this is where most travelers stop for home-cooked hot beef sandwiches, mashed potatoes, chicken and rice soup, pork chop sandwiches, and lake perch. Up the street, **Port Antiques,** 314 N. Franklin St., 262/284-5520, open daily 10–5, carries a strong collection of nautical antiques, hunting and fishing pieces, and 19th-century matted maps.

When you leave Port Washington, follow the lakeshore north and return to I-43 for an uneventful ride to Exit 120 for Highway OK (yes, it's literally "OK") toward Sheboygan. From here, you'll reach Highway LS, the lakeshore run that'll take you north. After a brief flirtation with farmland, you'll be in the city. It's a little hard to navigate here, so you may have to ask directions to 15th Avenue, which eventually turns to Highway LS north of town.

If you didn't eat at Harry's, when you reach the intersection of 15th and Geele, turn left and stop at the **Charcoal Inn,** 1637 Geele Ave., 920/458-1147, a corner diner where prices are as small as the dining room. A pork chop sandwich or bratwurst goes for $2.90, a chocolate sundae $1.25. Homemade soups and hand-dipped shakes round out the menu. Serves breakfast, lunch, and dinner.

After lunch, you'll make the great escape into Wisconsin farm country by taking LS North to Highway XX, where you'll turn right toward Manitowoc on Highway 42 and then on to Two Rivers. It was here in 1881 that Ed Berners, my nominee for a Nobel Prize in desserts, put chocolate sauce on a young girl's ice cream and the ice cream sundae was born.

The original site where the sundae was invented is long gone, but the historical society compensates with the **Washington House,** 1622 Jefferson St. (just a block off Hwy. 42), 920/793-2490. The restored saloon now houses Berners' Ice Cream Parlor, the town visitors center, and a museum. Docents claim the rare murals in the upstairs ballroom make it the "Sistine Chapel of Two Rivers." It's still early, but the Pope has yet to proclaim the Sistine Chapel the "Washington House of the Vatican."

This is the last gasp of city living you'll be subjected to since the road becomes even more placid as you ride through small villages like Kewaunee and Algoma and past longer and more luxurious expanses of Lake Michigan shoreline.

Following Algoma, Highway S takes you into dairy country for a gentle, easy ride straight to Sturgeon Bay, the portal to Door County. The combination of the fresh country air, reliable views of Lake Michigan, and the unhurried pace of it all is extremely satisfying, although you—like me—may be annoyed by other riders' lack of civility.

Whether it's the proliferation of Harleys, I'm not sure, but in Wisconsin, the part of riders' brains that controls basic motor skills (like waving) has atrophied. No matter how many times you wave, they will not wave back. Remember: Goofus never waves; Gallant always waves. Always.

You'll bypass Sturgeon Bay as you enter Door County, crossing a canal and then veering off to follow Highway 57 North on the eastern shoreline. It's a quieting ride as you pass through Jacksonport and work your way up to Baileys Harbor, where there are a few restaurants and the nice **Blacksmith Inn,** 8152 Hwy. 57, 920/839-9222 or 800/769-8619, www.blacksmithinn.com. With rates from $175–205, Blacksmith is expensive, but perfect if you don't want to be bothered by anything except a whirlpool tub, fireplace, CD, and TV/VCR.

I'd suggest pushing on to Fish Creek, which, judging from the proliferation of flowers, picket fences, and cottage shops, must have been the charm school valedictorian. From Baileys Harbor, turn west on Highway F and follow it past pristine farmland, cherry trees, and apple orchards until you roll into one of the most beautiful towns in Door County.

Door County Primer

This part of Wisconsin combines Cape Cod with the Berkshires. The "thumb" of the state is about 75 miles long and 10 miles wide, and its limestone base makes for fertile farmland. Door County produces 95 percent of Wisconsin's cherries and about 40 percent of its apple crop, giving the roads a pink and white hue when the blossoms spring to life.

Fish Creek, arguably the most popular destination on the peninsula, began with Asa Thorp, who arrived in 1854 to make his fortune. Building the first pier north of Green Bay, he began selling cordwood to fuel the steamers that plied Lake Michigan. Thorp increased his landholdings and then built a lodge for steamship passengers, charging $7.50 a week. When the Wisconsin legislature bought the land to create Peninsula State Park, the sawmills stopped, the small farms reverted to forests again, and tourism took the lead.

The nearby town of Ephraim was selected by *National Geographic* as one of the best small town escapes in America, the only Wisconsin town to win that recognition.

Which is the why you're here.

On the Road in Door County

The best part about basing yourself in Fish Creek is that you have easy access to most things worth seeing. Provided you were smart enough not to ride in peak tourist season, you're just a few minutes from peaceful country settings.

Point your bike in any direction, and a trace of your lost idealism will return. As you venture out in the countryside, you'll find that people here actually live on farms and actually make fresh foods. You'll see this as you pass signs tempting you with fresh fruit jams and jellies, cherries, applesauce, fish, fudge, cheese, milk, custard, and cakes.

It's easy to take a roughly circular ride around the county, but before leaving Fish Creek, wander around the village for a few hours. At the western tip of Main Street lies a small park offering an unobstructed view of Green Bay and its islands. Doubling back via Cottage Row and Spruce Street, you'll circle the block to arrive at a small marina. After that, drop in at any number of shops, many of which were converted from old motor courts.

When you do leave town via Highway 42 North, the first detour is at 3,700-acre **Peninsula State Park,** 920/868-3258, www.wiparks.net. After being cooped up for the winter, golfers tee up, couples kayak, and families bike and hike over every trail. Admission to the park costs $5—but it's free if you don't stop. I'm not talking about crashing the gate, I just mean there's an honor system and just not stopping as you ride through. Shore Road is fantastic for motorcycles, with small breaks in the tree line to expose the wide waters of Green Bay and provide you a place to pull over. Shore Road rolls by the 1868 Eagle Bluff Lighthouse and then Eagle Tower, a 75-foot observation

Kuralt: 1999 Buell Thunderbolt S3

"Kuralt"* for Wisconsin was the 1999 Buell Thunderbolt S3. After riding it for 450 miles, I'd suggest they re-christen this the "Teddy Roosevelt"—it is one rough rider. For those unfamiliar with the bike's pedigree, Erik Buell took a 101-horsepower, 1200cc Thunderstorm engine and mounted it on a sport-bike frame. It's fine at 50, rough at 60, and really rough at 70. Despite the saddlebags and small fairing, unless you're an aggressive 20-year-old who can handle the physical challenge, this isn't the bike for a long tour. For details on new Buell models, check www.buell.com.

*It was the travels of CBS correspondent Charles Kuralt that inspired me to explore America. I named each motorcycle I rode in his honor.

platform that offers a superb view of the park, bay, and neighboring villages. Don't be a wimp. It's worth the climb.

The road exits onto Highway 42 three miles north of Fish Creek, and simply by turning left, you'll be riding toward Door County's most picturesque town, Ephraim, founded in 1853 as a Moravian religious community. Today the steeples of Moravian and Lutheran churches reveal the town's spiritual values and love of natural beauty. Slow it down to take in all you see: handsome clapboard inns, sailboats at anchor, horse-drawn carriages, and white sand beach.

Though Ephraim has no true commercial district, everyone stops at **Wilson's Restaurant and Ice Cream Parlor,** 9990 Water St., 920/854-2041. You will, too. Here since 1906, the authentic family-owned diner serves fantastic hamburgers, soups, sandwiches, milkshakes, and sundaes (thanks, Ed Berners!). Don't miss this preserved look at Americana, and consider investing in the boat rental concessions across the street.

From Ephraim, follow Highway 42 to its northernmost point. The road is serene, traipsing through the villages of Sister Bay then Ellison Bay (check out the Pioneer Store) and past meadows and marshes to reach Gills Rock and its passenger ferry landing. You've reached the top of the thumb now, but if you continue riding east, 42 leads to one of the most incredible half-mile stretches of road I've seen. If you're riding in a group, get ready for some picture taking as you hit a winding, canopied road with some great moguls. The ride is as subtle as a Swiss cough drop, and you'll wish only for more land to keep the road going.

Alas, you've reached the end of the world. Here in Northport, the vehicle ferry is waiting if you'd like to leave the peninsula and sail north to **Washington Island,** 920/847-2546 or 800/223-2094, www.wisferry.com. On a motorcycle you'll pay $12 for the round trip ($8 for an extra passenger). Washington is the largest of Door County's islands and the oldest Icelandic community in the United States—but you knew that. Crossings of the "Straits of Death's Door" (named for the treacherous currents and unpredictable waves) are safer than in the early days, I think. When you reach the island, you'll find a pastoral setting, restaurants, shops, and more than 100 miles of country roads.

You'll have to backtrack on Highway 42 to head south, detouring onto Highway NP if you want to see the **Newport State Park U.S. Bird Refuge,** 920/854-2500, or are continuing to Ellison Bay. There, Mink River Road descends toward Rowley's Bay and Highway ZZ drops further south until it connects with Highway 57 and then Highway Q back down to Bailey's Harbor.

In other words, explore. When you're riding through Door County, there's no way to get lost.

And there's so much to find.

Pull it Over: Door County Highlights
Attractions and Adventures

In Door County, you're surrounded by water on three sides, which makes water sports the pastime. **Stiletto Catamaran Sailing Cruises,** South Shore Pier, Ephraim, 920/854-7245, www.stilettosailingcruises.com, offers seven sailings daily, with shorter cruises (75 minutes; $18.95) during the day and $25, two-hour sunset cruises. On a clear day, go for the sunset cruise—it's incredible.

If you don't see any ice floes, consider hitting the water. Boat rental rates at **South Shore Pier Boat Rentals,** Ephraim, 920/854-4324, range from $74 for two hours on a 21-foot deluxe pontoon boat to $261 for an all-day excursion on a 25-foot pontoon boat (gas extra). Split the cost with fellow riders and you've got your own sunset cruise. Traveling solo? Wave runners cost $65 per hour (gas included).

Hubbard Brothers Charters, 10919 Bay Shore Dr., Sister Bay, 920/854-2113, began as a family business in the 1920s and remains one of the more reasonably-priced fishing charters I've found. The $47 cost of the six-passenger charter includes a captain, poles, and tackle for a half-day excursion; you'll need to spring for the bait, refreshments, and fishing license ($10 for two days). Cash only, no cards. It's important to wear warm clothes and shoes, and know that these tough bastards don't cancel for rough seas, rains, or high winds. Say, you ever listened to "The Wreck of the Edmund Fitzgerald"?

the broad waters of Green Bay near the tip of the thumb in Door County, Wisconsin

© NANCY HOWELL

Like the Hubbard's, **Capt. Paul's Charter Fishing,** 921 Cottage Rd., Gills Rock, 920/854-4614, claims to be the longest-running charter in the state. Like the Hubbard's, this outfit offers four-hour trips in search of salmon and brown trout. The novelty here is that you are always fishing. Whenever someone snags a fish, you rotate to the next rod. The *Lady Linda,* a 32-footer, has a six-passenger capacity. Bait and tackle are included in the $58 fee; the fishing license is not.

Shake out your sea legs and head to the **American Folklore Theatre,** 920/854-6117, www.folkloretheatre.com, for an $11 evening performance held in Peninsula State Park's outdoor amphitheater. If you can endure the mosquitoes, you'll enjoy watching actors and musicians perform folk tales in a folksy setting—although the novelty can wear off before the last bow.

Shopping

Siobhan's, 9431 Spruce St., Fish Creek, 920/868-3353, is a small shop with some epicurean pleasures: a nice selection of California and European wines, as well as champagnes, liquors, cheeses, cognacs, and single malt scotches. A few cigars round out this small shop's inventory.

Blue-Plate Specials

As long as you're in Door County, you may want to invest your appetite in a fish boil (see sidebar on page 230 for a description of this culinary oddity). Several lodges, resorts, and restaurants host them, including: **Gordon Lodge,**

What the Bejeezus is a Fish Boil?

When I heard about the outbreak of fish boils in Door County, I placed a call to the surgeon general. Then someone put me wise. Fish boils are a staple of the Door County diet. Here's what happens, although I'm still not sure why:

Basically, it's a cookout. The process dates back to Scandinavian settlers and lumberjacks who tossed fresh whitefish into a pot of salted water, then added onions and potatoes, stacked flaming boards around the pot, and let the damn thing cook over a boiling fire. The same thing happens today at restaurants throughout Door County.

When everything is cooked to what people here call perfection, the chef completes the ritual. The pièce de résistance, the "boil over," comes when they toss kerosene over the flaming boards to spark a conflagration. This accomplishes multiple objectives: It boils the oils off the fish meat; it indicates that dinner is ready; and it singes the eyebrows off anyone who stood too close to the pot.

1420 Dr., Baileys Harbor, 920/839-2331; **Leathen Smith Lodge & Marina,** 1640 Memorial Rd., Sturgeon Bay, 920/743-5555; **Sandpiper Restaurant,** Hwy. 57, Baileys Harbor, 920/839-2528; **Square Rigger Galley,** 6332 Hwy. 57, Jacksonport, 920/823-2408; **Viking Grille,** 12029 Hwy. 42, Ellison Bay, 920/854-2998; **Wagon Trail Resort,** 1041 Hwy. ZZ, Ellison Bay, 920/854-2385; and **White Gull Inn,** 4225 Main St., Fish Creek, 920/868-3517.

For food that doesn't bubble up from a boiling cauldron of water, try breakfast, lunch, or dinner at **The Cookery,** Main St., Fish Creek, 920/868-3634, www.cookeryfishcreek.com., serving everything you want, done just right. Five breakfast specials start at $2.95. At dinnertime, they load you up on baked chicken, roast pork loin, stuffed pork chops, perch platters, and meat loaf.

Open for breakfast, lunch, and dinner, **Calamity Sam's,** Bluff Lane and Hwy. 42, Fish Creek, 920/868-2045, serves "real food for real people," such as $3.95 breakfast specials and big food dinner entrées like charbroiled pork chops, pot pies, turkey, chicken fried steak, fried chicken, meat loaf, and deep-fried catfish.

Watering Holes

Here since the 1930s, the **Bayside Tavern,** Main St., Fish Creek, 920/868-3441, is the only local hangout in town. It features a large curved bar, small tables, and the world-famous Bayside Coffee, a potent, flaming, liquor-filled concoction. For grub, sample Smiling Bob's Bar Room Chili. Bob whips up the spices at home and they're such a secret, even the cooks don't know the recipe.

Shut-Eye

If you travel in season, you would be foolish—yes, damn foolish—not to reserve a room in advance at one of Door County's many motels, hotels, condos, resorts, cabins, or campgrounds. For help finding one that fits your needs, call 800/527-3529 or www.doorcountyvacations.com

Motels and Motor Courts

Fish Creek Motel & Cottage, Fish Creek, 920/868-3448, www.fishcreek motel.com, is a combination of modern motel rooms and original rooms with soothing woodland views. Clean and neat, they promise "free bikes" but I'm certain they don't mean motorcycles.

The **Edgewater Cottages,** 4144 SR 42, Fish Creek, 920/868-3551, doesn't have much going for it in way of furnishings, but the log cabins and clapboard cottages are Bonnie-and-Clyde-hideout cool and provide a nice view of the cove. Quiet, comfortable, and some have kitchenettes.

Cedar Court, 9429 Cedar St., Fish Creek, 920/868-3361, gives you larger lodgings since this is really a compound with guest houses and a pool in back. One block from the bay and the shopping area, Cedar Court offers standard amenities in each room and whirlpool tubs in the choice ones. Off-season motel room rates start at $65 and go to $89 in season, with specialty rooms ranging from $98–128.

Indulgences

One place that fills up months in advance is the fabled **White Gull Inn,** 4225 Main St., Fish Creek, 920/868-3517, www.whitegullinn.com. Each room or suite ($115–250) has a porch or deck, fireplace, TV/VCR, and space to spread out. If you're riding with a group, their Lundberg Guest House ($310) sleeps eight. The inn also features a full restaurant.

A few miles away in Ephraim, the **Eagle Harbor Inn,** 9914 Water St., Ephraim, 920/854-2121 or 800/324-5427, www.eagleharbor.com, rests on five peaceful acres across from the bay. This quiet resort offers a complimentary breakfast and nice landscaping. Suites, which sleep up to six and go for

$165–199, have a whirlpool tub, fireplace, kitchen, CD/TV/VCR, and private deck. Room rates range from $89–149.

In the heart of the village, most rooms at the summers-only **Ephraim Inn,** 9994 Pioneer Ln., Ephraim, 920/854-4515, www.theephraiminn.com, afford great views of the harbor and tiered green bluffs. A continental breakfast is included in the $95–160 rate.

Related Side Trips

Wisconsin

Contributed by Sharon Haak

Wisconsin

Highway 171

Southwest Wisconsin

Head to Southwest Wisconsin and follow your nose. Tune into the fragrance of apple blossoms and it will lead you down Highway 171, a twisty, winding road that channels you through "apple orchard country." The blossoms bloom in spring, but the steep grades are year-round, with sharp twists and a 15-mph hairpin turn leading to the Kickapoo River.

Highway W

New Diggings General Store and Inn
Southwest Wisconsin

About 15 miles from Galena, Illinois, you'll find a funky store that opened for business back in '24. That's 1824. Hardly anything has changed since then. Hang out here on weekends in July and August and you can catch a free live concert.

Highway 60

Southwest Wisconsin

Between southwest Wisconsin's twin cities of Muscoda (pop. 1,287) and Gotham (pop. even less), Highway 60 bends and winds along with the banks of the beautiful Wisconsin River. It's a short run, but the canoe and cabin rentals invite you to stay a little longer, and you're never out of sight of the Wisconsin River and the eagles that nest along its banks.

Brewery Creek Inn

Mineral Point, Wisconsin

About 45 miles from Madison, you can reach historic Mineral Point via Highways 23 or 151. When you settle in at Brewery Creek, south of downtown, take in a pleasant slice of American touring: plank flooring and an oversized antique bar that sets the stage for a good homebrew.

Highway 35

Wooden Nickel
Ferryville, Wisconsin

A Mississippi River run heads up Highway 35 in Wisconsin. North of Prarie du Chien in Ferryville, the Wooden Nickel bar is decked out with thick, dark polished wood, and the tall round tables surrounding it are a welcome sight for riders. Order a brew (just one—you're riding) and treat yourself to the river's view and the best burgers between here and New Orleans.

Related Side Trips

Michigan

Contributed by Ken Gluckman

Michigan

Route 119

Perhaps the prettiest ride in Michigan's lower peninsula starts near the northern
tip in Harbor Springs. Route 119 North, along the shore of Lake Michigan,
curves through what locals call the "Tunnel of Trees." Take your time along the
waterfront and when you reach the end of 119 at Cross Village, stop for lunch
at the Legs Inn (www.legsinn.com), a quirky and unique restaurant.

Port Austin

Near Detroit, pick up Route 25 just north of Port Huron and follow it along the
shore to Port Austin. You've reached the "tip of the thumb" (Michigan's lower
peninsula is shaped like a mitten), a spot known for picturesque sunrises and
sunsets. Stay overnight in a motel or bed-and-breakfast and have dinner at the
Garfield Inn. Twice a day you can walk out on one of the piers and watch the
sun rise and set.

Resources for Riders
Wisconsin Thumb Run

Wisconsin Travel Information
Wisconsin Association of Campground Owners—970/725-9997 or
   608/429-3061
Wisconsin Department of Tourism—800/432-8747, www.travelwisconsin.com
Wisconsin Innkeepers Association—877/365-6994, www.lodging-wi.com
Wisconsin Road Conditions—800/762-3947
Wisconsin State Parks—608/266-2181, www.wiparks.net
Wisconsin State Parks Reservations—888/947-2757, www.reserveamerica.com

Local and Regional Information
Door County Chamber of Commerce—920/743-4456 or 800/527-3529,
   www.doorcountyvacations.com
Ephraim Information Center—920/854-4989, www.ephraim-doorcounty.com
Fish Creek Information Center—920/868-2316 or 800/577-1880
Greater Milwaukee Convention & Visitors Bureau—414/273-7222 or
   800/554-1448, www.milwaukee.org
Milwaukee Road Conditions—414/785-7140
Milwaukee Weather Information—414/744-8000 or 414/936-1212
Washington Island Chamber of Commerce—920/847-2179,
   www.washingtonislandwi.org

Motorcycle Shops
Hal's Harley-Davidson-Buell—1925 S. Mooreland Rd., New Berlin,
   262/782-1320, www.halshd.com
Corse's Superbikes—700 E. Milan, Saukville, 262/284-2725,
   www.corsessuperbikes.com
House of Harley-Davidson—6221 W. Layton Ave., Milwaukee, 414/282-2211,
   www.houseofharley.com
Milwaukee Harley-Davidson/Buell—11310 Silver Spring Dr., Milwaukee,
   414/461-4444, www.milwaukeeharley.com
Southeast Sales (BMW, Triumph, Honda, Kawasaki)—6930 N. 76th St.,
   Milwaukee, 414/463-2540, www.southeastsales.com
Suburban Harley-Davidson/Buell—139 N. Main St., Thiensville, 262/242-2464,
   www.suburbanharley.com
Route 43 Harley-Davidson—I-43 and Hwy. 28, Sheboygan, 920/458-0777,
   www.route43hd.com
Sheboygan Yamaha—N7402 Hwy. 42, Sheboygan Falls, 920/565-2213,
   www.sheboyganyamahainc.com
Stock's Harley-Davidson Motorcycles—3206 Menasha Ave., Manitowoc,
   920/684-0237, www.stockshd.com

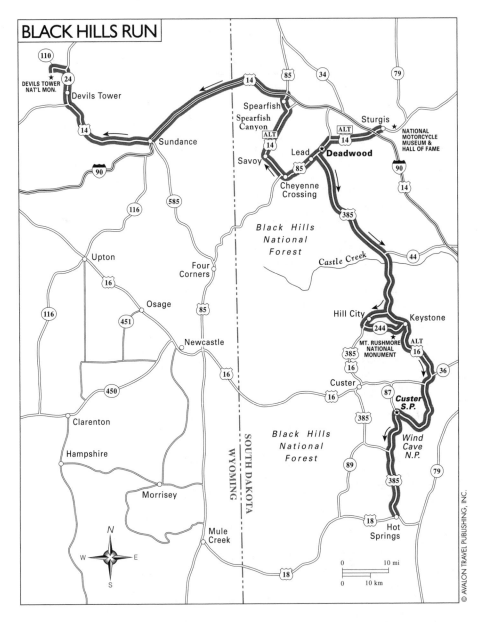

BLACK HILLS RUN

Route: Deadwood to Custer State Park via Devils Tower, Sturgis, Hot Springs, Mount Rushmore, Iron Mountain Road

Distance: Approximately 160 miles (with side trips); consider four days with stops.
- Day 1—Deadwood/Devils Tower • Day 2—Travel/Sturgis/Mount Rushmore
- Days 3 & 4—Custer State Park/Hot Springs

First Leg: Deadwood to Custer State Park

Helmet Laws: South Dakota does not require helmets.

Black Hills Run

Deadwood to Custer State Park, South Dakota

Thanks to the Sturgis Rally, South Dakota attracts its share of motorcycle travelers, but there's more to the state than a single week in August. In the Black Hills you will see things that teach you that the West isn't a location, but a lifestyle. There are towering structures and wide-open spaces, caves and fossil beds, natural beauty and a desire to preserve it. And when you travel during shoulder season (May or September), the roads are wide open and free.

Deadwood Primer

Gold was the key. When word got out that there was gold in Deadwood, tent cities were erected and the boom was on.

Folks here are still searching for gold, but now they do it in the small-stakes casinos. The casinos have turned Deadwood into a town of contradictions, but it's still the nicest place to base yourself before exploring the Black Hills.

Prior to 1989, this small town's Main Street was lined with restaurants and independent businesses. Then low-stakes gambling—uh, *gaming*—was introduced. Old inventory and displays were out; computerized slots were in.

At first glance everything seems perfect. The brick streets are clean, the people content . . . but then come those damned contradictions. At a casino called Chinatown, you listen to American rock classics, dine in a Mexican cantina, and stare at a London taxi. It is Vegas flashy without the success—the empty streets testify to that. Ask the locals and they admit that gambling seemed like a great idea at first, but most of them miss their old hometown.

It's not depressing, just out of sync.

On the Road in Deadwood

There are things to see in Deadwood, but the roads are more appealing. Then again, if you're a Kevin Costner fan you may never want to leave.

Costner, whose acting style follows his early role as a corpse in *The Big Chill,* opened the Midnight Star casino, displaying nearly every costume, prop, and script he ever touched.

More intriguing is a ride out to Devil's Tower via Spearfish Canyon. You won't need a passport to ride into Wyoming; just take Route 85 out of Deadwood toward the town of Lead (pronounced "leed"). The road isn't too attractive, but stay on it—it gradually improves.

About eight miles from Lead at the junction of Rte. 85 and Rte. 14A, turn right and take a break at the **Cheyenne Crossing Store,** 605/584-3510. Open daily 7:30–7:30, this is one of those old-fashioned combination café/lodge/souvenir stand/beer stop/bait shop/ filling stations. I'd like to see them expand their inventory to include plutonium, beetle larvae, and chimpanzees.

Although Spearfish Canyon is a national scenic byway, the scenery isn't fantastic. It does let you explore some backcountry, though. Spearfish Creek runs along a curving road, and when the road narrows, the ride gets more interesting. At the town of Savoy, you'll find a fancy restaurant, cultural center, and resort—too fancy for these parts. Keep heading north through the canyon, and the road ascends and descends rapidly, with other riders springing up in the oncoming lanes.

When you've completed the canyon, 14A takes you through the clean streets of Spearfish and onto I-90 West. You have fifty-plus miles to ride before reaching **Devil's Tower,** 307/467-5283, www.nps.gov/deto, and for now the road is low-key. When you reach Highway 14, head north and be prepared to slow down behind campers who got up a little earlier than you did. The landscape alternates between lush pine forests and open plains, but it's an easy ride to reach Highway 24, which you take north and veer off at 110.

From the road you'll see the 5,112-foot Devil's Tower monument thrusting into the sky. Numerous pullouts afford views. If you enter, you'll pay $3 per passenger (free if you've sprung for a money-saving National Parks Pass) and gain access to a steeply inclined three-mile road that leads to a museum, bookstore, and 1.3-mile paved trail surrounding the tower.

What formed this monolith? The Kiowa Indians believed eight children were playing when suddenly the lone boy among them turned into a bear. The girls climbed onto a talking tree stump and, as the bear tried to kill them, the stump rose so high that the girls turned into the stars of the Big Dipper. The long gashes on the tower are claw marks from the homicidal boy/bear. I spoke to my imaginary geologist friend Hank who confirmed that this is true.

After circling the tower, backtrack to Spearfish Canyon, then to Deadwood for a night at the casinos and another loving look at Kevin Costner's quiver.

Pull it Over: Deadwood Highlights
Attractions and Adventures

Three cemetery plots should gain your attention at Mount Moriah. Wild Bill Hickok, Calamity Jane, and local character Potato Creek Johnny are buried here. If Hickok's head wound hadn't killed him, the procession up this steep grade would've. Wild Bill's faithful following drop packs of "aces and eights" by his tombstone. Admission is $2.

If you're planning a heist, target some of the displays at **Nelson's Garage Car and Motorcycle Museum,** 629 Main St., 605/578-1909, at the Celebrity Hotel. They've stashed Evel Knievel's helmet and jumpsuit, James Bond's suit from *Diamonds Are Forever,* Sylvester Stallone's Ducati Paso 750 Limited, Steve McQueen's '66 Triumph 650, Clint Eastwood's Trans Am, and Paul McCartney's '73 Honda 125. Ship them to me in care of the publisher. Admission is $2.50.

No snapshots here—these are actually nice photographs at **Woody's Wild West Portrait Emporium,** 641 Main St., 605/578-3807. I know there are a lot of vintage photo places, but this one's better since the large studio features 25 settings and 600 costume combinations that allow women to dress in their bordello finest and men to become cardsharps and gunslingers. Another advantage is that riders can bring in their bikes for a Western-style shot. Open daily, hours vary.

Blue-Plate Specials

It's hard to find great food and a normal restaurant in Deadwood since you have to navigate a casino to do it. Up and down Main Street, you'll find home cooking and ethnic eateries, but only one stands out.

On the second floor of the Midnight Star, **Jake's,** 677 Main St., 800/999-6482, serves lunch and dinner. Expect fine dining in a nice atmosphere, with entrées

Rally: Sturgis

Why in the world do riders head to the barren landscape of South Dakota? Because of a rally started in August, 1938, by Indian Motorcycle dealer J.C. "Pappy" Hoel. Back then, nine riders raced on a half-mile dirt track for a $500 purse. What followed were crowd-pleasing stunts, such as head-on collisions with cars, board wall crashes, and ramp jumping. From this, the Jackpine Gypsies Motorcycle Club was born and the rally was proclaimed the Black Hills Motorcycle Classic. After World War II, the rally and race drew up to 5,000 people and 150 competitors, and by the 1960s, the Sturgis Chamber of Commerce was taking part by hosting barbecues in the park and awarding prizes to the rally queen, oldest rider, best dressed couple, and the longest distance traveler. During the rally's 45th anniversary, the governor proclaimed "Pappy Hoel Week" to honor its founder, and attendance peaked at 30,000. The big draw came during the 50th anniversary when as many as 350,000 riders flocked to Sturgis. The following year, 1991, the event was re-named the Sturgis Rally and Races and became (promoters wished) a "family event." In reality, it is a wild drinking, riding, racing party where inhibitions are checked at the door. By 2000, what started as a down-home event attracted 650,000 riders and watchers, making it the biggest outdoor event in America.

605/347-9190
www.sturgismotorcyclerally.com

like rack of lamb, steaks, and Cajun seafood. High rollers (a relative term in Deadwood) dine here. The third-floor sports bar is less fancy and less expensive.

Watering Holes

Casinos have cornered the market, but there are a few joints to check out. Friendly barkeeps at **Oyster Bay,** 628 Main St., 605/578-3136, may persuade you to sample the $1.50 "oyster shooter" concoction, created with an oyster, beer, Worcestershire sauce, tabasco, cocktail sauce, salt and pepper, and other stuff I'm running tests on. The beer and oyster bar attracts folks from around the world, whose signed dollar bills have become the bar's wallpaper.

Not the saloon where Wild Bill was blown away (that was across the street at 622), the **Old Style Saloon #10,** 657 Main St., 605/578-3346, www.saloon

10.com, does have his "death chair" (look over the door after you enter). The place feels authentic, with sawdust on the floor (used by saloonkeepers to camouflage dropped gold dust), an 1870s atmosphere, and a full liquor bar. Watch your back.

Shut-Eye

An organization called **Black Hills Central Reservations,** 800/529-0105, www.blackhillsvacations.com, can arrange rooms, adventures, and activities—and takes a five percent fee. Most hotels in Deadwood are along Main Street and all have a casino attached.

Among the better choices is the **Franklin Hotel,** 700 Main St., 605/578-2241 or 800/688-1876, www.deadwood.net/franklin, the grand dame of Deadwood. Undergoing restoration since 1989, the Franklin has large rooms that make up for the lack of fine furniture, and the owner's celebrity friends (Tom Brokaw, Mary Hart, Jann Wenner, et al.) don't seem to mind. Rates run $77–97, except during rallies when you won't find a room. There's a motor court across the street, but try to stay in the main hotel, which has a dining room and Durty Nelly's Irish Pub. Down the street, the **Bullock Hotel,** 633 Main St., 605/578-1745 or 800/336-1876, www.bullock-hotel.com, boasts the nicest rooms, which go for $69–159. Well decorated, they are separated from the noise of the casino and include king or queen beds, shower baths, and some whirlpools. A restaurant, casino, and full liquor bar downstairs mean that you can stay in for the night. The **Celebrity Hotel,** 629 Main St., 605/578-1909 or 888/399-1886, also where you'll find the motorcycle museum, features clean, functional rooms ($89–139) with a fridge, a TV, and a patio deck that lets you enjoy the weather if it's nice.

Chain Drive*
A, C, E, L, CC

*Chain hotels in, or within ten miles of town. See cross-reference guide featuring phone numbers and web addresses on page 405.

On the Road: Deadwood to Custer State Park

This next leg is like taking four rides in one. You could take a few days to do this, but here's one way to do it all at once if you wish:

From Deadwood, take 14A to Sturgis. Yes, Sturgis. When the rally's not here, there's little to see. Downtown is depressing and the National Motorcycle

Museum and Hall of Fame is gone. So when you leave Sturgis, return past Deadwood and follow Highway 385 South. Along the way you'll see signs reading "X marks the spot. Think." These are posted after riders lose their challenge with tight turns. Think.

Still, it's hard to resist accelerating into this steeplechase for bikes. The road spins up, then down, then around every terrain ever invented. The landscape alternates between boondocks, fields, and meadows, with an occasional general store popping up on the roadside.

Following the turnoff to Rapid City (skip it), the road returns to its unpredictable layout, taking you down hills and whipping around corners and past Pactola Lake, a picturesque spot with pullouts for photos and a National Forest information center on the opposite side.

When you reach Hill City, turn left onto Route 16 at the **Three Forks Country Store,** junction of Hwy. 385 and 16, 605/574-2554, and follow it six miles toward Keystone. Exit at Highway 16A and ride through cluttered Keystone, more touristy than anyplace you've seen.

From here, follow SR 244 toward **Mount Rushmore National Memorial,** 605/574-2523, www.nps.gov/moru, open daily 8 A.M.–10 P.M. You cannot deny the thrill when that first face peeks through the trees. Although you can go to the main parking lot ($8 for an annual pass), you can save some cash by watching for the "no-fee parking area" to your right, just beneath the summit. From here you'll be at Gutzon Borglum's studio, where steps lead to the monument.

Once you scale the steps, the crust of cynicism dissolves and lost idealism returns. This is not a cheap postcard, this is a 3-D testament to an experiment with democracy and the leadership of four great men. A $56-million renovation (using no tax dollars, just donations) created a new restaurant, a massive gift shop, an amphitheater you'll return to that evening, a theater and exhibit hall featuring original models and sketches, firsthand accounts about the construction, and an inspiring explanation of why these presidents were chosen for the honor (respectively, they symbolize the founding, development, growth, and preservation of the country). Instead of watching the faces with everyone else, find a quiet spot to sit and reflect on the massive undertaking.

Make plans to return here around 8 P.M. for a first-class presentation. Around 8:30 patriotic music plays in the amphitheater, and at 9, a ranger takes the stage to answer questions and explain the lighting ceremony. A short documentary is shown, and when the national anthem plays and the audience sings along, the faces are illuminated. As if you needed encouragement, this will make you proud to be an American.

When you leave Mount Rushmore, get ready for one incredible road. Peter Norbeck, the South Dakota senator and governor who was instrumental in the creation of Mount Rushmore, the Needles Highway, and the preservation of Custer State Park, rode on horseback to map out Iron Mountain Road. The result is a magnificent motorcycle run.

Turn south onto Highway 16A and the test-track tight turns begin adding alternating stretches of canopy roads, great countryside, 15-mph switchbacks, and the occasional "pigtail bridge," an ingenious invention that spans steep climbs within a short stretch.

This road is not for sissies. The turns throw you around like Nature Boy Rick Flair and pump your left leg to maximum density with all the shifting. This is a red hot, helluva fun road.

Occasionally it settles down to a nice ride through the forest, and then it rocks and rolls you over the countryside and into nearly vertical ascensions. You'll get an upper-body workout tackling these turns. Since the landscape hasn't been violated, even as you're tossed around like a rag doll, your spirits will lift.

It's a long ride to Custer State Park, but when you turn right and follow Highway 16A to the park entrance, you'll enter the park equivalent of Iron Mountain Road, a place filled with adventure, excitement, and natural beauty.

Custer State Park Primer

It was doomed General George A. Custer who led a scientific army expedition into the Black Hills in 1874. Although his team found gold, Custer seemed more interested in the area's natural beauty. Fortune seekers weren't so magnanimous. They arrived in droves and their presence took a toll on the area's wildlife.

By 1913, the South Dakota legislature created a state game reserve in the southern Black Hills where they would replenish the wildlife population with bison, pronghorn, elk, bighorn sheep, and mountain goats. Governor Peter Norbeck envisioned a 73,000-acre showcase for the area's spectacular resources. With that, the reserve became Custer State Park, which has all the appeal of Yellowstone and Yosemite, yet on a manageable level. It's as close to perfect a park as you'll ever find.

On the Road in Custer State Park

I'll start with a warning: You may be tempted to sign on for the Buffalo Jeep Safari, but based on experience I say you'll see just as much, if not more, by

The Wilderness Loop also features big buffalo roaming. They and the prairie dogs rule the roads at Custer State Park.

© NANCY HOWELL

riding your bike south on the Highway 87 section of the 18-mile Wildlife Loop Road.

From the State Game Lodge, turn left and follow Highway 16A West past meadows and creeks until you reach Highway 87 and head south toward Hot Springs. This is one of the top 10 rides you can make—provided you're not impaled by a buffalo. Get your camera ready: Chances are you'll spy enough wildlife to fill an ark while riding a road that twists like a knot.

If someone charged you with the task to build a road, this would be it. As you pass the Blue Bell Lodge and general store and cross French Creek, you couldn't ask for a better ride, complete with peaks and valleys. It narrows and most likely will put you in the midst of a buffalo herd. It's safer to be in a car when these 2,000-pound beasts are around, but you don't have that option. If they're blocking the road, wait patiently. Do not try to approach them. Although they appear to be as slow and stupid as a paint-sniffing monkey, they can hit at 30 mph and pierce you like a pincushion. Still, these damned beasts are fascinating.

Further on you'll hear a high-pitched chirping. A glimpse of a single prairie dog will suddenly reveal thousands of these creatures standing sentinel atop their holes or scattering like rats in front of traffic. You can spot the local drivers: They're the ones speeding through here, popping a few prairie dogs. If you're lucky and your vision is good, you may also see bighorn sheep, mountain goats, elk, deer, burros, coyotes, falcons, mountain lions, and bobcats—animals too big for the locals to kill.

When you reach the end of Highway 87, follow Highway 385 South and detour to the loop road that takes you to **Wind Cave National Park,** 605/745-4600, www.nps.gov/wica. Beneath one square mile of earth lies 83 miles of tunnels. For $8 ($20 if you're an adventurous psychopath eager to take the Wild Cave Tour, a strenuous four-hour caving class), you'll join a two-hour tour. If you've never been in a cave before, it's frightening at first, then you think you'll die, then you think about earthquakes, then you're fine, then the passages get narrow and the ranger turns out the lights and you're frightened again.

Although there are no grand stalactites or stalagmites or waterfalls, the cave is interesting and cool (53 degrees). The fact that the ranger carries barf and waste bags tells you that this tour isn't for everyone. Avoid it if you're claustrophobic.

When you're back on the road, ride south on 385 to Hot Springs, an ordinary old town with one interesting site about a mile out of town. The **Mammoth Site,** 605/745-6017, www.mammothsite.com, seems like it would be a tourist trap, but once inside it's like walking into an archaeological dig. About 26,000 years ago, a spring-fed sinkhole formed and dozens of mammoths who had dropped by for a drink, dropped in and couldn't get out. In the 1970s when a developer started to clear the land, diggers found bones and a tourist attraction was born. Archaeologists dig only in July, but it's fascinating to see this bone orchard. Outside of a Beverly Hills plastic surgeon's office, it's the only display of fossilized mammoths in America. The site is open daily 8–6. Admission is $6.

When you're ready to roll, return via the same roads, but when you reach Custer State Park again, watch for the eastern side of the Wildlife Loop Road and take that back to the State Game Lodge (or wherever you're staying) to complete the circle. And watch out for them prairie dogs.

Pull it Over: Custer State Park Highlights
Attractions and Adventures

The Needles, also known as Highway 87 North, comes fully equipped with narrow granite tunnels and hairpin turns. The name comes from the long, slender granite spires that border the road. The 14-mile thrill leads through rugged Black Hills to Sylvan Lake.

Although it's outside the park, it's worth seeing what will become the largest sculpture ever created. **Crazy Horse,** located on Highway 385, 605/673-4681, www.crazyhorse.org, is open daybreak–dusk. Admission is $4. Right now, only the face is complete because, out of respect for the subject, sculptor Korczak Ziolkowski turned down federal money. Why Crazy Horse? Ziolkowski admired the martyr (he was stabbed in the back under a flag of truce by a U.S.

soldier), and he sympathized with Crazy Horse and his people, who endured a string of broken treaties. Ziolkowski is dead now; his family continues his work.

To explore the park itself, rent a mount from **Blue Bell Stables,** 605/255-4571. Horseback rides last from one hour ($18) to a full day ($125), with a two-hour ($30) and half-day ($75) option in between. Do this in South Dakota and you'll be a cowboy, my friend.

Shopping

Each lodge at Custer has a general store nearby, but the oversized Coolidge General Store near the State Game Lodge gets my vote for best store in a state park. Minnesota shipbuilders built it in 1927 to accommodate the tourists and reporters who accompanied President Coolidge on his visit. Check out the ceiling and you'll see the hull of a ship turned upside down. Of course, the smaller general stores are perfect places to stop while you're out for a pleasure ride.

Blue-Plate Specials

As in Yellowstone, you can grab snacks and quick meals at snack bars and general stores in the park. For sit-down meals, there are also dining rooms where you can order breakfast, lunch, and dinner: the **Tatanka Dining Room** at the Blue Bell Lodge, 605/255-4535; the **Legion Lake Dining Room** at the Legion Lake Resort, 605/255-4521; and the **Lakota Dining Room** at the Sylvan Lake Resort, 605/574-2561. The nicest location may be the **Pheasant Dining Room,** 605/255-4541, at the State Game Lodge. Comfortable and rustic, the restaurant serves buffalo, salmon, trout, steak, chicken, and pheasant, and the service is excellent. Reservations are a smart idea at any park restaurant.

Shut-Eye

The park makes a great day trip, but staying here is even better. For reservations at any lodge, call 800/658-3530. Rates vary widely according to season and type of accommodation (cabin, hotel, or lodge).

It's easy to see why Calvin Coolidge extended his stay at **State Game Lodge and Resort** from three weeks to three months. The idyllic front porch overlooks a sweeping lawn; there's an artist in residence; and, like the park, it is not so large as to be overpowering. With rates of $81–99, the lodge features cool creek-side cabins along with hotel rooms, a small wooden church, and the Coolidge General Store nearby.

At 6,250 feet, **Sylvan Lake Resort** overlooks a picturesque mountain lake and offers cabins, lodge rooms, and a lounge. Rates run $95–145. You'll need to run the Needles Highway to reach your room. Not a bad deal. **Blue Bell Lodge** is a cowboy resort with cabins ($99–175) and a general store, gas station, campground, and laundry. Trail rides and cookouts leave from here. The least flashy of the lodges, **Legion Lake Resort** rents cabins from $85–135 that are complemented by a restaurant, gift shop, grocery store, and sport-boat rentals on the lake. For campsite reservations, call 800/710-2267.

Related Side Trips

Minnesota; Nebraska

Contributed by Sharon Haak

Minnesota

Highway 16

River roads usually provide the most satisfaction for riders. In Southeast Minnesota, Highway 16 follows the lead of the Root River. Between La Crescent and Dexter, the road surface is silky, while the surrounding rough bluffs beg bikers to stop and take souvenir pix. Keep an eye open for Spring Valley, which delivers on a full slate of narrows and twists.

Highway 14

Escape the breakneck I-90 traffic en route to the Sturgis Rally and take a casual cruise on Highway 14 through Minnesota. Riding north and parallel to the interstate, the advantage is a tour of small Minnesota towns and farms. If you've got the energy, stay on Highway 14 all the way through South Dakota and you'll arrive in jam-packed Wall.

Contributed by John M. Flora

Nebraska

U.S. 385

Carhenge

North of Alliance on U.S. 385 is an astronomically correct automobile replica of Stonehenge. Sculptor Jim Reinders designed the structure as a memorial to his dad, who once farmed this land. The bodies of 38 granite-gray cars were placed in a circle 96 feet in diameter, planted trunk down in five-foot-deep pits, while others were welded at their front bumpers to form arches. Carhenge is open 24/7, year-round.

Resources for Riders
Black Hills Run

South Dakota Travel Information
Bed & Breakfast Innkeepers of South Dakota—888/500-4667,
   www.bbonline.com/sd/bbisd
South Dakota Department of Tourism—605/733-3301 or 800/732-5682,
   www.travelsd.com
South Dakota State Parks—800/710-2267, www.campsd.com
South Dakota Road Conditions—605/773-3571 or 605/394-2255

Local and Regional Information
Black Hills, Badlands & Lakes Association—605/355-3600,
   www.blackhillsbadlands.com
Custer State Park—605/255-4515 or 800/710-2267, www.custerresorts.com
Custer State Park Resort Company—605/255-4772 or 800/658-3530,
   www.custerresorts.com
Deadwood Chamber of Commerce—605/578-1876 or 800/999-1876,
   www.deadwood.org

Motorcycle Shops
Sturgis Yamaha-BMW-Suzuki—2879 Vanoker Rd., Sturgis, 605/347-2636
Black Hills Harley-Davidson—141 E. Omaha, Rapid City, 605/342-9362,
   www.sturgishd.com
Black Hills Powersports—3005 Beale St., Rapid City, 605/342-5500 or
   888/642-5505, www.blackhillspowersports.com
Petersen Motors (Honda, Kawasaki, H-D) —422 S. Fort St., Pierre,
   605/224-4242, www.petersenmotorcycles.com

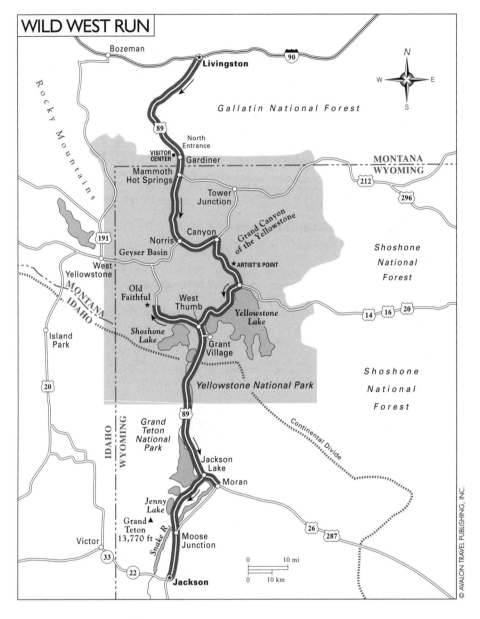

Route: Livingston to Jackson via Yellowstone National Park, Grand Teton National Park
Distance: Approximately 210 miles; consider six days with stops.
   • Day 1—Livingston • Day 2—Livingston/Travel • Days 3 & 4—Yellowstone
   • Day 5—Travel/Jackson • Day 6—Jackson
First Leg: Livingston to South Yellowstone (125 miles)
Second Leg: Yellowstone to Jackson (82 miles)
Helmet Laws: Montana and Wyoming do not require helmets.

Wild West Run

Livingston, Montana to Jackson, Wyoming

This tour may be the best run in the West. It begins in an authentic Western town, traverses a kaleidoscope of natural wonders, and comes to a close in another Western town—one with a nice twist.

The roads are not challenging in themselves, but the ride is unforgettable—for it offers the most magnificent scenery and wildlife in America. You can avoid harsh weather and tourists by riding in May or September.

Livingston Primer

Everything was going fine in Clark City until the Northern Pacific decided to relocate their line. That's when 500 people, six general stores, two hotels, and 30 saloons wound up in nearby Livingston. In 1872, when Congress established Yellowstone, the completion of the park branch of the Northern Pacific Railroad brought Livingston new business.

The town profited from the railroad and mining; in the 1880s, cattle, sheep, and grain became the major economic forces. Livingston hasn't grown much since then, although there's a distinct difference today. The town's year-round population of about 7,500 swells when part-time residents arrive to take advantage of the spells of good weather. Folks who call Livingston home at least part of the year include celebs like Jeff Bridges, Tom Brokaw, Meg Ryan, Dennis Quaid, and Peter Fonda. The veneer here may be pioneer, but the town's soul is sophisticated.

On the Road in Livingston

There are some great loop roads outside of town (ask for directions at the chamber), but it'll be hard to pull yourself away from the anachronism that is Livingston—the town is locked in the 1940s, which means that your senses won't be assaulted by franchises and chain stores when you arrive. Their absence makes wandering around downtown as satisfying as any ride.

On the surface, Livingston seems to be an ordinary Western town filled with rustic cowpokes. Dig a little deeper and you'll detect the town's sophistication, perhaps casually revealed in an art gallery, nice restaurant, or conversation with a rancher—who probably carries more money than the Federal Reserve.

So park your bike and look around. For now, the road can wait.

Pull it Over: Livingston Highlights
Attractions and Adventures

The great outdoors is big around Livingston, and several outfitters can take you to it. **River Services Ltd.,** 4 Mount Baldy Dr., 406/222-3746, www.river services.com coordinates boat and gear rentals, whitewater rafting trips, scenic floats, fishing excursions, rowing instruction, overnight kayak tours, canoe floats, and fishing guides—at a low, low, no charge to you.

Here as elsewhere in Montana, fly-fishing is big, and it all culminates at the **International Flyfishing Museum,** 215 E. Lewis St., 406/222-9369, www .livingstonmuseums.org or www.fedflyfishers.org. The old Lincoln School was turned into an enclave of sculptures, watercolors, and exhibits showcasing the lure and lures of the sport. The museum ($3) also offers free fly casting and tying lessons. What's so hot about fly-fishing? Practitioners claim it's more rewarding because you get away from 200-horsepower boat engines and into the rhythms of nature.

If your visit to the museum has inspired you, head to **Dan Bailey's Fly Shop,** 209 W. Park St., 406/222-1673 or 800/356-4052, www.dan-bailey.com. One of the most famous names in the sport owns one of the most comprehensive stores in town, packed to the gills with everything you need and hundreds of things you don't. How many times have you lost sleep wondering where you could find strung schlappen, hackle capes, and bumblebee popper foam? You'll rest easy after a visit here, open Monday–Saturday 8–6. Bailey's also organizes daylong fishing excursions from $250–375.

A more urban pleasure awaits you at the **Livingston Depot,** 200 W. Park St., 605/222-2300, a beautiful restoration of the Northern Pacific passenger depot. Open May–September, it features exhibits on Western life, art shows, and hosts annual events, such as railroad swap meets. Check out the building's ornate brickwork and lion's head accents.

Shopping

Gil's Got It, 207 W. Park St., 406/222-0112, open daily 9–5, carries everything you used to crave when your parents were lugging you around the country in the backseat of the Buick. Here since 1914, it survives by selling straw cowboy hats, popguns, and wallets with cowboys on them. Hip.

Customize one of the tepees available from **White Buffalo Lodges,** 522 E. Park St., 406/222-7390, www.whitebuffalolodges.com, and you've got it made. Choose Sioux, Cheyenne, Blackfoot, or Crow style, and dress it out with custom paintings based on traditional designs, stories, medicine symbols, and animals. Kits range from $465 (for two kids) to $2,000 (sleeps seven to eight adults) and include a liner, poles, carrying bag, rope, door cover, willow lacing pins, and stakes.

Pardner, if you collect Old West memorabilia, mosey by the **Cowboy Connection,** 110 1/2 N. Main St., 406/222-0272, www.thecowboyconnection.com. Stocked items include gambling mementoes, antique Colts and Winchesters, saddles, chaps, spurs and bits, Stetsons, artwork, bronzes, boots, frock coats, knives, and shotguns.

Blue-Plate Specials

For several reasons, I'd rank **Martin's Cafe,** 108 W. Park St., 406/222-2110, among America's top diners: Ranchers, cowboys, and working folks eat breakfast, lunch, and dinner here seven days a week; it debuted in 1902 as the beanery for Northern Pacific passengers; and it serves chicken fried steak, fried chicken, burgers, onion rings, and banana, coconut, and chocolate creme pies. Is it popular? Check out the well-worn counters where decades of elbows have rubbed the green formica clean.

At the corner of 8th and Park, **Mark's In and Out,** 406/222-7917, is a drive-in where you can fuel up on the four food groups: burgers, hot dogs, onion rings, and milkshakes. Clean as a whistle, Mark's service and prices are straight out of the 1950s—fitting, considering it opened in 1954. Burgers are 89 cents, cheeseburgers 99 cents. If you don't mind bypass surgery, order a mess of Cadillac fries with gravy, chili, or cheese sauce.

Filled with local characters who hang out at the bar (open 'til 2 A.M.), **The Stockman,** 118 N. Main St., 406/222-8455, also serves lunch and dinner to folks who believe that this small restaurant's got the best steaks in town.

Weekends are packed, so try to go on a weeknight for a hand-cut top sirloin, New York strip, or rib eye. Bring cash—credit cards aren't accepted.

The best thing about the **Sport Restaurant,** 114 S Main St., 406/222-3533, www.thesportrestaurant.com, is that it's not a sports restaurant. The original opened in 1909 when the popular sports were hunting and fishing, and women weren't allowed in until the late 1940s. This must-see restaurant has an authentic Old West atmosphere with mounted heads and archival newspapers. The menu advertises burgers, ribs, wings, seafood, homemade soups, chicken sandwiches, and Montana ranch steaks. The real sports bar, Sports Next Door, is the place to go if you've got a wager with Pete Rose and have to catch a game.

Watering Holes

I only drink to excess, so I had a hard time staying out of Livingston's bars. Each has the feel of a Western roadhouse: bartenders who can be sassy or sympathetic, and enough smoke to trigger the oxygen masks. They're all over downtown Livingston, but here are a few stand-outs:

The bar at the Murray Hotel, **Swingin' Door Saloon,** 201 W. Park St., 406/222-9816, features a pool table, seven beers on tap, a full liquor bar, live bands, and lots of energy. If you stepped into a time machine and were transported back to the '40s, you'd see just what awaits you at **The Mint,** 102 N. Main St., 406/222-0361. Break out the booze and have a ball. There used to be a brothel upstairs at the **Whiskey Creek Saloon and Casino,** 110 N. Main St., 406/222-0665, but no more—if there were, the ladies on call would be pushing 90. The bar still attracts locals who come early and stay late.

Shut-Eye

Motels and Motor Courts

Not a motel, but a legend, the **Murray Hotel,** 201 W. Park St., 406/222-1350, www.murrayhotel.com, premiered in 1905 and has since greatly enlarged its pleasant rooms ($65–92) while retaining the touches of an old-fashioned hotel. Check out the wash basins in the rooms, rocking chairs in hallway alcoves, and desk clerks who double as elevator operators. But be prepared—noise from the bar and nearby trains can keep you up at night.

Chain Drive*

A, C, G, L, CC

*Chain hotels in, or within ten miles of town. See cross-reference guide featuring phone numbers and web addresses on page 405.

Inn-Dependence

The **Greystone Inn,** 122 S. Yellowstone, 406/222-8319, www.montanagrey stoneinn.com, is a perfect bed-and-breakfast. Lin Lee is the proprietor and in addition to superbly comfortable rooms and hearty country breakfasts at the inn ($65–90), she opens up her country cabins (just $65–110) as well. The most popular cabin even includes a small kitchen, washer, and dryer. Whichever you choose, she'll make it feel like home.

On the Road: Livingston to Yellowstone

It's a straight 55-mile shot to Yellowstone National Park via Paradise Valley, but the ride doesn't compare to the park itself. When you do get out of Livingston, the land starts to look larger, a portent of things to come. The country ride brings mountains to your left and hills to your right, but it takes a while to notice that there is nothing out here; you are so swept up with the emptiness, you don't notice the absence of homes, stores, and billboards. The Yellowstone River shows up, brushing against the road and then retreating toward the mountains. For now, you have only to enjoy the sun and the mountains, pausing if you wish at a roadside chapel and rest stop about 30 miles south of Livingston. Later, the river starts picking up steam, rolling and boiling and churning along as it flows north. The road tries to match its energy, adding some curves and descents. This all builds up to your farewell to mighty Montana—a state that needs no improvement.

When you reach Gardiner, you'll find restaurants, motels, and service stations, but if you don't need them, roll around the corner to a great photo op. The Roosevelt Arch says more than the words inscribed on it: "Yellowstone National Park. For the Benefit and Enjoyment of the People. Created by Act of Congress March 1, 1872."

Unless you have a National Parks Pass (a $50 investment that gets you into every national park for one year), you'll pay $15 to enter Yellowstone (the pass is valid for the Grand Tetons as well). Even though you may have seen the park in elementary school filmstrips, you've never seen anything like the real thing.

Yellowstone Primer

Instead of its history, consider what makes up Yellowstone National Park: steaming geysers, crystalline lakes, thundering waterfalls, and panoramic vistas sprawled across 2 million acres of volcanic plateaus. This was the world's first national park and accounts for 60 percent of the world's active geysers. The Lower Falls on the Yellowstone River are nearly twice as high as Niagara's. The land rises in elevation from 5,282 feet at Reese Creek to 11,358 feet at Eagle Peaks Summit. Yellowstone is home to 12 tree species, more than 80 types of wildflowers, 58 mammal species, and 290 species of birds.

Yellowstone contains five "countries." Mammoth Country, a thermal area in the northwest, is home to elk, bison, hot springs, and limestone terraces. Geyser Country, in the southwest, encompasses Old Faithful, fumaroles, mud pots, and hot pools. Lake Country, in the southeast, is habitat to native cutthroat trout, osprey, and bald eagles, as well as moose, bison, and bear, which wander the 100-mile shoreline of Yellowstone Lake. Roosevelt Country, in the northeast, recaptures the Old West, and Canyon Country comprises the Lower Falls, Hayden Valley, and the Grand Canyon of the Yellowstone. Free ranger-led programs, sightseeing tours, fishing, boating, horseback riding, and more than 1,210 miles of marked hiking trails all conspire to help you explore the park.

Believe it or not, all of this takes up less than four percent of the park itself. The rest is wilderness. And it's there for you and your bike.

On the Road in Yellowstone

Why do I love Yellowstone? Let me count the ways . . . Commercial trucks are prohibited, it has more wildlife than a hundred zoos, it fulfills every image I had formed about it, and it delivers what the government intended when it protected these lands in 1872.

The road from Tower Junction to Canyon Junction over Dunraven Pass in the northeast corner is the first to close and last to open when snow hits, so there's a good chance you won't be able to ride it. If it's open, terrific; if not, start at the park's northwest section and head south, soaking in the views as you climb rapidly over 6,200 feet. Dealing with the campers that clog the road is discouraging at first, but soon you'll cross the 45th parallel, which marks the midway point between the equator and the North Pole. For some reason, at this point you'll calm down.

Your first stop should be the **Albright Visitors Center** to talk to a park ranger, get maps, and check on programs. From 1896–1916, this was the site of Fort Yellowstone, where the U.S. Army protected the park from poachers, vandals, robbers, and anyone or anything that threatened the preserve and its early tourists. Today's rangers can help you decide how and where to allot your time. Be selective in what you see if you're on a schedule.

An incredible shot—grizzly bear and cubs and the Kawasaki in Yellowstone. Nancy wanted to get closer for a better shot, but cooler heads prevailed. Note that Nancy took this. I was hiding in someone's car.

© NANCY HOWELL

Follow the road south to Mammoth Hot Springs, which builds tier upon tier of cascading terraced stone. These are interesting not only for their beauty but because, despite clearly visible warning signs, some idiots have scalded or burned themselves to death by walking out on and falling through the fragile layer of minerals.

Soon you'll smell a familiar aroma. This is no kitchen cleanser, it's the trees emanating the original pine-fresh scent. The geological wreckage of mountains is omnipresent, and when you approach Swan Lake Flat you're on top of the world. If you ride in the late spring, you may share my fortune and see a grizzly and her cubs—an experience that made me appreciate nature and wish my bike had automatic door locks. Moments like this remind you that, despite the roads here, this is wilderness and it doesn't belong to you, it belongs to the animals. Respect them.

Riding on, you'll spot the glacial green waters of North Twin Lakes and, past the Gibbon River, buffaloes grazing, which may cause gridlock. Steer clear of these brutes. They're big enough to wreck a Humvee and could easily disintegrate a bike.

Near the Norris to Canyon Road in the middle of the figure 8, the Norris and Firehole River Geyser Basins feature the largest display of geysers. Steamboat Geyser, at Norris, is the world's tallest, with infrequent, unpredictable eruptions that reach 400 feet. Next, head east on the middle road toward Canyon Village. The landscape isn't impressive here, but if you head straight until you reach the Grand Canyon of Yellowstone you won't mind the break. The 24-mile-long canyon sneaks up on you, and once in full view it is

Animal Sense

Riding a bike through Yellowstone poses an element of danger. People in cars can shield themselves from bears and bison, but you can't. Here are some tips that may save your life:

- Give animals plenty of space when they are crossing the road.
- If one animal crosses the road, wait to see if another is following behind before proceeding.
- Don't try to entice any animal with food.
- If you see an animal, try to park in an established turnout, not in the middle of the road.
- If you're shooting photographs, don't try to get closer. For a good shot, use a telephoto lens.

majestic. From 800–1,200 feet deep, 1,500–4,000 feet wide, it is marked by rainbow-hued cliffs of orange, yellow, pink, white, and tan.

At first you can only hear the 308-foot-high Lower Falls, then it appears through the trees and takes your breath away. You've reached a geological crossroads, where hot springs have weakened the rock and spout into the river to create an unusual confluence of waterfalls, cliffs, canyon, and geysers.

Down the road, a bridge crosses to Artist's Point on the opposite side of the canyon. When you get back on the road, the ride improves as the road follows the river's course and the frostbite on your fingers tells you you're reaching higher elevations. There's something in the air. . . bubbling, churning, sulfurous mud boils that smell worse than the awards ceremony at a baked-bean festival.

Depending on where you're staying, you could wrap up a long day by resting at the Lake Lodge or the Lake Yellowstone Hotel (see "Shut-Eye") or continuing the journey to Old Faithful. Either way, Yellowstone Lake opens up on your left. After miles and miles of riding, you could swear this lake would come to a close, but it has more stamina than you do. Big enough to create its own weather, the lake is a large crater formed by a volcano and filled by glaciers about 12,000 years ago.

Even after the lake is blocked by lush forests for miles, you round the corner and. . . it's still there. Eventually you'll adopt it as your riding buddy and hope it continues. After about 45 minutes, its 100 miles of shoreline finally come to a close and you're alone again as you ride to the West Thumb Geyser Basin.

This is where you'll find the Fishing Cone, so named because fishermen caught trout from the frigid lake and cooked them still on the hook in the cone's boiling waters.

Between here and Old Faithful, a long 17 miles away, the thrill of the road depends on the weather. When the snow is packed up high on the sides, it's like being in a bobsled race with the road rising and falling like the Roman Empire. There's not a lot to see, but this may be the best stretch for motorcycle travelers.

If you've timed it right, by the time you reach the exit to Old Faithful, you won't have long to wait before seeing the geyser blow. Approximately every 79 minutes, thousands of gallons of thundering, hissing, steaming water blast into the sky. An American icon, it's worth seeing. The benches close to the Old Faithful Inn (see "Shut-Eye") may afford the best view.

From here, you can double back and commence your trip south or check into whichever lodge you were smart enough to book in advance.

Pull it Over: Yellowstone Highlights
Attractions and Adventures

Yellowstone is less like a park than a country. Seven full-service gas stations and four auto repair shops function within the park. *Yellowstone Today,* a free newspaper available at visitors centers and at the entrance, carries seasonal news and current information about park facilities and programs.

The powers that be have also developed a complete retinue of tours and adventures. These include the **Old West Cookout** ($32–53), **Stagecoach Adventure** ($7.25), various guided tours ($9.25–33), horseback trail rides (one hour, $25; two hours, $37), guided fishing trips ($55–72 per hour), power boat rental ($30 per hour), and photo safaris ($40, offered June–September). The new **Firehole Basin Adventure** is a three-hour, $19 tour that leads to the geyser basin near Old Faithful and discusses the geothermal features of the area. Also new is the **Teton Vista Rendezvous,** $36, a daylong tour through the southern park and down to Grand Teton National Park, which you'll ride through later.

For complete details and reservations, call 307/344-7311 or www.travel yellowstone.com.

Blue-Plate Specials

Snack bars, delis, cafeterias, fast food joints, and grocery stores can be found throughout Yellowstone, but don't travel after dark for dinner. Mammoth

Hot Springs Hotel, Old Faithful Inn, Grant Village, Canyon Lodge, and Lake Yellowstone Hotel have dining rooms (also serving breakfast and lunch). Dinner menus include prime ribs, steak, seafood, and chicken; reservations are strongly recommended. Grant Village and Roosevelt Lodge feature family-style restaurants. If you've got a hankering for cowboy cuisine, an Old West Dinner Cookout leaves from Roosevelt Lodge. You'll ride on horseback through Pleasant Valley to Yancey's Hotel, arriving in time for a hearty dinner of steak, corn, coleslaw, cornbread muffins, homemade Roosevelt beans, watermelon, and apple crisp. For dining or cookout reservations, call 307/344-7311 or contact any lodging front desk, dining room, or activities desk.

Shut-Eye

Your best bet is the **Old Faithful Inn.** Built in the winter of 1903–04 with local logs and stones, it features a towering lobby with a 500-ton stone fireplace and a handcrafted clock made of copper, wood, and wrought iron. With rates from $69–164, this stunningly beautiful hotel offers a nice dining room, fast food restaurant, gift shop, and the Bear Pit Lounge. The inn shares a general store and service station with the **Old Faithful Snow Lodge and Cabins,** which opened in 1998 and charges rates of $68–134. Old Faithful Lodge Cabins from $40 and $65

If you disobey me and travel during summer tourist season, I cannot overemphasize the importance of making reservations well in advance by calling 307/344-7311 or checking www.travelyellowstone.com. Lodging options range from rustic cabins to fine hotels, but because of the park's remoteness, few rooms have phones, and none have televisions. Request a private bath if that's important. Among your in-park choices are those listed below.

Completed in the 1930s, **Mammoth Hot Springs Hotel and Cabins** offers hotel rooms and cabins with and without private baths, for $54–90.

A classic historic hotel, **Lake Yellowstone Hotel and Cabins** opened in 1891 and has been restored to the grandeur it enjoyed during the 1920s. The original wicker furniture has even been returned to service. The sun room, a sitting area designed for relaxation and conversation, affords wonderful views of the lake and is also a good place to relax with a cocktail and listen to the piano or chamber music in the evening. Choices range from deluxe historically renovated hotel rooms to more moderately priced annex rooms. Rooms are the most luxurious (and expensive) at $157–167, but annex rooms are $107 and cabins are $83.

cruising past the Grand Tetons south of Yellowstone

© NANCY HOWELL

You'll also find lodges and cabins (with and without baths) at the **Lake Lodge** ($51–112), **Canyon Lodge** ($56–123), and **Roosevelt Lodge** ($48–86), as well as 1,400 campsites ($15 per night). The motel-like **Grant Village** sits at the west thumb of Yellowstone, and a bed'll cost you $90–101.

On the Road: Yellowstone to Jackson

When you slip out of Yellowstone via Highway 89, you'll notice little to distinguish Yellowstone from **Grand Teton National Park,** 307/739-3399 or 307/739-3600, www.nps.gov/grte. In the pristine wilderness between Yellowstone and the Grand Tetons, you'll enjoy a quieting ride, interrupted only by the **Flagg Ranch Resort,** 307/543-2861 or 800/443-2311, www.flaggranch.com. If the overpowering scenery of the area wrestles you to a halt, you can rest easy here with camping and lodges as well as food and fuel.

Just past Flagg Ranch, the vistas have received a booster shot of scenery. In 1929, more than 500 square miles were set aside to preserve and protect the land around the Teton Range; that area was expanded in 1950 when John D. Rockefeller Jr. donated adjacent lands.

There's only one way to experience this park on a bike and that's via the Jenny Lake Loop. Actually, the first body of water you'll see is Jackson Lake, which deserves a dozen rolls of film and a four-hour miniseries. The lake mirrors the mountains, and the result is a surreal, colorful blend of green waters, white mountain peaks, and blue sky. As the mountain chain recedes in the distance, the peaks appear uniform in height and shape, a clue why French trappers called them Les Trois Tetons (the Three Breasts).

Four miles later, the road has risen in elevation to place you midway between the lake and the towering peaks. There's a museum, store, and gas station at Colter Village, but you may be so inspired by the visuals you'll just stick with the road. The mountain chain stays with you as you rocket toward Grand Teton (13,770 feet) the largest mountain in the chain.

In addition to seeing these most incredible peaks, you get to ride alpine runs, then pine-bordered roads and quick drops, where the valley floor opens and the road dives right into it. The road is seemingly custom-designed with bikes in mind, and after riding it, you'll probably need a cigarette—even if you don't smoke.

Where the road T's, turn right into vast emptiness and you are in Jackson Hole, the valley that actually begins just south of the Yellowstone entrance. It seems like a lonely, deserted land but just wait, cowboy. A few miles south and you'll be in the nicest town in the West.

Jackson Primer

Trailblazers have made their mark on this town. The territory was named Jackson's Hole (later Jackson Hole) after trapper David E. Jackson. Prior to Jackson's arrival, however, there were summer residents: the Shoshone, Crow, Blackfoot, and Gros Ventre Indian tribes.

With six trapping trails converging at Jackson Hole, it became a popular fur trading area, but around 1845 the trade—not to mention the animals—was in decline. For the next 40 years, the isolated area laid dormant until the Hayden Expeditions arrived in 1871 and 1878 and introduced the region to the rest of the country. Yellowstone was formed and big game hunters, foreign royalty, and East Coast "dudes" started showing up.

After the town was laid out in 1897, cattle ranching took hold. A hundred years later, this mix of hardworking locals and affluent outsiders still typifies the town, though tourism and skiing have long supplanted ranching. Less than three percent of Teton County is privately owned; the rest is contained within Grand Teton National Park, the Bridger-Teton National Forest, and the National Elk Refuge.

It's hard to imagine a more perfect town.

On the Road in Jackson

You can't disguise it. Jackson is a Cowboy Carmel. There's lots of money here, generated by tourism and movie executives who invest part of their time and fortunes here.

As in Montana, great rides await you on the outskirts of town, but wandering around Jackson is damned fun. Everything here centers around the town square, marked by the famed Antler Arches. Gathered each year by Boy Scouts who scour the nearby National Elks Refuge, most antlers are auctioned off on the third Saturday in May to western export houses, regional craftspeople, and Asian markets that believe that powdered elk horn works faster than Viagra. It doesn't. Trust me.

Wooden sidewalks lead you through numerous shops, bars, restaurants, and galleries. Take an afternoon, find some places on your own, check out a few listed below, and enjoy a pocket of civility in an otherwise harsh world.

Now git along, lil' dogie.

Pull it Over: Jackson Highlights
Attractions and Adventures

Whitewater rafting is the warm weather equivalent to Jackson's winter ski season. Most excursions run the same rapids and charge about the same rate (from around $30–55). Some trips combine whitewater and scenic float trips with the majestic Grand Tetons as a backdrop. Ask if trips include lunch and if overnight trips (roughly $100) are offered.

I haven't done them all so you'll have to make the call on selecting the best whitewater rafting outfitters. Avoid ones advertising high casualty rates. Try: **Charlie Sands Wild Water River Trips,** 307/733-4410 or 800/358-8184, www.sandswhitewater.com; **Dave Hansen Whitewater,** 307/733-6295 or 800/732-6295, www.davehansenwhitewater.com; **Jackson Hole Whitewater,** 307/733-1007 or 800/648-2602 or 888/700-7238, www.jhwhitewater.com; **Lewis & Clark Expeditions,** 307/733-4022 or 800/824-5375, www.lewisand clarkexpeds.com; and **Mad River Boat Trips,** 307/733-6203 or 800/458-7238, www.maddashriver.com.

Located two miles north of Jackson on Highway 89, is the **National Museum of Wildlife Art,** 307/733-5771, www.wildlifeart.org. You want to see this: the premier collection of wildlife art in America, from prehistoric carvings to art by mound dwellers to the sculptures and paintings of historic and contemporary Western American artists like W. R. Leigh, C. M. Russell, and Robert Bateman. In all, the museum showcases more than 2,000 paintings, sculptures, photographs, and works on paper by more than 100 wildlife artists. No unicorns and rainbows here—this is fine art that could turn a condo into a lodge. Admission is $6.

Shopping

Sure, you can buy a hat off the rack, but you'd end up looking like a dude. The nationally known **Jackson Hole Hat Company,** 245 N. Glenwood, 307/733-7687, www.jhhatco.com, can make you a custom-made beaver felt hat at cowboy prices. Not cheap, but it's an American original. If you like leather (and I'm sure you do), you gotta see the collection at **Hideout,** 40 Center St., 307/733-2422, packed with hand-painted custom clothing, moccasins, boots, chaps, Native American headdresses, flying helmets, and leather jackets with fringe and studs and buckles and zip-out linings and body armor. . . Having a nicotine fit? Head to **Tobacco Row,** 120 N. Cache, 307/733-4385, and check out the cigars, pipe tobacco, and hand-carved pipes.

Blue-Plate Specials

Whether they're cowboys or corporate execs, locals fuel up on breakfast and lunch at **Jedediah's,** 135 E. Broadway, 307/733-5671. Breakfasts are big, with inexpensive sourjack pancakes, Teton taters, eggs, waffles, and bacon. Afterwards you'll be waddling like a fat-camp teenager, but you'll have no regrets.

Bubba's BBQ, 515 W. Broadway, 307/733-2288, serves breakfast, lunch, and dinner for meat-eating mammals like you. The basic, pretty-inexpensive grub includes ribs, chicken, pork, sandwiches, baked beans, coleslaw, and corn on the cob.

Snake River Grill, 84 E. Broadway, 307/733-0557, www.snakerivergrill.com, was named Jackson's best restaurant by *Wine Spectator* so you can't expect the place to be diner cheap. For some, though, the premium has a payoff. The Grill serves only fresh fish, free-range veal and chicken, and more than 200 wines as well as ports and single-malt scotches. In this casual Western setting, you can order Chilean sea bass, venison chops, double-center-cut pork chops, and a bunch of other stuff I love to eat when somebody's buying.

Watering Holes

The **Million Dollar Cowboy Bar,** 25 N. Cache, 307/733-2207, www.million dollarcowboybar.com, is the absolute coolest bar you'll ever see. From the cutout stagecoach in the diorama, to the saddle seats at the bar, to the chiseled faces of the patrons, to the Western swing bands who lure the wallflowers out on the dance floor, this place has got it all. And the patrons aren't just drugstore cowboys. On weekends, ranchers who sowed their wild oats here 50 years ago return, their faces filled with more character than you'd find in a dozen Louis L'Amour novels.

Attached to the fancy Wort Hotel, the **Silverdollar Saloon,** 50 N. Glenwood, 307/733-2190 or 800/322-2727, accents the decor (actual silver dollars are embedded in the bar) with saws, antlers, and saddles. The saloon serves wines, microbrews, and bar food. I list it because it's popular, but it seems like contrived fun to me. Open daily 11:30–11.

Just north of town, the **Log Cabin Saloon,** 475 N. Cache, 307/733-7525, is theme-free and open 'til 2, which makes it a safe haven for locals who want to get some relief from the 3.2 million tourists who've descended from Yellowstone.

Shut-Eye

For such a small town, Jackson offers many options for bunking down. A central number for the **Town Square Inns,** 800/483-8667, www.town squareinns.com, puts you in touch with four reasonably priced, generic, and clean motels.

Motels and Motor Courts
The **Cowboy Village Resort,** 120 S. Flat Creek Dr., 307/733-3121 or 800/962-4988, www.townsquareinns.com, rents great little air-conditioned cabins (from $69 during shoulder seasons) equipped with combinations of queen beds, sofa sleepers, kitchenettes, TVs, tub/showers, covered decks, and BBQ grills. They also throw in a continental breakfast.

Chain Drive*
A, E, Q, S, CC

*Chain hotels in, or within ten miles of town. See cross-reference guide featuring phone numbers and web addresses on page 405.

Inn-Dependence
The **Parkway Inn,** 125 N. Jackson, 307/733-3143 or 800/247-8390, www.parkwayinn.com, borders on a motel, but the rooms are large and clean; it sits a few blocks outside the rush of town square; and they feed you a good breakfast, all for $119–169. The pool and hot tub are just right after a day on the road.

Indulgences

Read this only if you think you may want to park your bike for a week and rough it on the saddle of a real horse. Dude ranches and trail rides are a cottage industry (actually, a bunkhouse industry) around here, and while I can't attest to any of these, check 'em out if you'd like to live the life of Hoss. Among them are **Triangle X Ranch,** 307/733-2183, www.trianglex.com; **Gros Ventre River Ranch,** 307/733-4138, www.grosventreriverranch.com; **Rancho Alegre Lodge,** 307/733-7988, www.ranchoalegre.com; and the **Red Rock Ranch,** 307/733-6288, www.theredrockranch.com. Most dude ranches include one or a variety of activities, including trail rides, fly-fishing, swimming, horseback riding, float trips, pack trips, cookouts, hunting, square dancing, hiking, scenic tours, photography, breaking stock, and shoeing horses. Lodging will usually be in log cabins. Prices aren't inexpensive, but may be a bargain for what you get and how many people you can crowd into a group rate. Plus, at some places you get your own horse and a chance to ride like the Lone Ranger. Hi-yo!

Resources for Riders
Wild West Run

Montana Travel Information
Montana Bed & Breakfast Association—800/453-8870, www.mtbba.com
Montana Camping Reservations—800/280-2267, www.reserveusa.com
Montana Fish, Wildlife and Parks—404/444-2535, www.fwp.state.mt.us
Montana Road Conditions—800/332-6171
Montana Weather—800/226-7623
Travel Montana—406/444-2654 or 800/847-4868, www.visitmt.com

Wyoming Travel Information
Wyoming Game and Fish—307/777-4600, www.gf.state.wy.us
Wyoming Homestay and Outdoor Adventures—307/237-3526,
    www.wyomingbnb-ranch.com
Wyoming Road Conditions—307/772-0824 or 888/996-7623
Wyoming State Parks and Historic Sites—307/777-6323, www.wyobest.org
Wyoming State Parks Camping Reservations—877/996-7275,
    www.wyo-park.com
Wyoming Tourism—307/777-7777 or 800/225-5996, www.wyomingtourism.org
Wyoming Weather—307/635-9901 or 307/857-3827

Local and Regional Information
Jackson Hole Area Chamber of Commerce—307/733-3316,
    www.jacksonholechamber.com
Jackson Hole Central Reservations—307/733-4005 or 800/443-6931,
    www.jacksonholeresort.com
Livingston Chamber of Commerce—406/222-0850,
    www.yellowstone-chamber.com
Yellowstone National Park Visitors Services—307/344-2107 www.nps.gov/yell
Yellowstone Activities and Reservations—307/344-7311,
    www.travelyellowstone.com

Montana Motorcycle Shops
Alpine Yamaha—301 N. Main St., Livingston, 406/222-1211
Yellowstone Harley-Davidson—540 Alaska Frontage Rd., Belgrade,
    406/388-7684, www.yellowstoneharley.com

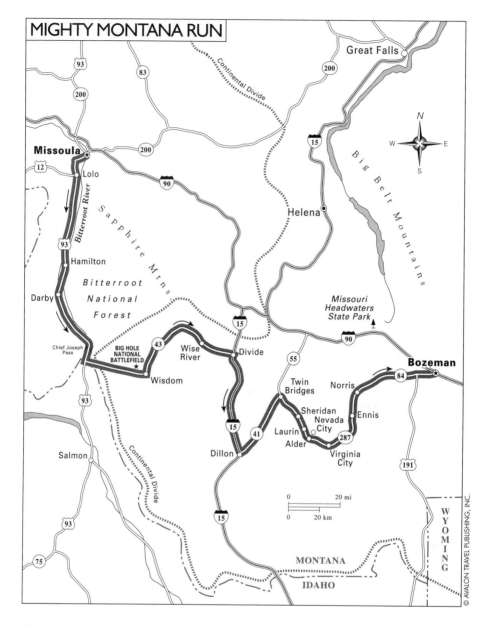

MIGHTY MONTANA RUN

Route: Missoula to Bozeman via Lolo, Hamilton, Big Hole National Battlefield, Divide, Dillon, Sheridan, Nevada City, Virginia City, Ennis, Norris

Distance: Approximately 335 miles; consider four days with stops.

• Day 1—Missoula • Day 2—Travel • Day 3—Dillon/Travel • Day 4—Bozeman

First Leg: Missoula to Dillon (210 miles)

Second Leg: Dillon to Bozeman (123 miles)

Helmet Laws: Montana does not require helmets.

Mighty Montana Run

Missoula to Bozeman, Montana

This is a grand ride, large in scope, large in scenery, and large in memories. Montana bursts with mountains, rivers, ghost towns, and saloons; Montanans project a refreshing self-reliance and strength of character. The essence of the state is palpable on this journey. May and September are good times to ride.

Missoula Primer

Geographically, this is the perfect setting for a town. The Flathead Indians called the area Nemissodatakoo, a term meaning "by or near the cold, chilling waters," an apt moniker considering that four trout-rich rivers—Rock Creek, Blackfoot, Lower Clark Fork, and Bitterroot—converge here. Lewis and Clark passed through this way in the early 1800s, but the first permanent settlement, Hellgate Village, wasn't established until 1860. Four miles from Missoula's current location, the town limits encompassed the flour and sawmills. When the railroad came to town, townspeople ditched Hellgate and changed the name to Missoula.

Missoula offers a great way to get used to Montana and for many reasons is a great starting point. The third-largest city in Montana, Missoula is easy to tour. It also reveals reasons to love this state: no sales tax, the saloons and roadhouses still have character, and the citizenry is a pleasing mix of university students, artists, and regular folks. *American Heritage* named Missoula a "Great American Place" in 1999.

On the Road in Missoula

Understand that fly-fishing is as popular here as jai alai is in Miami and purse snatching is in Central Park. Don't expect to ride into Missoula and stay indoors. The town is surrounded by some of the most pristine country and abundant waters in America.

The road south is a fine ride, but first spend a few hours wandering around downtown, the heart of the city, where independent merchants, junk shops, and watering holes haven't changed much in half a century. Ride Reserve and Higgins, the main thoroughfares, and you'll think you're in a 1950s time warp. On Saturday morning, local farmers and craftspeople set up shop on side streets to sell their plants, handcrafted rugs, jewelry, and weavings. Most appealing are places like **Ma and Pa's,** 531 N. Higgins Ave., 406/728-0899, peddling some of the best junk I've seen. The University of Montana is also near downtown as are bookstores, the historic and eye-popping Art Deco **Wilma Theatre,** 131 S. Higgins Ave., 406/728-2521, www.thewilma.com, and cool, dark saloons.

Pull it Over: Missoula Highlights
Attractions and Adventures

At the **Smokejumpers Center,** 5765 West Broadway (U.S. 10), 406/329-4934, www.smokejumpers.com, brave bastards learn how to skydive behind fire lines in the remote wilderness and fight forest fires. Open daily 8:30–5, the center features free tours, videos, a lookout tower, and exhibits showing the history and training requirements for these crazy asses. If riding across the country isn't exciting enough, they'll help you get started on a career as a smokejumper.

It's easy to be cynical when you're wearing more leather than a cow, but the **Carousel for Missoula,** 1 Caras Park, 406/549-8382, www.carrousel.com, is interesting. Chuck Kaparich wanted to give the community a carousel, so he carved four horses. Others got in on the act and donated time to carving mirror frames, gargoyles, and horses to create the first fully hand-carved carousel since the Depression. It's a Charles Kuralt moment when you see that the horses—with names like Bud, Cannonball, Hardhat, and Sweet Sue—have been "adopted" by local families. Open daily 11–7. Admission is a mere $.50.

Montana rivers and streams teem with trout: rainbows, cutthroats, browns, and brook. Guides can take you to where the fish are; most head out about 60 miles to find a favorite fishing spot. Some gear can be rented; licenses and other items must be purchased; and a tip is never included in prices that range from $250–350 for a day's outing. Fishing trips are offered by **Missoulian Angler,**

401 S. Orange St., 406/728-7766, www.missoulianangler.com, and **Grizzly Hackle,** 215 W. Front St., 406/721-8996 or 800/297-8996, www.grizzly hackle.com.

Montana's stretches of wilderness are so vast, it looks like a foreign world to those of us who live in towns and cities. In addition to exploring this relatively pristine frontier on your bike, you may want to see it from other angles with **Lewis and Clark Trail Adventures,** 406/728-7609 or 800/366-6246, www.trailadventures.com, which offers whitewater trips, including overnights, where all meals, tents, camping, and rafting gear are provided.

If you'd rather climb every mountain, **Trailhead Mountain Sports,** 110 E. Pine, 406/543-6966, www.trailheadmontana.net, rents gear for camping, climbing, kayak, and canoe excursions. Not a bad start for novices.

The fastest-growing wildlife conservation center in the country, **Rocky Mountain Elk Foundation,** 2291 W. Broadway, 406/523-4545 or 800/225-5355, www.rmef.org, works to preserve more than 2.4 million acres of elk country with exhibits, talks, and displays of stuffed dead elk. Inspiring for outdoorsmen. Open Monday–Friday 8–5, weekends 10–4.

Blue-Plate Specials

A northwestern-style downtown restaurant, **Iron Horse,** 501 N. Higgins Ave., 406/728-8866, has a good vibe with college students and mature people. Lunch and dinner fare includes steaks, quesadillas, hamburgers, and pub food. Pitchers of cold beer are particularly enjoyable at the sidewalk café. This is a good place to hang out since the bar's open 'til 2.

It was at the **Double Front Cafe,** 122 W. Alder, 406/543-6264, that I ordered a chicken and an egg just to see which would come first. They sold their first chicken in the 1930s and the current owners have been plucking and frying here since 1961. You can order burgers and seafood in the restaurant, but the big deal is the $6 chicken dinner chased by a glass of pop. Check out the full bar in the basement, then go back upstairs and get some more chicken. A Missoula legend.

Not overly impressive, **Doc's Gourmet Sandwich Shop,** 214 Higgins Ave., 406/542-7414, is just a nice retro diner serving breakfast and lunch. The menu includes soups, burgers, and a concoction known as "hangover stew."

Watering Holes

Drop in any bar along Higgins and you'll find a hole in the wall filled with cowboys and mountain men and a distinct personality. Here are a couple to try.

Enter the **Oxford,** 337 N. Higgins Ave., 406/549-0117, and you fall into a Steinbeck novel. It's been here since the 1880s, in its present location since the 40s, and it's open 24 hours a day. Step inside to a full liquor bar, an interior unchanged since the Depression, gun displays, a card room in back, pool tables, and local characters, including a guy who thinks he's a leprechaun. **Charlie B's,** 428 N. Higgins Ave., 406/549-3589, stays open 'til 2. As you enter, notice the wall of photos of regular patrons and, when your eyes get accustomed to the dark, check out the elk heads, pool tables, and mountain men.

Located in the skeleton of the old Palace Hotel is **The Ritz,** 208 Ryman, 406/721-6731. As the original bar from the Palace, The Ritz has remained an institution, serving patrons since the turn of the 1900s. Today, regulars crowd in for rock, blues, jazz, funk, and 32 beers on tap. A basement billiards hall adds to the appeal. Down the street, **The Rhino,** 158 Ryman St., 406/721-6061, www.rhinoceros.com, has a slightly-less-impressive lineage (it's only been around since 1988), but compensates by having 50 beers served on tap.

Shut-Eye

Most of Missoula's best lodging choices are chain hotels.

Chain Drive*
A, C, E, L, Q, BB, CC, DD

*Chain hotels in, or within ten miles of town. See cross-reference guide featuring phone numbers and web addresses on page 405.

Inn-Dependence
Goldsmith's, 809 E. Front St., 406/728-1585 or 866/666-9945, www.gold smithsinn.com, is connected to a riverfront restaurant, which is actually a plus since it has a great patio deck overlooking the Clark Fork River. The rooms ($104–144) are plainly furnished, however.

On the Road: Missoula to Dillon

As you leave Missoula, Montana doesn't assault your senses. It just grows on you until you realize there is no other state quite so attractive, no great outdoors quite so great. As Missoula recedes in your mirrors, the sky ahead opens and draws you forward.

an open-space ride on the Kawasaki outside Dillon, Montana

NANCY HOWELL

Highway 93, a wide four-lane road, sweeps you up and over Missoula toward Lolo, then south through the Bitterroot Valley toward Hamilton. The road opens into a straightaway and, spotting mountains far on the horizon, you get your first inkling of how large this trip will be.

The stretches of emptiness are long. When they are interrupted, it's usually by Montana businesses, such as the Antler Creation Gallery and the wood carver who claims he can carve you up a nice made-to-order totem pole. I ordered one that looks like Marcia Brady.

Hamilton appears after you cross the Bitterroot River, offering several opportunities for gas and food. The **Coffee Cup Cafe,** 500 S. First St. (Hwy. 93), 406/363-3822, serves great home cooking and mighty tasty pies and cakes that'll push you back into husky pants.

After Hamilton, the road is effortless. The slow curves don't ask much and thus begins a perfect combination of scenery and landscape, although the fires of 2000 took out thousands of acres of forest, which are now struggling to return. The road widens and gives you room to breathe and to think. Sheep graze in the fields and as you roll past small towns like Darby, you're witness to the American West without the pretense. Fewer than 900,000 people live in Montana, an average of six people per square mile, and the land reflects this pioneering spirit.

About 25 miles south of Hamilton, the road narrows and the riding becomes more challenging. As you enter the backcountry and head toward the Bitterroot River, the road leads through the valley and to the **Sula Country Store,** 7060 U.S. 93 S., 406/821-3364, www.bitterrootkoa.com, one of the cleanest and friendliest stops you'll make. "The coffee's always on and it's always on us!" is their slogan. Add to this cabins, gas, a diner, fishing licenses, and a nice front porch to kick back on, and there's every reason to stop and do absolutely nothing.

Civilization lies behind you and for the next 13 miles, you'll see every vision the name Montana brings to mind. The road wraps around mountains, swings into 25-mph curves, and propels you into snowcapped elevations. Keep one eye on the gravel and the other on the vistas that appear as you top this mountain chain. Pine trees puncture the snow cover, and when you reach the Lost Trail Pass at 7,014 feet, you're on top of the world.

This is only the beginning. On Highway 43 at the Montana/Idaho border, turn left to reach the Chief Joseph Pass (7,241 feet) and cross the Continental Divide. What follows are great descents, pristine woodlands, and the first of hundreds of miles of split-rail fencing. You're not riding through some puny East Coast farm country now. You're into something far greater. This is big.

Although the entrance to the **Big Hole National Battlefield,** 406/689-3155, www.nps.gov/biho isn't well marked, it's the only detour for miles, so you should be able to spot it on your left. It's as sad a place as I've seen and here's why: In the summer of 1877, five bands of Nez Perce had fled Oregon and Idaho to escape the U.S. Army and General Oliver Howard, who were trying to round them up and put them on a reservation. They outmaneuvered the army in nearly a dozen battles across 1,200 miles, but when they made it here, Colonel John Gibbon's Seventh U.S. Infantry attacked their sleeping camp on August 9 and 10, 1877, killing warriors, women, and children. Despite the surprise attack, the Nez Perce managed to kill or wound nearly 70 soldiers and drive them back.

The Nez Perce beat the army again at Canyon Creek, but surrendered in October 1877, at Bear Paw Battlefield. Nez Perce civil leader Chief Joseph had had enough. He told Colonel Nelson Miles, "Hear me, chiefs. I am tired; my heart is sick and sad. From where the sun now stands I will fight no more forever."

In my opinion, this reflects the very worst of American history. And while I shouldn't feel personally responsible for what happened here, I sure felt bad.

When you leave the center, the breadth of the land you see is phenomenal. There is enough earth here to build new planets. You're in the Big Hole Valley, riding at an average elevation of 1.2 miles. Even though the horizons are empty, the view is more inspiring and far more beautiful than you can comprehend.

A few miles later when you ride into Wisdom (pop. 78), you'll encounter something else to file in your growing collection of "on the road" stories. Pull into the **Big Hole Crossing Restaurant,** 406/689-3800, and you've entered an anomaly. The restaurant is no Montana greasy spoon. They serve up damn good food here, and have as backdrop a toasty fireplace, an art gallery, and a clothing store where handcrafted dresses sell for $250 and cool leather jackets for $1,000. If you're on a liquid diet, next door is **Antler's Saloon,** 406/689-9393, where cowboys shoot stick and locals work out with 16-ounce weights. The decorative touches, antlers and guns, recall an early roadhouse. I expect by now the sights have tempted you to become a part-time Montanan. Don't. If you're not ready to "earn your spurs," leave the state to the people who belong here, those who endure its hardships and deserve its rewards.

If your mind can handle it, the road and landscape following Wisdom improve exponentially. The Great Plains lays itself out beneath your wheels; sunlight falls in large shafts on the valleys below; and the landscape grows so large that even grazing horses look as insignificant as Shetland ponies. You're in the "Land of 10,000 Haystacks." By the time you're through riding, only reconstructive surgery will be able to erase the smile from your face.

Amid the straights and curves and low sloping hills, something is missing: This great land is uncluttered by houses, billboards, factories, gas stations, and strip malls. There is nothing but land and the road, which, when you get down to it, is really all you need.

The ride's grandeur sustains itself as you cruise alongside the Wise River, taking 40-mph turns as the water churns and boils on your left. When you do reach a town, you can usually count on a gas station and saloon like the **Blue Moon,** 406/267-3339, located a mile off I-15 in Divide and filled with friendly locals. When you head south on the lonesome interstate, it's worth noting that this may be the only federal highway that you can ride without seeing any other car, truck, or bike.

You'll ride 38 miles to reach Dillon, not because there's anything to do there, but because it gives you a place to sleep and prepare you for the next day's ride.

Dillon Primer

Dillon had an impressive start. It was born when the Utah and Northern Railroad was heading toward Butte in 1880, but the railroad stopped when it reached rancher Richard Deacon's spread. He wouldn't let the line continue

riding the range on the Kawasaki outside Dillon, Montana

until a group of businessmen raised enough cash to buy him out. While the railroad stalled during the winter of 1880–81, the town site was named after railroad president Sidney Dillon.

That's really all you need to know. Dillon also enjoyed a gold boom that went bust, and today the town relies on agriculture. There's not much else shaking here. Not much at all.

On the Road in Dillon

Thumb through this book and you won't find another town like Dillon. Usually even if there's nothing to see in a town, there's something to talk about. Not here. I won't belabor the point. There are a few chain motels, a grain silo, a quiet downtown, Western Montana College and, most importantly, a Dairy Queen. If you want to know more, stop by **Dillon Visitors Information Services** at 125 South Montana, 406/683-5511.

Pull it Over: Dillon Highlights
Shut-Eye

Chain Drive*
A, C, CC

*Chain hotels in, or within ten miles of town. See cross-reference guide featuring phone numbers and web addresses on page 405.

Inn-Dependence

The **Centennial Inn,** 122 S. Washington St., 406/683-4454, www.bmt
.net/~centenn, is the saving grace of Dillon. If you stay here, you'll be handled
with care by Jean James, a very gracious innkeeper. This is the way travel should
be. You roll into town and check into a clean and comfortable room ($89).
Although the pace in Dillon is slow, there are stories here if you look. For instance, the James family also owns a 3,000-acre ranch and runs the horrifically
named hunting/fishing guide service Bloody Dick Outfitters (T-shirt, anyone?).
They also oversee the Dillon Junior Fiddle League which has represented
Montana in Japan, New York City, and elsewhere around the country. In the
evening, the James family likes to sit around and jam on their fiddles and guitars. This is what makes travel great: meeting nice people who make good
down-home music.

On the Road: Dillon to Bozeman

Leaving Dillon on SR 41 North takes you right back to the prairie and photo
ops with a Rocky Mountain backdrop. The landscape varies little, so just let
your mind wander until you've gone about 25 miles to Twin Bridges, as close to
not being a town as any town I've seen. The road forks here; turn onto Highway
287 toward Virginia City.

About now you'll notice a few things: The fierce wind smacks your body as it
pours over the plains; every pickup you've passed since Missoula has a dog in
back (I believe they come standard with Montana trucks); and, finally, where
there is nothing to look at, there is a place to stop. Before Sheridan, **Traveling
Thru Time,** 3730 Hwy. 287, 406/842-5277, www.travelingthrutime.com, is
an unexpected gold mine of great old autos, accessories, and random motorcycle stuff. Gas pumps, model trains, parking meters, oilcans, cop spotlights, and
a few old Native American and Harley items are on display.

Sheridan fizzles to a close and merges with the prairie as you head out of
town. About five miles later you'll pass Robber's Roost on your right, where
desperadoes, rustlers, and Enron execs came to plan their heists. Beyond that,
random towns crop up when nothing else is around. This happens in Laurin,
Ruby Valley, and Alder, each of which grows progressively dirtier and more
lonesome.

The landscape rapidly changes into mining country. The ground is gritty
with sagebrush and mean brown creeks that penetrate the deadwood. This is
the perfect setting for Nevada City, a strange shambles of a place that's half

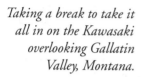

Taking a break to take it all in on the Kawasaki overlooking Gallatin Valley, Montana.

© NANCY HOWELL

ghost town, half museum. There's a hotel here worthy of *Gunsmoke,* a saloon where you can bring your own drinks, and a complete town hidden beyond the street-front buildings. Check out the darkened music hall and find nickelodeons, fortune telling machines, and the "famous and obnoxious horn machine" stashed inside. In the village, they've saved everything from outhouses to stores stocked with unopened merchandise.

A hundred years ago and a few miles north of Nevada City, six discouraged prospectors stopped to pan for enough gold to buy tobacco. Within three years, the Alder Gulch gave up $30 million in gold and **Virginia City,** 406/843-5555 or 800/829-2969, www.virginiacitychamber.com, was born. A more modern town than Nevada City, Virginia City is still a frontier town as well. It does have a few great shops and restaurants, such as the **Roadmaster Grille,** 126 W. Wallace, 406/843-5234, displaying old Buicks on hoists. Stop here for a great burger and shake and sit in a booth created from split cars.

Without embellishing, I can say the road to Ennis is as magnificent a road as you'll ever ride. Climbing into the hills, the glorious country is at your feet, and when you reach an overlook hundreds of feet above the valley floor, it will dazzle and humble you with mountains, rounded hills, broad beams of sunlight, and far more beauty than your mind can take in. Thank whatever gods you believe in for their handiwork.

Descending from the promontory is a kick. When you reach Ennis, turn left on Highway 287 toward Norris. Unlike in Washington, the scenery here never falters. Ride toward the brink of a cliff and look down the shaft of a long, empty valley where shadows of clouds smudge the ground. When you

Kuralt: Kawasaki Vulcan Nomad 1500

"Kuralt"* for Montana, Wyoming, and South Dakota was the 1999 Kawasaki Vulcan Nomad 1500. I really like this bike. It has the power of the Suzuki Intruder 1500 LC, the easy handling of the Yamaha Royal Star, the style of Harley's Electra-Glide Classic, and the comfort of the Honda Gold Wing. For me, everything was in the right place, and the '50s retro style and color combination (candy apple red and burgundy), plus two large, sleek, hard saddlebags, made this bike a pleasure to ride for thousands of miles. It started easily, was light enough to roll out of an inclined parking space, had a hinged gas cap and cooling fan, shifted smoothly, and accelerated well. In the American West I never got great gas mileage (strong headwinds) and there wasn't much pep in high gear, but other than that, this bike was perfect for me.

For details on new Kawasaki models, check www.kawasaki.com.

*It was the travels of CBS correspondent Charles Kuralt that inspired me to explore America. I named each motorcycle I rode in his honor.

reach Norris and the junction of 84, turn right and the terrain takes you back into hill country. The low, flat road gives you instant twists beside the fantastic Madison River.

Fishermen wade in the waters here, and the canyon turnouts are perfect for resting your bike, peeling off your boots, and cooling yourself with a walk into the river. Try this, and when you shut off your bike and listen to the silence, I defy you to imagine a more beautiful country.

As you continue into Bozeman, the land turns into farmland. Hear the wind pouring over your helmet and the engine's low-pitched, pulsing hum.

Combined with Montana, it is a symphony.

Bozeman Primer

Others arrived before Lewis and Clark, but they were the first to generate a written description of the valley, in 1805 and 1806. Decades later, when gold was discovered, Bozeman Trail became the chosen path west—and then east, when the prospectors returned here to create the town in 1864.

By 1883 the Northern Pacific Railroad had completed its line through the town, and the Montana Agricultural College held its first classes in 1893. With settlers arriving from around the country, Bozeman developed a unique local heritage. Today the town has eight historical districts and more than 40 properties listed on the National Register of Historic Sites.

While the outskirts of town look suspiciously like everyplace else, the heart of downtown still has a 1940s flavor, with 10-gallon hats, pointy-toed boots, drugstore cowboys, and antiquated signage at stores like Western Drug and Big Bair's Western Wear.

Mosey on down and check 'em out.

On the Road in Bozeman

As in Missoula, the road has been so generous that it's satisfying to stay in town and see what's shakin'. Main Street is the main part of town, more compact than Missoula's. Just a few hours up and down the street will acquaint you with the more interesting shops. Beyond that, just take it easy in the Old West.

Pull it Over: Bozeman Highlights
Attractions and Adventures

If you've never been fly-fishing, there's no better place to start than right here. What does it take to take up this sport? Money, mostly. Guides charge from $250–350 for a day of fishing, but as you learned in Missoula, that doesn't include gratuities, license, or equipment. In most shops you can rent a rod, reel, and waders, but you have to purchase gear and flies—unless you've got some plastered on your visor. Most excursions depart at 8:30 and return about nine hours later. Bear in mind that this is catch and release—you're fishing for the fun of it (if you think spending 300 bucks is fun). The shops below also arrange trips and guides.

Opened in 1944, **Powder Horn,** 35 E. Main St., 406/587-7373, is sacred ground for sportsmen, featuring books, rods, reels, clothing, boots, rifles, shotguns, shells, and cooking supplies. They also represent 20–30 local guides—not college students—who know where to go. Working with novice to serious fly fishermen, **Bozeman Angler,** 23 E. Main St., 406/587-9111 or 800/886-9111, www.bozemanangler.com, offers walk/wade or float trips on the Yellowstone, Beaverhead, Gallatin, Madison, and Missouri Rivers. A few miles outside of Bozeman in the town of Belgrade, Dave Warwood at **Bridger Outfitters,** 15100 Rocky Mountain Rd., Belgrade, 406/388-4463, www.bridgeroutfitters.com, can arrange a half-day horseback ride ($60), a full day with sack lunch ($125), or a mighty man adventure that lasts four days and

© NANCY HOWELL

miles of big sky and pristine road in the Treasure State

three nights ($700) and features overnight camps, cattle drives, horseback rides, and fishing in backcountry lakes and streams.

The biggest draw in Bozeman, the **Museum of the Rockies,** 600 W. Kagy Blvd., 406/994-3466, www.museumoftherockies.org, is a great source of data that centers around dinosaur fossils unearthed by local legend Jack Horner. I'm glad I came here. I was investing my money in coprolite until I learned that it's just fossilized dinosaur crap. On display are fake dinosaurs, CAT-scanned dinosaur eggs that reveal embryos, skulls of a triceratops and tyrannosaurus, and thoughtful exhibits on Native Americans and Lewis and Clark. Combined, the flood of information will wear your brain down quickly, so take in only the exhibits that catch your interest. Open Monday–Saturday 9–5, Sunday 12:30–5. Admission to the museum is $7, $3 to the planetarium.

The free **Gallatin County Pioneer Museum,** 317 W. Main St., 406/522-8122, www.pioneermuseum.org, pays tribute to the history of Bozeman and the pioneers who settled in the Gallatin Valley. Take a look at the travels of your spiritual ancestors, Lewis and Clark, who are honored in this old jail at the L&C library. Other exhibits include an 1870s log cabin, American Indian exhibits, a sheriff's room with a hanging gallows, a whiskey still, and more than 11,000 archival photos from the early days of the town.

Blue-Plate Specials

Serving lunch and dinner, **Boodles,** 215 E. Main St., 406/587-2901, features a refined setting, though not stuffy, a bar where you can smoke cigars, and food so good it's hard to believe. Excellent servers help you navigate through the wines and meals, and they never rush you—this is the perfect place for a leisurely dinner. When you're done, head to the full bar, a popular hangout.

Looie's Down Under, 101 E. Main St., 406/522-8814, rivals the setting of Boodles, but in a basement with a cool, 1940s, Sinatra-style piano bar. A nice retreat, Looie's features such entrées as lamb shank, blackened salmon, sea bass, and sushi.

The **Western Cafe,** 443 E. Main St., 406/587-0436, opens at 5 A.M.—just in time to serve early rising regulars tins of fresh-baked cinnamon rolls and pies. When lunch rolls around, they roll out the T-bone steaks, chicken fried steaks, homemade soups and stews, and dinner rolls. The only drawback? There's just not enough time to eat it all—closing time's 4 P.M.

Watering Holes

Famous for its hats, **Rocking R Bar,** 211 E. Main St., 406/587-9355, at its best is just a funky watering hole that keeps a full bar going for students, locals, and tourists. It's cool in a smelly, smoke-filled way, but I imagine oxygen masks deploy when things get too bad. Open daily 'til 2 A.M.

If you wear boots even when you aren't riding, you may be at home at **Crystal Bar,** 123 E. Main St., 406/587-2888, open daily 8 A.M.–2 A.M. This country cowboy bar opens a second-floor rooftop beer garden in the summertime; year-round you'll find a few pool tables and lots of beer—and it's clean.

The clientele changes throughout the day at **The Cannery,** 43 W. Main St., 406/586-0270, from doctors and lawyers after work, to college students after class, to real people later at night. Open daily 11 A.M.–2 A.M., this joint features sassy bartenders and a pool table attached to the ceiling.

Inside the cool old Baxter Hotel, the **Bacchus Pub,** 105 W. Main St., 406/586-1314, borders on a restaurant but may be worth a stop to see the bar—a reproduction of a medieval Munich winery.

Shut-Eye

Most chain hotels are located on Seventh Avenue and, since they're fairly close to the downtown district, may be your best option.

Motels and Motor Courts
The **Lewis and Clark,** 824 W. Main St., 406/586-3341 or 800/332-7666, www.lewisandclarkmotel.net, probably saw its best days in the '60s—it still

boasts a "dining room, coffee shop, and lounge." Still, the rooms ($73–89) are clean, large, and have two queen beds.

Chain Drive*
A, C, E, I, L, Q, U, CC

*Chain hotels in, or within ten miles of town. See cross-reference guide featuring phone numbers and web addresses on page 405.

Inn-Dependence
The nicest inn, the century-old **Voss Inn,** 319 S. Wilson, 406/587-0982, www.bozeman-vossinn.com, features spacious rooms (sans TVs) for $85–125. Kinda frilly, but some rooms are masculine with king beds. Morning brings a full breakfast in your room or the parlor.

Related Side Trips

Idaho

Contributed by John M. Flora

U.S. 20

Craters of the Moon National Monument

Arco, Idaho

About 18 miles southwest of Arco, Idaho, on U.S. 20, the landscape shifts dramatically from high desert to barren lunar vistas, with black cinder cones, lava flows and jagged boulders and ravines stretching out as far as the eye can see. Though this 618-square-mile lava field once confounded early settlers on their westward trek, U.S. 20—a main route across central Idaho—now cuts through its northwest corner. Sixty different lava flows range in age from 15,000 to just 2,000 years old.

Resources for Riders
Mighty Montana Run

Montana Travel Information
Montana Bed & Breakfast Association—800/453-8870, www.mtbba.com
Montana Camping Reservations—800/280-2267, www.reserveusa.com
Montana Fish, Wildlife and Parks—404/444-2535, www.fwp.state.mt.us
Montana Road Conditions—800/332-6171 or 800/226-7623 (ROAD)
Montana Weather—800/226-7623 (ROAD)
Travel Montana—406/444-2654 or 800/847-4868, www.visitmt.com

Local and Regional Information
Bozeman Chamber of Commerce—406/586-5421 or 800/228-4224,
    www.bozemanchamber.com
Bozeman Road Conditions—406/586-1313
Dillon Visitors Information Services—406/683-5511, www.bmt.net/~chamber/
Missoula Chamber of Commerce—406/543-6623 or 800/526-3465,
    www.missoulachamber.com
Missoula Road Conditions—406/728-8553
Missoula Weather—406/329-4840

Motorcycle Shops
Five Valley Honda-Yamaha—5900 U.S. Hwy. 93 S., Missoula, 406/251-5900
Big Sky BMW Kawasaki—1804B North Ave. W., Missoula, 406/728-5341
Al's Cycle—619 Hwy. 93 S., Hamilton, 406/363-3433
Mountain Motorsports and Marine—620 Hwy. 93 S., Hamilton, 406/363-4493
Sneed's Cycle—112 N. Montana St., Dillon, 406/683-2205
Team Bozeman Polaris/Kawasaki/Yamaha—403 N. 7th Ave., Bozeman,
    406/587-4671 or 800/830-4671
Yellowstone Harley-Davidson—540 Alaska Frontage Rd., Belgrade,
    406/388-7684, www.yellowstoneharley.com

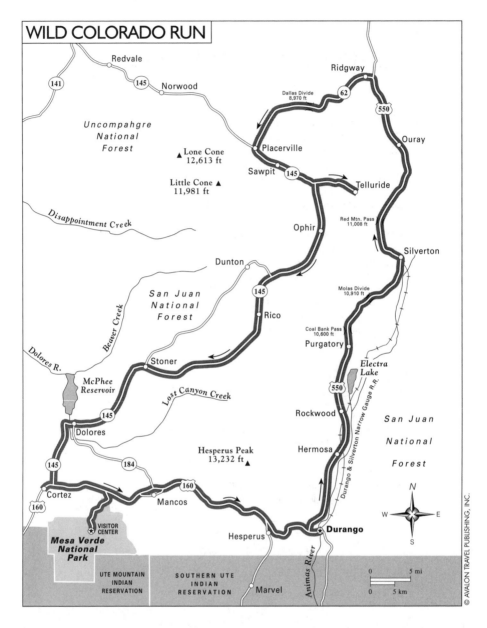

WILD COLORADO RUN

Route: Durango to Mesa Verde via Silverton, Million Dollar Highway, Ouray, Telluride
Distance: Approximately 200 miles; consider five days with stops.
 • Day 1—Durango • Day 2—Durango/Travel • Day 3—Telluride
 • Day 4—Telluride/Travel • Day 5—Mesa Verde
First Leg: Durango to Telluride (120 miles)
Second Leg: Telluride to Mesa Verde (80 miles)
Helmet Laws: Colorado does not require helmets.

Wild Colorado Run

Durango to Mesa Verde National Park, Colorado

This ride won't take very long, but it will last forever. Every Colorado beer commercial is evoked here. Feast your senses on waterfalls, switchbacks with sheer drops, frontier towns in no hurry to leave the 19th century, and a mysterious village frozen in time. You'll ride across mountain passes at 11,000 feet, with the option of renting a Jeep to ride past 13,000. . . if you don't mind a collapsed lung. Ride in early or late summer for prime riding weather and less traffic.

Durango Primer

After the Anasazi vanished and the Utes, Navajo, and Spanish came and went, Durango was born by way of the rails.

With the San Juan Mountains overflowing with gold and silver, the folks at the Denver and Rio Grande Railroad had a brainstorm. In 1879 they established the town of Durango as the base point for their railway. The tracks were completed by 1882 and by the time the line stopped in the 1960s, about $300 million worth of gold and silver had been removed from the hills.

Durango was a wealthy town at the turn of the century and, judging by the architecture, still looks well off today. But it's not just money that makes this town rich. It is its natural setting on the Animas River and the town's proximity to cool, lush forests and broad, powerful mountains. Arguably its greatest asset is its people. Their hospitality and lack of pretense make Philadelphians look like street thugs.

On the Road in Durango

Since the impending ride will satisfy your thirst for adventure, while you're in Durango you might as well hang out downtown or, if you have a day to invest, board a steam train for a real cliffhanger.

If you stay in town, the epicenter of activity stretches between 5th and 12th along Main Avenue. A showroom's worth of motorcycles typically sit at an angle along the curb because this is an Old West walking town that hasn't lost its flavor. Here, the independent merchants, local saloons, and historic buildings give Durango an edge that ordinary cities surrendered when mall developers flashed their cash.

Along Main Avenue you'll find leather and saddle shops, newsstands, old photo shops, a one-of-a-kind hatmaker, and one of the best melodramas in the West. After strolling Main Avenue, don't leave town by bike. Not yet. Seriously consider a run on the **Durango-Silverton Narrow Gauge Railway,** 479 Main Ave., 970/247-2733 or 888/872-4607, www.durangotrain.com. Back in the 1880s, about the time the Rolling Stones released their first wax cylinder, mining in Silverton was going full steam. The best way to get the goods down to Durango was via this narrow gauge railway.

If you think the San Juan Skyway is gonna be tricky on a 600-pound bike, surrender the job to the engineer of a circa 1923, 50-ton, coal-fired steam train as he creeps it along the cliffs of the Animas River Gorge. When you enter the mountainous terrain and peer 400 feet straight down, you'll understand why cruising at 10 mph makes sense.

The locomotive chuffs along the canyon for about three and a half hours, rising from 6,512 feet in Durango to 9,288 feet in Silverton (a town you'll see later on your bike even if you don't take the rail). The layover in town lasts only two hours—enough time to eat, down a beer, and buy a rubber tomahawk. If you've never ridden a steam train and get a kick out of historic modes of transportation, it's worth the $60 you'll pay for the nine-hour round trip. Reservations are recommended. Touring the museum and the railyard costs $5.

Back in Durango, rest up and get ready for an old-fashioned evening listening to a honky-tonk pianist at the Diamond Belle Saloon or booing the villain at the melodrama. When you're in Durango, this sure as shootin' beats a night at a sports bar.

Pull it Over: Durango Highlights
Attractions and Adventures

When you've got a river in your backyard, you'd be a dumbass not to use it. As in many towns in the West, outfitters in Durango wring maximum use out of the mighty Animas. From serene to extreme, the river runs offered by **Outlaw Rivers and Jeep Tours,** 690 Main Ave., 970/259-1800, www.out lawtours.com, last from one hour ($15) to two days ($325), and then they add Jeep rentals ($100 daily) and Jeep and Hummer tours to the mix. **Durango Rivertrippers,** 720 Main Ave., 970/259-0289 or 800/292-2885, www.durangorivertrippers.com, provides local folklore and wildlife observation from $20 (two hours) to $30 (half day).

Trimble Hot Springs, 6475 CR 203, 970/247-0111, www.trimblehot springs.com, doesn't qualify as a water adventure since white water appears only when someone does a cannonball, but you can ease them saddle-sore muscles here. The spa features Olympic pools, massages, herbal wraps, and waters at 85, 102, and 108 degrees. Open daily 8 A.M.–11 P.M. Admission is $8.50.

When you see the sublime setting of the airstrip at the **Durango Soaring Club,** 27290 U.S. 550 (three miles north of Durango), 970/247-9037, you

Rally: Four Corners

One of the newest major rallies, Four Corners attracts as many as 30,000 riders every Labor Day weekend. Founded by the local ABATE chapter, promoters, and Senator Ben Nighthorse Campbell, it was originally held at the Sky Ute Event Center in Ignacio, but the popular event outgrew its 40-acre birthplace. In 2002, the rally rolled over to a new 156-acre site two miles outside Ignacio, which is about 18 miles southeast of Durango, Colorado. Like other rallies, there are demo fleets, custom shows, the original "Biker Bull Riding" and a chorus line on wheels: the fabled Hardly Angels, www.hardlyangels.org, the first all-woman motorcycle drill team.

970/375-0777
888/284-9212
www.fourcornersrally.co

may never want to leave the ground. When you do, you'll soar up to 9,500 feet before popping off from the tow plane and soaking up tremendous views of the San Juan mountains, as far away as 100 miles, and see the Animas River snake through the valley. If you're in a pack, your friends will be nearly as content sunning themselves on the observation deck. Weight limit 260 pounds, reservations suggested. Flights cost from $85–150.

Shopping

Long before trendsetters beatified cigars, **Hall's Brothers Smoke Shop,** 113 W. College Dr., 970/247-9115 or 800/742-7606, www.durangosmoke shop.com, was smoking. Claiming to be the "tobacconist to the Four Corners," Hall's stocks many cigars, Zippo lighters, and risqué postcards.

Blue-Plate Specials

Francisco's Restaurante y Cantina, 619 Main Ave., 970/247-4098, is a local favorite for its homemade soups, great Mexican food, impressive wine list, and full bar, where margaritas are a specialty and locals gather to watch the big game. Expect a long wait if you travel in season. Serves lunch and dinner.

The rustic miner's shed that houses the **Ore House,** 147 E. College Dr., 970/247-5707, is a great setting for an evening's retreat. The chefs start with pan-fried steaks and work their way up to chateaubriand; in between, they whip up center cut bacon-wrapped filets stuffed with king crabmeat, steak ranchero, and the Ore House grub steak. Eat dinner here and annoy a vegetarian.

Inside a renovated Ford tractor showroom, the **Steamworks Brewing Company,** 801 E. 2nd Ave., 970/259-9200, www.steamworksbrewing.com, draws local college students and a smattering of tourists for lunch, dinner, and five regular and three seasonal microbrews. The style is basic, with cor-rugated tin walls, copper vats, and smooth cement floors. Oh yeah, the food: Mexican, chicken, pastas, sandwiches, and pizza. The patio deck is great for all this, plus a cold one and conversation.

The **Durango Diner,** 957 Main Ave., 970/247-9889, www.durango diner.com, is a local landmark, and they keep going thanks to their no-frills meals. Beyond serving breakfast all day, they spice up the menu with green chili, southwest salsa, and enchilada sauces sold here and across the country. If you're afraid you'll run out of gas on the San Juan Skyway, stop here first.

Watering Holes

You cannot *not* have a good time at the **Diamond Belle Saloon,** located in the Strater Hotel, 699 Main Ave. This corner bar, locked in the 1880s, boasts a full line of drinks, from beer to bourbon. From the flocked wallpaper to the honky-tonk piano player to the nude painting to the sign that suggests "work is the curse of the drinking classes," this is one of the best bets for bikers I've seen. Chances are you'll meet people from around the world. The only thing missing here is Festus. Open daily 11 A.M.–midnight.

If you're driven by thirst, check out **Lady Falconburgs,** 640 Main Ave., 970/382-9664, www.falconburg.com. open daily 11 A.M.–2 A.M. The rathskeller-style interior isn't that impressive (the basement of a shopping mall), but the establishment pours 125 types of bottled beer, 20 beers on tap, and a $4 sampler.

The bar for riders attending the nearby Four Corners Rally, **Players Pub and Pool,** 652 Main Ave., 970/259-6109, features four pool tables, an extra bar in back, 30 bottled beers, five on tap, and a full liquor bar. It calls itself a sports bar—true, if holding a pool cue makes you an athlete. Open daily 'til 2 A.M.

If your nights aren't fueled by beer, amuse yourself with the **Diamond Circle Melodrama,** held at the Strater Hotel, 699 Main Ave., 970/247-3400, www.diamondcirclemelodrama.com, an authentic melodrama where the acting is stuck in the 1800s. The rapid-fire action makes it hard to follow at first, but once you catch on, it's completely entertaining. Stick around for the vaudeville sketches that follow the show. In peak summer seasons, the curtain rises at 8 P.M. Monday–Saturday. Tickets go for $17.

Shut-Eye

The city operates a central reservations line for lodging, activities, and the Durango-Silverton train. Call 800/525-8855 or head to www.durango.org and you'll get the skinny. Most chain hotels are north of downtown on Main Avenue.

Chain Drive*
A, C, E, G, L, S, U, X, BB, CC, DD,

*Chain hotels in, or within ten miles of town. See cross-reference guide featuring phone numbers and web addresses on page 405.

Inn-Dependence

A block off the main drag, Kirk and Diane Komick run both the **Leland House** and **Rochester Hotel,** 721 E. 2nd Ave., 970/385-1920 or 800/664-1920, www.rochesterhotel.com. With rates from $109–179, both offer superb rooms. I liked the Rochester for its Western film–themed rooms and mighty manly decor (some with kitchens), huge breakfast, fresh cookies and tea, and the fact that it used to be a bordello. Yowsah! Then again, both give you the comfort of an inn with the conveniences of a hotel.

A larger and mighty more expensive choice is the magnificent **Strater Hotel,** 699 Main Ave., 970/247-4431 or 800/247-4431, www.strater.com. Built in 1887, it's one of the nicest restored hotels you'll have the pleasure of finding, with rates from $169–205. The antiques are real, the restoration flawless, and the saloon and melodrama (see "Watering Holes") will add flavor to your tour. Not only are the 93 rooms large and quiet, the elegant Gilded Age accouterments throughout the lobby will turn you into a frontier high roller. Western novelist Louis L'Amour loved room 222—he said the ragtime music from the bar below gave him inspiration for his plots and characters.

Indulgences

If you don't agree that **O'Farrell Hats,** 563 Main Ave., 970/259-5900 or 800/895-7098, www.ofarrellhats.com, has the finest hats in the world, drop by and have your head examined. Open Monday–Saturday 9–9, Sunday noon–5. The secret here is the "conformotour," an ingenious device invented in Paris 160 years ago that measures the subtle bumps and shapes of a person's head. Armed with two of these antique babies, O'Farrell's custom-fits hats for celebrities, cowboys, and bikers. Prices are steep—about $700—and the 100 percent beaver-skin hats and customized cedar inserts take six–eight weeks to make. Riders have reported that the perfectly-fit customized hats are wind-tested to 55 mph.

On the Road: Durango to Telluride

Before you saddle up for the San Juan Skyway, heed the advice offered by local riders: Plan to stay longer than you expect; be aware that at night it gets supernaturally dark; be careful for gravel on mountain corners; and watch for wildlife. Although I suggest Telluride as the first overnight, you'll

An impressive road warning sign high in the Rockies. This was along the San Juan Skyway south of Ouray en route to Telluride.

© NANCY HOWELL

ride through other intriguing towns where you can stay the night without disappointment.

When you leave via 550 North, the road rises slightly as you enter the San Juan National Forest. Soon you are surrounded by nothing but Colorado, where the purple mountains' majesty will elicit enough "Oh, my Gods!" to start a new religion. After Cascade Creek it gets trickier, but you will fear no mountain, even as you ride over 10,000 feet into thin air. If you parked your bike and trotted 50 feet, you'd be panting like a dog.

When you reach the Colbank Pass Summit at 10,640 feet, you may think you've hit the highest height—but you haven't. There's much more to come, but for now observe the waterfalls, great timber, alpine meadows, and switchbacks that open the trapdoor into valleys below, then rise again to 10,910 feet at Molas Pass. If you wanted to go underground, you wouldn't need the FBI's help. You'd just camp out here.

Ride with caution: What follows are miles of steep grade yet only a two-foot-high guardrail between you and eternity. When you reach the overlook outside of Silverton, make sure your seatback's in its upright position for the final approach.

Silverton (elevation 9,318 feet), the terminus for the narrow gauge steam train, is a Victorian mining town that dates to 1874. As you cruise into town, the information center lies on the right (open daily 9–5), followed by a small village of gift shops, bakeries, small hotels, and markets. The same is to be found on notorious Blair Street, where bordellos once thrived. If you never rode the Durango train, listen for its cacophonous grand arrival, then roam around town. Drop by **Handlebars,** 117 13th St., 970/387-5395, a combination bar and paraphernalia-cluttered restaurant, where you can order up big food for lunch or dinner, or a big brew.

What succeeds Silverton is a fantastic ride on Otto Mears's "Million Dollar Highway." Roadside creeks flow outside rainbow-wide curves. Be careful here since the air and the road thins and there's no margin for error in the mountains—especially when you approach Red Mountain Pass. At 11,075 feet, this is the highest pass on your journey.

From here, it's back to Monaco riding with more twists than in a Hitchcock film. Some of the sharpest banked curves are right here, and the road becomes schizophrenic, not knowing which way it's supposed to turn. The repetitive corners give way to high canyon walls and valley overlooks that will remain with you for years, especially as you approach the town of Ouray (elevation 7,706), an optional overnight. For lodging information check with the **Ouray Chamber of Commerce** at 970/325-4746 or 800/228-1876, www.ouraycolorado.com.

Like Silverton, Ouray (pronounced "you-ray") made and lost its fortunes through mining. Whether you stay overnight or not, don't miss **Box Canyon Falls,** 970/325-4464. If you venture across the steel grating ($2.50) to get close to the falls, the spring run-off thunders and throws the full weight of its freezing waters on you.

Ouray also has Jeep tours and rentals that peel you off your bike and thrust you into the country. **Colorado West Jeep Rentals,** 701 Main St., 970/325-4014 or 800/648-5337, www.coloradowesttours.com, and **Switzerland of America Jeep Rentals,** 226 Seventh Ave., 970/325-4484 or 800/432-5337, www.soajeep.com, rent Wranglers and Cherokees for half- and full-day excursions, although most riders seem to prefer leaving the driving to guides who know area history and the right roads to reach fields of wildflowers, mining districts, waterfalls, and alpine meadows. Either way, with a Jeep you can explore ghost towns, old mining camps, and gold mines in and around Ouray. Bring warm clothes, food, a camera, and between $50 (tours) and $130 (on your own).

If your body's aching after a long ride, head to Ouray's main attraction, the **Hot Springs Pool,** 970/325-4638, where you'll pay $7.50 to soak in waters ranging from pleasantly warm to a muscle-melting 106 degrees.

The most important must-see is the **Bachelor-Syracuse mine tour,** 970/325-0220, offered daily. Take 550 North to CR 14; turn right and follow a gravel road to the mine entrance. Save room for food—the cowboys here cook killer breakfasts and lunches. After boarding a rickety mine car, you'll head 3,350 feet through a CAT scan–style tunnel eight feet wide by eight feet tall. It's eerie as hell riding along the veins of gold and silver, and even worse when the guide turns out the lights. Guides will provide a historical perspective to give you an in-depth and painless education on the hazards faced by western miners. Don't miss it.

The second leg down to Telluride is easier than the first, starting atop a plateau that gives way to a valley floor. When you reach Ridgway, turn left at Highway 62. The landscape grows larger and more impressive, and the consistently nice road affords several photo ops. Understand, this is not a road to be hurried through. This is slow-paced cowboy country; chances are you'll be tempted to unscrew the footpegs and string up some stirrups instead. The curves, neither dangerous nor demanding, lead easily to Route 145, which turns south on the western side of the San Juan Skyway.

The road rides through vapid Placerville, into a canyon, and then beside red rock cliffs and into the Uncompahgre National Forest. Sixteen miles after accessing 145, Telluride comes into view as you stare in awe at staggering Bear Mountain Pass, a zigzag motorcycle-destroying road that scales the mountainside beside a gushing river.

A great introduction, and the follow-up will not disappoint.

Telluride Primer

Telluride's is a mighty strange history, friend. The nomadic Utes arrived in the Telluride Valley searching for elk, deer, and mountain sheep, and then they split. The Spanish arrived in the 1700s searching for an overland route to the Pacific Coast, but they didn't stay, either. The settler who decided to stick it out was a man with a reason to stay: prospector John Fallon.

Fallon staked his claim above the town in 1875, registered the Sheridan Mine, then struck it rich with zinc, lead, copper, iron, silver, and gold. This was the Silicon Valley of the 1870s, drawing fortune seekers from around the world: Finns, Swedes, Irish, French, Italians, Germans, and Chinese. Unlike the millionaire geeks in California, these boys had gambling halls, saloons, brothels, and friends like Butch Cassidy, who arrived to plan his first heist at the San Miguel Valley Bank in June 1889.

When the mining boom collapsed, the town suffered a slow decline, approaching ghost-town status in the 1960s. That's when a few resolute citizens realized that "white gold" (a.k.a. snow) could save their town. With a few shakes of entrepreneurial spirit, they transformed Telluride into a ski resort.

*another beautiful Colorado
mountain view*

© NANCY HOWELL

The result will keep you satisfied. There are hippies trying to re-create the halcyon days of Haight-Ashbury (minus the nuisance of personal hygiene); art galleries and a surplus of natural beauty; and handsome young ski bums who make life worth living for middle-aged women and comparably depressing for middle-aged men. And then there is money, lots of it, imported by recent transplants and celebrity residents.

Beneath it all, however, this is an ordinary mountain town. There are small markets and a hardware store, the "Free Box" where the needy or greedy filch donated surplus, and a calendar of festivals, from the Telluride Airmen's Rendezvous to the Bluegrass Festival to the legendary Telluride Film Festival.

It's a great little town. Have fun.

On the Road in Telluride

You entered a valley when you entered Telluride, so a pleasure ride isn't worth the effort—at least, not on a bike. There are ways to get around and experience the town, most of which you can do fairly easily.

I'd suggest starting before 9, when the morning light bathes the mountains in a rich gold and the streets are perfectly deserted for photos. After grabbing a breakfast with the locals at Sofio's, walk over to the gondola on the south end of Oak Street, 970/728-2662. When it's not hauling skiers in winter, it's hauling sightseers in summer. And it's free.

Wait for an empty car and start your 30-minute round trip. From this vantage point, the aerial views of the town and mountains grow increasingly more majestic—but wait for the return ride to take photos, when ski racks won't block your view. There are two stops along the way, the first at Sophia Station (just under 11,000 feet), the second at Mountain Village (9,545 feet), a picturesque yet oddly artificial affluent neighborhood. Return for a night-time ride to enjoy equally magical views.

When you return to town, roam on foot. Don't pressure yourself. Just savor the mountain air and views and the fact that you're not in an office.

Pull it Over: Telluride Highlights
Attractions and Adventures

You can wander around searching for individual outfitters and rental compa-nies, or you can save some shoe leather by stopping at **Telluride Adventures,** 150 W. Colorado Ave., 970/728-4477 or 800/828-7547, www.telluride sports.com. Since 1972 they've been a one-stop shop for all things outdoors: fly-fishing, whitewater rafting, hiking excursions, glider rides, horseback rid-ing, and kayaking. Prices range from $15 (mountain bike rental) to $65 (pad-dle boat rental)—although prices for guided excursions (see below) are much higher.

Roudy, the town character, offers "gentle horses for gentle people, fast horses for fast people, and for people who don't like to ride, horses that don't like to be rode." Choices at **Riding with Roudy,** off Highway 145 (call for directions), 970/728-9611, www.ridewithroudy.com, include a variety of trail rides from roughly $30 an hour, as well as dinner rides ($60) and custom pack trips. If you ride, ride with Roudy. He's good company.

Telluride Outside, 121 W. Colorado Ave., 970/728-3895 or 800/831-6230, www.tellurideoutside.com, is a full-service provider of fly-fishing and float trips, whitewater rafting, ballooning, Jeep rentals, and tours.

Shopping

Earlier, I told you that O'Farrell's in Durango makes the best hats in the world. Well, Steve King, proprietor of **Bounty Hunter,** 226 Colorado St., 970/728-0256, says forget that. He's created custom hats for Ted Nugent, Madeleine Albright, the Clintons, and other people who can easily afford his customized beaver-skin hats, boots, belt buckles, $3,500 hand-burned deer-skin jackets, and $4,200 beaded jackets. He can re-create your favorite riding jacket with new leather and beaded eagle designs. Now, if you can figure out how to put this on your company's expense account, you've got it made.

A cool little neighborhood spirits shop, **Telluride Liquors & Wine Shop,** 219 W. Colorado Ave., 970/728-3380, features some 450 wines, 100 in the wine cellar, and 250 bottled beers, as well as a small humidor with a good selection of cee-gars. They deliver.

Now that most antiques shops claim that Flintstone jars are collectibles, it's great to find a place like **Telluride Antique Market,** 324 W. Colorado Ave., 970/728-4323, which sells quality antiques, such as silver-plated Indian prints, cheesecake calendars, Art Deco items, and old travel posters and prints.

Blue-Plate Specials

Perhaps the best place to grab an early breakfast, **Sofio's,** 110 E. Colorado Ave., 970/728-4882, looks like a typical Mexican restaurant and is a favorite with locals who gather for big portions of eggs, pancakes, sausage, omelettes, and waffles made with fresh ingredients. Sofio's also serves dinner.

Open for breakfast, lunch, and dinner, **Eagle's Nest,** 100 W. Colorado Ave., 970/728-0886, www.eaglesbarandgrille.com, is one of the town's more active restaurants at night. The mix of creative spins on Mexican, pasta, pizza, seafood, chicken, ribs, and steak entrées may be the reason, or the corner location, or the casual interior, or the full bar . . . whatever it is, it works.

Noticing a dearth of affordable dining options, **Smugglers Brewpub and Grille,** 225 S. Pine St., 970/728-0919, opened in 1998 and gained an instant following for its 10 on-site microbrews, ribs steeped in BBQ sauce, drunken chicken breasts, Philly cheesesteak sandwiches, and interior created from an old miner's warehouse. Open for lunch and dinner, this casual, laid-back joint is a great place to grab a brew on the patio.

If you're on a writer's budget, you'll be pleased with **Baked In Telluride,** 127 S. Fir St., 970/728-4775, serving breakfast, lunch, and dinner. You can grab a baked breakfast, slice of pizza, deli sandwich, soda pop, or big salad. Nothing fancy, but the food's real groovy.

Watering Holes

There are two authentic hangouts in Telluride. **Last Dollar Saloon,** 100 E. Colorado Ave., 970/728-4800, is one of them. "The Buck" comes complete with hardwood floors, brick walls, tin ceiling, pool table, full liquor bar, bottled beers, and a few on tap. Can't do much better when you want a main-street view and a place to meet real people.

O'Bannon's Irish Pub, 121 S. Fir St., 970/728-6139, www.obannons .com, is the other authentic hangout. This one's a small, loud basement bar with $4 pints of Harp, Bass, and Guinness, a pool table, juke box, well-worn bar, and ceiling draped with flags of Ireland.

Sheridan Bar, 231 W. Colorado Ave., 970/728-3911, open daily 3 P.M.–2 A.M., has a more manufactured feel, but you may not notice due to the tin ceiling, upright piano, long bar, and mighty cool pool hall in back.

Shut-Eye

Lodging options abound in Telluride; rates peak during winter and are higher in summer than in spring and fall. **Resort Quest of Telluride,** 800/538-7754, www.telluridelodging.com, books inns, condos, hotels, and homes. Rates aren't cheap, but if you're traveling with a group, their houses may be an option. The town's own service, **Telluride Central Reservations,** 970/728-3041 or 888/288-7360, www.telluride.com, handles lodging, too, as well as air service, performance tickets, and activities. Keep in mind that some accommodations require two-night minimum weekend stays, and prices rise during special event weekends like the Film and Bluegrass festivals.

Chain Drive*
A, C, CC

*Chain hotels in, or within ten miles of town. See cross-reference guide featuring phone numbers and web addresses on page 405.

Inn-Dependence
The **New Sheridan Hotel,** 231 W. Colorado Ave., 970/728-4351 or 800/200-1891, www.newsheridan.com, is one of the town's best bets, with rates from $120 to twice that. It was built in 1891 and has since gotten itself gussied up with 32 spacious, tasteful rooms and suites with nice furniture and spa tubs. There are also a few condo-style suites. The full breakfast, library, and fitness room are impressive, but what puts it over the top are the two rooftop hot tubs with spectacular mountain views.

On the Road: Telluride to Mesa Verde

The overwhelming beauty of this run will either inspire you or cause cardiac arrhythmia. Leave Telluride via West Colorado and turn left after the service station on Route 145. You're back on the San Juan Skyway now and gearing up for scenery you cannot imagine.

Within minutes you're riding into the mountains for a view of wildflowers, lakes, cliffs, and valleys slung between jagged mountain peaks. The road is like your grandmother—while you'll spy a few curves, most of it is dropping. The ride takes your bike down into portions of these valleys like an elevator falling down a shaft.

This section of highway is where all your Colorado visions come together. The curves are not difficult, but the overwhelming combination of colors and textures is hard to fathom. Drink in multiple shades of green from the rail-straight pines, fields of brilliant wildflowers, black and white mountains, and surreal blue skies.

The road is reluctant to become routine, and the surge of energy it triggers may spark you to goose it—but watch your speed since some curves can be deceptively tight. You'll cross the 10,000-foot plateau once again and see tundra and meadows before descending to 8,827 feet into the town of Rico, where there's not much except a gas station.

After Rico the road transforms into an ordinary ride through the country. It may not be as inspiring as the earlier run, but when you consider the alternative—bending paperclips in an office or sitting in city traffic—you should have no complaints.

Ride past red rocks and, before you know it, you've reached the Colorado Plateau between the San Juan Mountains and Sonoran Desert. When you reach the end of Route 145, turn left onto Route 160 East toward Durango. As you ride toward Mesa Verde, look to your left; about 40 miles away you'll see the mountains you conquered a few hours earlier.

On Mesa Verde

"I saw a little city of stone asleep—that village sat looking down into the canyon with the calmness of eternity, preserved with the dry air and almost perpetual sunlight, like a fly in amber, guarded by the cliffs and the river and the desert."

—Willa Cather on Mesa Verde

From here it's only seven miles to Mesa Verde National Park, although if you opt to stay the night at Far View Lodge (the park's only indoor lodging option), you have another 15 miles to go.

Whether or not you stay inside the park, get ready for the grand finale to your nearly circular run. After springing for the $10 fee (free if you carry a National Parks Pass), you'll ride a road that rises like a phoenix, with fantastically sharp ascents that open up endless views of the desert plains.

Four miles later, the Morefield Campground has a laundry and café, as well as the park's only option for gas. The road continues with curves similar to those of the Pacific Coast Highway, with each corner opening up to an ocean of earth. Once you've risen to the top of the mesa, take everything you recognize—then erase it from your databank. That is what you'll see—absolutely nothing. The emptiness lasts for mile after mile, with the only constant being the shifting, braking, and cornering you'll undertake to reach the visitors center.

Now the mystery begins.

Mesa Verde Primer

Mesa Verde is a strange and mysterious place. Take the tales of ghost ships and the Lost Colony, multiply them by a hundred, and you still won't even begin to understand Mesa Verde.

The "Ancestral Puebloans" (the term now preferred over the previously common "Anasazi," a derogatory Navajo word meaning "the ancient enemies") settled here, carving homes into the cliffs and valleys. They were hunters, traders, artisans, and farmers, and this area was the heart of their civilization for nearly a thousand years.

They built stone villages on mesa tops and cliff dwellings within canyon walls, and created elaborate stoneworks, ceremonial kivas, intricately designed pottery, and four-story housing structures. Then, around 1300 A.D., the inhabitants of Mesa Verde packed it up. No one knows what they left with, but they left behind crops and personal belongings. Since they had no written records, to this day no one knows where they went or why.

Their very existence remained a mystery until 1888, when ranchers Richard Wetherill and Charles Mason rode through the area to round up stray cattle. That's when Wetherill saw the village hidden within the canyon. A few years later, amateur archaeologist Gustaf Nordenskiold arrived to document the dwellings and sites.

What's intriguing is that the mystery remains to this day. Even though the park and services aren't on the level of Yellowstone or Yosemite, Mesa Verde was still selected the world's number-one historic monument by readers of *Condé Nast Traveler*—ranking ahead of the Vatican even! In 1978, UNESCO, a United Nations organization, named it a World Heritage Cultural Site, and Mesa Verde was also the first park dedicated to the preservation of cultural resources. While it doesn't feature the multitude of services you can find in Durango and Telluride, it's a logical, archaeological, and fascinating place to wrap up your San Juan Skyway run.

On the Road in Mesa Verde

Unless you're an anthropologist or Indiana Jones, there's only one way to see—and really understand—Mesa Verde. Two tours depart from the Far View Lodge and Morefield Campground. Unless you are willing to marinate your head with the intelligence of trained guides, you'll simply be looking at a map and struggling to comprehend more than 4,000 identified sites and ruins. Although the ride around the park's juniper- and piñon-dotted landscape is pleasing, it's just not worth traveling solo—and really not worth traveling at all from mid-September–mid-May, when not all services and tours are available.

Start at the Far View Visitor Center and arrange a special ranger-led tour ($2.25) to either Cliff Palace, Balcony House, or Long House, since demand restricts guests to one site per day. Hold off on touring the museum—it will make more sense once you've taken a tour.

On just the half-day bus/walking excursion, I learned more here in three hours than I did in three years of high school. Anyway, the first sites you see are ordinary, but the stories and structures become increasingly more fascinating. Starting with the ruins of a simple kiva (ceremonial room), you'll eventually reach Spruce Tree House, an elaborate structure of 114 rooms and eight kivas that you can walk to and, in some sections, through. Keep in mind that many of these structures were accessible only by scaling cliff walls, so you can assume cross-eyed and knock-kneed children probably didn't live very long. You also have to walk a half mile down to reach it, although it seems like two miles coming back up. Wear comfortable shoes and carry your own drinking water—none is available at any site.

I can't even begin to explain what you'll see and learn here—just swing by the Far View Visitor Center, sign up for a tour, and dig information out of the rangers. When you're done, plan to return to some of the places you missed, such as the museums at the visitors center and Spruce Tree (open daily 8–6:30), where dioramas and exhibits on pottery, jewelry, tools, weapons, and beadwork will fill in some of the blanks. They also have well-stocked bookstores as well as cheap ($.25) and informative pamphlets on specific sites.

Pull it Over: Mesa Verde Highlights
Attractions and Adventures

The entire park is a historic site, with guided tours departing from **Morefield Campground** and **Far View Lodge,** 800/449-2288. Half-day tours ($34) leave at 8:30 and 12:30 from Morefield and at 9 and 1 from Far View. The full-day tour ($55) departs at 9 from Morefield and 9:30 from Far View. Make reservations, especially in season.

Adjacent to the Mesa Verde museum, Spruce Tree Terrace sells silver jewelry, etched and painted pottery, and sand paintings. There is also a shop at the Far View Visitor Center. At various times throughout the summer, Native Americans hold handicraft fairs and demonstrations in the park.

Blue-Plate Specials

There are few places to eat at Mesa Verde. Snack bars and cafeteria-style restaurants at Far View and Spruce Tree are adequate if you're not agile enough to kill and skin a rabbit with an *atl-atl* (a local native spear-throwing device). If you can swing it, the **Metate Room** at Far View Lodge is the park's signature restaurant. No corn dogs here—load up on roast turkey, chicken escalante, Rocky Mountain trout, broiled salmon, lamb chops, or buffalo fajitas. They even have BBQ rabbit probably iced with an atl-atl. The Southwestern-style dining room has wide bay windows revealing glorious views of the mesas and finger canyons.

Shut-Eye

If you don't stay in the park, the nondescript town of Cortez, 10 miles west, has loads of chain hotels. Durango is 60 miles east. The park offers two options. The exterior of the top-of-the-line **Far View Lodge** is 1970s ugly and the interior is generic hotel, but you get a balcony with stunning views from a 2,000-foot plateau. Rates here go from $103–115. The **Morefield Campground** ($19 tent, $25 full hookups), a popular spot if you don't mind roughing it, has 435 campsites with picnic tables, grills, and benches, as well as a grocery store, showers, and a laundry. Reservations for either can be made by calling 970/565-2133 or 800/449-2288.

Chain Drive*
A, C, E, G, L, CC, DD

*Chain hotels in, or within ten miles of town. See cross-reference guide featuring phone numbers and web addresses on page 405.

Resources for Riders
Wild Colorado Run

Colorado Travel Information
Bed & Breakfast Innkeepers of Colorado—800/265-7696,
www.innsofcolorado.org
Colorado Division of Wildlife—303/297-1192 or 303/291-7534,
www.wildlife.state.co.us
Colorado State Parks—303/866-3437, www.parks.state.co.us
Colorado Road and Weather Conditions—303/639-1111, www.cotrip.org
Colorado Travel and Tourism—800/265-6723, www.colorado.com
Distinctive Inns of Colorado—970/586-8683 or 800/866-0621,
www.bedandbreakfastinns.org

Local and Regional Information
Cortez Weather and Road Conditions—970/565-4511
Durango Area Chamber Resort Association—970/247-0312 or 800/525-8855,
www.durango.org
Durango Weather and Road Conditions—970/247-3355
Mesa Verde Country Visitors Information—800/253-1616, www.swcolo.org or
www.mesaverdecountry.com
Mesa Verde National Park—970/529-4465 or 800/449-2288,
www.visitmesaverde.com or www.nps.gov/meve
Mesa Verde Road Conditions—970/529-4461
San Juan Skyway Association—800/962-2493, www.sanjuanskyway.com
Silverton Chamber of Commerce—970/387-5654 or 800/752-4494,
www.silveton.org
Telluride Road Conditions—970/249-9363
Telluride Visitor Services—970/728-6265 or 800/525-2717, www.tvs.org

Motorcycle Shops
Fun Center Suzuki-Kawasaki—50 Animas View Dr., Durango, 970/259-1070,
www.funcentercycles.com
Handlebar Cycle (Honda-Yamaha)—346 S. Camino Del Rio, Durango,
970/247-0845
Ridgway Motorsports—566 Hwy. 62, Ridgway, 970/626-5112
Gene Patton Motor Company (Honda-Yamaha-Kawasaki)—2120 S. Broadway,
Cortez, 970/565-9322

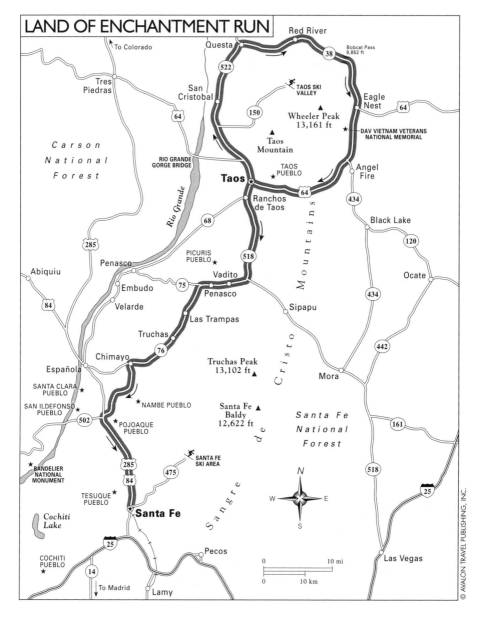

LAND OF ENCHANTMENT RUN

Route: Taos to Santa Fe via the Enchanted Circle, Red River, Eagle Nest, High Road, Peñasco, Madrid

Distance: 170-plus miles; allow three days.

    •Day 1—Taos/Enchanted Circle •Day 2—Travel •Day 3—Santa Fe

Helmet Laws: New Mexico does not require helmets.

Land of Enchantment Run

Taos to Santa Fe, New Mexico

You'll take a short ride along the "High Road" to Santa Fe, as well as a loop around the Enchanted Circle, a stretch punctuated by the creativity of Southwestern art. If you believe in the power of energy fields, this ride may give you a boost. Look for perfect riding weather and relatively quiet roads in late summer or early fall.

Taos Primer

I'll give Taos credit. Its ad campaign is so effective there's hardly a person in America who doesn't know about this town of 6,200. The short, soft name conjures images of bronzed Native Americans skillfully creating silver necklaces, copper bracelets, and turquoise rings. This isn't so much a compliment as it is an observation that Taos has created more out of less than any city I can recall.

When you talk to locals and ask what it is about Taos, they eventually admit, "The mountain either speaks to you or it doesn't." They're referring to Taos Mountain, which, some say, controls the lives of all who enter its domain: "If the mountain likes you, you must return. If you displease the mountain it will banish you forever." I must have done something to yank its chain.

Anyway, when you're here, you're in the Sangre de Cristo Mountains, where Indians arrived more than 1,000 years ago, followed by Spanish colonists who introduced the wheel, iron, horses, cattle, and disease. They were followed centuries later by French-Canadian trappers and then, in 1898, by two artists whose wagon broke down. Apparently the two pleased the mountain because they stuck around and turned Taos into an artist's colony.

On the Road in Taos

Though an artist's colony, Taos leans toward a monochromatic palette of brown and gray and mud and less-than-attractive streets. The city promotes the galleries and museums of Taos Plaza as well as the nearby Taos Pueblo. Each is worth seeing, but more intriguing is the 84-mile loop known as the Enchanted Circle. I've come to realize that New Mexico gives some attractions positive reinforcement to boost their self esteem—the circle isn't as enchanting as it is a good ride with some nice views.

You can hit the Taos Pueblo before or after your ride, which begins by taking Highway 64 (Kit Carson Road) North. At the junction of Highway 522, turn left on 64 and ride for seven miles to reach the Rio Grande Gorge Bridge, the "second largest suspension bridge on a national highway in America." (Everybody's got an angle.) Rest your bike; walk across the bridge; and look down into the gorgeous gorge 650 feet below.

Head back on 64 to take Highway 522 North on a clockwise run around the circle. It takes only a few miles to get into the groove; the plains create a surreal landscape, where clouds hover low to the ground and the valley stretches for miles. There are mile markers along the roadside, and at mile marker 10 in San Cristobal is the D. H. Lawrence Ranch, a gift to the writer from Mabel Dodge Luhan.

Six miles later, the winds and the views pick up as you enter Carson National Forest. When you reach Questa, turn right at the stoplight at Highway 38 and head east into a forest of spruce, Douglas fir, and ponderosa pine. If you're ever on a quiz show, remember that spruce trees have square needles and fir trees have flat needles and you'll be just fine.

Beyond the trees, the road jazzes things up. Although the terrain's not alpine and the Red River here is just a stream, the many curves and the rising elevation do expect you to pay attention. By the time you reach the town of Red River, you've climbed 8,750 feet into the hills and haven't broken a sweat.

Things have certainly changed here since the old days. Back then, there was only one hospital and the town's doctor was its only patient. Then he died, so they tore the hospital down. Today, the town is full of pizza restaurants, Mexican restaurants, trout fishing guides, and a few hotels and lodges—most here for the winter ski season.

The next 17 miles jack up the excitement. The road rises sharply and reveals a fantastic view of the valley below. At times it can be close to frightening, other times it's just really scary. Suddenly the trees aren't over your head, but falling

San Geronimo Church in Taos

away below as you cross Bobcat Pass at 9,852 feet and gun it into a series of steep grades and equally steep drops. Look to your right and you'll spot Wheeler Peak, which, at 13,161 feet, is the highest point in New Mexico.

Once you've tamed Bobcat Pass, you can pick up speed—at least until you reach a valley overlook that's perfect for yet another memorable motorcycle photo. From here the road is simple and empty until you reach the intersection of 38 and 64. Just past your fairing is Eagle Nest Lake, which you'll ride beside shortly. At the corner on your left lies a gas station/convenience store where you can buy everything from liquor to groceries, and where the clerks are as friendly as diner waitresses.

The town of Eagle Nest is to your left, and if you didn't grab a bite in Red River, there are some restaurants here. Otherwise, turn right and you're riding down Highway 64, the last road you need to return to Taos. Although desert states like New Mexico don't have much water, they do have reservoirs like Eagle Nest Lake, created by the largest privately built dam in the United States.

You'll ride beside the waterfront for several miles and there's no reason to stop, except for the **DAV Vietnam Veterans National Memorial.** David Westphall died in Vietnam in 1968, and his father created this site as a memorial to him and the 13 soldiers who died with him. Whether you're a vet or not, it's worth a moment to pay your respects to the soldiers and to the father who didn't forget.

Pass the winter resort town of Angel Fire and stay on Highway 64 for a heart-pumping ride. Almost immediately, you're into the sharpest and most consistent series of rises and twists along the circle. This beautiful ride takes you on winding roads, slows you down to 20 mph, and weaves back and forth as you re-enter Carson National Forest.

For several miles the road is hyperactive. Development is scant (a plus), trees plentiful, and turns tight. When you return to Taos County, the road becomes less curvy and cabins start cropping up along the river's edge. As in Vermont, people here make a living in the middle of nowhere, which is good if you're looking for a sculptor, carpenter, or a pit stop like the **Shady Brook Cafe and Inn,** 26219 Hwy. 64 E., 505/751-1990, which serves an inexpensive breakfast special.

After this, the road returns to normal and you're riding back into the heart of Taos. Walk around the plaza, see a museum, or blow it off, get back on your bike and do the whole ride counterclockwise.

Pull it Over: Taos Highlights
Attractions and Adventures

A clearinghouse for outdoor adventures, **Taos Mountain Outfitters,** 114 South Taos Plaza, 505/758-9292, www.taosmountainoutfitters.com, sells outdoor gear, but as a sideline they can help you arrange mountain climbing lessons and excursions, whitewater rafting, and hiking trips.

Van Beacham is a fourth-generation New Mexican who's carved out a nice niche—taking serious fishermen on a trip called Solitary Anglers. The retreat emphasizes year-round fly-fishing, without the crowds. Find him at **Los Rios Anglers,** 125 W. Plaza Drive, 505/758-2798 or 800/748-1707, www.los rios.com. Charging rates from $175 (two people, half-day) to $275 (two people, full day), he and his guides work with beginners and seasoned casters. Rod, reel, and wader rentals are available.

Since 1350, Taos Indians have lived in and near **Taos Pueblo,** 505/758-1028. Talk about rent control; this is the largest pueblo structure in America, a five-story creation of mud and straw, where residents still bake bread in outdoor domed ovens and sell the requisite baskets, pottery, jewelry, moccasins, and drums. Call in advance for a schedule of religious ceremonies, such as the Turtle Dance, Buffalo Dance, and Deer Dance—none of which ever made it to American Bandstand. The pueblo is open for tours ($10) daily 8–4:30. They also generate extra cash through pictures. Remember: If you take photos you're stealing the souls of the residents; but this minor transgression is overlooked if you slip them $10 for still photos and $20 for a video.

Shopping

If you're on the lookout for a leather jacket, you may want to postpone your purchase until you can come to **Overland Jacket Factory,** three miles north of

Taos Plaza on Highway 522, 505/758-8820, www.overland.com. Even if you think fur is murder, you'd die for one of their animal coats.

The folks at **Taos Drums,** Hwy. 68, 505/758-3796 or 800/424-3786, make and paint log, ceremonial, and hand drums out of rawhide and indigenous materials. They've been "Caretaker of the Drum" since 1951 and claim to have the world's largest selection of Indian drums. You can't beat that. Free drumming sessions and tours of the workshop are offered Monday–Friday at 11 A.M. and 2 P.M. This can be an inspirational stop. I was inspired to become "Caretaker of the Sousaphone."

If you're a doctor, optometrist, or medicine man, check out the old quack machines and medical instruments at **Maison Faurie Antiquities,** 1 McCarthy Plaza, 505/758-8545. The owner's a hoot (he's a Frenchman!) and the weird junk he has here is cool—and pretty expensive.

After awhile, Southwestern art starts to look the same. The difference at **Blue Rain Gallery,** 117 South Taos Plaza, 505/751-0066 or 800/414-4893, www.blueraingallery.com, is that the selection here is big enough to be different: baskets, sculptures, kachinas, glass, paintings, bronze, jewelry, photography, pueblo pottery, and blankets. The focus here is on the work of young Native American artists who "depict their native culture with elegant style and creative awareness." Not a bad mission. Open Monday–Saturday 10–6.

Blue-Plate Specials

The food's fancy and the setting's casual at the **Trading Post Cafe,** 4179 Hwy. 68, 505/758-5089. Dig into crispy garlic pork loin chop, Creole pepper shrimp, or Sonoma lamb chops—and send me your leftovers. **El Taoseño,** 819 Paseo del Pueblo Sur, 505/758-4142, is a locals' hangout for breakfast, lunch, and dinner. The menu features steaks, fish, Mexican, and Mexican-American offerings.

Michael's Kitchen, 304 Paseo del Pueblo Norte, 505/758-4178, has been cooking since 1974, whipping up chopped steaks smothered with gravy, onions, and potatoes, chicken fried steak, mammoth pork chops, fried chicken, trout, and Spanish dishes. Opens at 7 A.M., closes at 8:30 P.M., and serves all foods at all hours. Can't beat that.

Watering Holes

At **Eske's Brew Pub and Eatery,** 106 des Georges Ln., 505/758-1517, www.eskesbrewpub.com, the menu is strange (burritos, bangers and mash, nachos), but their New Mexican wines and nine varieties of beer on tap are fresh, unfiltered, and unpasteurized. Located in a 1920s flat-roofed adobe home, the outdoor setting is a good spot to discuss the day's ride.

The **Adobe Bar,** 125 Paseo Del Pueblo Norte, 505/758-1977, www.taos inn.com, is a hangout for locals and visiting artists and musicians. On Sundays, listen to flamenco guitarists; Monday is open mike; and the rest of the week brings musicians playing country, folk, and Western swing. You'll get a real sense of Taos by hanging out at this eclectic gathering spot.

Shut-Eye

Taos has a handful of chain hotels, but more inns. **The Taos Association of B&B Inns,** 505/758-4246 or 800/939-2215, www.taos-bandb-inns.com, represents 30 inns with rates from $70 to a honking-big $325.

Motels and Motor Courts
El Pueblo Lodge, 412 Paseo del Pueblo Norte, 505/758-8700 or 800/433-9612, www.elpueblolodge.com, is an adobe-style collection of motel and condo rooms within walking distance of the Plaza. The setting is secluded and private, a thick adobe wall concealing a heated swimming pool and hot tub. Rooms are just rooms, but a light breakfast sets this apart at reasonable rates from $70–89.

Sun God Lodge, 919 Paseo del Pueblo Sur, 505/758-3162 or 800/821-2437, www.sungodlodge.com, is further away (1.5 miles south of the Plaza), but you can justify the difference in distance. The God has 45 rooms and four kitchenettes, a hot tub, laundry facilities, picnic and BBQ areas, and six decked-out suites. They'll expect between $45–95 for a one bedroom, $49–109 for two rooms.

Chain Drive*
A, C, E, L, S, U, CC

*Chain hotels in, or within ten miles of town. See cross-reference guide featuring phone numbers and web addresses on page 405.

Inn-Dependence
Casa Benavides, 137 Kit Carson Rd., 505/758-1772 or 800/552-1772, www.taos-casabenavides.com, features Southwestern-style rooms with fireplaces, VCRs, antique furnishings, large beds, and room to spread out, with rates from $89 to more than you want to know. If you want to get out of Taos and back to nature, ride six miles to **Taos Creek Cabins,** Rt. 1, 505/758-4715 or 800/580-5434, www.taos creekcabins.com, where a stream flows below the mountain decks and you'll capture

views of Carson National Forest. Some cabins ($70–120) accommodate up to four people and include full kitchens, baths, glass-front woodstoves, large living rooms, and decks. So whad'ya think about that, Davy? Davy Crockett?

On the Road: Taos to Santa Fe

Instead of taking Highway 68 to Española and heading south, take the more exciting and life-affirming "High Road" to Santa Fe. You'll praise yourself later.

Leave Taos via Highway 68. Once you reach the outskirts of town, the plains open and the cliffs on the horizon look as insignificant as termite mounds. The road introduces some nice rises, and soon the scenery starts looking larger than life. The Rio Grande Gorge is in the distance, a monstrous gash in the earth, and over your right shoulder the landscape—with a dusting of snow—looks like the label on a Nestlés bar. This is one mighty view.

Hang a left onto Route 518 and let the joy begin. This first stretch is 16 miles of mountain riding. Stick with it and in less than a mile you'll see on your right the remains of a torreon, one of the round lookout towers that ranchers used for protection against nomads. Historic churches dot the landscape, but even more divine is the entrance into Carson National Forest for an exciting run toward Route 75. Run, forest, run.

Although the towns are poor, the roads are rich with daring corners and a splendid emptiness that gives you room to think. Everything here is scenic and natural—although there are so many icons of sliding trucks you'll think you're part of a convoy. You may even consider investing in a seatbelt.

Take the road past Vadito (nothing here) and six more miles to Peñasco, which looks like a major metropolitan area compared to everything else you've just seen. There are a few restaurants and a gas station, so fuel up with food and gas if you need it.

From here, take Route 76 South toward the towns of Las Trampas and then Truchas, a ghost town that hasn't given up the ghost. The road is great and the landscape as inspiring as any O'Keeffe painting. Keep watching because that's all you can do for the next 35 miles until you reach Chimayo. Settle back and reward yourself with a good ride.

It gets tricky around here. Highways aren't always marked and most roads have Spanish names that many Anglos have a hard time deciphering. Look for the entrance to 98 (a.k.a. Juan Medina Road) and head south. After the sporadic craft shops, haciendas, and restaurants, comes a wild road.

Roads 518 and 76 were just a prologue to this stretch. The road, which leads into 503, is like Nolan Ryan—it throws you curves when you don't expect it.

Then there are the moguls, the series of quick rises and falls that would be great in winter if you could lash some skis to your tires. Take advantage of this road. Treat it like a beast. Once you've mastered turns that switch directions when you crest a hill, it'll start to slow down into some graceful bends as it works its way toward US 84/285 north of Santa Fe.

Compared to your recent past, the road into Santa Fe is less than thrilling, but there's something to watch for: Camel Rock. I've seen rocks that look like things, but this rock really looks like a camel. Sadly, its hump was trampled into dust by generations of hyperactive climbing kids.

Hump-bustin' little brats.

Santa Fe Primer

La Villa Real de la Santa Fe Asis, a.k.a. Santa Fe, has seen its fair share of conquistadores. It's been the capital city for Spain, Mexico, the Territory of New Mexico, and New Mexico itself.

Francisco Coronado showed up in 1540 searching for gold, but he eventually gave up and left for Mexico. Priests started digging for souls instead of gold, and missions began springing up alongside the Native American pueblos. Not willing to accept defeat, more Spanish explorers returned to hunt for gold, and the capital moved around a few times before settling here in 1610.

Then Mexico overthrew the Spanish here in 1821 and Santa Fe became a commercial center. Apparently, the Americans who showed up with goods to sell liked the city, because they figured out a way to get it away from the Mexicans in 1846. The Americans didn't have it long, though, because in 1861, the Confederates took over—but I'm pretty sure the Americans got it back later.

Today Santa Fe is a large town that looks small, a historic community where everything is adobe, a religious town where faith lies somewhere between Christianity and Native American spirituality. There's not much beyond the historic district, but that alone is worth the trip.

And you don't have to please no damn mountain.

On the Road in Santa Fe

If you're wondering if your future holds a good ride through Santa Fe, consider Will Rogers' thoughts on the matter: "Whoever designed the streets in Santa Fe must have been drunk and riding backwards on a mule." That said, when you're in the historic downtown section, look at Santa Fe as a condensed walking town with enough authenticity to make you feel like you're not being ripped off. Even though the tourists look touristy, there are also hippies and Native Americans surrounding the plaza, probably the best place to hang out and watch people.

Although the city doesn't legislate interiors, it does have a say in "culturally appropriate exteriors." If it's Spanish, Native American, or early American Mexican architecture, then it's OK. This isn't a recent bureaucratic decision. In the early 1900s, artists thought Santa Fe was looking as uniform as other American towns, with new citizens bringing in Gothic, Romanesque, Queen Anne, and Italianate architecture from the Midwest. So they did something about it.

As in Charleston or Savannah, you can ride around the historic section and stare at buildings from your bike, but until you have a point of reference it won't mean a thing. When you've finished getting an insider's view, wander around and check out hidden courtyards and church interiors. Roam the plaza, where Native Americans sell jewelry and pottery on blankets. If you travel with a camera, ask before taking their picture—and then have 10 bucks ready to pay them for the privilege. You may do better with a postcard.

Since any tour takes only a couple hours, allow an afternoon for a ride down the Turquoise Trail. To reach it, take Highway 68 out of Santa Fe to I-25 and then exit at 278A onto Highway 14 South toward Albuquerque. It's always satisfying when an interstate doubles as a scenic road, and I-25 is just that, so when it leads to 14, the transition is seamless. Well, almost.

One of the first points of interest is the New Mexico State Penitentiary. If you have friends here, stop by and say hello. From here the road isn't as curvy as in Napa Valley, but the landscape seems similar. After passing 44A, the mountains seem rounder and the trees are of uniform height and shape.

This ride doesn't expect much from you. Just enjoy the afternoon since there's not much to see—except Madrid. Picture the Waltons, except poorer, and you can visualize this place. It's a strange old town, once thriving with coal mines, that sort of appears out of nowhere with the Madrid Country Store, art galleries, a bookstore, a bed-and-breakfast, a coffee shop, and the must-see **Mine Shaft Tavern,** 505/473-0743, which, judging by the rows of motorcycles, appears to be popular with riders. I imagine they serve miners, too.

Stay in Madrid or keep riding down past Golden, then to Highway 536, and turn right for a $3 ride up to **Sandia Crest,** 505/243-0605, www.turquoise-trail.org, elevation 10,678 feet. The view from "High Point on the Turquoise Trail," as from other high points, is tremendous. A restaurant and observation platform sit at the peak and, the views are all yours.

After descending the peak, head back on the Turquoise Trail. The road is extremely easy, but never mundane. It'll test your reflexes, but not expect you to be a motocross rider. The other advantage is that it seems lightly traveled; out here in the middle of nowhere, it's just you, desert cactus, and the world. Perfect.

Pull it Over: Santa Fe Highlights
Attractions and Adventures

Dig this: On the Ninth Day of Novena, the nuns at Loretto Chapel prayed to Joseph to create a way to get to the choir loft. Well, wouldn't you know it, a carpenter leading a donkey appeared and he got busy creating the "Miraculous Stairway": two 360-degree spirals in a staircase built without a central supporting rod! Then he left without a word! Even though historians know the fix-it man was a French master carpenter and not Joseph, the faithful don't let that interfere with a good story. Pay $2 to tour the **Loretto Chapel,** located at 207 Old Santa Fe Trail, 505/982-0092, www.lorettochapel.com.

More than 80 paintings, watercolors, drawings, pastels, and sculptures that O'Keeffe made between 1914 and 1982 are on exhibit at the relatively new **Georgia O'Keeffe Museum,** 217 Johnson St., 505/995-0785 or 505/946-1000, www.okeeffemuseum.org. It's open Tuesday–Sunday 10–5, until 8 on Friday. Admission is $8. If you ride and are inspired by the beauty of New Mexico, you're seeing O'Keeffe's vision. She felt she belonged here to paint the ragweed and scraggly maples and cow skulls. "That was my country," she said. "Terrible winds and a wonderful emptiness." I feel that way after I eat cabbage.

The "A Boot About" tour elevates you from a tourist to a student of history. When the two hours are over, you'll understand in detail what was shakin' around Santa Fe during the last 500 years. The $10 tour departs at 9:45 and 1:45 from the **Hotel St. Francis,** 309 W. San Francisco St., 505/988-2774, www.abootabout.com.

Riding at High Elevations

When you ride in the mountains, for the first few nights you may experience symptoms that accompany reduced amounts of oxygen: insomnia and headaches. By staying in good physical condition, you'll have better reserves to cope with the change in altitude. Still, if you'll be residing or riding at elevations over 6,000 feet, it's wise to gradually adapt to physical activities over several days.

The **Outback Tour,** 505/820-6101 or 800/800-5337, www.outbacktours .com, takes you out of the city and into the countryside on a variety of tours ($55–96) to Bandelier National Monument to explore Anasazi Indian ruins, to the Jemez volcano, and to O'Keeffe country, land of red rock canyons and O'Keeffe's Ghost Ranch. Other tours leading to remote mesas, juniper, and pine forests cover fossil safaris, history, and geology.

Several whitewater rafting operations run out of Santa Fe—although the water's out of town. Most feature half- and full-day whitewater rafting, as well as overnight trips, fly-fishing, canoe trips, and kayak instruction. Among the many operators, the **New Wave Rafting Company,** 505/984-1444 or 800/984-1444, www.newwaverafting.com, paddling since 1980, has tame trips as well as ones that navigate the Racecourse, which is five miles of white water, and the Taos Box, 16 miles of wilderness gorge. Ask for current prices and whether your excursion includes lunch and gear.

Blue-Plate Specials

The Razatos family has been on the plaza since 1918, and their old-fashioned diner is infused with their character. Serving breakfast, lunch, and dinner, **Plaza Restaurant,** 54 Lincoln Ave., 505/982-1664, is packed with locals who dine on standard diner meals (meatloaf, hot turkey sandwiches, burritos). I like the signage that marks a family restaurant. If you have a complaint, they list numbers for the police chief, mayor, governor, and president. You're also reminded not to talk back or fidget, and to keep your elbows off the table, be nice, and say thank you.

Bobcat Bite, Old Las Vegas Highway, 505/983-5319, has received applause for the best cheap eats in town and praise for their green chile cheeseburgers. Don't expect to spread out: Seating capacity's about 18 and often there can be a wait for a seat. Out of the way (about five miles north) but worth the ride.

Horseman's Haven, 6500 Cerrillos Rd., 505/471-5420, has been all in the family since the 1960s, whipping up breakfasts, burgers, burritos, chile, and authentic Mexican dishes. Yes, the sweat will pop out of your head almost as if you were dancing the bossa nova with Ann-Margret.

I love the name of the **Cowgirl Hall of Fame,** 319 S. Guadulupe St., 505/982-2565, and the food has worked its magic on me, too: Mesquite smoked BBQ ribs, chicken and brisket, grilled salmon soft tacos, jerk chicken, monster T-bones, and made-from-scratch *Chiles Rellenos.* The dozen draft beers, ales, and full bar are best savored on the deck. Check out the portrait library of honorees from the National Cowgirl Hall of Fame and walls crammed with memorabilia celebrating the American Cowgirl. Ride 'em, cowgirl.

Watering Holes

Although not a "biker" bar, **Evangelo's,** 200 W. San Francisco St., 505/982-9014, plays the blues and caters to bikers. If you arrive on your bike, they waive the cover—even when there's a band. The place features four pool tables, a downstairs bar, 150 kinds of beer, and a cool and comfortable look that mixes the South Pacific and Mediterranean. Right on the plaza.

El Farol, 808 Canyon Rd., 505/983-9912, www.elfarolsf.com, is a restaurant, but the draw is the bar, where you can listen to local musicians playing hot Spanish music, blues, country and western, Mexican flamenco, or rock—the format changes each night. Arrive after 10 P.M., when things start to cook—and go home to display your newfound flamenco dancing skills.

San Francisco Street Bar and Grill, 114 W. San Francisco St., 505/982-2044, also serves food (their hamburgers have been featured in *Esquire* and the *New York Times*), but you'll want to concentrate on the 14 wines, soft ice margaritas, tequilas, sangrias, spirits, and draft beer.

Shut-Eye

You can make one call to find a variety of places in Santa Fe. **Santa Fe Detours,** 505/986-0038 or 800/338-6877, www.sfdetours.com, is a reservation service for hotels, motels, inns, horse rides, river runs, and rail trips. Also try Santa Fe Central Resevations, 800/776-7669.

Chain Drive*
A, C, D, I, L, N, P, Q, S, T, X, U, W, BB, CC, DD

*Chain hotels in, or within ten miles of town. See cross-reference guide featuring phone numbers and web addresses on page 405.

Indulgences

If you can swing this one, more power to ya. The **El Dorado Hotel,** 309 W. San Francisco St., 505/988-4455 or 800/955-4455, www.eldoradohotel.com, is a grand Southwest hotel that fits Santa Fe perfectly. Rates run $269–299. Spoil yourself silly with butler service (really), balconies, rooftop swimming, a whirlpool, and exercise rooms. They also take reservations for the Inns of Santa Fe (three smaller properties within walking distance) and you can still use the facilities here.

Resources for Riders

Land of Enchantment Run

New Mexico Travel Information

Highway Hotline—800/432-4269
New Mexico Bed & Breakfast Association—505/766-5380 or 800/661-6649,
    www.nmbba.org
New Mexico Department of Tourism—800/733-6396, www.newmexico.org
New Mexico State Parks and Recreation—505/476-3355 or 888/667-2757
    (NMPARKS), www.emnrd.state.nm.us/nmparks

Local and Regional Information

Santa Fe County Chamber of Commerce—505/983-7317,
    www.santafechamber.com
Santa Fe Visitors Bureau—505/955-6200 or 800/777-2489, www.santafe.org
Santa Fe Weather Information—505/827-9300
Taos Visitors Center—505/758-3873, www.taoschamber.com
Taos Reservations and Recreation—800/732-8267, www.taosguide.com

Motorcycle Shops

Dave's Custom Cycle—214 Paseo Del Pueblo Sur, Taos, 505/758-4535
Centaur Cycles (BMW)—452 Jemez Rd., Santa Fe, 505/471-5481
Bobby J's Yamaha Inc.—4724 Menaul Blvd., Albuquerque, 505/884-3013
Chick's Harley-Davidson/Buell—5000 Alameda Blvd. N.E., Albuquerque,
    505/856-1600, www.chickshd.com
Motorsports—6919 Montgomery Blvd., Albuquerque, 505/884-9000
R & S Kawasaki-Suzuki—9601 Lomas Blvd. N.E., Albuquerque, 505/292-6692,
    www.teamrands.com

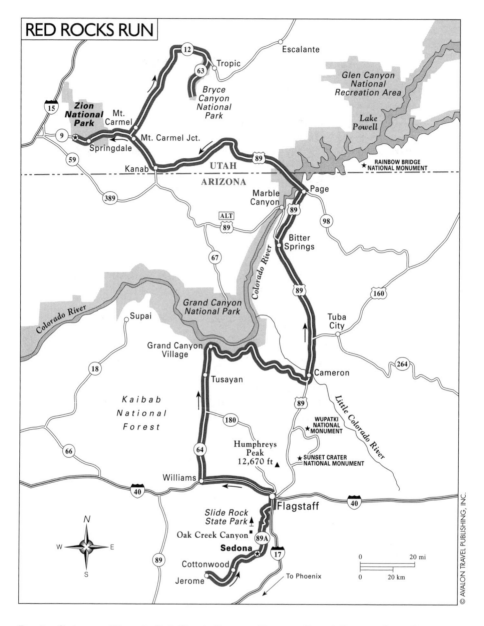

Route: Sedona to Zion via Oak Creek Canyon, Tusayan, Grand Canyon, Page, Bryce Canyon

Distance: Approximately 365 miles; consider six days with stops.
• Day 1—Sedona • Day 2—Travel • Day 3—Grand Canyon • Day 4—Travel
• Day 5—Page/Travel • Day 6—Zion National Park

First Leg: Sedona to Grand Canyon (110 miles)

Second Leg: Grand Canyon to Page/Lake Powell (143 miles)

Third Leg: Page/Lake Powell to Zion National Park (112 miles)

Helmet Laws: Arizona and Utah do not require helmets.

Red Rocks Run

Sedona, Arizona to Zion National Park, Utah

Over the next several days, you'll find that just as the Calistoga-Sausalito-Carmel run is a perfect showcase for California towns and roads, Sedona-Grand Canyon-Zion is the right blend for Arizona and Utah. With the exception of Sedona, the roads are not very challenging, but you may not mind too much. The vast openness of this part of the country is intriguing in its own way. The riding weather in early fall is ideal.

Sedona Primer

Sedona. It's a beautiful name for a beautiful place. I mean, would you feel the same way if you rode into Schnebly Station? That was the first name proposed by settler T. Carl Schnebly when he wanted to establish a post office here in the early 1900s. When the postmaster decided the name was too long for a cancellation stamp, the honor went to Carl's Pennsylvania Dutch wife, Sedona.

Turn back the clock and you'll see that it's taken nature about 350 million years to make Sedona what it is today. No standard issue brown and gray rocks here. Sedona's fire-red buttes and mesas, spires and pinnacles are the result of a prehistoric sea washing over, and receding from, the area seven times.

First settled around 700 A.D., the area was home to the Sinaguans, who stuck around until 1066, when a volcano blew. They left and the Anasazi arrived to take advantage of the recently fertilized soil and to introduce modern amenities like multi-storied pueblos and burglar-proof homes. Low doorways forced intruders to crouch upon entering, so the vigilant Anasazi homeowner could bash their brains out.

No one knows why the Anasazi left in the 1300s. In the 1500s, Spanish explorers came looking for gold and didn't find any; so they left, too. Prospectors, pioneers, and trappers began to arrive in the early 1800s and got along fine with the new tribes here, until the white man began fencing off Native hunting grounds. By 1872, the American army had heard enough complaining and shoved the Native Americans off their land in the infamous "March of Tears."

Despite the injustice, Native Americans are well represented throughout Sedona. Today, this is a major cultural center, with dozens of artists, actors, writers, and musicians gaining their inspiration from the beauty outside their doors. New Age disciples also congregate here, claiming Cathedral Rock is Sedona's most powerful female "vortex"—an electromagnetic energy force rising from within the earth. If you believe, you may find balance in health, relationships, work, and money.

Chances are you'll spend the majority of your time in Uptown Sedona, the older commercial district, or take a quick run down Oak Creek Canyon. There's nearly nothing you'd want to do indoors except sleep and eat, which makes this a natural for motorcycle travelers.

Wherever you ride, the roads will be right.

On the Road in Sedona

It's been said that God created the Grand Canyon, but He lives in Sedona.

Sedona *is* divine. When you arrive you'll see that the physical beauty combines the mountains of Vermont, the rocks of California, and the clay of Georgia back roads. If it looks at all familiar, you may have seen a similar landscape from Pathfinder's mission to Mars.

There's a lot to see on surrounding roads. Perhaps the most popular stop for motorcycle travelers is 24 miles away in Jerome, an old mining town, now a weird destination. From Sedona, the ride's not that nice, but if you didn't go there, your friends might beat you with sticks.

From Uptown Sedona, South Highway W. Hwy. 89A is a wide four-lane road that passes franchise restaurants, reduces to two lanes, and rides away from the red rocks—which look outstanding in your mirrors. The road remains the same until you reach Cottonwood, where you turn left at the Shell Station and begin your steep ascent. It's another four miles up the mountain, where the landscape was borrowed from a Saturday-morning cowboy matinee.

Chilling out by the red rocks in Sedona, Arizona.

© NANCY HOWELL

Next to Taos, Jerome has done the best job of creating something out of nothing. In its heyday as a copper mining community, it was the third-largest city in Arizona. Now there's no gas station or grocery, no doctor or pharmacy, and the bank is an ATM. It won't matter to you after you park your bike with all the others outside the **Spirit Room,** 144 Main St., 928/634-8809, and consider yourself at home.

This joint has become the base for riders making their way to high mountain country, low desert, red rocks, and canyons in an easy one-day ride. No fighting, no country music, no pointy boots, just a watering hole for riders who appreciate the lack of a cover, $2 brews, and Bloody Marys that can hurt you. You can add to the bar's collection of graffiti or donate a bra (if you wear one).

Further down on Main Street, **Paul and Jerry's,** 928/634-2603, has been a saloon since 1887. Today it serves beer and has a full bar and three pool tables in back. **Jerome Grill,** 309 Main St., 800/634-5094, www.innatjerome.com, built in 1899, is one of a few restaurants serving standard hamburgers, enchiladas, soups, and appetizers. For $100 they'll run down to Cottonwood and pick you up a Big Mac.

Unless you've got a mighty deep hankering for a drink, Jerome should take only a few hours. When you return to Sedona, you'll be tempted to examine the red rock monoliths that contrast beautifully with the green of piñon, juniper, and cypress trees. Pick up a Sedona map that identifies the monoliths, which are named for their appearance: Cathedral, Courthouse, Snoopy, Elephant. . . You'll have to find the local off-color favorite on your own.

Since you'll be running down Oak Creek Canyon on your way north, head down Highway 179 to Chapel Road and turn left to reach the **Chapel of the Holy Cross,** 928/282-4069. A labor of love, the chapel was purposely designed to appear as part of the rock formation. From its summit, you have an unobstructed view of Courthouse Butte, Bell Rock, and the Two Nuns. Time this for late afternoon and you'll be here to witness one of the most spectacular sunsets in the country.

Afterward, the town is yours to explore. Wander around uptown or go deeper into the desert on a Jeep tour. Sedona is a great town—you shouldn't cheat yourself.

Pull it Over: Sedona Highlights
Attractions and Adventures

The term "great outdoors" doesn't do justice to Sedona. It's greater than that—but inaccessible to touring bikes. Other modes of transportation—rental Jeeps, guided tours, and hot air balloons—can be almost as much fun, though. Most ground-based tours take you on rugged and historic trails leading to off-the-beaten-path canyons and mountains.

Ride with a guide on **Sedona Red Rock Jeep Tours,** 270 N. Hwy. 89A, 520/282-6826 or 800/848-7728, www.redrockjeep.com. Prices range from $36 for a 90-minute trip to $54 for an intro vortex tour and a horseback ride, led by experienced cowboys, on the Legends of Sedona Trails. Everyone needs a gimmick, and **Pink Jeep Tours,** 204 N. Hwy. W. Hwy. 89A, 928/282-5000 or 800/873-3662, www.pinkjeep.com, has made color theirs. These folks offer tours ranging from a $32, 90-minute Canyon West ride to the $60 Ancient Ruin ride. The 2.5-hour trip heads to a Sinaguan Indian cliff dwelling, where a guide points out and explains the rock art. For roughriders, try the Broken Arrow run, which offers two hours of heavy duty 4x4-ing.

A Day In The West, 252 N. Hwy. 89A, 928/282-4320 or 800/973-3662, www.adayinthewest.com, has an array of tours. Photo tours, Jeep tours, horseback rides, and chuckwagon trips are planned by guides "who've been riding these trails so long there's red dust in their veins." Prices range from $32 for the photography adventure to $95 for the western dinner.

Although you won't see the rocks up close, **Northern Light Balloon Expeditions,** 928/282-2274, offers the most peaceful way to see them—provided you can shake yourself awake for the sunrise flight. They'll pick you up at your place and get you worked up for an hour flight ($135), but the entire experience lasts up to four hours because of the inflation and post-flight lunch.

The payoff for the early day is that you'll feast on a brilliant palette of colors only found in nature. And Sedona.

If you're looking for a concentration of Southwestern art, you'll find it uptown or at **Tlaquepaque** (tah-lah-ca-pok-ee), Hwy. 179 at the bridge, open daily 10–5. Modeled after a Mexican village, the shopping district spreads out and rambles through shaded courtyards and ivy-covered walls.

Blue-Plate Specials

It looks like a hole in the wall, but at **Cowboy Club Grille & Spirits,** 241 N. Hwy. 89A, 928/282-4200, "high desert cuisine" goes hand in hand with Old West tradition and hospitality. Try the rattlesnake(!), pistachio-crusted halibut, buttermilk fried chicken, or buffalo(!) sirloin, low in fat, high in protein. The bar is great, too. Their margaritas are legendary, and the Prickly Pear is made with real cactus juice. The prices are fair here, the service excellent. Cowboy is open for lunch and dinner. Oh, and the *Cowboy Artists of America* was founded here.

I usually wake up well before breakfast so it was a boon to find the **Coffee Pot Restaurant,** 2050 W. Hwy. 89A, 928/282-6626, which can create—upon request and with no help from *confederates*—101 types of *omelettes.* I got mine with pencil shavings, string, and gravel. Here since the 1950s, the Coffee Pot is the place for locals (and celebrities) and anyone who wants a hearty breakfast or lunch.

Shut-Eye

For a complete listing of more than 20 bed-and-breakfast inns that are inspected and approved by the Sedona Bed & Breakfast Guild, check out www.bb sedona.net. The **Sedona Chamber,** 928/282-7722, www.sedonachamber.com, is a good source of information on the many cabins of Oak Creek Canyon.

Motels and Motor Courts

The **Sedona Motel,** 218 Hwy. 179, 928/282-7187, is just over a half-mile from the town center and offers 16 rooms with microwaves, coffee makers, and mini-fridges. Rates start at a reasonable $50 and go to $100, but note that the highway rolling past may break your sleep.

La Vista Motel, 500 N. Hwy. 89A, 928/282-7301 or 800/896-7301, is one of the most economical choices with rates from $49–65. Don't expect much, but for a place to bunk down, this is good enough.

Chain Drive*
A, C, E, J, K, L, S, T, CC

*Chain hotels in, or within ten miles of town. See cross-reference guide featuring phone numbers and web addresses on page 405.

Inn-Dependence
The **Creekside Inn,** 99 Copper Cliffs Dr., 928/282-4992 or 800/390-8621, www.creeksideinn.net, rests—ironically—right beside Oak Creek. Although the setting is wild, the inn is not—it's Victorian with swank guestrooms featuring jetted tubs and a furnished garden patio. A room here goes for $175–275. This is the place for husband and wife riders who've paid off the mortgage.

Indulgences

If you're traveling in a pack or need room to spread out, **Junipine,** 8351 N. Hwy. 89A, 928/282-3375 or 800/742-7463, www.junipine.com, features one- and two-bedroom creek-side cottages for $200–240 in the heart of Oak Creek Canyon. The cottages contain a fully-equipped kitchen, private deck, living room, and two fireplaces. The secluded wooded setting may make it hard to break away.

On the Road: Sedona to the Grand Canyon

If you couldn't resist temptation, you may have already ridden up this road. Not a bad idea because it's definitely worth a second look. The beginning of this run is a perfect goodbye to Sedona, since it is just as beautiful, albeit in a lush, more verdant way.

The topography changes immediately as Highway 89A slides into Oak Creek Canyon. From your seat, you command a vantage point not enjoyed by motorists. The canyon appears on your right, so close to the guardrail it seems much deeper than it actually is. The railing is low enough to flip you over the side if you're not careful.

So far, this gentle ride doesn't demand a lot, except that you pay attention to nature. Just when you didn't think it could get better, it does, with red rocks on one side and a canopy road on the other. You're descending into the canyon now and approaching **Slide Rock State Park,** 928/282-3034, a slippery run down the rocks that's worth a stop if you have a bathing suit in your bags. Admission is $7.

Continuing north, you'll pass small motels and creek-side cabins; gradually, the red rocks give way to white granite formations that look like El Capitan in miniature. Soon you begin your ascent into hearty pine forests, riding up to 6,000 feet and facing some exciting 20-mph twisties. You can see the challenge ahead when you look straight up and see the Babel-esque road winding overhead. This is a very nice road, and slightly safer since a sprawling chain-link fence keeps the mountain from falling on you.

At 7,000 feet, pull off at Oak Creek Vista, a great place for a picture, with the creek flowing 1,500 feet below. Joining you will be about 30 Native Americans who sell silver and turquoise jewelry and other handcrafted artwork.

Just as you're getting used to the curves, the road turns into a level pine forest and Oak Creek Canyon Road surrenders to I-17. Turn left (north) and drive a few miles to reach I-40 West. Arizona notes that I-40 is a scenic drive, but for the most part, it offers only wide, empty landscape, with the exception of **Grand Canyon Harley-Davidson,** W. Hwy. 66 at Exit 185, 520/774-3896, on your left. Unless you need yet another specialty H-D leather jacket or underwear, though, ignore it and follow Highway 180.

Ahead is Humphrey's Peak, which, at 12,633 feet, is the highest point in Arizona. The road skims along its base, which gives you the privilege of continuing the same pine forest run that's become a part of your life. Far more scenic than I-40, taking Highway 180 will provide your motorcycle tour with roughly 30 miles of road bordered by pines and mountain. You won't face the challenge of switchbacks, nor will you suffer from the hypnotizing effects of straights either. Instead, the road is marked by slow, meandering curves that glide across a fairly level landscape. As soon as you've grown accustomed to the richness and verdant green of the forest, nature decides to change the scene. You start dropping slowly and imperceptibly as you cruise into the high desert. As you ride steadily along 180, you'll ride across another 20 miles of desert and sagebrush before reaching the junction of Highway 64, which you'll take north.

Even though the road is flat, you may have the same gut feeling I did: that you're riding on the crest of an abnormally large mountain. In reality, you are. The Kaibab Plateau is a low, rounded mountain, and while you still have 30 more miles before hitting Grand Canyon, the ease and solitude of the landscape grants abundant time to relax and think. At mile marker 196, the land rises slightly and the plains spread out before you. On a clear day, you can see the Grand Canyon, from here just a black streak.

There's little to note between here and there, just straight riding until you reach the growing village of Tusayan and your destination.

Grand Canyon Primer

Each time a magazine or TV program does a "best of America" piece, you can bet you'll see an image of the Grand Canyon. For good reason. It's large; it's beautiful in an empty sort of way; and as a national park, it belongs to you.

Back in 1530, though, it belonged to Don Lopez de Cardenas, a captain in Coronado's expedition. It was de Cardenas who discovered the Grand Canyon—which was news to the Native Americans who were already here.

Fast forward to the 20th century. The Grand Canyon was named a national monument in 1908 and a national park in 1919. The reasons are clear: This canyon is far larger than anything you can imagine. When you stand at the rim and look down, you're seeing only a fraction of the entire canyon. The dimensions are staggering: Measured by river course, the chasm is 277 miles long, up to 18 miles wide, and has an average depth of one mile. It took 6 million years (give or take a few hours) to cut the Grand Canyon, and nature is not finished yet. Rain, snow, heat, frost, and wind are still sculpting new shapes, bluffs, and buttes. The reed-thin creek at the bottom is the Colorado River, which averages 300 feet wide and up to 100 feet deep. This sliver of water is the erosive force that carved the canyon.

Avoid visiting in the summer. Grand Canyon Village is packed and no vehicles—not even your faithful mount—are allowed on Western Drive. The road is open only from mid-October–mid-March. This and dense traffic detract from the experience. See it in autumn and in the morning, before the high sun washes out its colors. If you have the wherewithal, see it via mule train, helicopter, or raft.

On the Road in the Grand Canyon

Unless you start with an aerial tour, your first stop should be the park's visitors center. Here you can get a map of the park showing the best overlooks, watch an introductory film, and see a very large-scale model of the canyon that, in proportion, would make you as thin as a paper match.

If you can swing it (because it *is* pricy), invest in a helicopter tour that will define the canyon. Flying lower and slower than an airplane (although no one can fly beneath the rim), you'll cross the 18-mile-wide canyon twice at 100 mph and receive the benefit of the pilot's narrative. Among the stories guides tell is the story of Louis Boucher. When a settler encroached on Boucher by establishing a homestead two miles away, the silver miner retreated into the Grand Canyon for a little privacy.

Whether you see the canyon from a helicopter, airplane, mule, or standing on its edge, the Colorado River is a squirt-gun stream, and an 8,000-square-foot boulder appears no larger than a pebble. The canyon's architecture is far larger than you can comprehend. You can take pictures until you pass out, but unless you blow them up to actual size, they won't begin to reflect the breadth, width, depth, and grandeur of the canyon.

When you enter the park on your bike ($20) and tour the canyon rim, you'll find that the roads aren't designed for motorcycles and aren't exciting until you get to the vista points. When you do look over the side, however, what you'll see is Sedona in reverse. Every red rock is sucked down into the earth and the heroic hole loses all sense of dimension.

The view is different from each overlook, although one thing that remains the same is the sight of tourists gathering at the same protective barricade. Be bold. You can walk about 30 feet to either side and usually find a secluded spot where the view is just as nice and you can find a promontory to sit on. If you have time—and you should allow some—arrive near dusk and head down the Western Road to watch the canyon moon rise and the shadows fall like a sweep second hand.

Perhaps the most spectacular view is several miles east in Desert View. Climbing the 70-foot Watch Tower, built in 1932 as an observation station, places you a total of 7,522 feet above sea level. Of all the vista points at the Grand Canyon, this is definitely worth a stop, and the pictures are priceless.

Pull it Over: Grand Canyon Highlights
Attractions and Adventures

Grand Canyon: The Hidden Secrets is a must-see. For ten bucks, catch it at the **IMAX Theater,** Hwy. 64, Tusayan, 928/638-2203, www.grandcanyon imaxtheatre.com. The film captures great views of the canyon, offers a historical perspective, and earns your undying respect for the one-armed stuntman who portrays explorer William Powell shooting the rapids on the Colorado. How he didn't paddle in circles, I'll never know. Some scenes in this film are so scary you'd swear you're in the raft yourself. Outside, the tourist information center and gift shops are a convenient stop.

There are abundant (although expensive) opportunities to kick up your adrenaline. Helicopter and airplane tours are the most popular. If you do only one, choose the helicopter; they fly lower and slower than airplanes. Both depart from the Grand Canyon Airport, fly similar routes, and cost about the same. **Kenai Helicopter,** 928/638-2764 or 800/541-4537, www.flykenai.com, offers flights daily 8–6 during summer, daily 9–5 during winter. Cost is $104 for

near the Watch Tower at Desert View in the Grand Canyon

25–30 minutes, $164 for 45–50 minutes. **Papillon Grand Canyon Helicopters,** 928/638-2419 or 800/528-2418, www.papillon.com, flies daily from 9–4 and charges $99 for 25–30 minutes, $159 for 45–50 minutes. **Air Star Helicopters,** 928/638-2622 or 800/962-3869, www.airstar.com, also offers daily flights from 9–5. Cost is $99 for 25–30 minutes, $145 for 40–45 minutes, $165 for 50–55 minutes.

If you don't trust helicopters, opt for an airplane tour. **Grand Canyon Airlines,** 928/638-2407 or 800/528-2413, www.grandcanyonairlines.com, takes you up on a twin-engine Otter for one of the longest (45–50 minutes), most complete air routes permitted over the canyon. Operating since 1927, the Otters fly more slowly than other planes, and high wings and panoramic windows are designed for aerial sightseeing. Flights cost $75. Air Grand Canyon, 928/638-2686, 800/247-4726, www.airgrandcanyon.com, offers 30- to 40-minute flights for $74, 50 minutes for $89, and 90 minutes for $174. The longer flights fly over the western canyon so you can see waterfalls and the Native American village.

If you'd rather be on the river than up in the air, choose from nearly 20 Colorado River outfitters, who take either gentle cruises down the river or hair-raising, coronary-busting, life-threatening races through the rapids. Some are one-day affairs, most go overnight or longer. The best source for information on these companies is the **Grand Canyon River Trip Information Center,** 928/638-7843 or 800/959-9164, www.nps.gov/grca. The center also provides updates on which launch dates have been cancelled. Rafting is popular enough for me to recommend reservations up to six months in advance.

Less thrilling than a raft ride, **Grand Canyon Mule Trips,** 303/297-2757, www.amfac.com, nevertheless can be fun and save your feet. On one-day trips to Plateau Point ($120), you'll spend about six hours in the saddle, or you can be bold and take an overnight to Phantom Ranch ($338). The ranch is not luxurious, but you get a stew or steak dinner. Cabins include bunk beds and showers. Both are physically rigorous trips. There's a weight limit of 200 pounds, and prices can go lower if more people ride.

Outside the park, the center of Grand Canyon commerce lies in the **Tusayan General Store,** Hwy. 64, Tusayan, 928/638-2854. This grocery store serves double duty as a post office and gift shop.

Blue-Plate Specials

Choices are limited, but **El Tovar Hotel** has a fine dining restaurant. Get the full rundown on this and other GC choices by calling 928/638-2631. In Tusayan, the **Canyon Star,** inside the Grand Hotel, 928/638-3333, serves big food, such as hand-carved steaks and turkey, and features a large salad bar. The entertainment (folk singers or Native American dancers) doesn't cost you a dime.

Shut-Eye

For general Grand Canyon information, call 928/638-7888. More than 2,000 rooms are available in Tusayan and Grand Canyon Village, and the park has several campgrounds. **Mather Campground,** 800/365-2267, features full amenities, a store, and showers, and takes reservations in advance; fees are $15

A 30-Second History: Yamaha

While Suzuki started with spinning looms, Yamaha took a more sensible approach: They made reed organs. The company started in 1887, but the first bike didn't appear until 1954—a 125cc single-cylinder two-stroke based on a German DKW model. The YAI (a.k.a. the Red Dragonfly) was well received and sparked the introduction of a larger 175cc, twin-cylinder model. By 1959, the five-speed YDSI was in stores, followed in the 1960s by more powerful bikes, until in 1973, the company's production surpassed one million bikes. Now just look at 'em.

per night. Sites at **Desert View** ($10), also at 800/365-2267, are available on a first-come/first-served basis, but organized groups of nine–40 people may make advance reservations ($2 per person, plus $2.50 per campsite). Facilities include restrooms and picnic tables, but no showers. Have fun, Stinky.

Grand Canyon National Park Lodges, 303/297-2757, www.amfac.com, features the most prized lodging options, and reservations can be made two years in advance; same-day reservations are taken at 928/638-2631. The 78-room **El Tovar** is the most expensive ($114–279) and most beautiful lodge, although only four suites have a view of the canyon. Opened in 1905, the precursor to Yosemite's Ahwahnee features stone-and-timber design, concierge and room service, and fine dining at the on-site restaurant. Less than 40 steps to the rim, it also includes a gift shop and small general store. Other less attractive options include the **Bright Angel** ($60–116) and the ugly-ass **Thunderbird and Kachina Lodges** ($109–119).

Several chain hotels and suites lie along Highway 64 in Tusayan. There are two safe choices run by the same company. The **Grand Hotel,** 928/638-3333 or 888/634-7263, www.gcanyon.com, styles itself after an Old West

Kuralt: Yamaha Royal Star Tour Deluxe

"Kuralt"* for Arizona, Utah, Colorado, and New Mexico was a 1998 Yamaha Royal Star Tour Deluxe. If your first ride was a minibike, the handling may seem familiar. This bike is tight. Even with 1300ccs of power, it seems smaller and is smooth as silk on corners. It'll do a rapid 85 mph without breaking a sweat, although I didn't have much luck getting it goosed a lot faster on the open road—the result of its engine or high desert winds, I'm not sure. The style is sleek, probably the nicest cruiser design I've seen, with a great windscreen, saddlebags with locks on either side, and handlebars just the right height to make riding easy. I averaged around 40 miles per gallon, but with no gas gauge, I was surprised to find that I'd drained the tank and had nothing left in reserve in the middle of the desert. Fortunately, I was adopted by a friendly tribe of Native Americans and given the name Running-on-Empty.

For details on new Yamaha models, check www.yamaha-motor.com.

*It was the travels of CBS correspondent Charles Kuralt that inspired me to explore America. I named each motorcycle I rode in his honor.

national park resort, but is housed in a new and attractive building. The rooms ($70–138) are large and comfortable, and at night, it features Western entertainment and Native American dancers. It has a great restaurant, too. At its sister property, the **Grand Canyon Suites,** 520/638-3100 or 888/538-5353, www.gcanyon.com, every room is a suite with a king and a fold-out double bed, microwave, and wet bar. Suites are named after Western legends, such as Wild Bill, Zane Grey, Wyatt Earp, and Route 66. Rates start at $139.

Chain Drive*
A, Y, S

*Chain hotels in, or within ten miles of town. See cross-reference guide featuring phone numbers and web addresses on page 405.

On the Road: Grand Canyon to Page/Lake Powell

When you head east on 64, cruising along the South Rim, you'll see a little more of the Grand Canyon. The ride starts out gently, with pine forests on both sides and, occasionally, a turnout where you can pull over for one last, less crowded look. After Navajo Point, you'll pass the Watch Tower and then depart the park by the East Rim.

The road is nice and wide, and the way it's laid out, you can cruise into curves low and slow. The surrounds can be deceptive because when you leave the Grand Canyon, you'd assume the views were behind you, but you still have enough elevation to afford glimpses into tributaries. The natural beauty is interrupted only by the self-derogatory signs of roadside Navajo trinket stands: "Nice Indian behind you! Chief sez turn back now! Chief love you!" Sad.

Like the highway through Death Valley, Highway 64 is breathtaking in its desolation—that is, until you reach Highway 89 at Cameron. Turn left (north) and ride a few hundred yards to a good fuel and food stop. The **Cameron Trading Post,** 928/679-2231 or 800/338-7385, is a mini empire with a motel, artwork, fudge, gas, moccasins, cowboy hats, ponchos, rugs, replica weapons, jackets, and $400 Indian headdresses. Other than that economic anomaly, prices are fair here and the merchandise of surprisingly good quality. Get gas here—the next leg across the Navajo reservation is relatively empty. Speaking of empties, if you need evidence of the alcohol problem on reservations, just look at the roadside, where beer bottles bloom like sagebrush.

There's scant scenery as it's typically defined, but you'll feel satisfaction observing a different way of life. No suburbs or neighborhood beautification programs here, just old trailers that come complete with horse and truck.

Things pick up about 34 miles south of Page, where great red cliffs rise on the horizon. About 10 miles later, near Bitter Springs, you'll start to ride right into them. They are majestic and overpowering, and as you ride directly down the throat of one of these giants, the road turns and you ascend to one of the most amazing vistas on the trip. Stop here and take a long look. A gorgeous gorge opens up far below and a plain spreads out for hundreds of miles. When you saddle up again, around the corner is yet another fantastic sight: You're riding through a red cavern. Although it's only a few hundred yards long, the walls dwarf you and create a memorable motorcycling moment.

After twisting your bike through canyon walls, you'll encounter mile after mile of nothing but plains at 6,000 feet and cliffs rising higher. The desert floor is red and white and brown and yellow and speckled with sagebrush. Ride it at sunset, when the light reaches out to the farthest points on the horizon and over the wonderful buttes that dwarf manmade smokestacks. It sounds strange, but seeing this endless vista makes you feel as if you're part of infinity.

Allow time to let this scene fix itself in your mind. After that, you can turn to Page.

Page Primer

The Navajos thought that this barren land was a bewitched place, where the trees had died of fear. They didn't care too much after 1956, when they swapped 24 square miles of this land with the government for a larger tract in Utah.

Back then, Page was just a construction camp for workers building the nearby Glen Canyon Dam. When they weren't busy, workers applied their engineering skills to the sand and rock and turned this into a frontier town of metal structures.

Page was incorporated in 1975, and in the last quarter century this slow-paced town of 8,500 has become a base for water sports on Lake Powell, which now fingers its way up into Utah. There's not much to see here unless you plan on fishing, skiing, or sitting on a houseboat. Page is the hub of the "Grand Circle," though, and from here you can opt to continue the final 115 miles to Zion or 133 miles to Bryce Canyon, or go off script and ride the 235 miles to Mesa Verde National Park (see "Wild Colorado Run").

On the Road in Page

Page is too new to be of great interest, but if you stay over, ride down to the **Glen Canyon Dam Visitors Center,** 928/608-6404, for a tour of the dam and displays on geology, water, turbines, and dams. By any measure this is a damn big dam. 1,560 feet across, 710 feet high, and 300 feet thick at the bottom, it holds back the force of a 186-mile-long lake. Bear in mind that the dam only scratches the surface of the 1.25 million-acre **Glen Canyon National Recreation Area,** also at 928/608-6404, www.nps.gov/glca.

Since the roads here are relatively ordinary, you may be better off cruising on Lake Powell. To see every nook and inlet on the lake, you'd travel nearly 2,000 miles—nearly the width of America—and see blue waters lapping at cliffs, buttes, and gentle sands where the color of the canyon changes as evening shadows fall. The easiest way to get on the water is from the **Wahweap Lodge & Marina,** 928/645-2433, www.lakepowell.com, which has cornered the market on water sports. Five miles north of the visitors center on Highway 89, it's the recreation area's largest marina and lodging facility, with gift shops, campgrounds, laundry, showers, and a service station. From here you can rent houseboats, sailboats, canoes, and kayaks, and arrange a fishing excursion for bass, catfish, bluegill, crappie, trout, and walleye. Float down below the dam where the cold waters are a favorite spot for trophy trout.

Remember: Dam. Good fishing.

Pull it Over: Page Highlights
Attractions and Adventures

It's not an adventure per se, but the **Stix Market,** 5 Lake Powell Blvd., 928/645-2891, is Page's favorite fishing spot. Locals congregate here before dawn to swap fish stories and plan their fishing strategy. The store has everything: licenses, tackle, sporting goods, rod and reel rental, guide referral, groceries, snacks, pop, beer, liquor, coolers, ice, bait (live, plastic, or frozen), fresh anchovies, coffee, and donuts.

Colorado River Adventure, 50 S. Lake Powell Blvd. (outfitters store), 928/645-3279 or 800/528-6154, www.lakepowell.com, offers a calming half-day cruise ($62) into historical canyons first navigated by Major John Wesley Powell. Guides are part pilot, part historian as they explain ancient Anasazi petroglyphs. Bring a wide-brimmed hat, tennis shoes, bathing suit, and a camera. A bus will drive you 45 minutes to Lee's Ferry for the cruise, which includes a lunch buffet.

For a full list of activities or to make reservations for water sports on Lake Powell, call the **Wahweap reservations service** at 800/528-6154, www.lakepowell.com.

Blue-Plate Specials

Serving big food for lunch and dinner, **Ken's Old West,** 718 Vista, 928/645-5160, is appropriately accented with miner's lamps, sturdy wooden beams, and an old upright piano. Entrées include thick meats—steaks and BBQ ribs. The backroom bar and dance floor make it one of Page's few nightspots.

Finding an authentic, unpretentious '50s diner is a rarity, so don't miss **R.D.'s Drive-In,** 143 Lake Powell Blvd., 928/645-2791. Settle in a booth and pretend you're Fonzie. Open for breakfast, lunch, and dinner, R.D.'s serves all the good and occasionally greasy foods your parents fed you on road trips (before you heard about cholesterol), including flavorburst cones, chili, burritos, shakes, fries, and the "famous" R.D. burger. Good food, cheap.

Whiners, crybabies, penny pinchers, and complainers are barred from the **Dam Bar & Grille,** 644 N. Navajo, 928/645-2161, www.damplaza .com, a restaurant/saloon serving dinner, and the self-proclaimed "best bar by a dam site." The huge dining room serves all the basic food groups, including porterhouse steak, king crab, ribs, dirty Sonoran chicken, and pastas.

Watering Holes

Next door to the Dam Bar, the **Gunsmoke Saloon,** 644 N. Navajo, 928/645-2161, features a large rectangular bar, ten wide-screen TVs, four beers on tap, a fireplace, live rock 'n' roll, billiards, and darts. If you need a break, take your drinks to the patio (no view: It overlooks the parking lot).

Shut-Eye

Page has several chain hotels, so take your pick. At the **Wahweap Lodge,** 520/645-2433, www.visitlakepowell.com, the 350 hotel-like rooms go for $159–169. The lodge features a restaurant, convenience store, and gift shop, along with boat rentals, boat tours, and marina services.

Chain Drive*
A, C, D, E, G, L, Q, S, CC

*Chain hotels in, or within ten miles of town. See cross-reference guide featuring phone numbers and web addresses on page 405.

On the Road: Page to Zion National Park

As you rode north from the Grand Canyon, you may have noticed colorful examples of geological rioting. Over the last 10 million years, rock compressions, deformations, and uplifts created Grand, Zion, and Bryce Canyons, as well as cliffs that change color from chocolate to vermilion, white, gray, and pink as you drive north.

On your ride to Zion, you'll be cruising through the Vermilion Cliffs, which begin with scattered sagebrush and grazing cattle. About eight miles out of Page, you enter Utah. The rocks begin to turn white and take on new shapes; the force of wind, water, and erosion have applied a different finish to these cliffs.

After this, the scenery dissipates and the long, straight roads change little in elevation until you reach a section of Grande Escalante (Grand Staircase), 18 miles into Utah. Arches striped red, brown, and white dot the landscape, and you'll spot caves that'll tempt you to park your bike and go look for Injun Joe.

The lull in scenery reasserts itself and the lack of visual activity may break your concentration, but stay focused (the roadside monuments for dead motorists may rouse you). About 50 miles from Page, you'll see Kanab in the distance. Although folks in Page speak of Kanab with a reverence usually reserved for the Holy Trinity, there's not much here, save for one of the best roadside diners you'll find.

At **Houston's Trails End Restaurant,** 32 E. Center, 435/644-2488 or 800/599-2488, the "girls have guns on their hips and smiles on their lips." These pistol-packin' mamas carry Colt 45s and wrapped straws in their holsters, although when you ask why, they're not quite sure. Suffice it to say, the service and setting are exactly on target—a great place to pull over and rest your bike. Thankfully, this is no chain restaurant, just an authentic slice of America, where you can get a cowboy breakfast, sandwiches, and home-cooked lunches and dinners.

You're not far from Zion National Park, and Highway 89 continues winding across the plains. Foreshadowing what's to come, the cliffs add more swirls and colors to their composition, as if from a watercolor painting. Embedded in the coral pink rocks are designs suggesting knotted rope, tire marks, and the pattern you see when you stir cake batter.

When you reach Mount Carmel Junction, where 89 veers sharply north, you'll likely be tempted to detour 60 miles to Bryce Canyon. If so, you'll find an ordinary road, a few valleys, and a town called Orderville, where there's a rock shop, then another rock shop, and across the street a rock shop. A little further on the left, there's a rock shop. The road is easy, and the view is simple after seeing Sedona and the Grand Canyon. When you reach Bryce itself by following Highway 12 East toward Tropic, at first glance you'll know it was worth the ride. Not so much red as orange, the landscape beckons with short rock tunnels and arches; after these, you ride on a wide open plain with mesas.

At Highway 12, turn right and you'll see **Ruby's Inn,** 435/834-5341, www.rubysinn.com, a small town disguised as a gas station/hotel/restaurant/rodeo arena/store. Not a bad place to stay if you're tired of riding. A few miles more and you're at **Bryce Canyon National Park,** 435/834-4420, www.nps.gov/brca. Twenty bucks takes you and your bike to overlooks to see the fabled "hoodoos," pillars of red rock created about 60 million years ago in a prehistoric lake. If time is short, the first five pullouts should give you a sense of the park fairly quickly.

If you forsake Bryce, take Highway 9 into Zion National Park. For roughly four miles, you get a few twists and curves, and the speed limit drops to 30 mph, slowing not for curves but for cows. A few miles later you'll reach the east gate of Zion National Park. Although you may have booked a room at Zion Lodge, more likely your night's rest awaits in Springdale, a few miles beyond the southern exit. Either way, you'll get a small taste of Zion—enough to inspire you to feast on the park once you've settled down.

Zion Primer

It's no small praise that, even when compared to Yosemite and the Grand Canyon, Zion exudes a stronger sense of nature. Here, you and your bike make immediate contact with the environment. Zion National Park contains less than one-tenth of one percent of Utah's land area, but more than 70 percent of the state's native plant species. Within its 229 square miles are plateaus, canyons, waterfalls, creeks, and narrows. Differences in elevation, sunlight, water, and temperature have created micro-environments that nurture hanging gardens, forested side canyons, and isolated mesas. It is altogether a beautiful place.

If you're wondering where "Zion" came from, credit the Mormons, who borrowed the Hebrew word for "a place of safety or refuge" to name the area in the 1860s. Today Zion is a refuge for 2.5 million visitors a year, meaning you should ride well before or after the summer peak. From March–October, shuttles—not motorcycles—take park guests from Springdale into the far reaches of the park at the Temple of Sinawava. Only hikers, bicyclists, shuttle vehicles, and overnight lodge guests are allowed on the Zion Park Scenic Drive, although the rest of the park is open for riding.

With that in mind, accept this advice: Cash in your 401K; build a log cabin; live here; and be happy.

On the Road in Zion

What can I say about the perfect blend of road and land? Once you enter Zion (admission $5), you have nearly free rein to ride and gorge yourself on the impressive and endless views. From the east gate, the Checkerboard Mesa appears as its name implies. Unlike at other national parks, you have the freedom to park your bike and stride up rippled, textured rocks.

Around each copper-colored curve are rocks with fantastic shapes and variegated swirls ranging from dark red to light orange to pink and white. This wonderful ride connects 15-mph switchbacks with the magnificent motorcycle-friendly Zion-Mount Carmel Tunnel. Too small for motor homes, this tunnel offers one of the best biking experiences you'll ever have. As if a cosmic drill punched through the mile-long mountain, the passage loses daylight on both ends before you're halfway through. The adrenaline rush continues when you exit and see another mile or two of switchbacks ahead, the first of which propels you into the presence of a natural amphitheater created inside a cliff at least a quarter mile wide. On these curves, beware the low retaining wall that's just high enough to snag a footpeg and toss you over the side.

You can't help but gun it when you realize that the best LeMans roads aren't in Monte Carlo, but right here. The seven-mile Zion Park Scenic Drive is great if you can ride through, but it's open only to shuttle buses from May–October. Whether on a shuttle or on your cycle, head north and you'll pass the Zion Lodge; keep going and eventually you'll reach Angels Landing, Weeping Rock, and the Temple of Sinawava.

Plan to pull over frequently—around each bend another perfect photo beckons. To really get a sense of the park, hire a guide to take you beyond the implied barriers to see The Narrows, rock passages that are 60–100 million years old and tower some 1,500 feet. You've come this far, chicky-babe. Don't blow it.

Pull it Over: Zion Highlights
Attractions and Adventures

Zion Canyon: Treasure of the Gods offers a great introduction to the park, with shows daily on the hour 11–7 at **Zion Canyon Theatre,** 145 Zion Park Blvd., 435/772-2400, www.zioncanyontheatre.com. Tickets are $7.50. Few things can do justice to the beauty of this park, but this large-format film comes close. You'll travel back to meet the ancient Anasazi and experience what it's like to be a rock climber.

The average tourist heads down the scenic drive, walks down a sidewalk, sees some steps, and turns around. Zion boasts the best canyons in world, most of which are hidden behind the hills. Get off your bike and allow time to see what everyone else is missing.

The first stop you should consider making before wandering into the wilderness on your own is the **Zion Adventure Company,** 36 Lion Blvd., Springdale, 435/772-1001, www.zionadventures.com, which (for $16) provides the maps and gear you'll need to hike through the Narrows. Donning a drysuit and carrying provisions and a walking stick, you'll trudge through thigh- to waist-deep water and enter silent, sublime passages. The signature Zion experience, it may whet your appetite for their Jeep tours and rock climbing classes.

If you'd rather let a horse do the walking, **Canyon Trail Rides,** Zion Lodge, 435/679-8665, www.onpages.com/canyonrides, offers one-hour ($20) and half-day ($45) tours through the park. If you really want to test your mettle and leave your bike behind, they also offer the **Red Rock Ride** (www.redrock-ride.com), which is for the strong, the mighty, and the affluent. The seven-day trip costs a whopping $1,795 and includes all meals, hot showers, tents, and beds. This is no sissy trip. You'll ride the old trails used by cattle rustlers, Butch Cassidy and the Sundance Kid, and see Bryce Canyon, the Grand Canyon, and Zion National Park. Of course, you need to have riding experience—and motorcycle time doesn't count.

It's hard to capture nature's intricate beauty with a disposable camera, so Michael Fatali has done it for you. Lugging his camera to canyons and mountains you don't even know exist, he has spent weeks looking for the perfect shot. His efforts show in the colorful, passionate photographs on display at **Fatali Gallery,** 868 Zion Park Blvd., 435/772-2422, www.fatali.com. With the right light, shadow, and surreal natural colors, ordinary objects take on a different and far more interesting visage.

Blue-Plate Specials

The **Bit and Spur Restaurant and Saloon,** 1212 Zion Park Blvd., 435/772-3498, claims to be one of the best Mexican restaurants in Utah, but it's hard to judge since it's so packed, it's hard to get inside to eat the food. Serving dinner daily and breakfasts on weekends, the eatery uses locally grown produce in traditional Mexican favorites, and pours a great selection of Utah microbrews like Whip Tail Ale, Frogs Legs, Slick Rock Red Lager, and the Mormon favorite, Polygamy Porter—why have just one? To top it off, the restaurant features a garden patio, billiards, and sports TV.

Zion Pizza and Noodle Company, 868 Zion Park Blvd., 435/772-3815, www.zionpizzanoodle.com, located in an old church, serves lunch and dinner. Along with creative pasta dishes, salads, and Utah microbrews (Wasatch and Squatters), the menu features specialties like Thai chicken pizza and hot and spicy Southwestern burrito pizza. A back porch patio and front porch deck are perfect when the weather is right, and it usually is.

Shut-Eye

AMFAC, 303/297-2757, www.amfac.com, is the corporation that runs lodging operations at several parks: Grand Canyon, Bryce Canyon, Zion, and Furnace Creek and Stovepipe Wells in Death Valley. Make advance reservations through AMFAC, same-day reservations at the lodge itself.

The only place to stay inside the park, **Zion Lodge,** 435/772-3213 (same day) or 303/297-2757 (advance), www.nps.gov/zion, was designed in the 1920s, destroyed in 1966 by a fire, and rebuilt without the classic rustic design and historic appearance. The oversight was corrected in 1990 and now it looks like it should—an outdoors lodge in the heart of beautiful country. With 120 rooms and a restaurant, the lodge often fills up, so don't be disappointed if you can't get in. Rates run $107–135.

Springdale lodging is surprisingly diverse. The **Zion Park Inn,** 1215 Zion Park Blvd., 435/772-3200, www.zionparkinn.com, is a link in the Best Western chain, but very nice in a small town where conveniences are hard to come by. With rates from $82–135, the inn features a pool, hot tub, gift shop, guest laundry, state liquor store, large and comfortable rooms, and a terrific restaurant, the Switchback Grille. Slightly more upscale yet surprisingly reasonable is the **Desert Pearl Inn,** 407 Zion Park Blvd., 435/772-8888 or 888/828-0898, with rates from $98–123. Swank, cathedral-ceiling rooms come with a TV, fridge, and microwave; outside there is a waterfall and sparkling blue pool. The rooms are not quite suites, but with growth hormones they would be. Old-fashioned and reasonable describes the **Pioneer Lodge,** 838 Zion Park Blvd., 435/772-3233, 888/772-3233, www.pioneerlodge.com. For $59–69, it gives you what you want if you just want a bed, a pool, and a neat old motel diner that claims to be the "home of home-cooked cooking."

Resources for Riders
Red Rocks Run

Arizona Travel Information
Arizona Association of Bed & Breakfast Inns—800/284-2589,
www.arizona-bed-breakfast.com
Arizona Road Conditions—602/241-3100
Arizona State Parks—602/542-4174, www.pr.state.az.us
Arizona Travel Center—602/248-1480 or 888/520-3433,
www.arizonaguide.com

Utah Travel Information
Bed & Breakfast Inns of Utah—435/649-1904, www.bbiu.org
Utah Road Conditions—800/492-2400
Utah State Parks—801/538-7220 or 800/322-3770, www.stateparks.utah.gov
Utah Travel Council—801/538-1030 or 800/200-1160, www.utah.com

Local and Regional Information
Grand Canyon Chamber of Commerce—928/527-0359,
www.grandcanyonchamber.com
Grand Canyon Road and Weather Conditions—888/411-7623
Grand Canyon Switchboard—928/638-2631, www.nps.gov/grca
Grand Canyon Visitors Center—928/638-7644
Page/Lake Powell Chamber of Commerce—928/645-2741 or 888/261-7243,
www.pagelakepowellchamber.org
Sedona-Oak Creek Canyon Chamber of Commerce—928/282-7722 or
800/288-7336, www.sedonachamber.com
Zion Canyon Visitors Bureau—435/772-3757, www.zionpark.com
Zion Canyon Information—435/772-3256, www.nps.gov/zion

Arizona Motorcycle Shops
Sedona Motorcycles—1195 W. Hwy. 89A, Sedona, 928/282-1093,
www.sedonamotorcycles.com
Grand Canyon Harley-Davidson—I-40 at Exit 185, Belmont, 928/774-3896,
www.grandcanyonhd.com
Big Joe's Cycles—7911-C N. Hwy. 89., Flagstaff, 928/774-4662
Northland Motorsports—4401 N. Hwy. 89, Flagstaff 928/526-7959,
www.northlandmotorsports.com
Outdoor Sports Lake Powell—861 Vista Ave., Page, 928/645-8141

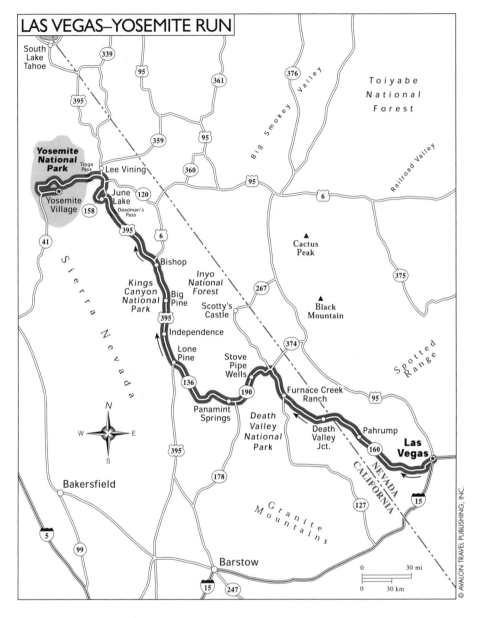

Route: Las Vegas to Yosemite via Death Valley, Lone Pine, Bishop, Lee Vining

Distance: Approximately 450 miles; consider six days with stops, add two days for optional Lake Tahoe run.

- Days 1 & 2—Las Vegas • Day 3—Travel • Day 4—Lone Pine/Travel
- Days 5 & 6—Yosemite

First Leg: Las Vegas to Lone Pine (240 miles)

Second Leg: Lone Pine to Yosemite Village (200 miles)

Third Leg (Optional): Yosemite Village to Lake Tahoe (200 miles)

Helmet Laws: Both Nevada and California require helmets.

Las Vegas—Yosemite Run

Las Vegas, Nevada to Yosemite National Park, California

Of all the runs profiled in this book, this is the most exciting, frightening, grueling, exhilarating, fascinating, inspiring, and humbling.

From the materialistic and surreal city of Las Vegas, the mood descends to the stark landscape of Death Valley. What follows are arguably the grandest vistas in America at Yosemite and, if you desire, the clear and clean waters of Lake Tahoe—a treasure to see on a spring or fall run. This ride will test your mettle and reward your efforts.

Las Vegas Primer

Las Vegas is a town steeped in excess. From multibillion-dollar themed hotels to less-than-discreet prostitution, Las Vegas is where the circus came to town—and never left.

Half a century ago, it was a way station in the middle of nowhere—until the Mafia saw an untapped oasis of cash. You know the rest: Sammy and Frankie and Dean begat Elvis and Engelbert and Wayne, and then the stakes were raised, and old hotels were blown up and corporations muscled in to build casinos disguised as hotels. The local convention bureau needed to fill more beds and positioned Las Vegas as a great family getaway—but it's not.

Vegas is crowded, expensive, noisy, profane, and no place for kids (unless you're teaching them about escort services and loan sharking). If you're an adult who's prepared for a juiced-up, high-tension, all-night bacchanal, however, it can be the fuel for a long and winding journey.

On the Road in Las Vegas

It's impossible to condense and define Las Vegas, especially for motorcycle travelers. You can ride your bike anywhere in the country and be content with yourself, your thoughts, and a few possessions stuffed in the saddlebags. A millisecond after you ride into Vegas, you're swept up in an orgy of greed and desire. Pray that it dissipates when you leave town or you'll be the most miserable sumbitch on the road.

This concludes the warning. From here, it's a pleasant surprise to find that most employees are hospitable and the roads easy to navigate. The city is laid out roughly like a grid, with Las Vegas Boulevard the main north-south artery. A portion of this street is "The Strip," where you're most likely to spend your time and money. The magnet for tourists and conventioneers, it is where hotels are destroyed and rebuilt, phoenix-like, as billion-dollar resorts.

The farther north you go, the less impressed you'll be. Fremont Street is clearly past its prime. It attracts chain-smoking seniors on gambling junkets and people trying to score bad food at cheap buffets. In these casinos, marathon slot-machine players press buttons in a sad choreography, looking like research monkeys awaiting banana-flavored pellets.

The stakes are raised as you ride south and pass the Sahara, Stratosphere, Stardust, Flamingo, Aladdin, and Circus Circus casinos. When you reach the Strip, you'll enter a universe of world-class hotels and high rollers. Yet there's a certain sameness to every venue: the ringing bells of an electronic arcade, the absence of windows and clocks, and VIP status applied not on the

Gettin' Hitched

Getting hitched in Vegas is either a romantic or pathetic amalgam of hormones, love, and kitsch. More than 50 wedding chapels operate in town, and if you want to get married (please, not to someone you just met through an escort service), the only requirement is a $50 license, which you can get at the seven-day-a-week **Clark County Courthouse**, 200 S. 3rd St., 702/455-3156.

basis of your worth as a person, but on your value as a loser. And that concludes the rant.

To be fair, you should experience Vegas for yourself. You won't be harassed by bums or hustlers, since casinos don't want them cutting in on their racket. Besides, it is not all gambling. It's a playground for adults, a place where you can feel the same freedom you experience on your bike.

Just save enough money for gas.

Pull it Over: Las Vegas Highlights
Casinos

Larger and louder than life, the most impressive casinos are found along the Strip. Each is a community unto itself with a distinct theme, headlining acts, guest rooms, restaurants, pools, and abundant services. Rates vary wildly—often daily and especially if there's a major convention in town. Suites are naturally higher. Those shown below reflect peak weekend rates in summer. Even if you don't stay, ask about the hotel's headliner—a very big draw here.

Luxor, 3900 Las Vegas Blvd., 702/262-4000, 800/288-1000 (room reservations), 800/557-7428 (show reservations), www.luxor.com, sports an Egyptian theme and a pyramid out front. You'll see its spotlight at night. Rates here run $59–259. Clean up NYC, multiply it by 10, and you have **New York New York,** 3790 Las Vegas Blvd., 702/740-6969, 800/693-6763 (room reservations), 702/740-6815 (show reservations), www.nynyhotelcasino.com. Rates range from $79–159. No theme (thank God) at **MGM Grand,** 3799 Las Vegas Blvd., 702/891-1111, 800/929-1111 (room and show reservations), www.mgmgrand.com, just a very large hotel with big shows and special events—including prize fights. A room here goes for $99–120. Siegfried and Roy are the stars at **The Mirage,** 3400 Las Vegas Blvd., 702/791-7111, 800/627-6667 (room reservations), 800/963-9634 (show reservations), www.mirage.com. You'll pay $99–159 a night here. At pirate-y **Treasure Island,** 3300 Las Vegas Blvd., 702/894-7111, 800/944-7444 (room reservations), 800/392-1999 (show reservations), www.treasureisland.com, the big show is Cirque du Soleil's *Mystere.* Rates run $60–390. An old favorite that attracts families, **Circus Circus,** 2880 Las Vegas Blvd., 702/734-0410, 800/634-3450 (room reservations), www.circuscircus.com, is not dirty, not clean. Somewhere in between, with rooms from $44–59. Theoretically, there's a magic theme at the **Monte Carlo,** 3770 Las Vegas Blvd., 702/730-7777, 800/311-8999 (room and show reservations) www.monte-carlo.com—good news for the headliner, Lance Burton, Master Magician! A night here starts at

$80 and goes up. **Caesar's Palace,** 3570 Las Vegas Blvd., 702/731-7110, 800/634-6661 (room and show reservations), www.caesars.com, is one of the city's traditional favorites. I'd give the waitresses here my vote for best costumes. They's sexy. Rooms run $99–500. **Excalibur,** 3850 Las Vegas Blvd., 702/597-7777, 800/937-7777 (room reservations), 800/933-1334 (show reservations), www.excaliburcasino.com, has a medieval castle theme. Why not? You'll pay $59–109 a night. A mixture of the tropical and mystical, **Mandalay Bay,** 3950 Las Vegas Blvd., 702/632-7777, 877/632-7000 (room and show reservations), www.mandalaybay.com, features a House of Blues, stage shows, and off-off-off-Broadway productions. Rates range from $109–399. The mighty large **Venetian,** 3355 Las Vegas Blvd., 702/414-1000 or 888/283-6423, www.venetian.com, materialized in June 1999 where the Sands once stood. The Italian-themed resort of 3,036 suites gets raves on the swank-o-meter and credit for hosting "Art of the Motorcycle."

Attractions and Adventures

If you'd like to experience skydiving and live to tell about it, **Flyaway Indoor Skydiving,** 200 Convention Center Dr., 702/731-4768, offers a one-hour program ($45) where you don skydiving clothes and step out over a monstrous bathroom blow dryer. No parachute, no worries. About 70 miles north of Vegas, the **Las Vegas Skydiving Center,** Mesquite Airport, 702/877-1010, shows you the city at 120 mph. They'll pick you up in Vegas and after a 20-minute lesson and brief flight, you and the instructor you're strapped to will then jump and free fall for 45–50 seconds. The memory will last a lifetime—or until you hit the ground—whichever comes first. Either way, you pay a steep $179.

In the flamboyant tradition of Gorgeous George and '70s Elvis, Liberace epitomized the vanity of Vegas. For riders, the highlights of the **Liberace Museum,** 1775 E. Tropicana, 702/798-5595, www.liberace.org, are many: an Excalibur car covered with rhinestones, a customized Bradley GT, a Rolls Royce Phantom V Landau limousine (one of only seven, this one dons the license tag "88 Keys"), as well as a custom rhinestone-covered Stutz Bearcat with a matching rhinestone-covered toolkit. The museum is open Monday–Saturday 10–5, Sunday 1–5. Admission is $6.95.

The accessory branch of Las Vegas H-D/Buell, the **Harley-Davidson Shop,** 4th and Fremont, 702/383-1010, www.lvhd.com, carries the requisite clothing, parts, and souvenirs. A bulletin board announces motorcycle-related products and services.

Blue-Plate Specials

Hundreds of restaurants line the Strip, both inside and outside the resort casinos. Surprisingly, the quality indoors is actually pretty good, and choices range from quick snacks to very elaborate meals.

If you feel that no one understands your passion for bikes, you'll find a sympathetic ear at **Harley-Davidson Cafe,** 3725 Las Vegas Blvd., 702/740-4555, www.harley-davidsoncafe.com. The cafe boasts plenty of parking out back, while the inside looks like an assembly line. Gleaming Harleys ride up and around the room, passing before a large map of Route 66 and a giant American flag created from red, white, and blue chains. What else? Oh, yeah. Food.

Shut-Eye

As Las Vegas turns into a convention clearinghouse, many of the 314 hotels and 127,000 rooms are booked months in advance. Make reservations as early as you can—perhaps as part of a gambling package, which will knock the rates down considerably. If not, you'll probably pay a premium to stay in a trashy hotel. Keep in mind that staying at a casino hotel can be soul rattling after a peaceful desert ride. A nationwide reservation service that covers Las Vegas may find you a room and save you some money; call 800/964-6835 (96-HOTEL) or check out www.hoteldiscount.com.

Motels and Motor Courts

OK, so they're not really motels, but here are a few places I really like. For peace and quiet without a premium, **La Quinta,** 3970 S. Paradise Rd., 702/796-9000, is a bargain with rates from $75–85 (includes continental breakfast). Just a few blocks from the action, it also has a pool. Even cheaper is the **Golden Gate Hotel and Casino,** 1 Fremont St., 702/385-1906 or 800/426-1906, where rooms go for $39–59. It offers cable, a free newspaper, and not much else besides a restaurant that's served 24 million giant shrimp cocktails since 1959. The **Hard Rock Hotel,** 4455 Paradise Rd., 702/693-5000 or 800/473-7625, www.hardrockhotel.com, hits the jackpot with great accents like Flying V door handles, a Beatles display case, and an H-D Hardtail Springer owned by Motley Crüe's Nikki Sixx. More inviting than the darkened casinos or even its younger clientele, the hotel charges $89–229 a night. The on-site restaurant is another reason to stay here—it displays one of Elvis's jumpsuits and Roy Orbison's Electra-Glide.

Chain Drive*
A, C, D, E, F, G, H, I, J, L, N, P, Q, S, U, X, Y, CC, DD

*Chain hotels in, or within ten miles of town. See cross-reference guide featuring phone numbers and web addresses on page 405.

Indulgences

One of the best things that's ever happened in my life was being invited to a class at **Freddie Spencer's High Performance Riding School,** 702/643-1099 or 888/672-7219, www.fastfreddie.com. It's like shooting 18 holes with Arnold Palmer. Spencer, who is a three-time World Grand Prix champion (and youngest ever), trains riders on super speedy Honda CBR600F4s. After getting decked out in full leathers, you ride a few blocks to the Las Vegas Motor Speedway and spend two or three days learning to ride fast. Very, very fast. Even if you're content cruising along at a casual clip, the principles you learn here for braking, cornering, and accelerating can be used on country roads and city highways. In the meantime, scraping your knee along the asphalt at the speed of light is one of life's greatest moments—if you've got the cash.

On the Road: Las Vegas to Lone Pine

Of all the rides you'll make in America, this one will require the greatest degree of guts. It demands that your bike be in peak condition, that your nerves be sure, and that you are ready to face the challenge of fierce, twisting curves in the Inyo Mountains and the barren loneliness of Death Valley.

Leaving Las Vegas on Route 159 West, it'll take a half hour to shake the Vegas glitter off your bike, just about the time you'll reach Red Rock Canyon, a magnificent sight and, if you ride the loop, one that affords possible views of bighorn sheep, gray foxes, and wild burros. Otherwise, head south toward Blue Diamond and Highway Rte. 160, then west to Pahrump; follow a shortcut to Route. 127 North, then to Rte. 190, which leads west across Death Valley.

Immediately, the road is a lonely stretch. There are no twists, no turns, just rolling desert. The road wakes up near Spring Mountain Ranch State Park, giving you curves to compensate.

Pahrump is just a lump of a town—an embryonic LA that spreads across the sands. Friendly clerks staff the well-stocked Mobil station (Highways 160 and 372), but here you wouldn't be surprised to see Kubrick's cavemen tossing bones into the sky. Instead of turning south to reach 190 via Shoshone, a few miles north of Pahrump an alternate route (Belle Vista Road) cuts west to Death Valley Junction. Take it.

Following four miles of twisties and 15 miles of straightaway, the big, empty desert starts to look like the Grand Canyon (minus the canyon). Roughly an hour later you're at the intersection of 190 and 127, poised for your ride across Death Valley. Definitely stop for a look (or an overnight) at the strange and fascinating **Amargosa Opera House and Hotel,** 760/852-4441, www.amargosa-opera-house.com. Built by the Pacific Coast Borax Company in the 1920s, the combination office space and hotel had fallen into disrepair by 1967. Then New York dancer Marta Becket drove through, had a flat tire, and fell in love with its desolation. She bought the forlorn complex and now rents rooms for $45-$60. As if that's not enough, on Mondays and Saturdays, Marta and friend Tom Willett still perform a ballet and mime revue in the adjacent opera house. Now, that's entertainment! No phones, no television, no food; but a place for some well-deserved rest before the upcoming ride.

Things get mighty strange here, sheriff. If you've ever judged times to reach distant points, don't expect to do it here. The land is so flat, it'll take 20 minutes to reach an object you can see halfway to the horizon.

Mile after mile this lasts. You're riding across the Amargosa Range, passing 20 Mule Team Canyon. If you're interested, before Zabriskie Point a one-way, 2.7-mile dirt loop road detours south again through the canyon and brings you back to the highway. Then nothing is something. A four-star resort, in fact. In an area where a snack machine could win the award for finest restaurant, why **Furnace Creek Resort,** 760/786-2345, www.furnace creekresort.com, is located here is a mystery. You can stay the night in below-sea-level luxury, go horseback riding, or take a break on the verandah and view the upcoming 104-mile challenge. If you want to play golf on the lowest golf course in the world, the one here is 214 feet *below sea level.* Despite its existence in exile, the resort is popular and their rates prove it: from $102–365. Reserve in advance if you think you'll stay. If not, get ready for a most incredible ride.

A few miles down the road, there's a gas station that will gouge you on gas, but fill 'er up again. You're about to start a heart-stopping ride.

As you start to descend into the valley, you'll see into the future. Car headlights can be seen from 10 miles away, and about 20 miles outside of Furnace Creek, the absence of life echoes around you. You may experience a most humbling and spiritual moment here. After running a satisfying series of mountain curves, you take a wide, sweeping left and then 3, 2, 1 . . . you've fallen hundreds of feet below sea level and are riding in the basin of Death Valley.

Picture yourself, a black speck alone in a place as flat and desolate as any on earth. Solo riders especially will feel the emotional deprivation of this silent world. If your bike is finely tuned, stop and experience the mystical solitude. It is as memorable as any experience you will have on a motorcycle.

When you turn your attention back to the road, the quiet continues until you reach **Stovepipe Wells,** 760/786-2387. It has an elevation of five feet, but don't let them sell you lift tickets. If you're tired of riding, Stovepipe offers an Einstein-smart option. They have 83 motel rooms, an RV park, gas, a general store, swimming pool, and saloon. A welcome sight, rooms here go for an affordable $50–92.

Between here and the next oasis, you'll ride through the anti-valley, some of the most harrowing and dangerous dips and twists you'll encounter. Six-degree grades and serious shifts in terrain roll on for miles at a time. Absent any guardrails, a moment's distraction can easily turn your bike into scrap metal, but if you stay focused, this ride is rich in adventure. Accelerating drops let you click into neutral and speed through twists at 60 mph, propelling you into valleys where the emptiness is sublime in its beauty. Realize that this is the same desert you may have flown over countless times, but now it is a planet you've tamed beneath your tires.

When you reach **Panamint Springs Resort,** 775/482-7680, www.death valley.com, you have another excuse to stay the night in a 15-room motel ($65–94), and reminisce about the ride. You may have doubted your resolve or the belief you could find beauty in this wasteland, but by now the desert has spoken to you. Chances are you'll be keyed up for the last 48-mile leg to Lone Pine.

From Panamint Springs, you're riding the backbone of a mountain range with sheer drops on your side and no barriers to break your fall. What you will find are infinite reasons to stop and shoot photos. Father Crowley Vista Point (elev. 4,000 feet) is a good bet, and I doubt you'll be hassled by oncoming traffic when you park your bike in the middle of the road. Look for the intersection of Highway 136 North, take it to reach U.S. 395, and turn north for a well-deserved rest in the historic Hollywood cowboy town of Lone Pine.

Yippeeiyay.

Lone Pine Primer

Lone Pine (elevation 2,000, pop. 2,060), the first town of any size west of Death Valley, flares up for a few blocks and then disappears back into the sand. Lexicographers believe the phrase "blink and you'll miss it" was coined here.

But there's more to Lone Pine than meets the eye. If you're old enough to recall matinee cowboys falling off cliffs only to return the following week, you'll have already seen Lone Pine. If you frequent antique shows, looking for a Hopalong Cassidy lunch box or Roy Rogers guitar, you'll have Lone Pine to thank.

More than 300 Westerns were filmed here, from serial episodes to full-length features. Capitalizing on this unique history, each October the Lone Pine Film Festival draws a few surviving stars of Hollywood's Old West movies.

Even if you were born too late to recall Lash LaRue and the Cisco Kid, being in Lone Pine and at the gateway to Mount Whitney is a purely American experience. After Death Valley, you deserve it.

On the Road in Lone Pine

One stoplight, three blocks, and years of history. It's enough for an interesting ride, primarily due to the Whitney Portal, a long and winding road to the majestic mountain. After defeating Death Valley, you may want to take a break from mountain roads, but if not, you can take a curvaceous 12-mile run to the base of Mount Whitney, California's highest peak (elevation 14,495).

Otherwise, stay a while in Lone Pine. After all, stopping in small towns offers some of the most enjoyable moments of a ride. If you're ready to rest, you can see downtown in about 25 minutes—a half-hour if you take your time. One must-see is at the lone stoplight. The **Indian Trading Post,** 137 S. Main St., 760/876-4641, was a favorite stop for stars such as Edward G. Robinson, Jack Palance, Errol Flynn, Chuck Connors, Maureen O'Hara, Gary Cooper, and Barbara Stanwyck, who scribbled their names on the walls and window frames while shooting in town. Today the walls are a priceless piece of Americana.

After the mountain and the town, there's not much else to do but settle back at the diner, grab a beer at the saloon (yes!), do your laundry, and, if you share my good fortune, see a real live prospector walking down the street with his pickaxe and shovel.

Pull it Over: Lone Pine Highlights
Attractions and Adventures

You're surrounded by natural beauty, and there are two places to visit to take full advantage of this. **Mount Whitney Ranger Station,** 640 S. Main St., 760/876-6200, www.r5.fs.fed.us/inyo, issues the wilderness permits you'll need to enter the Whitney Portal area. There's no charge, but if you want to camp here

back on the Whitney Portals—which leads to Mount Whitney, California's highest peak (elevation 14,495 feet)

($6–14), you'll need to make arrangements well in advance. A mile south of Lone Pine, at the junction of 395 and 136, the **Interagency Office, 760/876-6222,** stocks information about Death Valley, Mount Whitney, the Inyo National Forest, and other natural parks and sights.

Blue-Plate Specials

Besides a few pizza places and Mexican diners, eateries in Lone Pine are few, but it's easy to find some good USDA-approved road food if you know where to look. The largest joint in town is the **Mt. Whitney Restaurant,** 227 S. Main St., 760/876-5751. Here since the 1930s, the family-owned diner offers—dig this—venison, buffalo, ostrich, and veggie burgers. Ask politely and maybe they'll make you a real one with beef. Open from morning to evening, it's popular with riders thanks to the pool tables, pinball, beer and wine, and Monday night football on a 50-inch TV. Open 24 hours for breakfast, lunch, and dinner, **TJ's Bake and Broil Family Restaurant,** 446 S. Main St., 760/876-5796, serves breakfast anytime, beer and wine later on, and entrees include American favorites like chicken fried steak and chopped sirloin with mushrooms and grilled onions.

Watering Holes

One of the most enjoyable bars you'll find in America, **Jake's Saloon,** 119 N. Main St., 760/876-5765, is open daily 'til midnight. It's the home of the "notorious" Alabama Hills Gang, a loose affiliation of local characters who hold shoot-outs the second and fourth Saturday nights from May–September—or whenever they feel like it. They suggest you be ready for anything. Even when guns aren't blazing, the bar is a perfect place to settle down after your Death Valley run and crack your thirst with a cold beer.

Shut-Eye

Motels and Motor Courts

For a small town, Lone Pine offers more than adequate lodging choices. In the middle of town, the **Dow Villa Motel,** 310 S. Main St., 760/876-5521 or 800/824-9317, www.dowvillamotel.com, features clean rooms, a pool, outdoor spa, and rooms with TVs, VCRs, king and queen beds, and mini fridges. Expect to pay from $38–115, and be sure to check out the John Wayne exhibit in the den, which includes a poker table from a movie he shot here. At the south end of town, **Alabama Hills Inn,** 1920 S. Main St., the junction of 395 and 136, 760/876-8700, www.alabamahillsinn.com, is as clean as can be, with larger than normal rooms ($48), a nice view of Mount Whitney (in front), and the Alabama Hills (in back). Rooms feature two queen beds, bathtubs, mini-fridges, and microwaves.

Chain Drive*

A

*Chain hotels in, or within ten miles of town. See cross-reference guide featuring phone numbers and web addresses on page 405.

On the Road: Lone Pine to Yosemite Village

Aside from the monumental wall of wind, the ride north is easy—at least until you turn onto Highway 120 to reach Yosemite. That's when you may want to call your stunt double.

For now, the road out of Lone Pine stays true to form: impressive mountains and straight runs. Fourteen miles later, bypass Independence then slow down through well-patrolled Big Pine. Forty miles from here, Bishop's oasis of green lawns, trees, golf courses, and restaurants may entice you to stop.

When you continue north, the ride becomes comfortable as you blaze down the road with the Sierra Nevadas on your left and the Inyo Mountains on your right. Be thankful you've been freed from the confines of a car: The spicy fragrance of the desert is just as bracing as the chill of the mountain air. You're in the groove now, with another 120 miles of motorcycle-friendly road to ride. Forget the canopy lanes of New England; the wide-open road places you in God's Country.

After passing sprawling Lake Crowley on your right, the road rises forever, ascending to 7,000 feet and Sherwin Summit, then, miles later, Deadman's Pass, at 8,036 feet. The desert has been replaced by rich, green California forest. If you have time to prolong your ride and acquire other indelible images, turn left onto Highway 158 for the June Lake Loop. Most motorists bypass it, but it's worth the detour for motorcycle travelers.

A small creek running on your right soon spills into one of the most beautiful mountain lakes you'll encounter, and the combination of road, forest, lake, and sky is as picturesque as Switzerland's Lake Lausanne. This is a ski resort town, so the off-season traffic is lighter and makes it easy to stop for coffee in the small lakefront village.

On the road again, you'll cruise quietly past snowcapped mountains, log cabins, and waterfalls until, suddenly, you'll notice an eerie silence. There is an absence of movement and people, and the landscape has an unusual science fiction design. See it for yourself. Weird.

Highway 158 connects back with 395, so turn left and ride to Lee Vining, a nice town with a few motels and restaurants. If you're scared of heights or aren't prepared for the demanding two-hour, 74-mile push to Yosemite Village, you should stop here. You'll also be stopped when 120 closes following the first big snowstorm after November 1. Otherwise, turn left onto 120 and, after about a quarter mile, you'll see on your left the **Tioga Gas Mart,** 22 Vista Point Dr., 760/647-1088. The supermarket-sized Mobil station lets you stock up on food and supplies for Yosemite. If the weather's nippy, now's the time to get comfortable in a survival suit before heading for the mountains.

Already at 8,000 feet, you'll head up a steep grade on your way to the even higher Tioga Pass (elevation 9,941 feet). Muscle-flexing turns are rampant for the

The Bear Facts

Although lead poisoning killed off California grizzlies in the 1920s (they were shot), other bears are still sniffing out food in Yosemite Village. They can easily tear a car to shreds when searching out uncovered food, so when you leave your bike, take anything perishable with you. Better yet, leave items in your room. If you're camping, invest in bear-proof containers. Maybe buy one large enough to sleep in.

first several miles, and the road demands attention. At the ranger station, pay $10 per vehicle and $10 per passenger (unless you've purchased a $50 Golden Eagle or National Parks Pass) and enter the mother of the mother of all national parks. The simple and helpful park pamphlet will be tempting to look at, but chances are you'll be focused on wilderness scenery that'll leave your jaw on your gas tank.

The two-lane road is fairly wide, and a collection of slow curves and pine forests soon gives way to boulders and cliffs. Guardrails are few and drops precipitous, so be on your best biking behavior. You'll be sucked into several tunnels and spat out to glimpse coming attractions in the distance, but what is unusually noticeable are the textures you can distinguish. Wood, rock, water, or light, everything appears—if this makes any sense—to be better than nature.

Speeds can reach 60 mph on straights and drop to 20 mph on tight curves, and even though you could make the trip from Lee Vining in two hours, allow an extra hour just to stop at turnouts, shoot pictures, or savor the visual feast of twisting roads and the golden glow of autumn leaves.

About 55 miles into this leg, you'll reach Highway 41. Turn left and follow the signs to Yosemite Village. It is bigger and better than anything you can imagine.

Yosemite Primer

Yosemite conjures up thousands of images and raises expectations to dizzying heights. You'd think it would fail to deliver, but it doesn't. It is just as beautiful, wild, tame, rich, and sublime as you'd expect.

It's tempting to think the rest of America would look like this if we hadn't beat Mother Nature into submission, but there is only one Yosemite. Initially set aside by President Lincoln in 1864, Yosemite Valley and the Mariposa Grove of giant sequoias were to be "held for public use, resort and recreation . . . inalienable for all time."

In 1890, an act of Congress preserved 1,170 square miles of forests, fields, valleys, and streams equal in size to Rhode Island. Today it is traversed by 263 miles of roads and 840 miles of hiking trails and is home to 240 species of birds, 80 species of mammals, and 1,400 species of flowering plants.

The park is as bold and as beautiful as America. Enjoy it.

On the Road in Yosemite

While you could take your bike and explore the park on your own, I'd suggest you start by putting yourself in the hands of Yosemite's park rangers. They are knowledgeable, courteous, and will likely be able to answer every question you have.

Although it's high cheese, the tram tour (or bus tour in cold weather) is the best way to see Yosemite Valley, the most visited section of the park. The tour also stops at Bridal Veil Falls, Half Dome, and monumental El Capitan.

While the size of the high granite edifice may not impress you at first, look closely until you spot a pinpoint dabbed on the mountain and you'll get an instant education in proportion. That is a mountain climber. Focus on the parsley-sprigs ticked in slivers of rock. Those pine trees you are looking are 80 feet tall. Soak this in and respect for those pin-headed climbers increases.

The tour takes you by lush meadows that make up only 20 percent of the park but support 80 percent of its flowers. Information like this flows without restriction—tour guides think they're at a Jeopardy! audition and freely fling out data on botany, geology, and forestry. The tour lasts two hours, after which you'll have plenty of time to ride back to the highlights, this time with knowledge about what you're seeing.

Exploring on your own may be the most rewarding experience of Yosemite. At Curry Village and Yosemite Village, you can fill up a backpack with water, snacks, camera, and film, and the park is yours. Hiking trails, which range from easy to grueling, deliver you to impressive sights, such as boulders the size of Marlon Brando and trees as wide as Cadillacs. The woods are welcoming in their solitude and open your senses to every movement, sound, and fragrance. Rustling leaves recall a rushing stream; flaked bark peels off the gnarled trunks of cedar trees; acorns drop; and pine cones fall with a soft splat.

Stopping to feel the environment is akin to slowing down on a great ride, and far more satisfying. Allow time to rest when you want, where you want, and realize that the "real world" is hundreds of miles away, your office even farther. If you absolutely have to do something, check the lodges for listings of daily events, such as fishing, photography classes, and nature talks.

When night falls, the sky looks more white than black, since stars can be counted by the millions. It's only been two days since leaving Las Vegas. There, the city demanded you stay up late. Here, the rewards of Yosemite are offered when you rise early and take advantage of another day in paradise.

Pull it Over: Yosemite Highlights
Attractions and Adventures

If you plan to fish at Yosemite, you need a fishing license, available at the Sport Shop in Yosemite Valley, the Wawona Store, and the Tuolumne Meadows Store. If you want to take the first step towards tackling El Capitan, sign up for climbing lessons by calling the **Mountaineering School** at 209/372-8344.

A 30-Second History: Suzuki

About 60 years ago, Suzuki's main product was spinning looms. It wasn't until June 1952 that they entered the motorcycle market, introducing a 36cc single-cylinder two-stroke called Power Free. The bike's innovations (such as a double-sprocket gear system like today's moped) earned the company a financial boost from the patent office, which Suzuki used to develop Power Free's two-speed transmission and, later, a 60cc version called the Diamond Free. This was followed by 1954's Colleda CO, a relatively massive 90cc single-cylinder four-stroke. Remember, all this started in a spinning loom factory.

Several sightseeing tours are available; call 209/372-1240 for details on each. The most popular is the introductory **Valley Floor Tour** ($20.50), which lasts two hours and travels 26 miles through the heart of Yosemite. The **Glacier Point Tour** is $29.50. A full day's adventure, the **Grand Tour** ($55) winds through Glacier Point and Mariposa Grove, site of the famous giant Sequoias. Each tour is led by a park ranger who knows more than is natural about the park.

Yosemite's "downtown" is Yosemite Village, complete with post office, groceteria, pizza parlor, deli, auditorium, museum, cemetery, a few hotels, and the Ansel Adams Gallery, which features works for sale by Adams and other wildlife photographers. At the Visitor Center station, you can sign up for photo courses or ranger-led activities, check road conditions, or buy some books. Over at Curry Village, there are gift shops, a tour center, bike rentals, and snack shops.

Blue-Plate Specials

After a day of grazing on picnic grub or at concession stands, experience lunch or dinner at the **Ahwahnee** hotel , 209/372-1489. The original Western lodge, the setting is extraordinary. The big food and flawless service match the design and character of this massive room. Call me and I'll join you.

Shut-Eye

Yosemite used to reach peak popularity between Memorial Day and Labor Day; today, stretch that from April to the end of November. Make reservations as far in advance as possible. For hotel reservations within the park, call 559/252-

4848 (Fresno), www.yosemitepark.com; for campground reservations, call 800/436-7275.

The park boasts a range of facilities, from dirt-cheap rustic to over-the-top indulgent. Located in the heart of the park, Yosemite's fabled **Ahwahnee,** 209/372-1407, tops the price list. One of the most beautiful inns in America, it was built in 1927 and is breathtaking in design, superb in service. You'll find character and tradition in the grand fireplace, massive timbers, Great Room, and baronial dining room. Reserve one of 123 rooms (an eyebrow-arching $326) as far in advance as possible. Other choices offer greater variety—for example, private baths, cabins, or canvas tents. Choose from the motel-style **Yosemite Lodge** (about $112–136), **Wawona Lodge** ($101–161), or Curry Village tents and cabins ($54–125).

Kuralt: Suzuki Intruder 1500 LC

"Kuralt"* for the Wild West was a Suzuki Intruder 1500 LC, perhaps the most powerful warhorse I'd ridden. When I had to force my way through the snow while crossing Donner Pass, the Intruder plowed through it like a Zamboni. Power was only part of the attraction. For a short-legged rider, the low and extra-wide saddle was perfect for marathon rides like these. With the wide windscreen (optional), I was able to ride for hundreds and hundreds of miles without fatigue. Other pluses included the well-positioned handlebars and back seat, which provided unexpected lower back support. No strain, no pain.

One drawback, however, was the absence of a fuel gauge. A low-fuel light lit up when I was approaching reserve, which didn't comfort me on the already nerve-wracking ride across Death Valley. Also, the stingy 4.1-gallon fuel tank (awkwardly accessed beneath a flap near the seat) was blocked by a metallic T, which made it difficult to trigger the emission-controlled gas pumps in California. Other than that, the bike's style, ergonomics, and power made it especially good for the long, butt-numbing haul.

For details on new Suzuki models, check www.suzukicycles.com.

*It was the travels of CBS correspondent Charles Kuralt that inspired me to explore America. I named each motorcycle I rode in his honor.

Side Trip: Yosemite to Lake Tahoe

The road so far has been rich in both kindness and treachery. If you feel it's been more of the latter, leave Yosemite Village on 120 West and head for home. Otherwise, get ready for another adventurous 200-mile run, returning via 120 East to 395 and on to Lake Tahoe. Warning: Make this a daytime ride since tight curves can be dangerous after dark.

Even if you never ride another mile, you'll have experienced the most complicated blend of riding in terms of terrain, scenery, sociology, psychology, and climate. And there's more to come.

About three miles north of Lee Vining, Mono Lake reveals itself from a highway vista. Now drying out like a Miami retiree as folks in Los Angeles drain the lake for their lawns and bathwater, the exposed white sands are a curiously surreal landscape.

Six miles later, you're at 7,000 feet and climbing, with the vast Mono Basin in the distance on your right. This run soon places you back in a desert landscape, a curious fact when you cruise past 7,700 feet and look back to see Yosemite's Tioga Pass. The altitude also introduces winds that can kick your tires out from under you. Keep a low profile, Bugsy.

It's difficult to fathom that these changes are occurring during one incredible journey. And to prove its power, nature will once again change environments on you. After you cross the Conway Summit at 8,138 feet, the desert leaves the stage and you enter California ranch country. Small cow towns come into view. Scan the horizons and you may spy snow falling in one section, clear blue skies in another, rain in a third. It is altogether impossible to absorb the varying expressions of nature that surround you, but you don't really need to. Just file this information away under Memorable Motorcycle Run.

Past Bridgeport, the slow winding roads get their act straightened out and whisk you into Devil Gate's Summit, at 7,500 feet. This will sharpen your senses for the impending pinball run, but for now the hills are low and rolling and fun.

Although you've already defeated the toughest terrain, now you face Walker Creek Canyon. After 10 miles of tranquility, the winding roads snatch you back into the challenge of rushing water, boulders, pine needles, and fallen trees. As you catch fleeting glimpses of red rocks and black rocks and sand, you'll be making mental notes to thank the highway engineers and sign up for the Sierra Club.

When the canyon breathes its last, you'll enter the tiny town of Walker, where nothing seems to be living, and then Coleville (pop. 43), which makes Walker look like Chicago. The next town, Topaz, is your cue to look for Highway 89; if it's open, it will be on your left.

For a minor road, 89 is amazingly beautiful. Three miles into it you climb to 6,000 feet and enter a fertile valley rich with fields of pines and sagebrush. You have no choice but to keep riding, and you won't be disappointed. The higher you ride—and you will—the more spectacular the view. As your attorney, I advise you to stop at the peak and look back over the valley. It is an image that will stay with you for a long, long time. You can look for miles down the valley's breadth, and with keen eyesight may make out stacks of logs that are, in fact, remote cabins locked within the breeches of behemoth mountain walls.

No picture can do it justice; only your memory will capture the scope of this incredible vista. Desert, snow, mountains, valleys . . . From here, you are the king of the world, and command all that you survey. It is as inspiring as it is humbling.

You are nearing Monitor Pass at a mighty 8,300 feet, and the imminent descent is a gift to enjoy. Drop it into neutral and rest your engine for several miles as you glide your bike into easy curves and experience the decline of western mountain ranges.

Continue on 89 toward Markleeville, 32 miles south of Lake Tahoe. You may stop for several reasons: If the sun is setting, the mountains you just crossed will look like a Maxfield Parrish landscape painted with pinks, violets, blues, and crimson. The **Cutthroat Saloon,** 14830 Hwy. 89, 530/694-2150 offers up another good reason. It's quite popular with riders due to the Western Victorian decor and the ladies underwear pinned on the ceiling. Maybe you'll find something in your size. I did.

From here, the road is pleasing and predictable and leads to South Lake Tahoe. The city's population, 21,000, is why you're riding to the less populated northern shore, although you will find motels, hotels, and cabins here.

Highway 28 along the west shore gives you a final burst of excitement. Unlike most lakefront roads that blend into the shoreline, this one has dangerously high cliffs, Jordache-tight switchbacks, and eye-popping glimpses of Lake Tahoe from inlets and alpine vistas. In a way, this heart-throbbing run is the natural counterpoint to the artificial fun of Las Vegas.

Shut-Eye

Chain Drive*
Countless cabins and cottages surround the lake, as well as a number of chains: A, E, G, H, J, Q, S, Y, CC, DD

*Chain hotels in, or within ten miles of town. See cross-reference guide featuring phone numbers and web addresses on page 405.

Resources for Riders

Las Vegas—Yosemite Run

Nevada Travel Information
Nevada Road Conditions—702/486-3116
Nevada State Parks—775/687-4370, www.state.nv.us/stparks
Nevada Tourism—800/638-2328, www.travelnevada.com

California Travel Information
California Association of Bed & Breakfast Inns—831/464-8159, www.cabbi.com
California Division of Tourism—800/462-2543, www.gocalif.ca.gov
California Highway Patrol Road Conditions—916/657-7261
California Road and Weather Information—916/445-1534 or 800/427-7623
California State Parks—916/653-6995, www.parks.ca.gov

Local and Regional Information
Bishop (Lone Pine) Weather Bureau—760/873-3213
Lake Tahoe Central Reservations Service—530/581-6900,
    www.mytahoevacation.com
Lake Tahoe Forecast and Road Conditions—530/542-4636
Las Vegas Chamber of Commerce—702/735-1616, www.lvchamber.com
Las Vegas Visitors Information Center—702/892-7573, www.vegasfreedom.com
Lone Pine Chamber of Commerce—760/876-4444 or 877/253-8981,
    www.lonepinechamber.org
Yosemite Information—209/372-0200, www.yosemite.com or
    www.nps.gov/yose
Yosemite Road Service—209/372-0200

Nevada Motorcycle Shops
Desert Motorsports—3535 W. Tropicana Ave., Las Vegas, 702/795-2000,
    www.desertmotorsports.com
Kawasaki of Las Vegas—3800 N. Rancho Dr., Las Vegas, 702/382-8615
Las Vegas Harley-Davidson/Buell—2495 E. Sahara Ave., Las Vegas,
    702/431-8500, www.lvhd.com
Motorcycle City—4260 Boulder Ave., Las Vegas, 702/456-1600,
    www.azmotorsports.com

California Motorcycle Shops
Golden State Cycle—1220 N. Main St., Bishop, 760/872-1570,
    www.goldenstatecycle.com

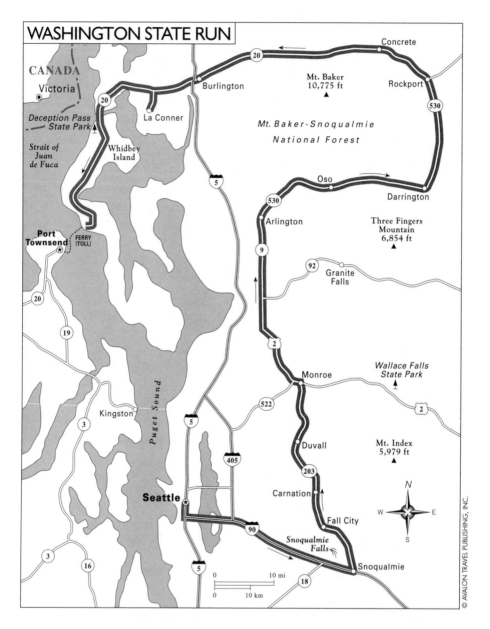

Route: Seattle to Port Townsend via Snoqualmie, Fall City, Carnation, Duvall, Monroe, Arlington, Darrington, Whidbey Island

Distance: Approximately 245 miles; consider four days with stops.
- Day 1—Seattle/Travel • Day 2—La Conner • Day 3—La Conner/Travel
- Day 4—Port Townsend

First Leg: Seattle to La Conner (196 miles)

Second Leg: La Conner to Port Townsend (46 miles)

Helmet Laws: Washington requires helmets.

Washington State Run

Seattle to Port Townsend, Washington

Washington is a big state with more than its share of natural beauty. The mountains are snowcapped even in summer, and the glacier lakes, bays, and islands are more striking than any postcard you've seen.

Unlike other rides described in this book, this tour has no perfect beginning point. The downside of Washington is that many back roads are poorly marked, and blue highways are often clogged with local traffic and logging trucks. Additional drawbacks include the small window of warm riding time (summer), perpetual rains west of the Cascades, and towns either too small or too large to enhance a ride. Consider this an introduction to a state too vast to condense in a single chapter.

On the Road: Seattle to La Conner

From Seattle, you can ride to Mount Rainier, Mount St. Helens, or the Olympic National Forest, but there's never a perfect combination of roads and walking towns within reach. On the other hand, you can get a good glimpse of the Washington countryside by leaving the Seattle area en route to some small towns.

I-90 out of Seattle reveals why this state is so popular. Even this federal highway is scenic. The road extricates you from city traffic and suddenly you're riding a wide, flowing road past lakes and mountains and then, when you reach the exit for Snoqualmie, into even more desolate countryside. If you ever watched the cult favorite *Twin Peaks,* you'll recognize the speck known as Snoqualmie by its main attraction: Snoqualmie Falls. Follow the signs to the village and ride to the **Salish Lodge,** 425/888-2556 or 800/826-6124, www.salishlodge.com.

Outside the lodge, park at the adjacent parking area and walk to the gazebo, a great spot from which to watch and hear the thunderous waters. At 270 feet, Snoqualmie is 100 feet higher than Niagara and kicks out spray for hundreds of yards. Be sure to pack a lunch, and then settle at a picnic table or, if you have time and a healthy heart, take the half-mile trail that winds down to the riverbanks. Add the fragrance and brilliance of the flowers and the sounds of nature and this is a must-see. If you can swing the price (from $189), the Lodge may be a good place to start—or stop. The spa here combines the styles of Asia and the Pacific Northwest. Fireplace-equipped rooms are indulgent, and the setting is a visual tranquilizer.

If you're ready to move on, the falls are a perfect introduction to a road that runs, briefly, through a dynamite combination of woods, rivers, and hills. Canopy roads give way to country roads, and soon you reach the junction of Rte. 203 at Fall City. Turn right onto 203 or, if you ride another hundred yards past the bridge, you may elect to make a stop at the **Last Frontier Saloon,** 425/222-5640. Here since 1941, it's the only place I've seen where the bartender seemed more gassed than the barflies.

When you return to 203, head north toward Carnation and Monroe. The two-lane road is level and winds slightly on the way to Carnation, a nice small town, but what comes next is more appealing. On your way out you'll cross a bridge and then enter green fields and great valleys, a subtle version of Vermont's Route 100.

After riding through Duvall, you'll reach Monroe, which is also a small town but features a few restaurants and pubs. Although maps show 203 continuing north to Granite Falls, the road actually ends here, and unless you're Ernest T. Bass or a logger, you won't be able to navigate the unmarked mountain roads. Instead, you'll have to bite the bullet and ride Highway 2 West, which navigates dense growth before freeing you into miles of farmland and then dumping you onto Highway 9 North. This isn't a great road, but the Mountain Loop Road to Darrington usually is not an option since there's a long section of gravel (or late snows) that makes it impassable. Option B takes you up to Arlington, where the ride gets nice in a hurry.

Get onto Route 530 toward Darrington, a short 25 miles away. This is what you've been waiting for. Instantly, the road gets better and wider, and you're riding between mountains that are Washington majestic. The smells are hearty; the grass is plump. Tufts of clouds stuffed between the summits slowly tug at their granite mooring, break free, and drift away. Even in early summer, slivers of snow from the peaks pierce into the woods below.

Past the town of Oso, pull off alongside the creek, and everything is perfect—with the glaring exception of clear-cut forests that have scarred the mountain tops.

Then comes Darrington. Stay on Route 530 North through the Mount Baker-Snoqualmie National Forest for another great moment in motorcycling. After every slow corner comes a magnificent run through a tunnel of 50-foot straight-as-nails pines. This wonderful road runs beside and over the Sauk River, not terribly far from the dense urban traffic surrounding Seattle and Puget Sound.

The woods continue on both sides and the air is fresh. At mile marker 60, the river, woods, and mountains converge and the twisty roads drop you past meadows, moss, and an almost fluorescent green landscape.

When you reach Highway 20 at Rockport (there's a gas station here), turn left. Around here, natural beauty takes a backseat to small towns like Concrete and larger ones like Sedro Woolley. Be prepared for a decent, though not breathtaking, ride. Once you cross beneath I-5, the mood of the road switches instantly from commercial to agricultural.

Farmland stretches from horizon to horizon. When you reach the turnoff to La Conner, ride on over to tulip town.

La Conner Primer

A town built on a trading post, shipping industry, canneries, and farms, La Conner ultimately became a retreat for artists and writers. On a point of land inaccessible by rail, folks had to make an effort to reach it. Not much has changed since then. Commercial development hit Skagit County, but distance has preserved La Conner. It remains a waterfront community relatively unaffected by the explosion of technology and music a few hours south in Seattle. Victorian-era buildings are still in use a hundred years later; pleasure boats are moored in the Swinomish Channel; and countless acres of fields burst into a rainbow each April when the tulips are in bloom. In fact, La Conner claims to export more tulip bulbs than the whole of Holland.

Take that, you friggin' wooden-shoed punks.

On the Road in La Conner

At first glance, it doesn't seem as if La Conner would be intriguing or popular. But it is and here's why:

In addition to springtime's omnipresent tulips, the town has reinvented itself as an artists colony. There are galleries and pubs and antique shops and restaurants in one condensed area, so you can park your bike and easily explore everything on

A 30-Second History: Kawasaki

American Kawasaki is a relatively new company—it opened in March, 1966, headquartered in an old meat warehouse in Chicago. They had no customers and no distributors, but that didn't stop them from selling a small, two-stroke bike called the Omega. It seemed to click, so Kawasaki built the Samurai and Avenger, a pair of rotary valve twins. In 1969 came the 500cc Mach III two-stroke triple followed in 1973 by the four-cylinder 900cc Z1. Kawasaki was a player.

foot. The other advantage La Conner has is its location. Equidistant from Seattle and Vancouver, the town is invaded every Friday by weekenders from both cities.

This is the kind of town I prefer on a ride—not so large you think you've missed something and not so small you go stir crazy. You can ride past the flower fields on the way out of town, but first just park your bike and walk down to 1st Street.

This could fill an afternoon and give you a place to relax at night. Notice the street window display artwork: Based on nature, most wood carvings, glassware, and paintings include grizzly bears, eagles, wolves, or a combination of the three.

The chamber of commerce offers tours of historic homes, and whale-watching cruises are available, but you don't really need to do anything. Just enjoy the town at a leisurely pace; give yourself time to relax; ride across the Rainbow Bridge once or twice; and then just kick back and watch the flowers grow.

Pull it Over: La Conner Highlights
Shopping

Of La Conner's antique shops, **Marketplace Antiques,** 106 1st St., 360/466-3187, is the best place in town to rummage around for good junk, old gadgets, magazines, paintings, and so on. It's open daily 9–5.

Jon Peterson's got a limited market, but if you collect antique fishing tackle, pay a visit to **Plug Ugly,** 313 E. Morris St., 360/466-1212. Open Thursday–Sunday, 11–5, this place sells duck decoys and marine gear as well.

Good thing La Conner has a well-stocked grocery store like **Pioneer Market,** 416 Morris St., 360/466-0188. This way, you can stock up on road food and supplies before you go. Even better, it's open 'til 10 every night.

The Roozengaarde Gardens outside La Conner, Washington. La Conner exports more tulip bulbs than the whole of Holland.

Blue-Plate Specials

Located on the outskirts of town just off Highway 20, **The Farmhouse Restaurant,** 13724 La Conner-Whitney Rd., 360/466-4411, serves old-fashioned big road food for breakfast, lunch, and dinner. Within this cavernous restaurant you can get platters filled with steak, ham, chicken 'n' dumplings, grilled pork chops, hot turkey sandwiches, pies, and cakes. After dinner here, I ballooned to 438 pounds.

Not only is **La Conner Brewing Company,** 117 S. 1st St., 360/466-1415, www.laconnerbrewing.com, a warm and intimate little restaurant serving wood-fired pizzas, soups, wings, quesadillas, and salads for lunch and dinner. They also have a great and active bar serving wines, ales, lagers, porters, stouts, pilsners, and dopple bocks.

La Conner Seafood and Prime Rib House, 614 1st St., 360/466-4014, is a traditional waterfront hangout open for lunch and dinner. Using only fish and meat, this restaurant has created about 100 different dishes—firecracker prawns, shrimp-smothered red snapper, Cajun prime rib, and more.

Watering Holes

If the Brewing Company's too tidy, **La Conner Pub,** 702 S. 1st St., 360/466-9932, is the alternative. This blue-collar bar has two pool tables, some old guys, a few young'uns, bottled and tap beers, and a full bar open until at least 1 A.M. Why there's a family restaurant attached is beyond me.

Kuralt: Kawasaki Concours

"Kuralt"* for Washington was a 1999 Kawasaki Concours. Few other sports tourers offer the same amount of motorcycle at this price. That's the biggest advantage. A 997cc engine will get you where you're going, and hard saddlebags and a molded fairing make this motorcycle look much larger than a modified street bike.

While this bike doesn't do any one thing with excellence, it does everything well. Acceleration is good; fuel consumption is good; the instrument panel and its two trip meters are good. But, unlike larger touring bikes, it has an omnipresent roughness: in shifting, in the rough rattle of the engine when you're cruising, in the nagging forward lean. If you can deal with the absence of bells and whistles and appreciate a bike that gives you all the basics at a good cost, then try this one on for size.

For details on new Kawasaki models, check www.kawasaki.com.

*It was the travels of CBS correspondent Charles Kuralt that inspired me to explore America. I named each motorcycle I rode in his honor.

Shut-Eye

La Conner offers relatively limited lodging choices, most of them inns. Motels are more than ten miles east or west of town. Call the Chamber (La Conner Chamber of Commerce) at 360/466-4778 or 888/642-9284, www.laconner-chamber.com, for additional recommendations.

Chain Drive*

A

*Chain hotels in, or within ten miles of town. See cross-reference guide featuring phone numbers and web addresses on page 405.

Inn-Dependence

The **Wild Iris Inn,** 117–121 Maple Ave., 360/466-1400, www.wildiris.com, has 20 large rooms—12 with hot tubs—and provides a full breakfast at rates from

$109–189. More basic, the **La Conner Country Inn,** 107 S. 2nd St., 360/466-3101, www.laconnerlodging.com, provides its guests with generic, motel-like rooms (some with king beds) for $95–120. The homemade breakfast is included.

On the Road: La Conner to Port Townsend

When you're ready to leave La Conner behind, look for Morris Street, which bypasses Highway 20. This short detour will take you to a patch of beautiful farmland. Less than a half mile from town, Morris Street zigzags and turns into Chilberg; once you've ridden past Best Road, start looking for Beaver Marsh Road. Turn left here and cruise down a few more miles to **Roozengaarde,** 15867 Beaver Marsh Rd., 360/424-8531, a small garden of multicolored tulips that will give you an idea of what the fields look like when they're in bloom. Though an excellent photo op, remember not to ride your bike over the flower beds. Open Monday–Saturday 9–5. Admission is free.

When you leave, follow Beaver Marsh to your right and then take another right at McLean Road, where, if you you need some supplies, you can stop in at the **Evergreen Grocery Store,** 16016 McLean Rd., 360/424-4377. After you've picked up supplies at the general store, a few blocks ahead is Avon-Allen Road, where you'll hang a left to wind back up on Highway 20—the last number you'll have to think about for the next several days.

With the Washington breeze in your face, you'll pass sporadic mountains and a few commercial enterprises before turning left to follow 20 toward Whidbey Island. The island's just about a dozen miles away and marks the entrance to the Olympic Peninsula. Once you make this turn, images from rides past will flash into mind; the start of this ride is comparable to the Berkshires, Yosemite, and the Blue Ridge Parkway.

On your right, you'll see glacier lakes that look frigid even at the height of summer. Near mile marker 43, watch for Pass Lake and a pullout where, if you're riding in a group, you can get a shot with the lake and mountain as a backdrop.

This level of scenery continues for several miles, bringing to mind the look of a 1940s *Field and Stream* magazine. Ahead, the Straits of Juan De Fuca can be seen to the right, but one of the most impressive sights of the trip arrives as you round the corner and approach Deception Pass. Where the Canoe Pass and Deception Pass bridges span a huge gorge, the vista is breathtaking. At the bottom, blue-green water rushes to the sea and you'll spy massive trees washed ashore like twigs. It's a larger-than-life scene, and crossing this span is more thrilling than running the Golden Gate.

On the opposite side of the 976-foot bridge are rest rooms, a parking area, and a trail that you should walk down even if you have a heart condition, gout, and a wooden leg. The views around each bend in the trail are fantastic and the pine forest scents are reminiscent of a Christmas tree farm.

Less than a mile later, consider pulling into the free, 4,128-acre **Deception Pass State Park,** 360/675-2417 or 360/675-7277, www.parks.wa.gov. Built primarily by the Civilian Conservation Corps in the 1930s, this marine and camping park boasts 30 miles of hiking trails, 19 miles of saltwater shoreline, three freshwater lakes, 246 campsites, freshwater swimming, fishing, and canoeing. The old growth forest is sprinkled with cedar, spruce, yew, apple, and cherry trees, as well as fields of foxglove, lupines, rhododendron, and roses. Due to the temperate climate here, wildlife thrives, and there's a strong chance you'll spy bald eagles in flight.

Now, I hate to have to break this to you, but following this spectacular introduction to Whidbey Island, the scenery fizzles. From here to Port Townsend, the landscape is pockmarked by random development, so even after you get your mojo going on a good run, it withers out when you encounter trailer parks and hideous commercial sprawl.

From here, all you need to do is watch for the turnoff to the **Port Townsend Ferry,** 206/464-6400. For $3, you and your machine can take a 30-minute sea cruise to one of the nicest towns on the peninsula.

Port Townsend Primer

Before Port Townsend was infected with quaintness, it was a real town—a real get-drunk-in-the-bar-have-a-whoopin-good-time kind of town. A century ago, Port Townsend was home to 40 saloons and 17 brothels (the most prosperous of which was located adjacent to City Hall). A writer visiting town remarked that the "stench of whiskey permeates Port Townsend to a depth of nine feet"—although no one knows how he measured it and I lost the scent at four feet.

It was an affluent town that accommodated a thriving maritime port and the consulates of 17 countries. As in other resurrected cities, a period of decline was eased by the arrival of hippies in the 1970s. From the luxury of their smoke-filled VW buses, artists and writers emerged and fueled a creative spark that sustains itself today. The hippies grew up and learned business and restored old homes, and rich Californians came in and bought the homes and turned them into inns. And the town was turned around.

Oddly, citizens seem to take obsessive pride in the movie *An Officer and a Gentleman,* filmed here about 20 years ago. If you walked into a hospital with a spear through your head, the doctor would tell you that "Richard Gere never had a spear through *his* head when he was here filming *An Officer and a Gentleman*." The film has become a religion.

What you'll see today is a tight-knit community that combines new money, young hippies, established businesses, and trendy shops in Woodstock-era ambiance.

Far out.

On the Road in Port Townsend

Port Townsend poses a dilemma. If you check the map, **Olympic National Park,** 360/565-3130, www.nps.gov/olym, seems close, and a ferry trip to Victoria, British Columbia, looks tempting. I chose to hang out in town for several reasons. A trip to Victoria makes for a very long day—the ferry trip lasts several hours and reaching the boat takes about as long. Olympic National Park didn't pan out either because, after riding halfway there, I realized that the road was beating me into submission with slow-moving traffic and a disturbing lack of scenery. Port Townsend calmed me down and kept me entertained. I was content. If your schedule affords you more time, give them both a try.

Port Townsend is a great walking town and the people are friendly. If you hang around town, definitely stop at **Bergstrom's Antique and Classic Autos,** 809 Washington St., 360/385-5061. Based on the building's exterior, you wouldn't expect to find much, but inside you'll see motorcycle stuff, a '47 Cushman scooter, a '53 Triumph, and a '35 Cadillac, plus garage memorabilia, hubcaps, lighters, and technical manuals representing a fleet of antique cars.

A short ride away lies **Fort Worden State Park,** 360/344-4431 or 360/344-4400, www.olympus.net/fortworden, which is where they filmed. . . *An Officer and a Gentleman*! The base is closed now, which makes it even more intriguing to ride through. It looks like Fort Knox after Goldfinger's ladies sprayed the soldiers with knockout gas. There are parade grounds, officers quarters, gun batteries, an artillery museum, a natural history museum, a theater, and a performing arts center, as well as nice shoreline beside the frigid waters of the straits. If you're traveling with a large group, you can reserve lodging space in some of the older, renovated barracks.

With a decent map, you'll likely find some nearby back roads to satisfy your desire to explore, and you shouldn't miss the stretch of restaurants and stores in the section of town known as uptown Port Townsend, which is higher up the bluff. Aside from that, just appreciate the broad waters of the Straits of Juan De Fuca and the magnificence of Port Townsend Bay.

Pull it Over: Port Townsend Highlights
Attractions and Adventures

If you don't mind devoting touring time to a movie, you may as well do it at the restored **Rose Theatre,** 235 Taylor St., 360/385-1089, www.rose theatre.com. Show tickets cost $6. Buy some licorice and Necco wafers at the counter, and then sit back and listen to owner/preservationist Rocky Friedman introduce and explain the upcoming film—just the way it should be.

A center for maritime education, the **Wooden Boat Foundation,** Cupola House, Port Hudson, 360/385-3628, www.woodenboat.org, teaches people how to build wooden boats. If you're a craftsman or woodworking hobbyist, this impressive collection of traditional vessel building materials, tools, and supplies may spark your interest.

You cannot avoid fly-fishing in the Northwest. Do not even try. The folks at **Port Townsend Angler,** 940 Water St., 360/379-3763, www.ptangler.com, have all the gear and arrange guides for fishing in streams and on the Sound. They claim this to be the best spot for wild steelhead fishing in the lower 48. An expensive hobby, a full day of fly-fishing will cost around $200, and gear will tack on another $35. A McFish sandwich costs $2.

Shopping

Joe Euro runs **Wine Seller,** 940 Water St., 360/385-7673 or 888/286-7674, www.winespt.com, the oldest wine shop on the peninsula. Open daily 10:30–6, the small shop features an array of wines (including generic "cheap white" and "cheap red" wines), plus cigars, gourmet cheese, smoked salmon, and free back issues of *Wine Spectator.*

Blue-Plate Specials

Silverwater Cafe, 237 Taylor St., 360/385-6448, www.silverwatercafe.com, serving lunch and dinner, features creative spins on fresh seafood, meat, and vegetarian entrées. The meals are upscale but the clientele are casual—an unusual mix, but it works here. In its quiet corner location, you can dine in peace.

Also open for lunch and dinner, **Waterfront Pizza,** 951 Water St., 360/385-6629, sells take-out by the slice downstairs, but the upstairs dining room serves pizza that keeps the locals coming back.

Watering Holes

Maxwell's Tavern, 639 Water St., 360/379-6438, sits on the site of the old Town Tavern, and features an 1800s bar, three pool tables, two fireplaces, and a dozen beers on tap (six of them brewed right here).

Sirens, 823 Water St., 360/379-1100, open 'til 2 A.M., is a real hipster's hootenanny, with local musicians playing jazz, blues, or rock to a packed bar of locals. The back porch looks out over the bay, making it a great spot to work on a pitcher of beer.

More coffeehouse than bar, **Upstage,** 923 Washington St., 360/385-2216, pours wine and draft microbrews. An eclectic entertainment calendar changes nightly, featuring everything from open mike to blues to swing.

Shut-Eye

Surprisingly remote, Port Townsend does not have many chain hotels. It does, however, have plenty of inns. Check with the chamber of commerce (Port Townsend Visitors Center 360/385-2722 or 888/365-6978, www.ptguide.com) for the full slate, and consider this list just the tip of the iceberg.

Inn-Dependence

The **Quimper Inn,** 1306 Franklin St., 360/385-1060 or 800/557-1060, www.olympus.net/quimper, a large 1888 home, rests on a hill overlooking Port Townsend. Elegant without the clutter, its rates run between $88 and $150. Kick back on the second-story terrace or relax in the living room and talk to innkeeper Ron Ramage about his Porsche collection and rebuilt trio of Triumphs. The **Palace Hotel,** 1004 Water St., 360/385-0773 or 800/962-0741, www.olympus.net/palace, is a nicely restored hotel on the town's main drag. Large rooms and suites (ask for a private bath) sport an Old West look and go for $119–169.

Related Side Trips

Oregon

Contributed by John M. Flora

U.S. 101

Tillamook Air Museum

U.S. 101 is a fabulous ride down the Oregon coast from the mouth of the Columbia River near Astoria. When the road turns inland at Tillamook, you can reach the largest clear-span wooden structure in the world: a massive hangar built in 1943 to house U.S. Navy blimps searching for Japanese submarines. Nearly 200 feet tall and 1,072 feet long, it encloses enough space for six football fields. Today, it's a museum housing more than 30 historic aircraft, including a great assortment of World War II warbirds.

Wasco-Deschutes Canyon Loop

Here's a fabulous ride with plenty of variety. South of the Columbia River Gorge, from I-89 at Biggs, take Exit 109 and find Wasco. Ride up the steep slope to the golden prairie above. Follow U.S. 97, which leads to Grass Valley, until you reach Oregon SR 216, where the undulating plateau offers a great view of Mt. Hood to the west, Mt. St. Helens to the northwest, and other Cascades volcanoes to the southwest. Descend via tight switchbacks along the steep canyon to the Deschutes River. U.S. 197 North completes the 90-mile detour and drops you off at I-89 at The Dalles.

Resources for Riders

Washington State Run

Washington Travel Information

Washington State Ferries—206/464-6400 or 888/808-7977,
    www.wsdot.wa.gov/ferries/
Washington State Parks—360/902-8844 or 888/226-7688, www.parks.wa.gov
Washington State Road Conditions—800/695-7623
Washington State Tourism—800/544-1800, www.experiencewashington.com

Local and Regional Information

La Conner Chamber of Commerce—360/466-4778 or 888/642-9284,
    www.laconnerchamber.com
Mt. Baker-Snoqualmie National Forest—206/470-4060, www.fs.fed.us/r6/mbs
Olympic Peninsula—360/437-0120, www.olympic-peninsula.com
Olympic Peninsula Bed & Breakfast Association—www.opbba.com
Port Townsend Visitors Center—360/385-2722 or 888/365-6978,
    www.ptguide.com
Whidbey Island Information—www.visitwhidbey.com

Motorcycle Shops

Renton Motorcycle Co.—900 Lind Ave., Renton, 425/226-4320,
    www.rmcmotorsports.com
I-90 Motorsports—200 N.E. Gilman Blvd., Issaquah, 425/391-4490,
    www.I-90motorsports.com
Bellevue Kawasaki—14004 N.E. 20th St., Bellevue, 425/641-5040
Bellevue Suzuki-Ducati-Polaris—13029 NE 20th St., Bellevue, 425/747-7360,
    www.eastsidemotosports.com
Everett Powersports—215 S.W. Everett Mall Way, Everett, 206/343-7980,
    www.everettpowersports.com
Port Townsend Honda—3059 Sims Way W., Port Townsend, 360/385-4559

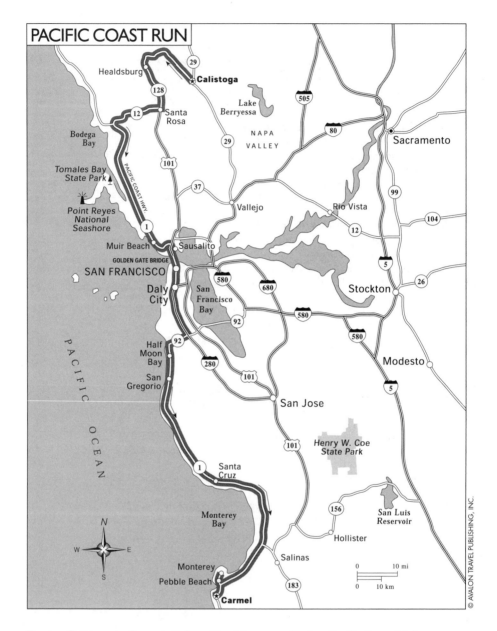

PACIFIC COAST RUN

Route: Calistoga to Carmel via Sausalito, Monterey, Big Sur, Pacific Coast Highway
Distance: Approximately 200 miles; consider 10 days with stops.
  • Days 1 & 2—Calistoga/Napa Valley • Day 3—Travel • Days 4 & 5—
  Sausalito/San Francisco • Day 6—Travel • Days 7 & 8—Carmel/Monterey
  • Day 9—Travel • Day 10—San Simeon
First Leg: Calistoga to Sausalito (80 miles)
Second Leg: Sausalito to Carmel (120 miles)
Third Leg (Optional): Carmel to San Simeon (112 miles)
Helmet Laws: California requires helmets.

Pacific Coast Run

Calistoga to Carmel, California

As evidenced by the ride through Death Valley, Lone Pine, and Yosemite, eastern California was designed by God specifically for motorcyclists. He did a pretty good job on the West Coast, as well. Napa Valley is the closest you'll come to riding along Mediterranean roads, unless you ship your bike to Piraeus. Although the region is marked by affluence, you don't have to be rich—the roads are free. From the luxury of Calistoga's spas to the pure beauty of the San Francisco skyline, from Carmel's fantasy architecture to the dream world of Hearst Castle, this run features short rides on roads that are just right. What's more, the journey from valley to hill to coastal highway creates a satisfying blend of environments, especially during late summer or fall.

Calistoga Primer

Some motorcycle travelers make a critical error when visiting Napa Valley by staying in the valley's namesake, Napa. Far more appealing is the town of Calistoga. As your advance team, let me tell you why you need to stay here:

Several thousand years ago, a volcano named Mt. Konocti erupted twenty miles away and plopped about five feet of ash on the valley floor. Around the 1500s, the Wappo Indians realized the ash had mixed with the naturally heated mineral water and started bathing in the mud and water. They finished up with a sweat wrap and they felt good. Damn good. The Wappos called the valley Tu-la-ha-lu-si ("Oven Place").

When Sam Brannan, California's first Gold Rush millionaire, arrived here in the 1860s, he saw the potential for a resort spa town. At a promotional supper, he proclaimed that this would be the "Calistoga of Sarifornia!" The slip became a marketing ploy, and Calistoga was born. Sorry, Wappos. For decades the town showed promise—at least until 1876, when it was abandoned.

The town rose and fell over the next century, but it appears to be riding the crest of a prosperous wave again. Spas and businesses that were closed just a decade ago are thriving now, as "wine sippers" from San Francisco flock to town for vineyard runs and body wraps. More importantly, motorcycle travelers park up and down Lincoln Avenue, frequenting small saloons and planning sorties into the surrounding mountain roads. One of the state's more pleasing towns, it is the perfect starting point for this journey.

On the Road in Calistoga

The best towns to visit are those where you can ride in, park for free, and check out the town on foot. Calistoga is just such a place and one of the best motorcycle towns you'll ever find—especially if you like drinking wine and having someone upgrade the condition of your muscles to happy. From Dr. Wilkinson's Hot Springs and Mud Baths to the fine restaurants, this is the Old West with a 21st-century facelift.

Unfortunately, you'll have to wait to see all that it offers because the roads of this region are so damn tempting, you'll be hard pressed to sit still.

The number of riding options rivals that of vineyards here. The Greek Peloponnese, Swiss Alps, and Italian Dolomites are all here for your pleasure. Within minutes you can take comfort in roads as curvaceous as Marilyn Monroe, hills that are soft and low, ride over green creeks and past drooping brown trees and pumpkin patches and groves bursting with almonds, avocados, and black walnuts. Not only will your ride be visually exciting, it will be redolent with the fresh, fragrant aroma of nut trees, strawberries, grapes, and flowering plants.

It is a thrilling experience to be here, where the outdoors are treasured, not tamed. You should see all of this and travel beyond the hills, but also consider a manageable trip to the region north of Napa Valley.

Although the larger wineries are in the southern Napa Valley, head north on Highway 29 (a.k.a. Silverado Trail), on the east side of the valley. Turn left on Tubbs Lane, then right at Highway 128. Soon you're on twisting canopy roads that offer some of the finest motorcycle riding in the country. Motorcycles springing up and over the hills look like ants on a mound, but be careful when the afternoon sun and shadows play tricks on the pavement.

Head north and you'll be riding into Alexander Valley. Although there are no major towns, you must stop in Healdsburg at the strangely well-stocked **Jimtown General Store,** 6706 Hwy. 128, 707/433-1212, www.jimtown.com. Think back a few decades—your childhood is right here: Mary Jane candies, bubble-gum cigars, Chinese finger traps, whoopee cushions, old toys from the '40s and '50s, a convenient deli, and, if your name is Jim, a chance at immortality by signing their autograph hound.

From here, you can head further north, south, east, or west to explore other valley back roads. Like those around New Hope, Pennsylvania, all roads lead to a great ride.

Pull it Over: Calistoga Highlights
Attractions and Adventures

If you want a spa treatment without feeling obligated to stay at a resort, you have two options; both have stood the test of time. Established by town founder Sam Brannan in 1871, **Indian Springs,** 1712 Lincoln Ave., 707/942-4913, www.indianspringscalistoga.com, is the oldest continuously operating thermal pool and spa in California. Spread across 16 acres of volcanic ash are mud baths, thermal geysers, massages, and a mineral pool. Yowsah! **Dr. Wilkinson's Hot Springs,** 1507 Lincoln Ave., 707/942-4102, www.drwilkinson.com, was founded in 1951 by Doc Wilkinson. Aside from a great name and continuous family ownership, the spa features mud baths, mineral whirlpools, steam rooms, facials, and an indoor mineral pool.

One of the main reasons you're here is because of the more than 150 wineries located in this region. You can get information and directions to all of them by making a few calls or doing a little online research. The hunt is well worth it since the roads to the vineyards are unusually seductive. For more information contact the **Napa Valley Vintners Association** at 707/963-3388, www.napa vintners.com; the **Sonoma County Wineries Association** at 707/586-3795, www.sonomawine.com, or **Alexander Valley Wine Growers** at 888/289-4637, www.aleaxandervalley.org.

The terrain and mood throughout these valleys is unique in America, and the experience of soaring above it all is as extraordinary as the price ($175) with **Napa Valley Balloons,** 707/944-0228 or 800/253-2224, www.napavalley balloons.com. The steep fee includes breakfast before the launch from the

What's in a Mud Bath?

You know how you can get achy after 10 hours in the saddle? A mud bath will loosen you up faster than an Ex-Lax smoothie. A mud bath is a mixture of heated mineral water and volcanic ash and/or peat moss. After you settle into this gloop, the thick mixture heats up to penetrate your body, relax your muscles, and alleviate stress, tensions, aches, and pains. Ten–twelve minutes should be enough, more if you're really keyed up.

Domaine Chandon Winery and flights of up to two hours. The **Bonaventura Balloon Company,** 133 Wall Rd., Napa, 707/944-2822 or 800/359-6272, www.bonaventuraballoons.com, is another option, with similar rates from $175–195—but the flights last 3–4 hours. Each operation adds options for breakfasts, picnics, or champagne brunches. Before deciding on either flight, ask how many passengers share your basket.

Ben Sharpsteen made good by becoming an Academy Award-winning animator, producer, and director for Walt Disney. His love for his adopted hometown led to the creation of the surprisingly intriguing **Sharpsteen Museum,** 1311 Washington St., 707/942-5911, www.sharpsteen-museum.org. The downtown museum provides a great introduction to Calistoga and the history of upper Napa Valley. With careful detail, its 32-foot diorama depicts 1860s life at the opulent resort. Sam Brannan's cottage is connected to the main museum, which is open 11–4 year-round. Admission is free—but they'd appreciate it if you slipped 'em three bucks.

Blue-Plate Specials

Off the beaten path, southeast of Calistoga on Highway 128, the **Corners Cafe and Saloon,** 6005 Monticello Rd., Lake Berryessa, 707/258-8138, is the starting line and rest stop for riders embarking on weekend runs. Riders of every racing stripe and model fuel up with breakfast, arrive to play pool or pinball, or sit in the bar and watch the game on a large-screen TV. A great place for breakfast, burgers, and pork chops, as well as the inside scoop on hidden roads.

Perhaps the nicest restaurant in town, **Brannan's Grill,** 1374 Lincoln Ave., 707/942-2233, www.brannansgrill.com serves lunches and dinners that are elegant, simple, and creative. The wide-open dining room and fireplace is settling, and the pace never seems rushed, even when it's packed. The menu changes seasonally, so check their website for current appetizers and entrées.

A low-key local favorite, **Pacifico,** 1237 Lincoln Ave., 707/942-4400, www.pacficorestaurant.com, serves traditional Mexican food for lunch and dinner. They win high marks for their chips, salsa, guacamole, and hand-shaken margaritas. The full bar is a rarity in Napa Valley.

Watering Holes

Open daily 'til 2 A.M., **Susie's,** 1365 Lincoln Ave., 707/942-6710, is literally a hole in the wall. Head down a narrow hallway and you end up here, at a cool, dark refuge in the netherworld between "dive" and "joint." Regulars are quick to befriend strangers, and you'll soon settle in at the only pool tables in town. You're also welcome to try your hand at the piano (provided you can play). Happy hour? All day long. The Redwood Empire HOG Chapter dubbed Susie's a biker-friendly bar.

Shut-Eye

Calistoga is so perfect, you may want to extend your stay by a year or two. Most lodging options include a spa, so plan on at least one massage to complement your visit. **B&B Style,** 707/942-2888 or 800/995-8884, www.bandbstyle.com, is a free information service for lodging in Wine Country.

Motels and Motor Courts
Nance's Hot Springs & Motel, 1614 Lincoln Ave., 707/942-6211, has rates from $72–125. Since 1923, Nance and her kneady descendants have been rubbing people the right way with massages, mineral baths, and mud baths. Lodging is clean and basic at this motel-like facility. The **Roman Spa,** 1300 Washington St., 707/942-4441, www.romanspahotsprings.com, has ordinary rooms but lush landscaping and a laid-back atmosphere. After a ride, you can rest outside in a mineral pool, jet spa pool, or sauna. Their spa services include the standard lineup of mud baths, mineral baths, and massages. Rates here run $94–178.

Chain Drive*
A, C, J, Q, U, DD

*Chain hotels in, or within ten miles of town. See cross-reference guide featuring phone numbers and web addresses on page 405.

Inn-Dependence

One of the most pleasing places you can stay is the **Cottage Grove Inn,** 1711 Lincoln Ave., 707/942-8400 or 800/799-2284, www.cottagegrove.com. These luxurious Napa Valley cottages, shaded by towering trees, feature whirlpool tubs, fireplaces, private porches, and distinct themes (fly-fishing, equestrian, Audubon, musical, etc.). The price at Cottage Grove is a yowsah-inducing $235–295, but they *do* include breakfast . . . Check them out; you may feel it's worth it just to be able to park your bike out front and walk downtown. No loud pipes, please.

Indulgences

Not any pricier than Calistoga's spa treatments, this option is just more. . . unusual. At **Osmosis,** 209 Bohemian Hwy., Freestone (west of Calistoga), 707/823-8231, www.osmosis.com, following a Japanese tea ceremony, you strip down to your absolute bare nakedness and settle into a wooden tub filled with antiseptic cedar fiber, rice bran, and 600 active enzymes. An attendant covers you up and you spend the next 20 minutes in the compost heap, throwing off more sweat than Secretariat. After you're dug up, you're hosed down and invited upstairs for the pièce de résistance—a massage. Surreal, yet relaxing. The enzyme bath for one is $75; add a massage for a total of $150.

On the Road: Calistoga to Sausalito

From Calistoga, you have several options, two of which are quite different. For a fast, ordinary, straight shot, ride west to Highway 101, and then drive south until you reach Sausalito. Here's the alternative for experienced riders:

Route 12 South (also called Calistoga Road) heads about 30 miles due west past Santa Rosa toward Bodega Bay (the setting for Alfred Hitchcock's *The Birds*) and then reaches the Pacific Coast Highway.

Let me warn you: The road to the coast can be wonderful at first but soon gives way to city traffic in Santa Rosa and then less than spectacular scenery until you reach fabled Highway 1 (a.k.a. the Pacific Coast Highway or PCH). Also, the stretch south can be pretty spooky unless you've replaced your tires with mountain goats. Seriously. Curves are very sharp, safety rails nonexistent, the twists can be hypnotic, and sometimes the road's layout can range from impassable to impossible. If you're ready, here's what you'll experience:

After you get on Highway 1, the road sweeps east and beyond the view of the coast. To compensate, there are great straightaways and your path follows the rise and fall of the mountains. You'll ride toward Tomales Bay, a long drink of water, where the rustic cabins of fishermen crop up every few miles.

Scenery remains a constant until you pass Lima. About eight miles later, the run approaches Dogtown, which, despite its elegant moniker, is a simple village that is seven times older than it looks. The road leads into a forest and a brief but most enjoyable series of 20-mph turns and shady, slow twists. A few miles later, as you rumble along the slow, graceful bayside, flecks of water may hiss on your pipes as you follow the curving shoreline on this mighty low road.

When you reach Point Reyes Station, you can follow the path blazed by other bikers and head out to the Point Reyes Lighthouse. It's a popular run for locals, but I didn't get much out of it. If you pass it by, the next big show lies south of Stinson Beach.

The ability to ride from here to Highway 101 is what separates man from animal. Throw back a few Maalox tablets and get ready to attack the road between here and Muir Beach, a paved funhouse of gravel, dangerously sharp turns, and very steep drops. Maybe it was because I was riding a monster bike, but I often tapped it into first and took turns at a speed exceeded only by tree sloths. For several miles, my mood alternated between excitement and sheer terror. Just about the time I was thinking, "What hell is this?" I was dumped out into level-headed Tamalpais Valley and then onto Highway 101 for a short, citified ride in Sausalito.

About damn time.

Sausalito Primer

It's almost a cliché to find that a quaint seaside town was once a hotspot for drunken sailors, bawdy saloons, and come one, come all bordellos—but I still get a kick knowing that all this happened in Sausalito. Today the place is so refined, it makes white sugar look rough. It has the feeling of the Cote d'Azur, and the European style is no accident. The town was discovered by Juan Manual de Ayala in 1575 and later became a favored shelter for full-rigged sailing ships from around the world. Today, those ships have been replaced by private yachts.

During World War II, Sausalito was a major ship-building site, with Liberty ships, landing craft, and tankers taking shape here. Afterward, the area became a haven for writers and artists—as evidenced by the galleries along Bridgeway Street.

It's an uncommonly exotic town, and I guarantee you'll enjoy it—or my name isn't Orville Redenbacher.

On the Road in Sausalito

You've already enjoyed a ride from the northeast, and later you'll embark on a great ride south. For now, just park your bike and enjoy the town. You'll never tire of the view, which is even more impressive than that of Camden, Maine, where the Appalachians dissolve into the Atlantic.

Sausalito also has plenty of restaurants and galleries and pubs, and if you need even more, simply head over to San Francisco via ferry or the mighty Golden Gate Bridge.

I chose to continue the low-key theme I'd grown accustomed to in Calistoga and decided to stay in town. Not a bad choice. The heart of Sausalito is as foreign as any village along the Mediterranean and evokes the loveliness of the Riviera.

Besides, the views from here rival any in the world, from the San Francisco skyline to the fogbanks rolling over the bay. The only thing missing is the Golden Gate Bridge, hidden from view behind some ill-placed hills.

In town, the Plaza de Vina Del Mar Park has a visitors center and, more prominently, two 14-foot-tall elephant statues created for the Panama-Pacific Exposition of 1915. The architecture defies generic business district, instead blending Victorian, French, Spanish, and Irish accents. Not only are the people friendly and the setting perfect, as you explore the central district you'll find the town to be as cosmopolitan and as relaxed as any you'll find.

This is clearly a town of affluence. As a double-naught spy, I deduced this from the forest of yachts I saw at the marina, which is just a short and pleasant walk from the park. As you roam the town, a few shops are worth exploring in greater detail. The **Venice Gourmet Delicatessen,** 625 Bridgeway St., 415/332-3544, www.venicesausalito.com, has been here since 1966 and continues to be the local favorite. The shop is cluttered with copper kettles, baklava, dried sausage, soft drinks, and premium wines. A few doors down, **Golden Gate Harley-Davidson,** 605 Bridgeway St., 415/332-1777, www.gghd.com, sells original art, jackets, clothing, and books.

If you finish making the rounds early, you may opt to visit San Francisco, or head north on Bridgeway to reach Caledonia Street, which is an authentic Sausalito neighborhood.

Then in the evening, as ferryboats start knocking through the waters, shuttling workers back from San Francisco, you can relax on the promenade or inside a waterfront restaurant and watch the most spectacular city skyline in America come to light.

Pull it Over: Sausalito Highlights
Attractions and Adventures

While an inmate on Alcatraz, I was only able to cruise the bay on my inner tube. For you, the alternative is traveling in style aboard the 103-foot **Hawaiian Chieftain,** 415/331-3214, www.hawaiianchieftain.com. The tall ship cruises around the bay during three-hour sunset sails ($35) and Friday sunset sails ($40, includes hors d'oeuvres and beverages), Saturday adventure sails ($45), and Sunday brunch cruises ($50). Get the captain drunk and maybe he'll actually take you to Hawaii.

It's great riding into SF, but you can cruise there cheaply and see it from a different perspective. **Blue and Gold Ferry,** 415/773-1188, www.blueandgold fleet.com, departs Sausalito several times daily ($6.75 one way, $13.50 round trip) for Fisherman's Wharf. From there, you can catch tour boats to Alcatraz. Be sure to make advance reservations for the $13 trip, which includes a cell house audio tour. **Golden Gate Ferry,** 415/923-2000, avoids Fisherman's Wharf and goes to the foot of Market Street; fares are $5.30 one way, $10.60 round trip. Sorry, no room for motorcycles.

Mark Reuben Vintage Gallery, 34 Princess St., 415/332-8815 or 877/444-3767, displays thousands of vintage photographs, many taken from the original negatives. Matted and framed original pictures include those of the Davidson brothers, the Beatles, and Marlon Brando in *The Wild One.* You could spend days in here. Topics cover sports, history, entertainers, political figures, and other photos perfect for the office and home. Shipping's available and dig this: The store manager was the Harley Queen of York, Pennsylvania.

Blue-Plate Specials

A great way to start the day is at the **Bridgeway Cafe,** 633 Bridgeway St., 415/332-3426. With a great view of the city and the bay, this friendly little diner serves all-day breakfasts, lunches, and dinners, and the waitresses are kind and considerate.

When the evening falls, consider **Horizons,** 558 Bridgeway St., 415/331-3232. In addition to its rich woods and high ceilings, the wide bay windows and patio dining reveal a breathtaking view of San Francisco. Serving lunch and dinner, the waterfront restaurant features fettucini jambalaya, five-cheese spinach cannelloni, and lobster tails. It's also a fact that the dining room manager owns a Vincent, a few BSAs, and a 1919 Harley.

Watering Holes

Two bars in town are among the best I've had the pleasure to discover. At the **No-Name Bar,** 757 Bridgeway St., 415/332-1392, there's character in abundance, a fireplace inside, and a garden patio outside. Owner Al Stanfield rides and often makes the 2,000-mile jaunt to Sturgis. His place delivers live jazz on weekends, blues on weekdays, and pub food in the afternoon. Beers and spirits abound in this mighty beautiful bar.

Since the late '60s, **Paterson's,** 739 Bridgeway St., 415/332-1264, has been frequented by spirits—and ales and more than 100 kinds of malt whiskey. In fact, Bill Paterson stocks a variety of rums, from $6-a-shot brands to a top-of-the-line Glen Grant for $30 a sip. This place rivals the best British pub, and it does it with style. During the day, the clientele changes from locals to tourists to commuters to younger locals. Anytime you arrive is the best time to be here. Another plus: pints are 20-ounce imperials.

Shut-Eye

I'd suggest making every effort to stay the night in Sausalito, but across the bridge in San Francisco exists every chain hotel known to man.

Chain Drive*
A, B, C, E, G, H, K, L, N, Q, R, S, T, U, Y, AA, CC, DD

*Chain hotels in, or within ten miles of town. See cross-reference guide featuring phone numbers and web addresses on page 405.

Inn-Dependence
There are four unique and (thankfully) non-generic hotels in Sausalito. I wish they were cheaper, but they're not. The **Alta Mira,** 125 Bulkley Ave., 415/332-1350, has been around since the '20s and hasn't changed much since. On Sausalito's high ground, it's the most moderately priced hotel downtown, with rooms starting at $85. The hotel's Mediterranean interior and commanding views of the bay alone are worth the price of admission. The rooms are somewhat small, but the balcony opens them up. The **Casa Madrona Hotel,** 801 Bridgeway St., 415/332-0502 or 800/567-9524, www.casamadrona.com, opened in 1885, features single cottages, and elevated rooms with perfect bay views. The staff is friendly; the rooms are plush; the garden-like atmosphere soothing; and it's all within sight of one of America's largest and loudest cities. Room 315 lets you soak in the tub while

watching the city lights. Included in the rate of $195–300 is an evening social hour that affords the opportunity to get looped on some free wine. On the park, **Hotel Sausalito,** 16 El Portal, 415/332-0700 or 888/442-0700, www.hotelsausalito.com, is the most European of the four, with rates from $145–270. The rich, warm, gold tones of this hotel perfectly mirror the sunrise over the bay. The hotel offers 16 1920s-style rooms and suites with modern amenities and views of the park or harbor. As the name implies, The **Inn Above Tide,** 30 El Portal, 415/332-9535, 800/893-8433, www.innabovetide.com, is on the waterfront. All 30 rooms face the hillside city, although they are more modern than I prefer. You may be lured by the free breakfast and sunset wine and cheese receptions. Rooms run $235–370.

On the Road: Sausalito to Carmel

The next leg of the journey revs you up for some spectacular scenery and the unforgettable experience of riding across the Pacific Ocean in less than five minutes.

When you leave Sausalito, take Bridgeway Street and follow it south. Three minutes from the center of town, you'll round the bend and see the twin towers straight ahead. Before you cross the bridge, get in the right lane and watch for a lightly trafficked access road that affords one of the best souvenir photos you'll ever take. Turn right, and a few hundred yards ahead, pull off and pose with your bike—the Golden Gate Bridge, bay, and city behind you help create photos suitable for framing.

When you get back on the road, you'll pay three bucks to cross the bridge, and even though you'd think they'd have the bridge paid for by now, it's worth it. To your left is the bay, to your right the Pacific Ocean, which will be your traveling companion for the next 100-plus miles.

Navigating through town to reach PCH is a little tricky, and trying to explain how to do it can drive a man to drink. The abridged version is this: After crossing the bridge, veer to the right to reach 19th Avenue (which is also Highway 1), and work your way through a tunnel, then into residential neighborhoods and toward Daly City. Stay on Highway 1. At I-280 the road splits. Veer left to take 280 further south to Rte. 92, where you turn west toward Half Moon Bay. Veer right onto PCH if you want to get right to the coast. Not a bad idea at all.

But after slow city traffic, I wanted to blow out the cobwebs, so I took I-280. Surprisingly, it wasn't bad. The farther from the city you get, the greater the pleasure, as you see buildings and urban sprawl wither away into the natural landscape.

The next surprise was taking 92 West. I was back in the land of curvy roads and nice lakes, and I also passed miles of flower farms—a far sweeter aroma than I had sniffed in Amish country.

The road ends at PCH, and from here it's 100 miles south to the Monterey Peninsula. Unlike PCH north of San Francisco, the road here is fairly flat, straight, and ordinary. Based on the inventory I spied at roadside produce stands, I deduced that the farmers of this fertile region raise artichokes, pumpkins, carrots, hot dogs, and soft drinks.

It's impossible to explain how easy this road is. Flat and smooth, the pleasure is in the tranquility of the environment. This lasts for about 60 coastal miles until you reach the Santa Cruz county line. Thus ends the scenic route.

Unfortunately, you have to run a gauntlet of urban ugliness to reach your final destination. You're in for fast food joints, cheap gas, bike shops, and a crappy highway that lasts for more than 10 miles.

Sadly, the ocean remains hidden behind miles of land, and there's not a damn thing you can do about it except get to one of the most enchanting towns in California. After passing Monterey, look for Ocean Avenue, turn right, and head straight into a dreamscape called Carmel.

Most extraordinary Carmel.

Carmel Primer

Carmel may be the crown jewel in the Monterey Peninsula, one of California's more naturally beautiful regions. The Essalen Indians knew it when they made it their home from 3000–500 B.C. Next the Ahlone Indians showed up and were doing fine until their time started running out in 1542, when Spanish explorer Juan Rodriguez Cabrillo sighted the white sand beach and pine forest. Even though Cabrillo couldn't land because of rough waters, he claimed it for Spain anyway.

Yes, he did. And I own Japan.

Several explorers later, in June 1770, Father Junipero Serra, a Spanish governor and a Franciscan priest, proclaimed the area the military and ecclesiastical capital of Alta, California.

With natural beauty and easy access to the ocean, it was obvious people would covet the Monterey Peninsula. Mexico owned it, then surrendered it to the U.S. Navy without a fight. In 1906, refugees from the San Francisco earthquake made it their new home. And in 1916, in Carmel itself, bohemian artists with no architectural training showed up and formed the village on Halloween.

An artist in his outdoor studio on 17-mile Drive near Carmel, California.

From the town's earliest days, art was in the forefront. When Hugh Comstock's wife asked him to build a separate house for her doll collection, he ended up building 20 whimsical cottages that are still highly prized (and liveable) today. While best known as Clint Eastwood's domain (he served as mayor from 1986–1988), the town of 4,500 remains true to the original vision of its founding artists and preserves an oasis of art and extraordinary beauty.

On the Road in Carmel

Before you start wandering around the village, you may want to stock up on film. You could easily burn up a dozen rolls shooting every picturesque building, alcove, courtyard, and garden throughout the town.

On one street, you may photograph a Swiss village, turn the corner and enter a Spanish mercado, and then spy the rounded archways and thatched roof of an English cottage. This is a town that will always be a village. Restrictions prohibit neon signs, street numbers, parking meters, high rises, plastic plants, and high heels.

Here you have the option of walking a few blocks to the beach, resting at a sidewalk café, or hanging out. The best way to understand the essence of the village is with **Carmel Walks,** 831/642-2700, www.carmelwalks.com, which offers two-hour guided tours through secret pathways, courtyards, and side streets, complete with some insider information. Tours ($20) are given Saturdays at 10 and 2, Tuesday–Friday at 10.

Touring downtown is only the beginning. Off Ocean Drive you can access the Carmel Gate of 17-Mile Drive. Dammit, sarge, only residents and employees can bring in motorcycles, but if you're determined (and you should be since this is a hyper-fun run), **Rent-A-Roadster,** 229 Cannery Row, 831/647-1929, www.rent-a-roadster.com, in Monterey rents reproduction 1929 Model A's for $30–35 per hour. With the top down and sea winds blowing, it's the next best thing to a bike.

Anyway, after paying the $7.25 toll, you'll get a map listing points of interest along 17-Mile Drive and can drive in and out from various gates around the loop. Theoretically, road signs should direct you on the tour, but they're often hard to follow. Just stick close to the coastline and have your camera ready.

Several points jut out into the Pacific, each with turnouts that reveal the sheer beauty of this rugged coastline. At Pescadera Point, white foam wraps around rocks, and at Cypress Point, a lone tree is the inspiration for one of California's signature icons. A little further, at Bird Rock, the seals and birds bark and caw without pause.

Although you may not have your favorite clubs with you, it'd be a shame to miss **Pebble Beach,** 800/654-9300, www.pebblebeach.com. Golfers consider this America's St. Andrews and are charged accordingly: non-residents pay a whopping $375 for 18 holes. Personally, I'd invest that money in a troupe of juggling monkeys. Even if you don't golf, it's worth driving through, just to see the dynamic shoreline.

You can exit at the Pacific Grove gate to visit a town of bungalows, Victorian homes, and a neat main street. There's something else about this village: Each October, swarms of monarch butterflies return here just as sure as vultures return to roost in Washington, D.C.

Eventually, the roads and advice of well-intentioned friends will guide you to Monterey and Cannery Row. According to brilliant American writer and native son John Steinbeck, Cannery Row was "a poem, a stink, a grating noise, a quality of light, a tone, a habit, a nostalgia, a dream." Now it's all this, plus some tacky tourist shops. Fisherman's Wharf is part carnival midway where merchants seem to believe that the world's problems could be solved if everyone ate "chowder in a bun," which is a concoction that looks suspiciously like a bread bowl full of vomit.

The definitive attraction is the **Monterey Bay Aquarium,** 886 Cannery Row, 831/648-4888, www.mbayaq.org. More than 100 galleries and exhibits highlight the diverse habitats of the bay, and most are larger than life. In addition to the million-gallon outer bay exhibit, there are whale skeletons, a stingray petting pool, and an otter exhibit (did you know otters have pockets?). If you don't scuba dive, the aquarium is a good substitute, and the outdoor promenade puts you on the 50-yard line of the pounding waves. Admission is $17.95.

From here, you can return to Carmel via 17-Mile Drive or work your way over to PCH and take the Ocean Avenue exit. The village is easily worth a day or maybe 10 years of walking.

Pull it Over: Carmel Area Highlights
Attractions and Adventures

John Steinbeck was one of our greatest writers, and his favorite topic, America, places his works among the best road reading material you'll find. The **Steinbeck Center,** 1 Main St., Salinas, 831/796-3833, www.steinbeck.org, celebrates the author's life and work. Open daily 10–5, the center exhibits items taken from the pages of his books, but the focal point is his GMC camper, Rocinante, from *Travels with Charley*—the inspiring cross-country journey he made with his poodle. If you love Steinbeck, you'll love the 30,000-piece archives, which include original manuscripts, oral histories, first editions, and photographs. The center includes a museum store and café. Pay $8 at the door.

Hey, Nanook! Wanna see a seal up close? Kayaks are big in this area, and you can rent them for $30 a day from **Adventures by the Sea,** 299 Cannery Row, 831/372-1807, www.adventuresbythesea.com. Tours are also available, for $45. Also check out **Monterey Bay Kayaks,** 693 Del Monte Ave., 831/373-5357, www.montereybaykayaks.com, which charges $30 per day. As you paddle among the harbor seals, you'll also see kelp forests, sea lions, otters, snowy egrets, and tourists. The bay is protected from large swells, so it should be smooth paddling.

Besides the sea, there are ranch lands inland. You can ride trails in Carmel Valley at **The Holman Ranch,** 831/659-6054 or 831/659-2640, www.holman ranch.com, a private 400-acre working horse ranch. Rides are $40 and up per person per tour, which are named after cowboy heroes: Hopalong Cassidy, Gene Autry, and the Lone Ranger (the one you want if you're an experienced rider with a sense of adventure).

Okey-doke, Icarus, I've got some aerial adventure as well. At **Western Hang Gliders** in the town of Marina (off PCH at Reservation Road), 831/384-2622, www.westernhanggliders.org, you may find a sport that provides more freedom than motorcycling. The beginner course ($98) includes classroom instruction, ground school, and at least five flights. You won't soar over the ocean (just about eight feet off the ground) but you can get started on a new hobby. Lessons begin at 10 A.M. Wear long pants and tennis shoes. Forty-five minutes away in

Hollister (where a biker's bacchanal inspired *The Wild One)*, **Bay Area Glider Rides,** Hollister Airport, 800/696-7627, www.bayareagliderrides.com, features sailplane rides from $135. The expensive one-hour trips ($250) will glide you back to Monterey and over the Pacific.

People who call you crazy for riding a motorcycle would bust a vessel if they saw you cavorting with the folks at **Skydive Monterey Bay,** 3261 Imjin Rd., 831/384-3483, www.skydivemontereybay.com. After 15–20 minutes of training, you can take a tandem fall. If you're motivated, they offer accelerated free fall and static line training programs. Reservations suggested.

The draw at Laguna Seca, a county park and campground about 20 minutes northeast of Carmel, is the **Laguna Seca Raceway,** 800/327-7322 (SECA), www.laguna-seca.com. Only one motorcycle race is held here each year, but that may be enough to make it worth a visit. In July, the Superbike World Championship draws SBK and AMA riders to a super showdown.

Shopping

Even though there are stores within stores within stores in Carmel, you can have a good time just window shopping and then dropping into at least two must-sees. **Wings America,** Dolores and 7th, 831/626-9464, www.wingsamerica.com, presents aviation accent pieces, signed pictures, nearly full-sized models, and aerodynamically dynamic accessories designed with an aviation theme. Buy a tile from space shuttle *Columbia* for $2,200. Buy several thousand and build your own spacecraft. The same person owns **Boatworks,** Ocean Ave. at Lincoln, 831/626-1870, www.boatworkstore.com, which is nautical and nice. They sell cool clothes, great steamship posters, ship models, and smaller items. If you made the mistake of ordering the optional boat rack from your bike dealer, you can put it to use with a sleek $28,000 wooden canoe. Both are open daily 9:30–6.

Blue-Plate Specials

Katy's Place, Mission between 5th and 6th, 831/624-0199, www.katysplace carmel.com, has one of the largest breakfast and lunch menus in Californi-yi-yay, even offering 10 varieties of eggs benedict. Joining the line-up: blintzes, pancakes, hash, burritos, omelettes, french toast, buckwheat cakes, bacon, sausage, steak, eggs, cereal, bagels, and muffins.

In a cozy cottage with a fireplace, **Em Le's,** Pantiles Court Delores between 5th and 6th, 831/625-6780, is hot at breakfast with french toast, omelettes, pancakes, and fresh OJ (not the kind that kills you). At lunch, the menu switches to burgers, sandwiches, soups, and salads. In addition to a soda fountain, they serve beer and wine.

There's a fine Italian restaurant (**Il Fornaio**), Ocean Ave. at Monte Verde, 831/622-5115, but I'd recommend trying their adjacent bakery for a casual breakfast. This is where the locals go for conversation, coffee, and quiet. It's not fancy, but it smells great and the rounded, draped room features a fireplace and newspapers.

You'll look like a local if you drop in for breakfast or lunch at the **Tuck Box,** Dolores between Ocean and 7th, 831/624-6365, www.tuckbox.com, a non-linear fairytale cottage/breakfast nook. One of Comstock's original cottages, it feels like somewhere beyond the looking glass. Here since 1940. Opens at 7.

Watering Holes

It's hard, but not impossible, while in Carmel to find a place to have a quiet brew and talk with friends. If there's a designated rider, Cannery Row nightspots in Monterey have replaced sardines as the main source of commerce.

A local tradition for food and drink, **Jack London's Bar & Grill,** Dolores between 5th and 6th, 831/624-2336, is tucked inside Su Vecino Courtyard. Here since the early '70s, the menu of burgers, calamari, and Mexican dishes are just precursors to a pint in the outdoor setting. Kick back here and take advantage of the full bar, seven TVs, and 10 beers on tap.

Forge in the Forest, 5th Ave. and Junipero, 831/624-2233, also has a cool outdoor dining area and an even cooler bar. If you travel in a pack (like the animal you are), set up your summit meeting at the brick-thick 15-foot table. The place is cluttered with antlers, skates, maps, and dozens of restroom signs, which you'll give thanks for after polishing off a Bass or Spaten Pils.

Shut-Eye

About 50 bed-and-breakfasts and hotels dot the peninsula. And even though Carmel reeks of wealth, rates are remarkably reasonable. If everything's booked in town, numerous chain hotels can be found in nearby Monterey.

Chain Drive*
A, B, C, E, F, G, J, L, N, Q, S, U, CC, DD

*Chain hotels in, or within ten miles of town. See cross-reference guide featuring phone numbers and web addresses on page 405.

Inn-Dependence

Tops in my book (and it *is* my book) is **La Playa,** Camino Real and 8th, 831/ 624-6476 or 800/582-8900, www.laplayahotel.com, a large and gorgeous Mediterranean hotel a few blocks from the ocean. The building's design, character, gardens, pool, and flowers all combine to make this a spectacular choice. A second-floor terrace restaurant and five cottages make it even nicer. Rates run $160 and up. Also in the heart of the village, the **Normandy Inn,** Ocean Ave. and Monte Verde, 831/624-3825 or 800/343-3825, www.normandyinn carmel.com, is an excellent choice with a collection of buildings and cottages connected by shaded courtyards. The large rooms ($79–190) feature featherbeds and mini-fridges; some have fireplaces and all include a complimentary continental breakfast. There's also a pool. Trust me, Carmel offers more than enough choices, but the **Seven Gables Inn,** 555 Ocean View Blvd., 831/372-4341, www.pginns.com, in appealing Pacific Grove, is another nice option. The classic

Hearst Castle

Hearst Castle, 800/444-4445, www.hearstcastle.org, reminds me of my first apartment—except this place has 165 rooms and 127 acres of gardens. If not for Hearst Castle, San Simeon (pop. 18) would be nothing surrounded by nothing else. But after losing three runs for political office, William Randolph Hearst decided that his bid for immortality would come not through ballots but through building.

Everything begins at the Visitor Center, where you buy tickets for the mansion ($14) and the IMAX movie ($7), which describes how the castle was designed, built, and decorated. Then you'll board a bus for a long and winding ride to the mansion.

The scale here is off the scale: Guest houses are the size of fat mansions; the gardens are Edenic; the dining room is royal. A seductive and sensual outdoor pool holds 345,000 gallons of spring water, and a smaller indoor Roman pool contains a paltry 205,000 gallons. Furnishings are equally dazzling, and it's worth noting that Hearst had enough stuff stashed in a warehouse that he could have built five more castles. At least, that's what Bob the Tour Guide said.

The home is now owned by the citizens of California. Don't be jealous. They also own San Quentin.

Victorian, with rates from $175–385, may seem a far cry from what motorcycle travelers are looking for, but the view from the bay window is more than enough to compensate. A full breakfast, four o'clock tea, and a park across the street round out the amenities.

Indulgences

It'll put a mighty dent in your wallet, but **Stonepine,** 150 E. Carmel Valley Rd., 831/659-2245, www.stonepinecalifornia.com, may provide you with the most memorable evening of your ride. The rates start at $275 (and zoom to $1,200 for a massive wing of the house), but that hasn't stopped guests like Bill Gates, Warren Buffett, and Arnold Schwarzenegger from dropping by for a long weekend. On this 330-acre estate is a majestic 1920 French chateaux home with grand rooms, a large fireplace, and private lounge. The opportunity to rest and dine in such luxury is thoroughly self-indulgent and satisfying. If this is a once-in-a-lifetime stay, you'll thank yourself when you're relaxing by the pool or quiet pond, worlds away from all sounds except those of nature. Bring binoculars and you may spy Doris Day at her home about a half mile up the hill. Bring an extra helmet and she may take a ride with you. . . que sera, sera.

Side Trip: Carmel to San Simeon

If you have a fear of heights, consider this ride a pleasant form of aversion therapy. As natural forces continue to pound boulders into pebbles, you'll rise above it all on this 112-mile route that scribbles along the Pacific Ocean. There's a reason why this is one of motorcycle travelers' most favored rides. It combines slow curves, sharp turns, and elevations magnified by the view of mountains and sea.

Watch for the sign south of Carmel: curves ahead next 74 miles. But unlike the psychologically brutal Stinson Beach/Muir Beach/Tamalpais Valley ride, you can experience these slow curves and broad vistas without fear of death. In other words, this ride doesn't challenge your mortality; it affirms your vitality.

As you ride south, get used to miles of weaving curves that foreshadow upcoming jolts of adrenaline. Make sure your brakes are in working order because you'll stop often to photograph the handsome cliffs and endless ocean—but watch for loose gravel and unpaved shoulders. This is a sustained pleasure that spikes about 30 miles into the run, when you take your bike across the Bixby Creek Bridge. Get those cameras ready, folks.

Construction on the "Rainbow" started in 1919 and took until 1937 to complete, but it was worth the wait. Thanks to some anonymous engineers and the fact that you wanted to get out of the house, you're riding 260 feet above sea level on a 718-foot race to the other side of the mountain.

After this jolt, the road is like a Chesterfield—it satisfies for the next 20 miles. When you arrive in Big Sur, you may start looking for the commercial district. You won't find it here, Wilma. Big Sur is a decentralized region, where residents enjoy the solitude and don't feel compelled to build city halls and shopping malls. It's why writers and artists come here, and it's where Henry Miller redis-covered his creative spark (while living in an abandoned convict labor camp).

The most active address on this stretch of road is **Nepenthe,** 831/667-2345, www.nepenthebigsur.com, a stop as necessary for motorcyclists as breathing. Constructed around a log cabin Orson Welles had built for Rita Hayworth, Nepenthe (Greek for "sorrow banisher") was expanded by Rowan Maiden, a disciple of Frank Lloyd Wright. Today it is a restaurant/overlook where lunch includes such fare as broiled swordfish sandwiches and the famous Ambrosia Burger; sunset dinners focus on steaks and fresh fish. Even if you're not hungry, you must stop here to feast on the view from the terrace, 800 feet above the shoreline. The surf sounds like muffled cannons from this height, and is yet another magical experience you'll add to your journey.

A quarter mile south, the Henry Miller Library is more of an artists' village than a library, but people still stop. Beyond this, PCH gets back into the rugged and exhilarating coastline you've come to love. Within miles, you'll be riding past different environments—ocean, desert, pine forests—each constantly in-terchanging.

There are few places in the nation more suited to your purpose. Take advan-tage of turnouts, where you can just park it and watch the water swallow rocks the size of mountains and pound the hell out of monoliths. In some spots, the water seems as clear as the Caribbean, and a few miles later the coastline disap-pears into fog.

As you drive south, you'll experience a sense of contentment, knowing that you're six feet closer to the ocean than those poor bastards in the oncoming lane. To reward yourself for this insight, when you reach the town of Gorda, buy yourself a sodee pop at the service station/general store.

Resuming the run, the rises are subtle. At times, the ocean appears without warning, 200 feet down a cliff. Be careful—you'll be contending with riders and drivers who see this as a test track.

The final miles to the Hearst Castle lose their scenic punch, but I promise that you will look back on this run and agree that this—and like your ride across America—was everything you expected it to be. It was dangerous within limits, vast beyond measure, and beautiful beyond description.

Resources for Riders
Pacific Coast Run

California Travel Information
California Association of Bed & Breakfast Inns—831/464-8159, www.cabbi.com
California Division of Tourism—800/462-2543, www.gocalif.ca.gov
California Highway Patrol Road Conditions—916/657-7261
California Road and Weather Information—916/445-1534 or 800/427-7623
California State Parks—916/653-6995, www.parks.ca.gov

Local and Regional Information
Calistoga Chamber of Commerce—707/942-6333, www.calistogachamber.com
Carmel Visitors Center—831/624-2522 or 800/550-4333, www.carmelcalifornia.org
Monterey Peninsula Visitors Bureau—831/649-1770 or 888/221-1010,
    www.montereyinfo.org
Napa Valley Visitors Bureau—707/226-7459, www.napavalley.com
Pacific Grove Chamber of Commerce—831/373-3304 or 800/656-6650,
    www.pacificgrove.org
Sausalito Chamber of Commerce—415/331-7262, www.sausalito.org
Sonoma County Visitors Bureau—707/996-1090, www.sonomacounty.com

Motorcycle Shops
Jim & Jim's Yamaha—910 Santa Rosa Ave., Santa Rosa, 707/545-1672,
    www.jjyamaha.com
North Bay Motorsports—2875 Santa Rosa Ave., Santa Rosa, 707/542-5355,
    www.northbaymotorsports.com
Santa Rosa BMW—606 Santa Rosa Ave., Santa Rosa, 707/542-4491,
    www.santarosabmw.com
Santa Rosa Vee Twin—1240 Petaluma Hill Rd., Santa Rosa, 707/523-9696,
    www.indianvtwin.com
Golden Gate Harley-Davidson/Buell—13 San Clemente Dr., Corte Madera,
    415/927-4464, www.gghd.com
BMW of San Francisco—1675 Howard St., San Francisco, 415/863-9000,
    www.bmwsf.com
Dudley Perkins Harley-Davidson—66 Page St., San Francisco, 415/703-9494,
    www.dpchd.com
Golden Gate Cycles—1540 Pine St., San Francisco, 415/771-4535,
    www.ggcycles.com
Magri Motorcycles—1220 Pennsylvania Ave., San Francisco, 415/285-6735
Monterey Peninsula Powersports—Del Monte and Auto Center Pkwy., Seaside,
    831/899-7433, www.montereypowersports.com
Cycle Stop Honda—511 Abbott St., Salinas, 831/394-8889
Warren's Harley-Davidson—321 N. Main St., Salinas, 831/424-1909,
    www.warrenshd.com
Yamaha of Salinas—330 Kings St., Salinas, 831/422-3232

Appendix

Top Motorcycle Web Sites
Moto-Directory
www.moto-directory.com
More than 10,000 links to events, rallies, magazines, videos, tours, stolen bike listings, riding clubs, rental operators, dealers, and salvage yards.
Motorcycle Shopper
www.motorcycleshopper.com
Quick access to clubs, salvage yards, new and used bikes, parts and shipping, tours, and feature articles.
Ronnie Cramer's Motorcycle Web Index
http://sepnet.com/cycle/
4,500-plus links.

Other Motorcycle Sites
All About Cycles
www.allaboutcycles.com
More than 1,300 links to dealers, cycle sales, events, and clubs.
American Motorcycle Network
www.americanmotor.com
News and more than 1,000 articles on events, rallies, and manufacturers.
Motorcycle Online
www.motorcycle.com
Fantastic digital motorcycle magazine with bikes, products, reviews, videos, clubs, events, rides, classifieds, financing, and chats.
Motorcycle Accessories Warehouse
www.accwhse.com
Parts, supplies, and thousands of links to clothes and close-outs, from goggles to tank covers. Also at 800/241-2222.
Rider Magazine
www.riderreport.com
Links to Rider, American Rider, Woman Rider, and Cruising Rider magazines and archives.

Selected Manufacturers
Most manufacturers' sites will lead to showrooms, accessories, clothing, riders clubs, FAQs, dealers, and riding products.

BMW
(dealer location information)
800/831-1117
www.bmwusacycles.com
Buell
800/490-9635
www.buell.com
Ducati
www.ducati.com
Excelsior-Henderson
612/873-5800
www.excelsior-henderson.com
Harley-Davidson
(dealer location information)
800/258-2464 (CLUB-HOG)
www.harley-davidson.com
Honda
(dealer location information)
310/532-9811
www.hondamotorcycle.com
Indian Motorcycles
408/847-2221,
www.indianmotorcycle.com
Kawasaki
(dealer location information)
800/661-7433
www.kawasaki.com
Moto Guzzi
www.motoguzzi.it
Suzuki
(dealer location information)
800/828-7433
www.suzukicycles.com
Triumph
770/631-9500
www.triumph.co.uk
Victory
612/542-0500
www.victory-usa.com
Yamaha
(dealer location information)
800/889-2624
www.yamaha-motor.com

Selected Motorcycle Organizations
American Motorcyclist Association
800/262-5646 (AMA-JOIN)

www.ama-cycle.org
If you belong to one motorcycling organization, make it the AMA. They sponsor thousands of sanctioned events and provide a monthly magazine, trip routing, hotel discounts, and club information for approximately 250,000 members. Spring for the $75 Diamond Level membership and you'll get a free copy of my book. Spring for the $150,000 über-platinum level and I'll personally write a book for you.

Motorcycle Events Association
605/224-9999 or 800/675-4656
www.motorcycleevents.com
Provides information on Daytona, Sturgis, Laconia, Four Corners, Hollister, and other major rallies.

Motorcycle Industry Council
714/727-4211 or 800/833-3995,
www.motorcycles.org
Marketing clearinghouse for motorcycle-related news items and consumer information.

Motorcycle Product News
608/249-0186, www.mpnmag.com
Lists products, distributors, manufacturers, parts, and accessories; primarily used by dealers and rental operators. Password required.

Motorcycle Riders Foundation
202/546-0983 or
800/673-5646 (MRF-JOIN)
www.mrf.org
Lobbying group for riders' rights, with links on this site.

Motorcycle Safety Foundation
800/446-9227
www.msf-usa.org
Offers courses throughout the United States; participation can lower your insurance rates. Also features information on rider training and industry contacts.

Selected Riding Clubs
State-by-state listings at www.motorcycle .com/mo/clubs.html

American Gold Wing Association
www.agwa.com

Blue Knights
207/947-4600 or 877/254-5362
www.blueknights.org
International organization of retired law enforcement officers: 14,000 members in 428 chapters in 17 countries.

BMW Motorcycle Owners of America
636/537-5511
www.bmwmoa.org

Christian Motorcyclists Association
870/389-6196
www.christianlink.com/clubs/cma

Gold Wing Road Riders Association
800/843-9460
www.gwrra.org

Harley Owners Group
800/258-2464
www.hog.com

Honda Riders Club of America
800/847-4722
www.hondamotorcycle.com/hrca

Kawasaki Good Times Owners Club
800/433-4862
www.kawasaki.com

Motorcycle Clubs & Associations
www.moto-directory.com/clubs.htm

Women on Wheels
800/322-1969
www.womenonwheels.org
Founded in 1982, WOW has 65 chapters with more than 2,500 female members.

Selected Rallies
Each year across the country, there are figuratively more than a million rallies of all shapes and sizes. Here are links to some of the largest. Most rally sites include information on registration, rides, vendors, lodging, histories, and entertainment.

Americade Motorcycle Rally
718/444-7626
www.tourexpo.com

Bike Week and Biketoberfest
386/255-0981
www.officialbikeweek.com

Four Corners Iron Horse Motorcycle Rally
970/563-4171 or 888/284-9212
www.fourcornersrally.com

Honda Hoot
www.hondahoot.com
Laconia Rally
603/366-2000
www.laconiamcweek.com
Sonomafest
800/870-7223
www.searspoint.com/pages/events/vmd
Sturgis Rally and Races
605/347-9190
www.sturgismotorcyclerally.com

Selected National Tour Operators
Adventure Cycle Tours
763/449-4908,
www.winternet.com/~act/
Offers 16 tours of the Midwest and Canada.
America Harley Tours
310/487-1047
www.ridefree.com
Rides across the West on Harley-Davidsons.
Insurance, food, lodging, and road support
provided.
Arkansas Cycle Touring and Training
501/665-2202
www.arkansascycle.com
Rides through the Ozarks.
Bob Duffeys Motorcycle & ATV Tours
505/523-1700
www.zianet.com/bobduffey
Ride your own bike on guided tours of
southwestern New Mexico.
Classic Motorcycle Adventures
510/849-1499 or 888/339-4262
www.cmatours.com
Great site describing all-inclusive tours of the
Sierra Nevadas and the desert Southwest.
Country Roads Motorcycling Tours & Rentals
973/560-9009
www.mctours.com
Tours in New Jersey and Florida on BMWs
and Harley-Davidsons.
EagleRider Motorcycle Rental
310/536-6777 or 888/900-9901
www.eaglerider.com
Nationwide service renting fully equipped
Road Kings, Softails, Fat Boys, and Electra
Glides. Locations in Los Angeles, San
Francisco, San Diego, Phoenix, Las Vegas,
Denver, Chicago, and Orlando.

Freedom Tours
800/643-2109
www.twisty-roads.com
Tours range from a three-day weekend, to
an eight-day Colorado Rockies run, to a
15-day marathon.
Lone Eagle Tours
888/566-3345
www.loneeagleyours.com
Rides in the Colorado Rockies.
Montana Motorcycle Tours
406/449-6362
www.montanamotorcycletours.com
Guided tours of Montana, Wyoming, and
Canada.
Pacific Rim Motorcycle Tours
www.pacificmotorcycle.com
Three-week rides across Oregon, Idaho,
Arizona, California, Wyoming, Utah,
Nevada, Montana, and Washington.
Rebel USA Tours
858/292-6200
www.rebelusa.com
Specializes in Harley adventure tours of Baja.
Ride the Dream
505/660-5274
www.ridethedream.com
Tours of the Southwest on Harleys.

Selected National Rental Companies
Albuquerque Motorcycle Rentals
505/830-9500
www.abqrentacycle.com
American Hog Motorcycle Rentals and Tours
636/451-4464
www.americanhog.com
Based in Gray Summit, Missouri, with info
on tours Ozarks, Branson, and River Road.
Boar Bikers Harley Rentals (Dallas, Texas)
214/351-1158
www.boarbikers.net
Budget Harley & Honda Rentals
888/622-0210
www.renthog.com
Rents Harleys in Maine.
*California Motorcycle Rentals
(La Jolla, California)*
858/456-9577
www.calif-motorcyclerental.com
Specializes in BMWs.

Cruise America
800/327-7799
www.cruiseamerica.com
Stocks Harleys, Buells, and Hondas in dozens of cities.
Harley Motorcycle Rental
(San Rafael, California)
415/456-9910 or 888/812-9253
www.harleymc.com
Iron Horse Rentals (Orlando, Florida)
407/426-7091
www.hogride.com
Motorcycle Rental Resource Page
www.harleys.com/mrrp.html
Rental operators listed by state.
Route 66 Riders Motorcycle Rentals
858/292-6200
www.route66riders.com

Miscellaneous Travel Information

Campground Reservations
800/280-2267
www.reserveusa.com
A one-call-books-all national company that handles reservations for 130,000 campsites at 2,000 national forest campgrounds in 44 states. Does not include national or state parks.
Historic Hotels of America
800/678-8946
www.nthp.org
Affiliated with the National Trust for Historic Preservation, HHA is a diverse collection of uniquely American lodgings, from rustic inns to elegant hotels. Rates at these member properties may be on the high end, but if you split the costs, you may do alright.
Kampgrounds of America (KOA)
www.koa.com

Information on more than 500 campgrounds nationwide.
MapQuest
www.mapquest.com
Trip planning, route, and mileage information.
National Forest Service
www.fs.fed.us
Links to national forests and campgrounds.
National Parks Reservations
800/436-7275
http://reservations.nps.gov/
Road Trip USA
www.roadtripusa.com
Eleven cross-country riding routes to get you off the beaten path.
Road Conditions
www.usroadconditions.com
Links to road conditions in every state.
Road Images
www.pashnit.com
Great road photographs and expert route suggestions.
Sport Fishing Information
800/275-3474 (ASK-FISH)
State and National Park Links
www.llbean.com/parksearch
State Helmet Laws
www.ama-cycle.org/amaccess/laws/
State Parks
www.dnr.(state abbreviation).us
(note: does not work for all states)
Weather Channel
www.weather.com
Yahoo! Travel
www.yahoo.com/recreation/travel
Starting point for links to books, maps, restaurants, and lodging.

Helpful Information

National Parks Pass

Each year, America's National Parks are visited more than 265 million times, a figure totaling more fans and guests than visit NFL games, Disney parks, and Universal Studios attractions combined. If you plan to visit more than one national park, invest in the National Parks Pass. For $50, the Pass will provide admission to any national park for a full year. The Golden Eagle Pass offers the same benefits, plus admission to many fee areas of the U.S. forest service. How far will your fifty bucks go? As far as 80.7 million acres of park land at 379 national parks ranging from Acadia in Maine, to Zion in Utah, all cared for and explained by more than 20,000 rangers, archaeologists, historians, biologists, architects, laborers, and gardeners.

Food Faves

One of my favorite vocations while riding is finding great roadside diners along the highway or in a village. Two of my favorite American writers are Jane and Michael Stern who, in addition to writing the classic Elvis World, wrote Eat Your Way Across the USA: 500 Diners, Lobster Shacks, Buffets, Pie Palaces, and Other All-American Eateries. While my book can lead you to a handful of restaurants, their book is a buffet of great American greasy spoons, hash houses, doughnut shops, cafeterias and small-town cafes.

Offbeat USA

If your motivation to ride is partially fueled by the chance discovery of kitsch Americana, check out www.roadsideamerica.com. This site is the online guide to offbeat tourist attractions, and may provide you with some sidetrip ideas when you're in the vicinity of places like the Zippo Lighter Visitors Center in Bradford, PA, or the giant advertising statues that still plug businesses across the U.S.

Selecting An Organized Tour

As the popularity of motorcycles grows, so does the proliferation of motorcycle tour operators. If you decide to ride on a pre-arranged trip, there are two constants you'll encounter: You will need a major credit card and a motorcycle endorsement on your license. There are also several variables. For instance, you may or may not need to bring your own bike, helmet, or raingear.

With these variances, play it smart by asking the "stupid" questions. Ask who covers specific expenses: lodging, meals, tolls, fuel, laundry, tips, insurance. And what type of lodging can you expect? Is it a flophouse, campground, or inn? Private bath? Shared rooms? Carrying a passenger will cost extra—how much? As you sift through these questions, also ask if you'll be allowed to break away from the group and meet them later. Is there a guide? A support vehicle? A trained mechanic? Does the ride include overnights or do you return to the same city each evening?

Make sure that if your ride is cancelled due to inclement weather, your deposit will be refunded (you may want to safeguard your investment by taking out traveler's cancellation insurance).

Chain Hotel Guide

A) *Best Western*
800/528-1234
www.bestwestern.com

B) *Clarion*
800/252-7466
www.choicehotels.com

C) *Comfort Inn*
800/221-2222
www.choicehotels.com

D) *Courtyard by Marriott*
800/321-2211
www.marriott.com

E) *Days Inn*
800/329-7466
www.daysinn.com

F) *Doubletree*
800/222-8733
www.doubletree.com

G) *Econo Lodge*
800/553-2666
www.choicehotels.com

H) *Embassy Suites*
800/362-2779
www.embasssy-suites.com

I) *Fairfield Inn*
800/228-2800
www.marriott.com

J) *Hampton Inns*
800/426-7866
www.hampton-inn.com

K) *Hilton*
800/445-8667
www.hilton.com

L) *Holiday Inn*
800/Holiday
www.holiday-inn.com

M) *Howard Johnson*
800/446-4656
www.hojo.com

N) *Hyatt*
800/233-1234
www.hyatt.com

O) *Knights Inn*
800/843-5644
www.knightsinn.com

P) *La Quinta*
800/687-6667
www.laquinta.com

Q) *Motel 6*
800/466-8356
www.motel6.com

R) *Omni Hotels*
800/843-6664
www.omnihotels.com

S) *Quality Inn*
800/228-5151
www.choicehotels.com

T) *Radisson*
800/333-3333
www.radisson.com

U) *Ramada*
800/272-6232
www.ramada.com

V) *Red Carpet Inn*
800/251-1962
www.reservahost.com

W) *Red Roof Inn*
800/843-7663
www.redroof.com

X) *Residence Inn*
800/331-3131
www.mariott.com

Y) *Rodeway*
800/228-2000
www.hotelchoice.com

Z) *Scottish Inns*
800/251-1962
www.reservahost.com

AA) *Sheraton*
800/325-3535
www.sheraton.com

BB) *Sleep Inn*
800/627-5337
www.hotelchoice.com

CC) *Super 8*
800/800-8000
www.super8.com

DD) *Travelodge*
800/578-7878
www.travelodge.com

General Index

Accommodations Index

Restaurant Index

About the Author

© LEE McKEE

Blessed with the chiseled features of a matinee idol, writer/rider Gary McKechnie is also a Florida native, a fourth-generation motorcyclist, a professional speaker, and founder of the Charles Kuralt Travel Society. He lives in Mount Dora, Florida.

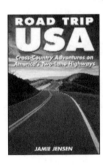